Dare to Share: Germany's Experience Promoting Equal Partnership in Families

OECD
BETTER POLICIES FOR BETTER LIVES

Please cite this publication as:
OECD (2016), *Dare to Share: Germany's Experience Promoting Equal Partnership in Families*, OECD Publishing, Paris.
http://dx.doi.org/10.1787/9789264259157-en

ISBN 978-92-64-25914-0 (print)
ISBN 978-92-64-25915-7 (PDF)

The statistical data for Israel are supplied by and under the responsibility of the relevant Israeli authorities. The use of such data by the OECD is without prejudice to the status of the Golan Heights, East Jerusalem and Israeli settlements in the West Bank under the terms of international law.

Revised version, February 2017.
Details of revisions available at: http://www.oecd.org/about/publishing/Corrigendum-DaretoShareGermany.pdf

Latvia was not an OECD member at the time of preparation of this publication. Accordingly, Latvia is not included in the area totals.

Photo credits: Cover © akindo/DigitalVision Vectors/Getty Images ; © yuoak/DigitalVision Vectors/Getty Images

Corrigenda to OECD publications may be found on line at: *www.oecd.org/about/publishing/corrigenda.htm*.

Foreword

Across OECD countries, the smallest gender gaps in time spent on household chores and caring are associated with the smallest gender gaps in employment rates. Time spent at home with the family affects time spent at work and vice versa. The traditional male-breadwinner model no longer reflects an efficient resource allocation in the labour market nor the aspirations of many fathers and mothers. Indeed, many fathers nowadays would like to have more time to spend with their children and many mothers would like to have more time to pursue their labour market aspirations and potentials.

German family policy and attitudes among Germans towards organising work and family life have changed considerably over the past 15 years, and it is timely to take stock of these changes also from an international perspective. This review outlines the advantages of a balanced sharing of work and family life, and provides an assessment of the situation in Germany and illustrates good policy practice and experience with examples from other OECD countries.

This report was prepared by Willem Adema, Chris Clarke, Valerie Frey, Angela Greulich (Université Paris 1 Panthéon Sorbonne), Hyunsook Kim, Pia Rattenhuber and Olivier Thévenon with support by Ava Guez, Annalena Oppel, Natalie Lagorce, Elma Lopes and Marlène Mohier and under the supervision of Monika Queisser, Head of the Social Policy Division. It was edited by Ken Kincaid and benefitted from editorial comments by Kate Lancaster. The German Federal Ministry for Family Affairs, Senior Citizens, Women and Youth provided financial support for this internationally comparative study into the promotion of equal partnerships in Families. The report accounts for comments by the German Federal Ministry for Family Affairs, Senior Citizens, Women and Youth on an earlier draft.

Table of contents

Acronyms and abbreviations 11
Executive summary 13

Chapter 1. **Dare to share: Germany's experience with promoting equal partnership in families** 15

1. Introduction 16
2. Sharing pays for families 17
3. Sharing pays for society as a whole 25
4. Preparing for sharing: Social policies can promote partnership in families 26
References 32

Chapter 2. **Partnerships, family composition and the division of labour: Germany in the context of the OECD** 37

1. Introduction and main findings 38
2. Most children live in couple families, but many families still have few children 39
3. Inequality and inefficiency in the labour market: German women work, but mothers are often trapped in part-time jobs 43
4. Inequality in unpaid work: women still do the lion's share of work at home 54
5. Germans feel the pinch of work-life conflict 56
6. Can Germany's labour force afford equal partnership? 60
7. Concluding remarks 63
Notes 65
References 66
Annex 2.A1. Estimating the effects of changes in male and female patterns of paid work on the German labour force and German GDP per capita 69

Chapter 3. **Policies to support equal partnerships in families in Germany** 75

1. Introduction and main findings 76
2. Families benefit from gender-equal family policies 78
3. Financial incentives to encourage both parents to work 85
4. Parental leave policies can change fathers' parenting behaviour and help mothers resume work more quickly 90
5. Policies towards a flexible "family working-time model" 97
6. Rolling out a comprehensive early childhood education and care policy and supporting parents as children grow older 99
7. Time for work and the family: policies and stakeholder agreements to promote flexible work schedules 108
8. Concluding remarks 113
Notes 115
References 117
Annex 3.A1. Tax-benefit models: Methodology and limitations 126
Annex 3.A2. Estimating the effects of a hypothetical "family-working time" scheme on the size of the German labour force 128

Chapter 4. **Earning and working unequally: Partnered parents in paid work** 133

1. Introduction and main findings 133
2. Coupled parents' working-hour patterns vary across the OECD 135
3. Mothers contribute less than fathers to household earnings in couple families across the OECD 150
4. What makes mothers choose full- or part-time employment? 155
5. Concluding remarks 161

Notes 162
References 163
Annex 4.A1. Working hours of mothers and fathers and fathers' reasons for part-time work 166
Annex 4.A2. Predicted probabilities of full-time employment among mothers with a dependent child 169

Chapter 5. **How partners in couples share unpaid work** 171

1. Introduction and main findings 172
2. Sharing among couples 173
3. Sharing among couples of working age 178
4. Sharing among parents 186
5. Concluding remarks 199

Notes 200
References 202
Annex 5.A1. Overview of the time use surveys analysed 207

Chapter 6. **Equal sharing and having children in Germany and France** 209

1. Introduction and main findings 210
2. Fertility trends in Germany and the OECD 212
3. The gap between actual and desired family size 215
4. Combining work and family formation: a key determinant of fertility 217
5. What influence of reconciliation policies? 223
6. Concluding remarks 224

Notes 226
References 227
Annex 6.A1. Jobs or babies? A comparison of fertility behaviour in Germany and France 231

Tables

Table 2.A.1. Summary of the effects of assumed changes in male and female patterns of paid work on overall labour force participation rates and overall average usual weekly working hours in Germany 71
Table 2.A.2. Summary of the potential effects of assumed changes in male and female patterns of paid work on GDP per capita and growth in GDP per capita in Germany 73
Table 3.1. Germany's new parental leave system encourges equal sharing between partners 96
Table 3.2. Statutory rights to flexible work arrangements for family reasons, selected countries 109

Table3.A2.1. Summary of the number of German employees potentially eligible for family working-time benefit and average working-hours amount those potentially eligible employees 129
Table 4.1. Own and partner characteristics are important for mothers' probability of full-time employment against part-time employment 158
Table 4.2. Partners' earnings are more important for mothers' probability of full-time against part-time employment in Country Group 1 160
Table 4.A2.1. Predicted probabilities of full-time employment against part-time employment.. 170
Table 4.A2.2. Predicted probabilities of full-time against part-time employment by country group 170
Table 5.A1.1. Main features of the time use surveys 208
Table 6.A1.1. Relationships between working patterns and fertility 234
Table 6.A1.2. Associations between fertility and partners' characteristics 236

Figures

Figure 1.1. Supporters of paid parental leave in favour of parents sharing parental leave period (equally) 17
Figure 1.2. Working mothers in Germany mainly work part-time 19
Figure 1.3. German-speaking countries have large within-couple gender gaps in work hours and earnings 21
Figure 1.4. Women do more unpaid labour than men across the OECD 23
Figure 1.5. Fewer hours on chores and child care are associated with higher female employment rates 24
Figure 1.6. Fathers and mothers of young children prefer that their partner work fewer hours 24
Figure 1.7. Enrolment in child care is catching up in Germany 28
Figure 2.1. German children are more likely to live with married parents and less likely to live with cohabiting parents than children in most other European OECD countries 40
Figure 2.2. The share of children living with two parents has fallen over the past couple of decades 40
Figure 2.3. Cohabitation is particularly common among younger people in Germany 41
Figure 2.4. Fertility rates in Germany are persistently low 42
Figure 2.5. The German population is both ageing and declining 43
Figure 2.6. In Germany as in most OECD countries, young women are more likely to complete higher education than young men 44
Figure 2.7. German women are under-represented in science, technology and engineering, but not mathematics 45
Figure 2.8. German women's employment rates rose significantly between 2000 and 2014 46
Figure 2.9. In most OECD countries, female employment has been growing faster than male employment since 2000 46
Figure 2.10. Women work fewer hours than men throughout the OECD 47
Figure 2.11. Working mothers in Germany work mainly part-time 48
Figure 2.12. Few families share paid work equally with both partners working reduced full-time hours 51
Figure 2.13. The gender wage gap persists but has narrowed since 2000 in most OECD countries including Germany 53
Figure 2.14. Female entrepreneurs often earn a lot less than male entrepreneurs 54
Figure 2.15. Women continue to do more unpaid labour than men throughout the OECD 55
Figure 2.16. German women continue to do more housework and child care than German men 55

Figure 2.17. German parents are more likely than most of their peers in Europe to report work-life conflict 57
Figure 2.18. Fathers and mothers of young children prefer that their partner work fewer hours 58
Figure 2.19. Opinions of working mothers have improved slightly over time 59
Figure 2.20. Female labour participation rates and working hours tend to be higher, and male working hours a little lower, in countries with more equal divisions of paid and unpaid work than Germany 61
Figure 2.21. Shifting towards patterns of paid work similar to those in countries with more gender-equitable divisions of paid and unpaid work would (at worst) do little damage to the size of the German labour force 63
Figure 3.1. Public spending on family benefits in cash, in kind and through tax measures in selected OECD countries 82
Figure 3.2. Public investment in children often dips after a good start 84
Figure 3.3. In most OECD countries, dual-earner couples are better off than single-earner couples 86
Figure 3.4. Paid leave available to fathers has increased over the past 15 years, while leave available to mothers has remained fairly constant 92
Figure 3.5. Young mothers in Germany have resumed paid work more quickly in recent years .. 93
Figure 3.6. Fathers' take-up of parental leave increased in Germany 95
Figure 3.7. Germany is investing more in early childhood education 99
Figure 3.8. Several OECD countries have developed extensive ECEC systems, though at different times and in different ways 104
Figure 3.9. Out-of-pocket centre-based child care costs in Germany are below the OECD average 105
Figure 3.10. Denmark leads the OECD in out-of-school hours care provision, while Germany has room for improvement 106
Figure 3.11. Germany is among the five countries where the most companies offer flexible working time arrangements 112
Figure3.A1.1. Net transfers to government in different couple-family earnings combinations at 200% of the average wage 127
Figure3.A2.1. Under certain assumptions, a family working time model would do little or no damage to the size of the German labour force 131
Figure 4.1. German gender gaps in employment are narrower than the OECD average, but not when working hours are taken into consideration 136
Figure 4.2. Women rather than men adapt their working hours over the life course 138
Figure 4.3. Countries with women in long-term part-time work (e.g. Germany) and polarised female labour force behaviour (e.g. Italy) have wider gender gaps in working hours 139
Figure 4.4. German mothers work relatively short part-time hours 141
Figure 4.5. In most countries family responsibilities are the main reason for mothers working part-time 142
Figure 4.6. The hours worked by German mothers in full-time jobs are relatively long 145
Figure 4.7. Partnered mothers are less likely to work full-time in German-speaking countries than in selected OECD countries 146
Figure 4.8. German-speaking countries have large within-couple gender gaps in working hours 147
Figure 4.9. Few families share market work equally with both partners working between 30 and 39 hours per week 148
Figure 4.10. Within-couple gender gaps in working hours are greater in Germany than in France 150

Figure 4.11. Mothers in couples earn lower shares of household earnings in German-speaking countries ... 151
Figure 4.12. Mothers work least and contribute least to household earnings in German-speaking countries ... 152
Figure 4.13. Mothers' contribution to household earnings increases with educational attainment and decreases with partner earnings ... 153
Figure 4.8. Career breaks reduce pension entitlements ... 154
Figure 4.A1.1. Part-time working hours of German fathers are higher than for mothers ... 166
Figure 4.A1.2. In most countries labour demand shortages are the main reason for fathers working part-time ... 167
Figure4.A1.3. Full-time working hours for German fathers are relatively high ... 167
Figure 4.A1.4. Average working hours of (self-)employed mothers and fathers ... 168
Figure 4.A1.5. Average working hours of mothers and fathers ... 168
Figure 5.1. Women do more unpaid work than men in all countries ... 173
Figure 5.2. Overall, partnered women work more than partnered men across different age groups ... 176
Figure 5.3. For similar hours of paid work, partnered women do more unpaid work than partnered men ... 179
Figure 5.4. Even dual-earner couples with similar paid hours do not share housework equally ... 181
Figure 5.5. Unpaid work is unbalanced even in couples where the woman earns the higher income ... 183
Figure 5.6. Couples share more evenly in countries with higher female employment rates ... 184
Figure 5.7. Highly educated couples share unpaid work more equally in most countries ... 185
Figure 5.8. Couples with higher household income share unpaid work more equally ... 186
Figure 5.9. The Netherlands have high proportions of women and men in part-time work compared to other OECD countries ... 187
Figure 5.10. The time that women in the Netherlands spend on unpaid work has fallen, but the gender gap persists when children are present in the household ... 188
Figure 5.11. Young, working-age partners share aggregate work and unpaid work less equally, particularly in countries with lower female employment rates, when they have children ... 189
Figure 5.12. Young working-age parents share paid and unpaid work more traditionally than their childless peers ... 190
Figure 5.13. Children spend similar amounts of time with fathers and mothers when the mother works full-time ... 194
Figure 5.14. Partnered fathers are less involved than mothers with young children, but the gender gap seem smaller during weekends and when children start school ... 195
Figure 5.15. Highly educated couples participate more equally in child care activities ... 196
Figure 5.16. Although fathers spend less time with young children, a greater share of that time is "quality time" ... 197
Figure 5.17. Partnered men are less likely to care for adult household members than partnered women in first place, but once they are involved in care giving they devote similar amounts of time ... 199
Figure 6.1. Fertility rates seem to be edging up in Germany in recent years ... 213
Figure 6.2. Women in France are most likely to have two or more children, while women in Germany are more likely to remain childless ... 214
Figure 6.3. Definitive childlessness in Germany is double the level in France ... 215
Figure 6.4. Two-child families: a dominant ideal in Germany ... 216
Figure 6.5. Mean ultimately intended family size, 2011 ... 217
Figure 6.6. Birth rates are often higher in countries with high female employment rates ... 218

Figure 6.7. Having children has a more adverse effect on female employment in Germany than in France 219
Figure 6.8. How many hours would you like to work? 220

Acronyms and abbreviations

AW	Average wage
BMFSFJ	Federal Ministry for Family Affairs, Senior Citizens, Women and Youth (*Bundesministerium für Familie, Senioren, Frauen und Jugend*)
DEM	Deutsche Mark
DGB	Confederation of German Trade Unions
DIHK	German Chamber of Commerce
ECEC	Early childhood education and care
EU LFS	European Union Labour Force Survey
EU SILC	European Union Statistics on Income and Living Conditions
FTE	Full-time equivalent
FWTA	Flexible working-time arrangement
GDP	Gross domestic product
GRB	Gender-responsive budgeting
IAB	Institute for Employment Research (*Institut für Arbeitsmarkt- und Berufsforschung*)
ISCED	International Standard Classification of Education
ISSP	International Social Survey Programme
OSH	Out-of-school hours
PISA	OECD Programme of International Student Assessment
PPP	Purchasing power parity
STEM	Science, technology, engineering and mathematics
TFR	Total fertility rate
WSI	Institute of Economic and Social Research (*Wirtschafts- und Sozialwissenschaftliches Institut*)
ZDH	German Confederation of Skilled Crafts

Executive summary

Germany has made great strides in reforming policies that support working families and promote equal partnership among parents in couple families. In the past, labour market institutions, public policies, and social norms reinforced traditional gender roles especially in West Germany, but social policy reforms over the last decade – such as parental leave reform and greater public investment in early childhood education and care (ECEC) supports – have increased opportunities for parents to find a better work/family balance.

This policy shift was accompanied and influenced by significant changes in attitudes and perceptions in Germany. The share of the population in Germany, for example, that believes mothers should not work at all when they have a pre-school aged child has halved in the decade to 2012. After Sweden, the population in Germany now is the most egalitarian in their attitudes towards the sharing of parental leave between the mother and the father. Compared to 2007, there are now fewer concerns over the financial cost of having children and more Germans consider their country as child-friendly. Yet, despite recent increases the total fertility rate (TFR) in Germany is still below the OECD average and German parents are still more likely than most in Europe to report work/life conflict.

Considerable challenges to parents' work-life balance persist. Overall, the main earner model continues to dominate in German families, albeit in a modified form: partnered fathers work, often long hours, while partnered mothers now tend to work part-time, rather than not at all. At home women do most of the unpaid work and spend much more time with the children than fathers.

A new German family policy approach aims to provide parents and children more time together through fostering a more equal partnership in the sharing of work and family life responsibilities ("Partnerschaftlichkeit"). Extending ECEC supports gives both parents better opportunities to combine work and care commitments. Building on the 2007 reform, the 2015 parental leave reform facilitates parents' ability to take leave on a part-time basis and grants a partnership bonus for at least four months when both parents work around 25-30 hours per week. Furthermore, efforts are underway in co-operation with social partners and other stakeholders to make working conditions more consistent with family life.

A more equal sharing of work/life balance opportunities and responsibilities between partners is good for the well-being of families. Equal sharing allows fathers to spend more time with their children, which in turn supports child development. And it gives mothers greater scope to pursue their labour market aspirations, strengthens their long-term labour force attachment and pension entitlements, and strengthens both their financial independence and their families' resources.

This report places the German experience with promoting equal partnership in families in an international perspective. It provides an overview of outcomes, driving factors, issues and policies to overcome obstacles to families spending more time together and a more equal gender balance in employment. These obstacles include:

long working hours, especially for fathers, that complicate combining paid work with family life; insufficient child care and after-school supports for working parents; and traditional gender patterns that develop at home after child birth, especially when mothers rather than fathers take time off or reduce working hours to care for young children. For that reason the debate in Germany over working-time flexibility and a more equitable sharing of work and family responsibilities between parents with small children involves "vollzeitnah" or "reduced full-time working hours" – a term not in common international use.

Promoting partnerships in which fathers and mother share the responsibility for children equally is good for families and their well-being, and also produces a range of less tangible, albeit important, social goods, like better father-child bonding and promoting egalitarian gender norms across generations. A family working-time model as currently debated in Germany could provide families with more time for each other and, if fathers and mothers were both to work reduced hours on a temporary basis, pursue their labour market career on a full-time basis as children grow up, could sustain labour supply and contribute to a marked reduction of gender pay and pension gaps. In all, a more gender-balanced sharing of work family responsibilities could ensure inclusive growth in future.

This review aims to support the German Government in its policy to promote equal partnerships in families. Recommendations include (for the full list see Chapter 1):

- *Continue to encourage more fathers to take up parental leave*, and monitor the effect of the 2015 "ElterngeldPlus" reform on fathers' uptake of leave, and the sharing of working hours between the fathers and mothers of young children.
- Building on the experience with "Elterngeld" and "ElterngeldPlus", *continue to develop family-policy measures*, including options for parents with young children to work reduced full-time hours for a specific period of time during which they may receive associated financial support.
- Having established the right to reduce working hours for family reasons, introduce the *right to increase working hours to full-time work* – or another level that fits their changing family circumstance – within a specified time frame.
- Building on the good progress in improving public investment in ECEC over the past 15 years, *continue to increase investment in, and ensure broader access to ECEC supports for young children.*
- Compared to investment in ECEC, Germany has to catch up regarding investment in out-of-school-hours (OSH) care supports: *greater investment and broader access to, out-of-school-hours care supports* for primary-school age children is needed.
- *Adjust the German tax-benefit system in order to encourage couples to share paid work equally* by improving financial incentives to work for second earners in couple families through, for example, a separate tax-free allowance for second earners.
- *Further extend the co-operation with social partners and other stakeholders to make workplace practices more conducive to family life*, through measures such as teleworking or allowing flexible work schedules.
- *Continue raising awareness of the benefits of equal partnerships in families*, also through initiatives aimed at fostering and sharing best practices at the local level.

Chapter 1

Dare to share: Germany's experience with promoting equal partnership in families

This chapter introduces the background to and issues at stake in promoting equal partnerships in families in Germany. It encourages German policy makers to build on the important reforms of 2007 and 2015 to enable both fathers and mothers to combine work and family commitments, and commends families to "dare to share". To those ends it places Germany's experience in an international comparison, and draws from the experience of, for example, France and the Nordic countries, which have longstanding policies to support work-life balance and strengthen gender equality. The chapter begins with an explanation of why and how equal sharing pays: it is good for family well-being, child development, female employment opportunities, fathers' working hours (Sections 2 and 3) and sustaining fertility rates. Section 4 examines policies to promote partnership, looking both at persistent shortcomings and progress achieved through reform since the mid-2000s. The chapter closes with a set of policy recommendations designed to enable parents to share work and family responsibilities more equally.

The statistical data for Israel are supplied by and under the responsibility of the relevant Israeli authorities. The use of such data by the OECD is without prejudice to the status of the Golan Heights, East Jerusalem and Israeli settlements in the West Bank under the terms of international law.

1. Introduction

The balance of work and family outcomes is changing in German families. Fathers continue to be the main breadwinners in couple families, but whereas they previously did not participate in the labour force, German mothers are typically in work nowadays, albeit on a part-time basis. German women aged 25 to 34 years old are now more likely to obtain a university degree than young men. This rise in educational attainment has contributed to the large increase (11 percentage points) over the past 15 years in the female employment rate to 70% in Germany: the highest proportion of women in the paid workforce outside of the Nordic countries and other OECD countries where women are frequently in part-time employment such as the Netherlands. This increase in labour force participation was associated with a decline in time spent on unpaid home and care work, but in Germany as elsewhere in the OECD, women still bear the brunt of unpaid work and fathers spend a lot less time with children than mothers. German parents are more likely than their fellow Europeans to report work/life conflict and, despite recent increases, the total fertility rate (TFR) in 2014 was 1.47, below the 2013 OECD average of 1.67 (Chapter 2).

In the past, labour market institutions, public policies, and social norms reinforced traditional gender roles, especially in West Germany. However, since the mid-2000s social policy reform has increased opportunities for parents to find a better work/family balance. Parental leave reform has effectively reduced the duration of the paid leave spell that mothers take and induced many fathers to use paid leave entitlements, often for two months at a time (Chapter 3). At the same time public investment in early childhood education and care (ECEC) increased markedly with public spending as a per cent of GDP and the proportion of children participating coming from behind to overtake the OECD average (Chapter 3).

Attitudes towards work and care opportunities have changed too. The share of the population in former West Germany that believes a mother should not work *at all* when they have a pre-school aged child has dropped from 46.6% in 2002 to 21.8% in 2012, and over the same period that proportion halved to below 10% in East Germany (Chapter 2). Furthermore in terms of who should take paid parental leave, fathers or mothers, in 2012 the German population was one of the most egalitarian after Sweden (Figure 1.1).

The new German family policy approach aims to provide parents and children more time with each other also by promoting a more equal sharing of responsibilities in reconciling work and family life – "Partnerschaftlichkeit" (BMFSFJ, 2015a). This is reflected in 2015 parental leave reform, which facilitates both parents to take leave on a part-time basis and provides a partnership bonus for at least four months when both parents work around 25-30 hours per week. This reform is part of a more general policy drive to make working conditions in companies more conducive to family life in co-operation with employers, unions and other stakeholders. In Germany currently many mothers work short part-time hours and many fathers work more than 40 hours per week. For that reason, the debate in Germany over working-time flexibility and a more equitable sharing of work and family responsibilities between parents with small children involves "vollzeitnah" or "reduced full-time working hours" – a term not in common international use.

Public policy also increased ECEC capacity, but considerable policy challenges remain including for example, regarding out-of-school-hours (OSH) care support and providing both parents with equally strong financial incentives to work (or work more) through the tax-benefit system.

2. Sharing pays for families

A more equal sharing of work/life balance opportunities and responsibilities between partners is good for the well-being of families and its individual members. This is perhaps most obvious for couple families – the focus of this report – but all families benefit from an equal sharing of responsibilities in reconciling work and family life, also when parents are separated and do not live together on a permanent basis. It gives more time to fathers to spend with their children which also supports child development; while it gives mothers more scope to pursue their labour market aspirations and career opportunities, strengthen their long-term labour force attachment and pension entitlements, enhancing both their financial independence and their families' resources. It could also have benefits for the economy and society as a whole as a better allocation of labour market resources can spur on economic growth.

Figure 1.1. Supporters of paid parental leave in favour of parents sharing parental leave period (equally)

Distribution of responses to the question "Consider a couple who both work full-time and now have a new born child. Both are in a similar work situation and are eligible for paid leave. How should this paid leave period be divided between the mother and the father?"

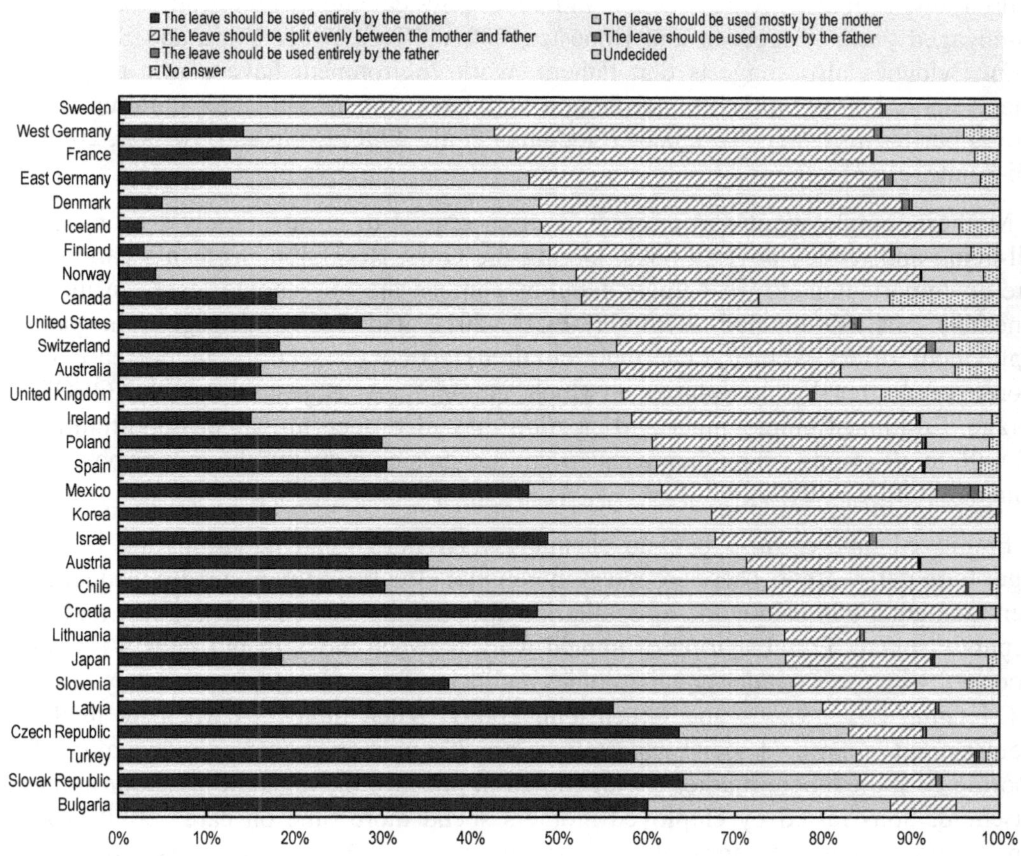

Note: Question only asked to those who think paid leave should be available to parents.

Response options "Father 100%, mother 0%" and "Leave should mostly be taken by father and some by the mother" lumped into one category due to low response rate.

Source: International Social Survey Programme (ISSP) 2012.

Parenthood proves to be a crucial moment in couple's lives. Parents' behaviour around the birth of a new child is important for determining later roles and responsibilities within a family (Baxter, 2008; Schober, 2013; Barnes, 2015). Up to parenthood many couples share paid and unpaid work relatively equally. But upon birth of the first child couples often revert to traditional roles and even as children grow older mothers do not always return (fully) to the labour market. Too often, partners' behaviours feed into an unfortunate circle: men engage more in paid work, women engage more in unpaid work and individual aspirations are not fulfilled.

Children benefit from spending time with their fathers: Greater paternal involvement is associated with positive cognitive and emotional outcomes (Lamb, 2010; Huerta et al., 2013; Schober, 2015) as well as physical health benefits for the child (WHO, 2007). Children can also benefit from their mothers' employment, as mothers' participation in the labour market increases household income. It may also change the allocation of resources within households as it gives mothers more control to increase child-related expenditures (Lundberg and Pollak, 1996; Woolley, 2004).

Fathers benefit from spending more time with their children: fathers who contribute more to unpaid work (including child care) face a lower risk of divorce than less-involved fathers (Sigle-Rushton, 2010), while fathers who engage more with their children report greater life satisfaction and better physical and mental health than their less-engaged peers (Eggebeen and Knoester, 2001; WHO, 2007; Craig and Swrikar, 2009). Evidence also suggests that fathers' work environment have a role to play: fathers report higher work-life satisfaction and involvement with their children, the more father-friendly their workplace (Goodman et al., 2008; Craig and Swrikar, 2009; Ishii-Kuntz, 2013).

Mothers' employment participation is often crucial to ensure family's economic well-being and reduce poverty risks. During the Great Recession, women's earnings were an important factor in helping families compensate for income losses in more vulnerable, male-dominated sectors (OECD, 2012 and 2014). Engaging in paid employment offers women (and their children) economic security in the case of divorce or partnership dissolution – which in Germany is just above the OECD average. Continued employment participation may also open up career opportunities and will, in all events, strengthen pension entitlements so reducing the risk of poverty in old age (OECD, 2015a).

Employed mothers also help to change gender norms and equal sharing in the longer term perspective. There are intergenerational effects on future gender inequality when mothers are in paid work, as egalitarian attitudes are shaped both at home and in the public sphere. Equal sharing of unpaid work between mothers and fathers is also associated with more gender-equal attitudes and behaviours of children once they grow up (McGinn, 2015; Davis and Greenstein, 2009). When mothers participate in the labour market, children's social expectations are that women should enjoy equality of opportunity in the labour market – with all that implies for the division of labour in the household. Sons raised by employed mothers spend more time on care activities at home as grown-ups than sons of stay-at-home mothers. As for daughters raised by employed mothers, they too, are more successful on the labour market. Their jobs are better, their pay higher and their paid hours longer than among the daughters of stay-at-home mothers (McGinn et al., 2015; Olivetti et al., 2015; Cunningham, 2001).

But most German families share paid and unpaid work unequally

The "main-earner model" continues to dominate in Germany, albeit in a modified form. Most children in Germany grow up with a full-time working father and a mother who often works part-time and does the bulk of the unpaid work around the house, including child care. In 2013, 47% of couples with a child under 18 followed the main-earner model (BMFSFJ, 2015b).

Nonetheless, over the past 15 years, employment rates among working-age women in Germany have increased by over 11 percentage points, from 58.1% to 69.5% (Chapter 2). The average change in this period across the OECD was only 4.7 percentage points. Germany's increase represents the second-largest increase in female employment in the OECD in this period, after Chile, and in 2014 Germany had the highest proportion of women in the paid workforce outside of the Nordic countries and Switzerland.

The gains in female employment in Germany have largely been driven by mothers entering part-time work, often working relatively short hours. More than half of the German mothers in employment work part-time: only the Netherlands – at 70% – has a higher proportion of employed mothers in part-time employment (Figure 1.2). Because of the prevalence of part-time work among employed women, the gender gap in full-time equivalent employment (which accounts for the working hours of those in employment) remains large at 24.6 percentage points, compared to a gender gap of 8.5 percentage points in employment rates in Germany (OECD, 2016a).

Figure 1.2. Working mothers in Germany mainly work part-time

Maternal employment rates by part-time/full-time status, mothers aged 15-64 with at least one child aged 0-14,[1] 2013 or latest available year[2]

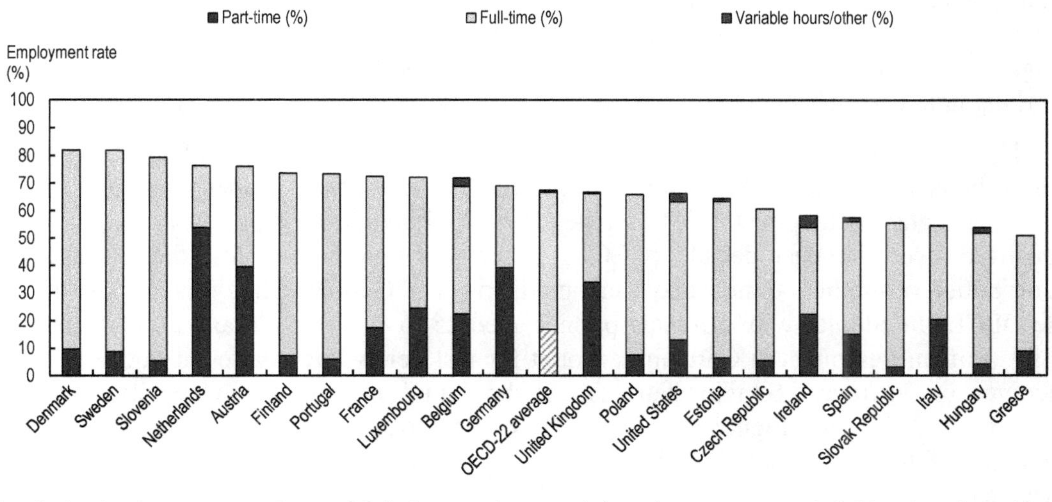

Note: The distinction between part-time and full-time employment is based on a common definition (usual weekly working hours of less than 30 in the main job). "Variable hours/other" refers to women whose usual hours cannot be given because hours worked vary considerably from week to week or from month to month. The definition of "employed" and "employment" follows ILO guidelines (http://laborsta.ilo.org/applv8/data/c2e.html) and covers those in both paid (dependent) employment and in self-employment (including unpaid family workers).

1. For the United States, children aged between 0-17.

2. Data for Denmark, Finland and Sweden refer to 2012.

Source: OECD calculations based on EU LFS for European countries and Current Population Survey for the United States.

At 42 hours per week on average German fathers often work long hours compared with many other OECD countries (Chapter 4). The time fathers spend at work takes away from the time they could spend with their family and caring for their children – an important factor in father-child relationships. Every third German father wishes to have more time for his children (Destatis, 2015a) and most fathers would prefer shorter paid work hours (BMFSFJ, 2015b).

Within-couple gender gaps in working hours and earnings in Germany are wider than in other European countries and the United States (Figure 1.3, Panels A and B). In couple families with a female partner aged 25 to 45 years old and at least one child, mothers are in paid work for an average of 17 hours, and in Austria, Italy and Switzerland this is also less than 20 hours per week on average. By contrast, the figure among partnered mothers aged 25 to 45 years old in Denmark, Norway and Sweden is 30 hours per week or more (Chapter 4).

German fathers, for their part, tend to put in relatively long hours. Most men in Germany work over 40 hours per week, and the share of partnered fathers working over 44 hours is higher in Germany, Austria, and Switzerland than in Finland, Norway and Sweden. "Dual reduced full-time work" households – for which the working definition used in Chapter 4 is those in which both parents work between 30 and 39 hours per week – are still uncommon in Germany. They account for below 2% of couples with children, far less than Denmark and Norway where they make up over 25% (Chapter 4). With 18%, the Netherlands is the country that has the highest proportion of couple households with children in which men work 30 to 39 hours per week and women work part-time: twice as many as in any other European country and three times more than in Germany (Chapter 4).

Given the patterns in working hours among partnered parents, the average within-couple gender gap in paid working hours in Germany and other German speaking countries is at 25 hours per week wider than in many other OECD countries (Figure 1.3, Panel A and Chapter 4). By contrast, within-couple gender gaps in working hours are less than ten hours per week in Denmark, Portugal and Sweden.

This difference in couples' work hours contributes to the persistent gender pay gap within households and at the national level. Germany's full-time gender wage gap of 13.4% is slightly below the OECD average (15.5%), although Germany's wage gap has narrowed over the past decade (OECD, 2016a). Within households, the average contribution of mothers to household income is lower in Germany than it is in most of the OECD. In couples with a female partner aged 25 to 45 years old and at least one child, women's earnings in Germany account for just below one-quarter of household incomes on averages. Similar patterns can be found in Austria and Switzerland (EU SILC, 2012 and Figure 1.3, Panel B). By contrast, in France, Sweden, and Denmark, female partners contribute over 35% to household income, on average (Chapter 4).

Figure 1.3. German-speaking countries have large within-couple gender gaps in work hours and earnings

Average within-couple gender gap in usual weekly working hours and average relative within-couple female share of earnings, for couples with a female partner aged 25 to 45 and at least one child, selected countries, 2012[1]

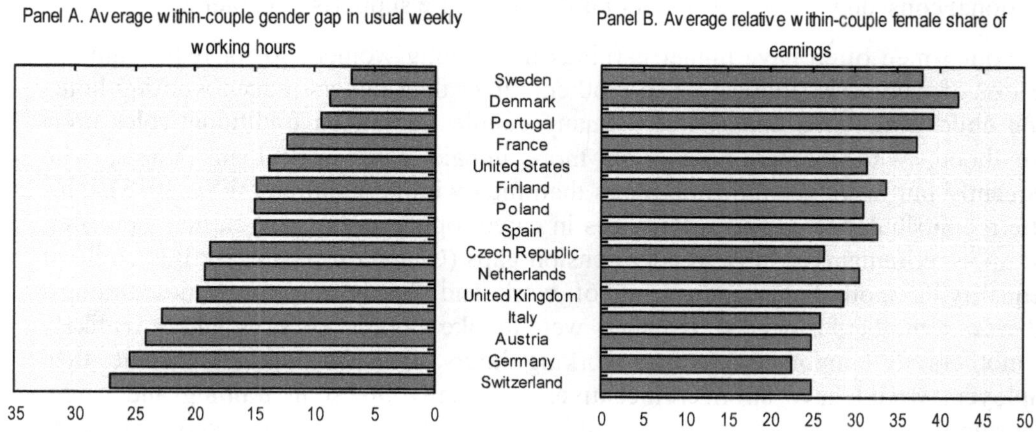

Note for Panel A: Data refer to the average absolute gap in usual weekly working hours between the male member and the female member of a couple (male partner's usual weekly working hours – female partner's usual weekly working hours). Couples with both partners not working are excluded. In Sweden, for example, male partners work on average nearly seven hours more per week than female partners.

Note for Panel B: Data refer to the average female share of a couple's total earnings [female partner's earnings / (male partner's earnings + female partner's earnings)]. Couples with both partners not working are excluded. In Denmark, for example, female partners earn on average 42.13% out of the couple's total earnings.

1. For the within-couple gap in usual weekly working hours, data refer to 2012 (2014 for the United States). For the female share of earnings, the income reference year is 2011 (2013 for the United States).

Source: OECD calculations of EU SILC 2012, and Current Population Survey (2014) for the United States.

Despite the tendency among partnered fathers in Austria, Germany and Switzerland to work long hours, the pay-off to excessively long hours is not better productivity (Chapter 2). While productivity does increase with hours worked, it only does so to a point: a large body of research finds that productivity reaches a maximum at around forty hours per week (Penceval, 2014; Business Roundtable; 1980; Thomas and Raynar, 1997). After five eight-hour days, productivity plateaus and then declines as workers' anticipate adding extra hours and produce less in each hour. Furthermore, the risk of accidents and errors increases and miscommunication and poor decisions are more likely (Dembe et al., 2005; Rogers et al., 2004; Flinn and Armstrong, 2011). Workers' health suffers (Virtanen et al., 2012) as well, which contributes to diminished productivity. Confronting excessively long hours requires cultural shifts within organisations, as well as sufficient policies protecting workers.

One way to bypass the constraints of full-time employment is to become an entrepreneur, which may provide more flexibility in the setting of working hours but does not necessarily imply shorter hours. German women, however, are also less likely to be entrepreneurs than German men. In 2013, only 2.5% of working women in Germany were their own employer, compared to 6.7% of men. Furthermore, German female entrepreneurs earn much less, on average, than their male counterparts: female earnings from self-employment in Germany were nearly 43% lower than male earnings from self-employment, which is larger than the OECD average gender gap in entrepreneur earnings (36.1%). The earnings gap can be explained by the lower capitalisation of female-run companies, the choice of sector, a lack of managerial experience, and the lower number of hours female entrepreneurs on average devote to their businesses, as they are more likely than men to combine paid work with family commitments (OECD, 2012). Lower earnings for female entrepreneurs may also be an additional consequence of insufficient public child care supports (Chapter 2).

Young men often have higher earnings than young women, so for many families the loss of income is smallest when mothers rather than fathers reduce working hours upon child birth. This contributes to many couples taking on traditional roles upon parenthood, with mothers taking on more unpaid care work than fathers, who frequently put in longer full-time hours than men without children (WSI, 2015). This pattern contributes to gender differences in career opportunities and earnings profiles, and upon retirement, to large gender pension gaps (Chapter 4). To break this circle of inequality, a more balanced sharing of work and family responsibilities amongst fathers and mothers is needed. If fathers were to take more leave, or would be as likely as mothers to temporarily reduce working hours upon becoming a parent, then employers would have stronger incentives to equally invest in training and career opportunities of mothers. If mothers could engage in employment on a similar basis as fathers, this would underpin their economic security in case of divorce or partnership dissolution and reduce their risk of pension-related old-age poverty. If fathers and mothers were both to work reduced full-time hours on a temporary basis, and pursue their labour market career on a full-time basis as children grow up this would contribute to a marked reduction of gender pay and pension gaps in future.

Women's unpaid work at home affects their engagement in paid, full-time employment

No OECD country has achieved equality in paid and unpaid work, and in all OECD countries women do more unpaid work at home than men (Figure 1.4). Female partners spend, on average, twice as much time on housework and child care as their male partners. Indeed, in nearly all OECD countries, men actually work *less* than women when adding up *total* hours spent in paid and unpaid work (Chapter 5).

Across countries, male-breadwinner couples tend to adhere to a more traditional division of paid and unpaid labour: when a male partner works full-time, the female partner predominantly manages housework and child care (Chapter 5). In dual-earner couples, in contrast, male partners take on a larger share of housework than male breadwinners. Yet even when both partners work full-time, the division of household labour is rarely a 50-50 split: the female share of unpaid household labour varies across countries, from 62%, on average, in Germany to 88%, on average, in Korea. Women tend to do less unpaid housework and child care as their share of household earnings goes up, but the relationship is not linear; there is some evidence that high-earning women often do more housework in order to conform to gender norms at home, if not in the workplace, an example of so-called "doing gender" behaviour (Bittman, 2003; Bertrand et al., 2015).

Although there has been an increase in the number of German women entering the labour market, and despite small improvements in the amount of work German men do around the house, the within-household distribution of unpaid labour is still unequal. Women (in the 30-to-44 year-old age bracket) spend an average of 4.73 hours per day on child care and other unpaid work, whereas men of the same age spend an average of only 2.52 hours per day on these tasks (Destatis, 2015b). Women's time spent on unpaid labour has decreased over the past decade, but this was driven largely by improvements in technology and automation, rather than a large increase in time spent by men on housework.

Time spent on housework affects time spent in the labour market, and vice versa. A disproportionate burden on women to care for children can deter mothers from (re-entering full-time work and can make employers less likely to hire mothers or women of childbearing age. In Germany, women who work part-time are most likely to cite housework or caregiving responsibilities as the reason they work fewer than 30 hours per week (Chapter 4). In contrast, countries with high female employment rates, more gender-egalitarian attitudes, and widely accessible ECEC and OSH-care services (like Denmark and Sweden) also tend to have more equal sharing of household labour (Figure 1.5).

Figure 1.4. Women do more unpaid labour than men across the OECD

Average minutes per day spent on child care and other unpaid work (15-64 year-olds[1]), by sex, latest available year[2]

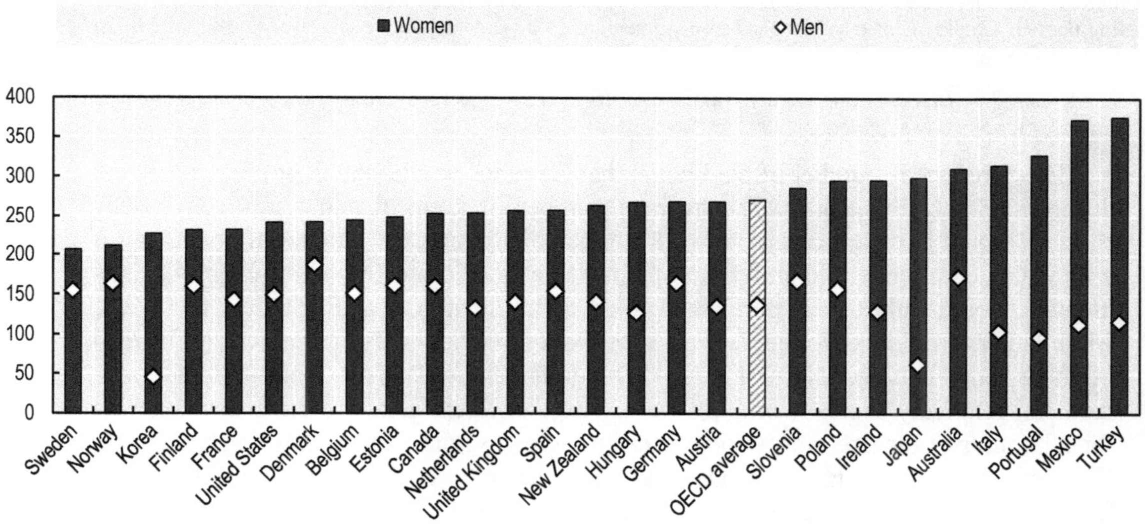

1. Data are for 15-64 year-olds, except for Australia (15+ year-olds), Hungary (15-74 year-olds) and Sweden (25-64 year-olds).

2. Reference years are: Australia: 2006; Austria: 2008-09; Belgium: 2005; Canada: 2010; Denmark: 2001; Estonia: 2009-10; Finland: 2009-10; France: 2009; Germany: 2001-02; Hungary: 1999-2000; Italy: 2008-09; Ireland: 2005; Japan: 2011; Korea: 2009; Mexico: 2009; the Netherlands: 2005-06; New Zealand: 2009-10; Norway: 2010; Poland: 2003-04; Portugal: 1999; Slovenia: 2000-01; Spain: 2009-10; Sweden: 2010; Turkey: 2006; the United Kingdom: 2005; the United States: 2014.

Source: OECD Gender Data Portal 2016.

Figure 1.5. Fewer hours on chores and child care are associated with higher female employment rates

Minutes per day spent on unpaid work by partnered men and women

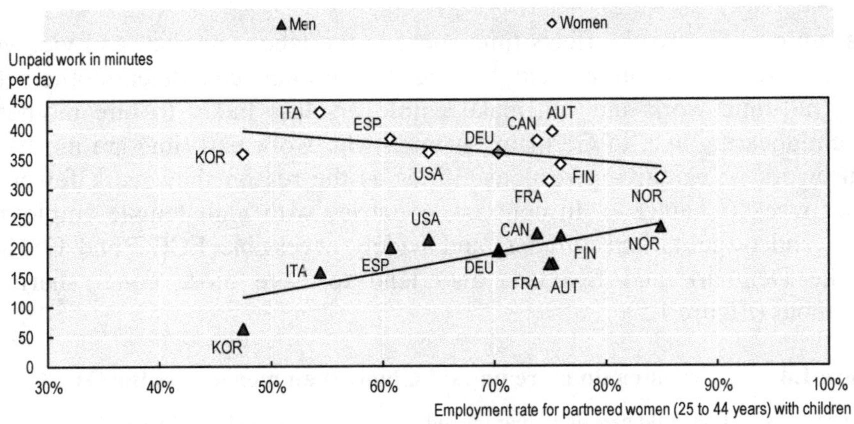

Note: Time use data for partnered men and women aged 20 years or above who live in the same household as a spouse or cohabitating partner. Employment rates for partnered women aged 20 years and above who live in the same household as a spouse or cohabiting partner. Employment rates for Norway for partnered women between 15 to 75 years.

Source: *OECD Time Use Database* and German Statistical Office, OECD Secretariat estimates of female employment rates. Employment rates for Norway supplied by Statistics Norway.

The "preferred" number of paid hours that Germans would like their partner to work differs markedly by gender. The average number of hours that mothers with young children would like their partner to work is much higher than the number of hours fathers with young children would prefer their partner to work (Figure 1.6). On average, German mothers would rather their partners worked approximately five hours less per week, while fathers would like to see their partners work three hours fewer per week (Chapter 4 offers a more detailed discussion of German fathers' relatively long – and German mothers' relatively short – working hours). These different gender preferences hold true for all countries but are more pronounced in Germany, the Netherlands and the United Kingdom than, for instance, in Denmark, France or Sweden, where support systems facilitate fathers and mothers to realise working hours in a less constrained manner.

Figure 1.6. Fathers and mothers of young children prefer that their partner work fewer hours

Average responses to the inquiry of partners' average working hours, and partners' preferred working hours, 2010

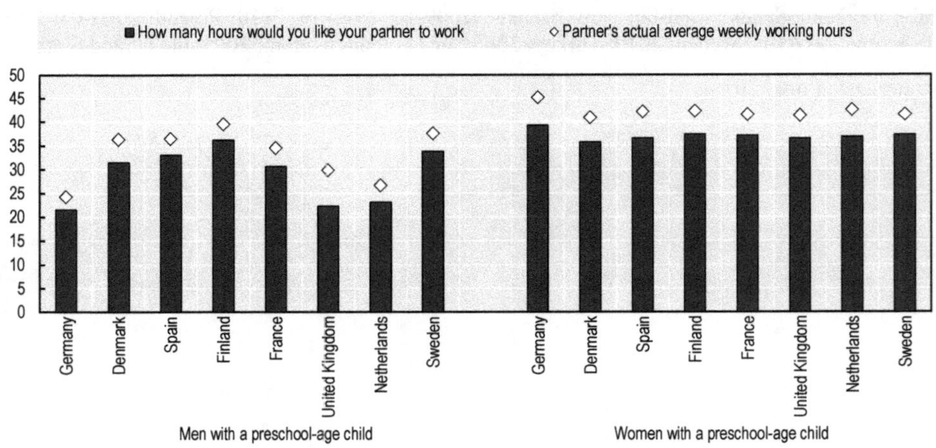

Source: European Social Survey (2010).

3. Sharing pays for society as a whole

Germany faces mounting demographic pressures. Promoting a better reconciliation of work and family life can deliver a double dividend to the German labour market: it will help the German labour market both in the short term – as more mothers work and/or work longer paid hours – and potentially limit the decline of the overall population, by promoting higher birth rates.

Realising women's professional potential in the labour market benefits the German economy

OECD projections suggest that GDP would increase by 12% over the next 20 years if labour force participation rates among women in OECD countries reached male levels (OECD, 2012). One of the areas of greatest untapped potential in the German labour force is inactive and/or part-time working mothers. Better sharing of unpaid work at home accompanied by coherent public policies helps mothers to maintain labour market attachment and continue their careers.

Given that women's levels of educational attainment now matches or outpaces men's in most OECD countries, there are potentially large losses to the economy when women stay at home or work short part-time hours. Young German women are well-educated in comparison to young German men: 32.1% of 25 to 34 years-old women have completed tertiary education, compared to 27.9% of their male peers (Chapter 2). OECD (2012) found that, across OECD countries, increases in educational attainment accounted for around 50% of all economic growth between 1960 and 2008, over half of which was due to increased female educational attainment.

More equal sharing of paid work between men and women can counteract the projected decline of the German labour force. In Sweden (one of the most gender-equal countries with a strong family support system) men's (fathers and non-fathers) paid work hours are about an hour less than in Germany on average and women's (mothers and non-mothers) paid work hours more than three hours more per week compared to Germany. If, by 2040, German men and women aged 25 to 54 emulated the labour market behaviour of Swedish men and women in the same age bracket, the projected decrease in the German labour force would be slowed and GDP per capita could increase, if it is assumed that changes in labour force participation rates or weekly working hours do not affect the labour demand (see Chapter 2 for a detailed discussion of different scenarios).

When employment and childbearing conflict, fertility rates suffer

Women's educational attainment and participation in paid employment increase the cost of interrupting their career for childrearing. In countries with limited support for reconciling work and family life, child birth often implies a significant reduction in family income, as at least one partner has to stop (or reduce) their employment participation in order to care for the new child.

There is significant tension between paid work and family commitments in Germany. The number of children in a family has a greater adverse effect on female employment in Germany than in many other OECD countries, and German women are much more likely to remain childless than women elsewhere (Chapter 6). In 2012, 36% of 25-to-49 year-old women were childless, compared to only 28% in France where definitive childlessness is also much less frequent than in most European countries (Miettinen et al., 2015). There is also a sizeable gap between women's preferences for childlessness and actual childlessness in Germany. Seven percent of women in Germany state that having no children is their "ideal" – this is 4% on average across the OECD (Eurobarometer 2014), which suggests that many households experience "unwanted" childlessness in Germany. Large families – those with three or more children – are also relatively uncommon in Germany.

The challenges in reconciling work and family life have contributed to persistently low total fertility rates (TFRs) in Germany (OECD, 2011). Since 1990, its TFR has hovered around 1.3 to 1.4 children per woman, although it edged up to 1.47 in 2014. Nevertheless, this is lower than the OECD average of 1.67 and well below the population replacement rate of 2.1 children per woman. Stagnating fertility rates are a particularly important issue for Germany: aside from the personal satisfaction derived from raising children, fewer babies means fewer workers in the future, with pernicious consequences for the economy.

Birth rates in Germany vary with women's educational attainment, occupation, and earnings (Dorbritz, 2008; Kreyenfeld and Konietzka, 2013; Bujard, 2015). German women with higher educational attainment are less likely to have children, as are women engaged in paid work and (especially) women engaged in full-time paid work. Women with higher earnings are also much less likely to have a child than women with lower earnings, as lower-income women often live with a male breadwinner. Differences in gender roles are less dramatic in France, where the likelihood of giving birth actually increases with a woman's earnings (Chapter 6). Fertility behaviour is also less dependent on women's working hours in France where the supply of child care, preschool and out-of-school care services is typically high.

International literature suggests that fathers' involvement in caring for a first born child is positively associated with the likelihood of families deciding to have a second child (Duvander et al., 2010; Aassve et al., 2015; Miettinen et al., 2015; Cooke, 2004). However, there is little scholarly consensus regarding the relationship between the general household division of labour and fertility, as studies vary in how gender equality is measured and typically do not measure "sharing" behaviours. This is an important avenue for future research.

4. Preparing for sharing: Social policies can promote partnership in families

Socioeconomic and demographic factors affect the degree to which household labour is shared. More equitable within-household divisions of labour are generally observed in couples who are unmarried, dual-earners, well-educated, younger egalitarian in their attitudes, and childless. Households in post-communist countries also share housework more equally.

A bird's eye view of recent policy change in German

German families face considerable challenges to spending more time together and achieving a more gender-balanced reconciliation of work and family life. Family policy can play an important role and Germany has already made substantial progress in supporting families ahead of and after the birth of a child (Chapter 3). In 2007, parental leave transfers were changed from a flat-rate, means-tested child-raising allowance to an earnings-related parental leave benefit with floors and ceilings.

Payments were set for 12 months, with another two months possible for the partner (typically the father) if s/he used at least two months of parental leave.

The 2007 reform significantly increased the probability of mothers to return to work after the expiry of the benefit, and particularly supported highly educated mothers' return to full-time work (Kluve and Schmitz, 2014; Kluve and Tamm, 2013). As parents (mostly women) return quicker and in greater numbers to the labour market, much of any additional cost of the scheme is likely to be offset by increases in tax receipts and decreases in other public expenditures associated with inactivity: Estimates by the research institute RWI suggest that even in its first few years as much as 25% of the additional cost was cancelled out by increases in government revenues and decreases in other expenditure (Bechara et al., 2015).

The 2007 reform to the parental leave system in Germany was a good step forward in ensuring that fathers engage more in parenting, and this policy reform was in line with international best practice, as it is similar to examples in Iceland, France, Portugal and Sweden (Adema et al., 2015). Following the German reform, the share of fathers claiming the parental leave allowance doubled to one-third over the 2009-13 period (Destatis, 2015b).

The parental leave reform of 2015 further encourages fathers' leave taking and provides financial incentives to couples to develop (and ideally sustain) a more balanced division of paid and unpaid work. The 2015 reform facilitates combining part-time work and leave taking ("ElterngeldPlus"), and better leave sharing among partners in couple families), as couples in which both partners work 25 to 30 hours per week for at least four months are now rewarded with a partnership bonus equal to four additional months of parental leave benefit (the "Partnerschaftsbonus"). Greater acceptance of fathers' reducing working hours and taking leave when children are young is another corner stone of equal sharing between mothers and fathers. When men present a greater "risk" of temporarily leaving a job around child birth, child-bearing age women may encounter less hiring discrimination and/or earnings and career penalties associated with taking leave. By further increasing father's take-up and generating better sharing among fathers and mothers, this reform as well as information campaigns targeted at employers would also help to "destigmatise" fathers' leave among employers and help improve gender diversity in workplaces.

Public policy models in countries such as Denmark, France and Sweden aim to provide families with a continuum of support throughout childhood. Apart from paid leave arrangements, this involves the provision of affordable quality ECEC and OSH services that allow parents to combine children with full-time paid employment, including during school holidays. Since the mid-2000s Germany has also increased considerably investment in ECEC services, to the benefit of children and their parents (OECD, 2011). Nevertheless, capacity rather than affordability appears to be an issue. Out-of-pocket centre-based child care costs for German parents are similar to those for Danish and Swedish parents (Chapter 3), but – despite a marked increase in recent years – ECEC participation rates are still below the OECD average (Figure 1.7).

Figure 1.7. Enrolment in child care is catching up in Germany

Participation rates for 0-2 year-olds in formal early childhood education and care services,[1] 2006[2] and 2013[3]

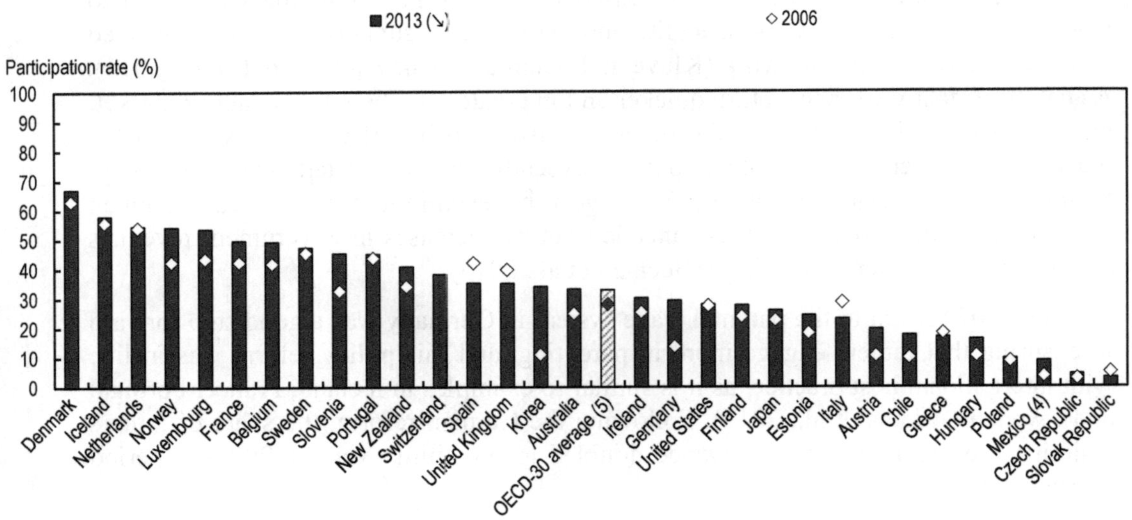

1. Data generally include children in centre-based services, organised day care and pre-school (both public and private) and those who are cared for by a professional child-minder, and exclude informal services provided by relatives, friends or neighbours. Exact definitions may however differ slightly across countries.

2. Data for Australia refer to 2005.

3. Data for Japan refer to 2010, and for Australia, Chile, Mexico and the United States to 2011.

4. Data for Mexico do not include services provided by the private sector.

5. Unweighted average for the 30 OECD countries with data available at both time points.

Source: *OECD Family Database*, http://www.oecd.org/els/family/database.htm.

In addition, there are initiatives to extend all-day schooling and out-of-school-hours (OSH) care, although there is still room for improvement: some 15% of German 6-10 year-olds use OSH services, compared to around 80% in Denmark and Sweden. Before (and after) the school day starts and ends, children can do their homework or take part in leisure activities organised by the local authorities. Parents thus benefit from longer, more flexible, publicly provided child-care hours.

Flexible working arrangements are crucial as they can give employees greater autonomy in managing their working hours to better reconcile work and family life, while they can contribute to maintaining the knowledge base in the workforce and limit hiring costs for employers. Since the mid-2000s, policy in Germany has moved to promote a more gender-equal sharing of time for child care and work, and in this sense it is ahead of most OECD countries, except perhaps the Nordic countries. There are a range of publicly-supported initiatives involving different stakeholders in the private sector, which include initiatives towards greater sharing of best practices amongst stakeholders and audits of family-friendly companies. Most recently, in 2015 various stakeholders (including employer associations and unions) signed a memorandum on the "New Reconciliation" of work and family life ("Die Neue Vereinbarkeit"). The memorandum identifies areas of progress (e.g. greater awareness of flexible working hours in companies) but also challenges (e.g. encouraging longer paid work hours of mothers), and it develops guidelines for successfully balancing work and life across the life cycle for employees and companies. This includes promoting reduced full-time working hours, i.e. less than 40 hours per week, particularly with regard to employees with care responsibilities for small children.

The 2015 parental leave reform ("ElterngeldPlus") can be seen as a stepping stone towards a "family working time model", which aims to support parents with young children who want to equally share work and family responsibilities. One proposal for such a model (Müller et al., 2013) involves offering an income supplement to coupled parents when both partners change their work hours to reduced full-time working-hours employment ("vollzeitnah") for a period of three years. On average this would involve shorter paid work hours of fathers and longer paid work hours of mothers with positive implications for family incomes and wellbeing, fathers' time with children, women's career progression and wages. A lower paid workload could allow fathers to invest more time in their children at a young age and set the basis for greater paternal involvement as children grow up.

Any type of dual-reduced full-time schedule would also give most mothers more paid hours, as most mothers in Germany currently work part-time, and it may provide a stepping stone for part-time mothers to transition to longer hours as children age. OECD estimates show that under these assumptions the "family working-time model", increases in female working hours would almost entirely cancel out any decreases in male hours, and should thus have a limited overall effect on German labour supply (Chapter 2). Furthermore, a period of reduced full-time work when children are very young could facilitate an increase to full-time work for both parents (which is very difficult when starting from a short-hours base), and further stimulate German labour supply in the long-term, which will be essential to cope with population ageing.

The German public is ready for change. Surveys suggest that many Germans are unhappy with their work-life balance: working parents in Germany are more likely than most other parents in Europe to report that their job interferes with time they would like to spend with their family. And although parents of young children express a preference for their partner (both mothers and fathers) to work fewer hours outside the home, Germans have become more prone to the idea of mothers of young children entering the paid workforce (Chapter 2): 61% of the German population believe that it is important to support parents with children under 3 years in a way that facilitates the employment of both partners (Allensbach Institut für Demoskopie, 2015), and many parents feel that enterprises could do more to promote a better reconciliation of work and family life (BMFSFJ, 2013).

Policy recommendations for Germany

To further facilitate an equal sharing of work and family responsibilities and achieve a better reconciliation of work and family life, this review recommends German policy makers to:

- *Continue to encourage more fathers to take up parental leave*. The 2007 reform of the parental leave system in Germany was in line with international best practice and a great step towards a more gender-balanced division of paid and unpaid work. Evaluations have shown that it significantly increased the probability of mothers to return to work earlier than before upon expiry of the benefit, and markedly increased father's use of parental leave.

"ElterngeldPlus" reform in 2015 facilitates combining part-time work and leave taking and provides financial incentives to encourage both partners in couple families to engage in paid work for 25 to 30 hours per week for at least four months. The impact of this reform should be closely monitored in order to see whether it contributes to a further increase in fathers' uptake of leave, fathers reducing their full-time working hours for a limited period of time and mothers increasing their hours in paid work.

- Building on the experience with "Elterngeld" and "ElterngeldPlus", *continue to develop family-policy supports* including options for parents with young children to work reduced full-time hours for a specific period of time during which they may receive associated financial support as currently debated in Germany under the notion of the "family working-time model". Reduced full-time hours could help many fathers to invest more time in their children at a young age, while compared to long-term short part-time hours, working reduced full-time hours on a temporary basis is likely to have positive effects on women's earnings and career opportunities.
- Having established the right to reduce working hours for family reasons, introduce a *right to increase working hours to full-time work* – or another level of working hours that fits their changing family circumstances – within a specified time frame. Parents could use working-time flexibility to match their work and family commitments – also as children grow up.
- *Continue to increase investment in, and ensure broader access to, child care for young children.* Parenthood is a crucial time for couples to set patterns in paid and unpaid work, and the adequate and affordable provision of early childhood education and care (ECEC) is key to enabling both parents to work while having a family. Germany has improved public investment in ECEC over the past 15 years. Yet more investment is needed to ensure that supply meets demand, especially in regions where ECEC is underprovided, and to meet parents' needs more flexibly.
- Compared to investment in ECEC, progress in OSH-care supports in Germany has to catch up: *greater investment and broader access to, out-of-school-hours supports* for primary-school age children is needed. Child care issues do not stop when children enter primary school, and full-time workers in Germany need to arrange care before and/or after school hours. Public policy in Germany should invest more in OSH-care supports that help parents with school age children to combine full-time work with family life, also during school holidays.
- *Adjust the German tax-benefit system in order to encourage couples to share paid work equally.* Tax-benefit policies in about one-third of OECD countries encourage equal sharing of paid work within couples, mainly due to individual progressive taxation. By contrast, the joint income tax system, free co-insurance of spouses, and the cap on social security contributions in Germany, ensure that the tax burden on household labour increases strongly when a second person takes up employment unless s/he engages in a tax free minijob with income of up to EUR 450 per month. Financial incentives to work for second earners in couple families could be improved in different ways, as for example through a separate tax-free allowance for second earners, or assessing health contribution on basis of the number of adults who are insured, with compensation for low-income families (see OECD, 2016c and Chapter 3 for more detail).

- *Further extend the co-operation with social partners and other stakeholders to make workplace practices more conducive to family life.* Continue to promote a range of family-friendly workplace measures as in the scope of the "Neue Vereinbarkeit Memorandum", including reducing the number of hours in a typical full-time workday, encouraging fathers' leave taking, facilitating remote work, and allowing flexible work schedules.
- The German authorities are encouraged to *continue* with their work *raising awareness of the benefits of equal partnerships in families*, through public information campaigns, promotion of role models, high-visibility events, and other means of communication. Maintain support to initiatives aimed at fostering and sharing best practices at the local level such as the local alliances for families ("Lokale Bündnisse für Familie") taking into account the peculiarities of Länder and the role of municipalities.

Promoting partnerships in which fathers and mother share the responsibility for children equally is good for families and their well-being, and also produces a range of less tangible social goods, like better father-child bonding and promoting egalitarian gender norms across generations and enabling better work-life balance. In turn, a more balanced sharing of work and family responsibilities amongst fathers and mothers, as for example debated in the context of a "family working-time model", could provide families with more time for each other and enable men and women to reach their full potential in the labour market. If fathers and mothers were both to work reduced full-time hours on a temporary basis, and pursue their labour market career on a full-time basis as children grow up this would contribute to a marked reduction of gender pay and pension gaps and sustain labour supply of men and women thereby ensuring inclusive growth in future.

References

Aassve, A. et al. (2015), "What Is your Couple Type? Gender Ideology, Housework Sharing, and Babies", *Demographic Research*, Vol. 32, No. 30, pp. 835-858.

Adema, W., C. Clarke and V. Frey (2015), "Paid Parental Leave: Lessons from OECD Countries and Selected U.S. States", *OECD Social, Employment and Migration Working Papers*, No. 172, OECD Publishing, Paris, http://dx.doi.org/10.1787/5jrqgvqqb4vb-en.

Allensbach Institut für Demoskopie (2015a), "Familienbilder in Deutschland und Frankreich – Vergleich der Ergebnisse von Repräsentativbefragungen der Bevölkerung im Alter von 16 bis 49 Jahren in beiden Ländern", Allensbach.

Allensbach Institut für Demoskopie (2015b), "Weichenstellungen für die Aufgabenteilung in Familie und Beruf", Allensbach, http://www.ifd-allensbach.de/fileadmin/IfD/sonstige_pdfs/Weichenstellungen_Bericht_FINAL.pdf.

Barnes, M.W. (2015), "Gender Differentiation in Paid and Unpaid Work during the Transition to Parenthood", *Sociology Compass*, Vol. 9, No. 5, pp. 348-364.

Baxter, J. (2015), "Children's Time with Fathers and Mothers over the Pre-School Years: A Longitudinal Time-Use Study of Couple Families in Australia", *Family Science*, Vol. 6, No. 1, pp. 302-317.

Baxter, J. and D. Smart (2010), "Fathering in Australia Among Couple Families with Young Children", *FaHCSIA Occasional Paper*, No. 37, Department of Families, Housing, Community Services and Indigenous Affairs, Canberra.

Baxter, J., B. Hewitt and M. Haynes (2008), "Life Course Transitions and Housework: Marriage, Parenthood, and Time on Housework", *Journal of Marriage and Family*, Vol. 70, No. 2, pp. 259-272.

Bechara, P., J. Kluve and M. Tamm (2015), "Fiskalische Refinanzierungseffekte des Elterngeldes –Projektbericht zum Forschungsvorhaben des Bundesministeriums für Familie, Senioren, Frauen und Jugend", Rheinisch-Westfälisches Institut für Wirtschaftsforschung.

Bertrand, M., E. Kamenica and J. Pan (2015), "Gender Identity and Relative Income within Households", *Quarterly Journal of Economics*, Vol. 130, No. 2, pp. 571-614.

Bittman, M. and J. Wajman (2000), "The Rush Hour: The Character of Leisure Time and Gender Equity", *Social Forces*, Vol. 79, No. 1, pp. 165-189.

BMFSFJ – Federal Ministry for Family Affairs, Senior Citizens, Women and Youth (2015a), "Family Report 2014, Benefits, Effects, Trends", Bundesministerium für Familie, Senioren, Frauen und Jugend, Berlin, December.

BMFSFJ (2015b), "Dossier Väter und Familie – erste Bilanz einer neuen Dynamik", Bundesministerium für Familie, Senioren, Frauen und Jugend, Berlin.

BMFSFJ (2013), "Family Report 2012 Benefits, Effects, Trends", Bundesministerium für Familie, Senioren, Frauen und Jugend, Berlin, December.

Brandth, B. and I. Gislason (2012), "Family Policies and the Best Interest of Children", in B.G. Eydal and I. Gíslason (eds.), *Parental Leave, Childcare and Gender Equality in the Nordic Countries*, Nordic Council, Copenhagen.

Bujard, M. (2015b), "Kinderlosigkeit in Deutschland: Wie interagieren Bildung, Wohnort, Migrationshintergrund, Erwerbstätigkeit und Kohorte?, Zeitschrift für Familienforschung, 27(3)– Journal of Family Research, pp. 1-25.

Business Roundtable (1980), "Scheduled Overtime Effect on Construction Projects: A Construction Industry Cost-effectiveness Project Report".

Cooke, L. (2004), "The Gendered Division of Labour and Family Outcomes in Germany", *Journal of Marriage and the Family*, Vol. 66, No. 5, pp. 1246-1259.

Craig, L. and P. Sawrikar (2009), "Work and Family: How Does the (Gender) Balance Change as Children Grow?", *Gender, Work & Organization*, Vol. 16, No. 6, pp. 684-709.

Cunningham, M. (2001), "Parental Influences on the Gendered Division of Housework", *American Sociological Review*, Vol. 66, No. 2, pp. 184-203.

Davis, S. and T. Greenstein (2009), "Gender Ideology: Components, Predictors, and Consequences", *Annual Review of Sociology*, Vol. 35, pp. 87-105.

Dembe, A. et al. (2005), "The Impact of Overtime and Long Hours on Occupational Injuries and Illnesses: New Evidence from the United States", *Occupational and Environmental Medicine*, Vol. 62, No. 9, pp. 588-597.

Destatis – German Statistical Office (2015a), "Wie die Zeit vergeht, Ergebnisse zur Zeitverwendung in Deutschland 2012/2013", Statistisches Bundesamt, Wiesbaden.

Destatis (2015b), "Kinder und tätige Personen in Tageseinrichtungen und in öffentlich geförderter Kindertagespflege am 01.03.2015 – Bundes- und Ländererergebnisse", Statistisches Bundesamt, Wiesbaden.

Dorbritz, J. (2008), "Germany: Family Diversity with Low, Actual, and Desired Fertility", *Demographic Research*, Vol. 19, No. 17, pp. 557-598.

Duvander, A., T. Lappegard and G. Andersson, (2010), "Family Policy and Fertility: A Comparative Study on the Impact of Fathers' and Mothers' Use of Parental Leave on Continued Childbearing in Norway and Sweden", *Journal of European Social Policy*, Vol. 20, No. 1, pp. 45-57.

Eggebeen, D. and C. Knoester (2001), "Does Fatherhood Matter for Men?", *Journal of Marriage and Family*, Vol. 63, No. 2, pp. 381-393.

Eichhorst, W. et al. (2012), " Geringfügige Beschäftigung: Situation und Gestaltungsoptionen im Auftrag der Bertelsmann Stiftung", IZA Discussion Paper, Bonn.

Flinn, F. and C. Armstrong (2011), "Junior Doctors' Extended Work Hours and the Effects on their Performance: The Irish Case", *International Journal for Quality in Health Care*, Vol. 23, No. 2. pp. 210-217.

Goodman, W. et al. (2008), "Paternal Work Characteristics and Father-Infant Interactions in Low-Income, Rural Families", *Journal of Marriage and Family*, Vol. 70, No. 3, pp. 640–653.

Huerta, M.C. et al. (2013), "Fathers' Leave, Fathers' Involvement and Child Development: Are They Related? Evidence from Four OECD Countries", *OECD Social, Employment and Migration Working Papers*, No. 140, OECD Publishing, Paris, http://dx.doi.org/10.1787/5k4dlw9w6czq-en.

Ishii-Kuntz, M. (2013), "Work Environment and Japanese Fathers' Involvement in Child Care", *Journal of Family Issues*, Vol. 34, No. 2, pp. 252–271.

Kluve, J. and S. Schmitz (2014), "Mittelfristige Effekte der Elterngeldreform in Ost- und Westdeutschland", *Vierteljahrshefte zur Wirtschaftsforschung*, Vol. 83, No. 4, pp. 163-181.

Kluve, J. and M. Tamm (2013), "Parental Leave Regulations, Mothers' Labor Force Attachment and Fathers' Childcare Involvement: Evidence from a Natural Experiment", *Journal of Population Economics*, Vol. 26, No. 3, pp. 983-1005.

Kreyenfeld, M. and D. Konietzka (2013), *Ein Leben ohne Kinder: Ausmaß, Strukturen und Ursachen von Kinderlosigkeit in Deutschland*, Springer.

Lamb, M. (2010), *The Role of the Father in Child Development*, Fifth edition, Wiley, New York.

Lundberg, S. and R. Pollak (1996), "Bargaining and Distribution in Marriage", *Journal of Economic Perspectives*, Vol. 10, No. 4, pp. 139-158.

McGinn, K., M. Ruiz Castro and E. Long Lingo (2015), "Mums the Word! Cross-national Relationship between Maternal Employment and Gender Inequalities at Work and at Home", *Harvard Business School Working Paper*, No. 15-094.

Miettinen, A., L. Lainiala and A. Rotkirch (2015), "Women's Housework Decreases Fertility: Evidence from a Longitudinal Study among Finnish Couples", *Acta Sociologica*, Vol. 58, No. 2, pp. 139-154.

Miettinen, A. et al. (2015), "Increasing Childlessness in Europe: Time Trends and Country Differences", *Families & Societies*, Working Paper, No. 33, Stockholm.

OECD (2016a), "The OECD Gender Data Portal", OECD Publishing, Paris, http://www.oecd.org/gender/data/.

OECD (2016b), *The OECD Family Database*, OECD Publishing, Paris, http://www.oecd.org/els/family/database.htm.

OECD (2016c), *OECD Economic Surveys: Germany*, OECD Publishing, Paris, http://dx.doi.org/10.1787/eco_surveys-deu-2016-en.

OECD (2015a), *Pensions at a Glance 2015: OECD and G20 indicators*, OECD Publishing, Paris, http://dx.doi.org/10.1787/pension_glance-2015-en.

OECD (2015b), *In It Together: Why Less Inequality Benefits All*. OECD Publishing, Paris, http://dx.doi.org/10.1787/9789264235120-en.

OECD (2014), *OECD Employment Database 2014*, http://www.oecd.org/employment/onlineoecdemploymentdatabase.htm.

OECD (2012), *Closing the Gender Gap: Act Now*, OECD Publishing, Paris, http://dx.doi.org/10.1787/9789264179370-en.

OECD (2011a), *Doing Better for Families*, OECD Publishing, Paris, http://dx.doi.org/10.1787/9789264098732-en.

Olivetti, C., E. Patacchini and Y. Zenou (2013), "Mothers, Friends and Gender Identity", *IZA Discussion Paper*, No. 7704, Bonn.

Pencavel, J. (2014), "The Productivity of Working Hours", *IZA Discussion Paper*, No. 8129, Bonn.

Rendall, M. et al. (2014), "Employment Impacts on Partnership and Parenthood Entry in Different Family-Policy Regimes", European Population Conference, http://epc2014.princeton.edu/.

Rogers, A. et al. (2004), "The Working Hours of Hospital Staff Nurses and Patient Safety", *Health Affairs*, Vol. 23, No. 4, pp. 202-212.

Schober, P. (2015), "Increasing Father Involvement in Child Care: What Do We Know About Effects on Child Development?", *DIW Roundup: Politik im Fokus*, No. 79.

Schober, P. (2013), "The Parenthood Effect on Gender Inequality: Explaining the Change in Paid and Domestic Work when British Couples Become Parents", *European Sociological Review*, Vol. 29, No. 1, pp. 74-85.

Sigle-Rushton, W. (2010), "Men's Unpaid Work and Divorce: Reassessing Specialization and Trade in British Families", *Feminist Economics*, Vol. 16, No. 2, pp. 1-26.

Thomas, R. and K. Raynar (1997), "Scheduled Overtime and Labor Productivity: quantitative Analysis", *Journal of Construction and Engineering Management*, Vol. 123, No. 2, pp. 181-188.

WHO (2007), "Fatherhood and Health Outcomes in Europe", WHO Regional Office for Europe, Copenhagen, Denmark.

Wood, J., J. Vergauwen and K. Neels (2015), "Economic Conditions and Variation in First Birth Hazards in 22 European Countries between 1970 and 2005", in K. Matthijs et al. (eds.), *Population Change in Europe, the Middle-East and North-Africa : Beyond the Demographic Divide*, Ashgate Publishing, pp. 45-80, http://www.ashgate.com/isbn/9781472439567.

Woolley, F. (2004), "Why Pay Child Benefits to Mothers?", *Canadian Public Policy*, Vol. 30, No. 1, pp. 47-69.

WSI – Institute of Economic and Social Research (2015), "Gender News: Große Unterschiede in den Arbeitszeiten von Frauen und Männern, Ergebnisse aus dem WSI GenderDatenPortal", *WSI Report*, No. 22, Wirtschafts- und Sozialwissenschaftliches Institute, Düsseldorf.

Chapter 2

Partnerships, family composition and the division of labour: Germany in the context of the OECD

German family policy seeks to promote equal partnerships in families in furtherance of its objective of enabling parents to have children, spend more time with them, and participate in the labour market. This chapter seeks to provide context and perspective. It begins by looking at demography in Germany and other OECD countries, with particular focus on fertility, family make-up, marriage and the rise of cohabitation. Section 3 addresses women's role in the labour market. It finds that, although there has been strong growth in female employment over the last 15 years, German women continue to earn less than men and are all too often confined to part-time work. Yet they are increasingly well educated, and often better educated than men. The next section finds that inequality also prevails in unpaid work in the home, where women still do the lion's share of housework and parenting. Section 5 considers widespread dissatisfaction with the struggle to balance work and family life, while the final section examines how a more equal gender distribution of paid work might impact on the German labour force and German economic performance.

The statistical data for Israel are supplied by and under the responsibility of the relevant Israeli authorities. The use of such data by the OECD is without prejudice to the status of the Golan Heights, East Jerusalem and Israeli settlements in the West Bank under the terms of international law.

1. Introduction and main findings

Most German children live with two married or cohabiting parents.[1] Indeed, the proportion living in couple families is slightly higher than the average for European OECD countries. Clearly, therefore, sharing practices in such families are an important parameter to factor into evaluations of family policy and gender equality in Germany and elsewhere.

Time spent at work affects family time and vice versa. Couple families where the man is the main earner are common in Germany, as in much of the OECD. Germany, however, faces unique challenges in its efforts to bring parents to share home and workplace responsibilities equally. A relatively high number of women – many of whom are mothers – are in part-time work. Although both families and society benefit when women work longer hours, parents' efforts to combine full-time work with family responsibilities are complicated by the fact that full-time jobs in Germany entail relatively long hours and public child care provisions, while recently extended, are still being further developed. Parents also do not share unpaid housework and care-giving equally, with women still doing more than their male partners. Patterns in parents' sharing of paid and unpaid work exert macro-level effects. Indeed, countries where the gender gap in time spent on housework and caring is narrowest are also those where it is narrowest in employment rates, with considerable consequences for economic growth and socioeconomic equality.

This chapter reviews the environment in which family life currently unfolds in Germany, as policy seeks to help parents and children spend more time together by fostering *Partnerschaftlichkeit* (partnership) in the sharing of work- and family-related responsibilities. It describes time-sharing trends in the home and the workplace over the past 15 years, seeking to identify areas in Germany and the OECD where there has and has not been progress. The chapter also looks at international indicators of family well-being and gender equality that relate to equal partnership in families (Chapter 3).

Section 2 describes demographic conditions in Germany and other OECD countries, focusing particularly on family composition, living arrangements, and fertility. Section 3 addresses couples and paid work, looking at men's and women's levels of educational attainment, their employment statuses, and the prevalence of part-time work, particularly among women. Section 4 concerns itself with gender differences in unpaid household work and finds that German women still do more than men. Section 5 examines changes in attitudes to work-life balance and the roles of parents. Finally, Section 6 considers how the gendered distribution of paid work may affect growth in coming years. Overall, Germany has made great strides in improving the gendered distribution of paid and unpaid labour. There is still plenty of room for further progress, however.

Main findings

- Most children in Germany live with two parents, many of whom are married. However, as cohabitation becomes more common, more and more children are growing up in households with two cohabiting parents.
- Germany's total fertility rate (TFR) has been low since the 1970s and remains well below the population replacement level. However, since a historic low of 1.24 children per woman in 1994, the TFR has risen by 0.23 points to 1.47 in 2014.

- Many German parents are dissatisfied with their work-life balance, and both fathers and mothers of young children would prefer their partner to work fewer hours per week.
- Although Germans have become more positive towards mothers of young children going out to work, many think mothers should work only part-time, not full-time.
- Young German women are more likely than young men to have higher education qualifications. However, they are still underrepresented in fields like engineering and science, although they have made significant inroads into mathematics- and statistics-related occupations since 2000.
- German women have entered the labour market in large numbers over the past 15 years. However, most are in part-time employment. German men continue to account for the bulk of full-time jobs, and many work long hours. The gender gap in working hours contributes to the persistent gender pay gap at the national level and in households.
- Women in Germany are less likely to be self-employed than men, and earn nearly 43% less from self-employment too.
- Although many more German women are now in paid work, the within-household distribution of unpaid labour has changed little. They continue to do more housework than their male partners.
- The size of the German labour force is projected to fall sharply over the next few decades as the population ages and the number of people of working age shrinks. Closing the gender gap in paid work so that it is similar to those in France or Sweden would help mitigate looming shortfalls in labour supply. But Germany can address labour shortages comprehensively only if women's patterns of paid work move towards and eventually converge with men's.

2. Most children live in couple families, but many families still have few children

Most children live with two parents, and often with two married parents

In Germany, like elsewhere in the OECD, most children grow up in households with two parents (Figure 2.1). In 2014, about 83.1% of children (0-to-17 year-olds) were living in a household with two parents, slightly above the average for European OECD countries (82.5%). German children are, however, far more likely to be living with married parents than children in many other European OECD countries – about 75.6% of German children were living with two married parents in 2014, compared to less than 60% in France and many of the Northern European OECD countries (Estonia, France, Iceland, Norway and Sweden).

The share of German children living with two parents has fallen slightly over the past two decades or so (Figure 2.2). According to data from Destatis (2015a), the share of children (0-to-17 year-olds) living in two parent families declined by almost 6 percentage points between 1996 and 2014. This is entirely on account of a drop in the number of children in families with two married parents, which fell by more than 10 percentage points between 1996 and 2014. Over the same period, the share of children living in families with two cohabiting parents more than doubled from 4% to the 9% – mirroring an increase in cohabitation in the adult population (see Box 2.1).

Figure 2.1. German children are more likely to live with married parents and less likely to live with cohabiting parents than children in most other European OECD countries

Distribution (%) of children (0-to-17 year-olds) by presence and marital status of parents[1] in the household, 2014

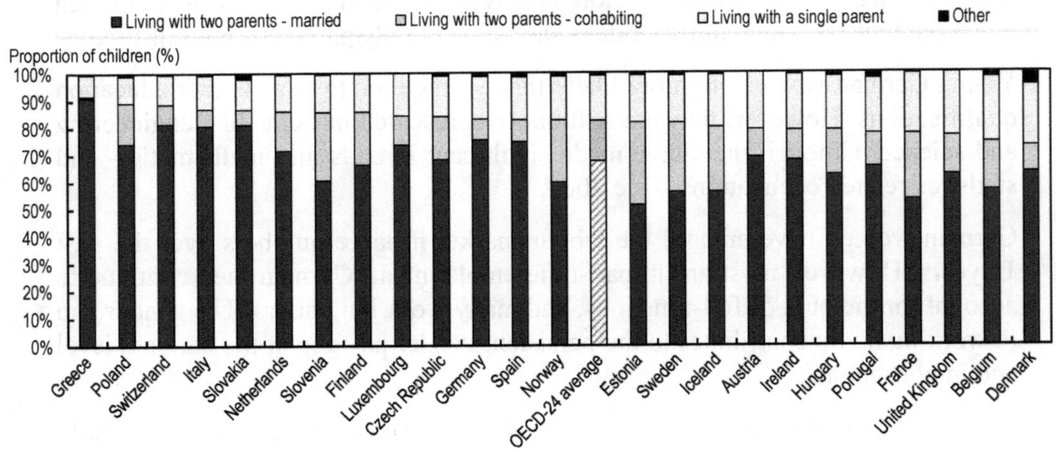

Note: Data for Estonia, Iceland, Ireland and Switzerland refer to 2013.

1. "Parents" refers to both biological parents, step-parents, and adoptive parents. "Living with two parents – married" denotes a situation where children live in a household with two married parents. "Living with two parents – cohabiting" refers to a situation where children live with two parents who are not married. "Living with a single parent" refers to a situation where the child lives in a household where only one adult is reported as a parent. "Other" denotes situations where children live in a household where no adult is reported as a parent.

Source: Eurostat, http://ec.europa.eu/eurostat/data/database.

Figure 2.2. The share of children living with two parents has fallen over the past couple of decades

Distribution (%) of children (0-to-17 year-olds) by family type,[1] Germany, 1996-2014

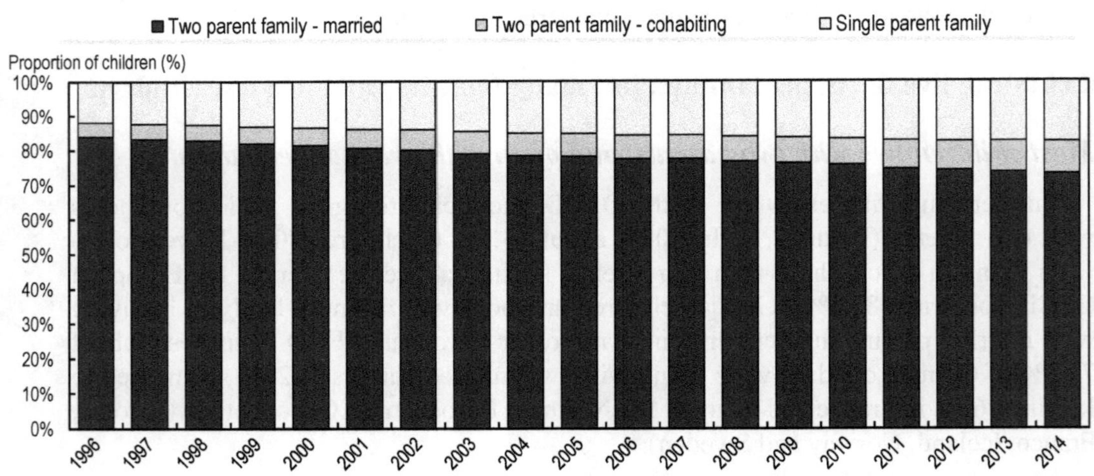

1. "Family type" refers to situations where two or more people live in the same household either as partners or as parent and child. "Parents" refers to both biological parents, step-parents, and adoptive parents. "Two parent family – married" denotes a family where children live with two parents who are married to each other. "Two parent family – cohabiting" denotes a family where children live with two parents who are not married to each other or are in a same-sex registered partnership. "Single parent family" refers to a situation where children live with one parent without a spouse or partner in the same household.

Source: Destatis (2015a).

Box 2.1. Partnership patterns are changing in Germany

In Germany, as in many other OECD countries, patterns of partnership are changing. In 1996, just over 48% of the total German population – around 39.2 million adults – reported living as a part of a married couple. By 2014, that proportion had fallen to a little under 43.7%, or around 35 million (Destatis, 2015a).

Long-run falls in the numbers of people getting married and increases in those divorcing are the main drivers behind the decline in the number of married couples. The marriage rate in Germany is moderate compared to many OECD countries (OECD, 2016a), but has dropped markedly over the past 40 years – from 7.4 marriages per 1 000 people in 1970 to 4.6 in 2013 (Eurostat, 2016). At the same time, the crude divorce rate – also moderate in comparison with some other OECD countries (OECD, 2016a) – climbed from 1.3 in 1970 to 2.1 in 2013 (Eurostat, 2016). Both marriage and divorce rates have stabilised over the past decade, with the number of marriages having actually increased very slightly and the share of marriages ending in divorce having decreased somewhat since the mid-2000s (Eurostat, 2016; Destatis, 2016). Still, far fewer people are getting married, and more are getting divorced, now than three or four decades ago.

Many Germans are instead opting for alternative forms of partnership. Between 1996 and 2014, the proportion of the population that reported living in a cohabiting couple grew by over 60% – from around 4.5% of the total population, or 3.7 million people, to just under 7.3% of the population, or a little over 5.8 million (Destatis, 2015a). The increase in cohabitation is related in part to rises in the prevalence of same-sex couples. Over the same period, the number of people who reported living in a same-sex couple climbed from around 75 000 to just over 175 000. But opposite-sex couples, too, are increasingly likely to cohabit. In 1996, about 3.6 million people reported they were in living in an unmarried opposite-sex cohabiting couple. By 2014, the number had climbed to just under 5.7 million (Destatis, 2015a).

Cohabitation is particularly popular among younger age groups (Figure 2.3). Data from the 2011 European Union Population and Housing Census showed that, in Germany, around 18.5% of 30-to-34 year-olds and almost 22% of 25-to-29 year-olds were living in a couple with a cohabiting partner. In fact, among young people between the ages of 20 and 29, cohabiting was more widespread than marriage. Many of those in a cohabiting couple may of course go on to get married in later life. Nevertheless, and among the youngest generations in particular, there is clear and growing acceptance of cohabitation as an alternative to marriage.

Figure 2.3. Cohabitation is particularly common among younger people in Germany

Proportion (%) of people in private households living in a married couple or registered partnership or cohabiting, by age group, Germany, 2011

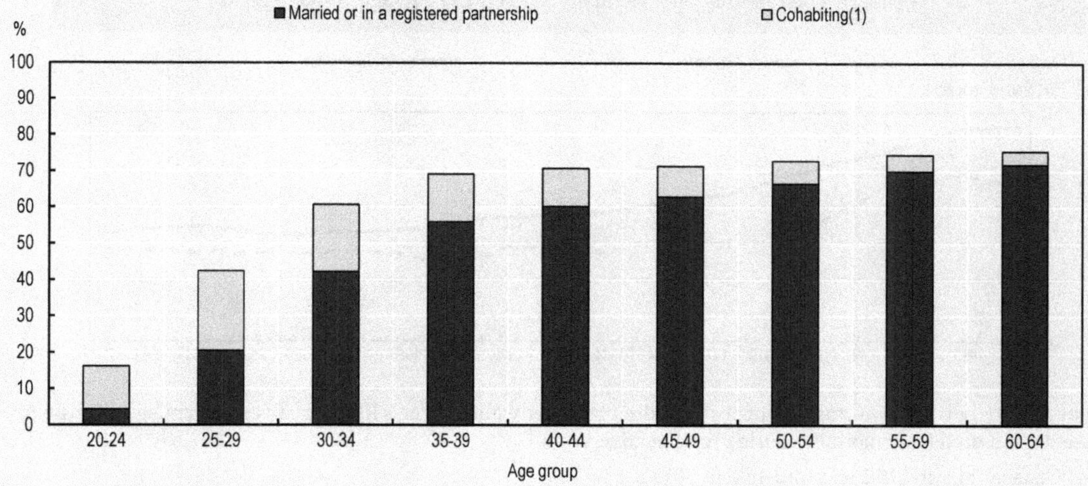

1. "Cohabiting" includes people in same-sex and unmarried opposite-sex couples.

Source: European Union Census on Population and Housing, 2011, https://ec.europa.eu/CensusHub2.

Fertility rates in Germany are persistently low

Fertility rates in Germany are lower than in many OECD countries (Figure 2.4, Panel A). In 2014, the total fertility rate[2] (TFR) was 1.47, below the OECD average (1.67) and well short of the population replacement rate of 2.1 children per woman. However, Germany is not alone in registering below-replacement-rate levels of fertility: in 2014, only three OECD countries (Israel, Mexico and Turkey) had a TFR above 2.1, while ten had rates that were lower than Germany's. In Portugal and Korea, TFRs were as low as 1.2 children per woman.

Low levels of fertility are not a recent development in Germany (Figure 2.4, Panel B). Its TFR slumped during the 1960s and early 1970s and has not touched the population replacement level since 1969. It has levelled out since the early 1980s, and has actually increased slightly in recent years – following a historic low of 1.24 children per woman in 1994, it grew by 0.23 points over the next 20 years. Nevertheless, the increase is small and far from enough to bring fertility up to the 2.1 children per woman needed for a stable population.

Figure 2.4. Fertility rates in Germany are persistently low

Panel A. Total fertility rate,[1] 2014[2]

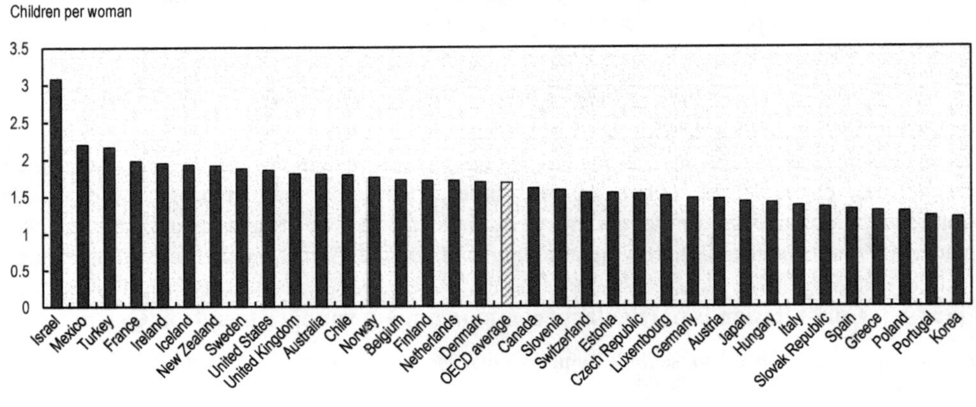

Panel B. Total fertility rate, Germany[3] and OECD average, 1960 to 2014

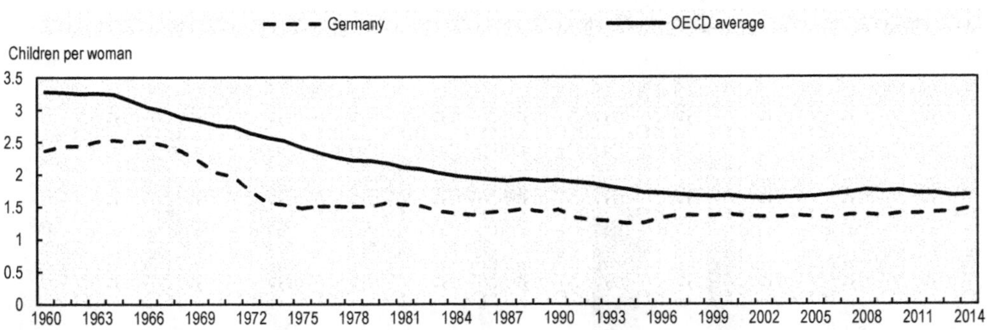

1. The total fertility rate is the average number of children born per woman over a lifetime, given current age-specific fertility rates and assuming no female mortality during reproductive years.

2. Data for Canada refer to 2012 and for Chile to 2013.

3. Data for Germany prior to 1990 include only West Germany. Data for Germany from 1990 onwards include both (former) East and West Germany.

Source: *OECD Family Database*, http://www.oecd.org/els/family/database.htm.

This prolonged period of low fertility has had (and will continue to have) a considerable impact on the size and age structure of the German population (Figure 2.5). The German population has been declining for over a decade now, from a peak of just over 82.5 million in 2002 to roughly 81.3 million in 2015. Projections suggest that the downward trend will persist and probably accelerate over coming decades, with the population projected to fall to as low as 76.1 million by 2050 (Destatis, 2015c and notes to Figure 2.5). At the same time, the age distribution of the German population is shifting too, particularly as the large cohorts born during the post-war years move into retirement. Those aged 65 and over already make up about 21.3% of the population, and that share is projected to increase to around 30.4% by 2050. Conversely, the share of those most likely to be looking for work – 15-to-64 year-olds – is expected to fall from 65.7% today to about 57.7% in 2050. Population ageing is not, of course, unique to Germany. Many other OECD countries, particularly in East Asia, also have to contend with similar shifts in the age distribution of their populations. However, combined with the projected decline in the size of the overall population, the decrease in the working-age share of the population means that the German working-age population could fall by almost 10 million over the next three-and-a-half decades – from around 53.5 million today to about 43.9 million in 2050.

Figure 2.5. The German population is both ageing and declining

Actual (1990-2013) and projected (2014-50) population by age group, Germany, 1990-2050

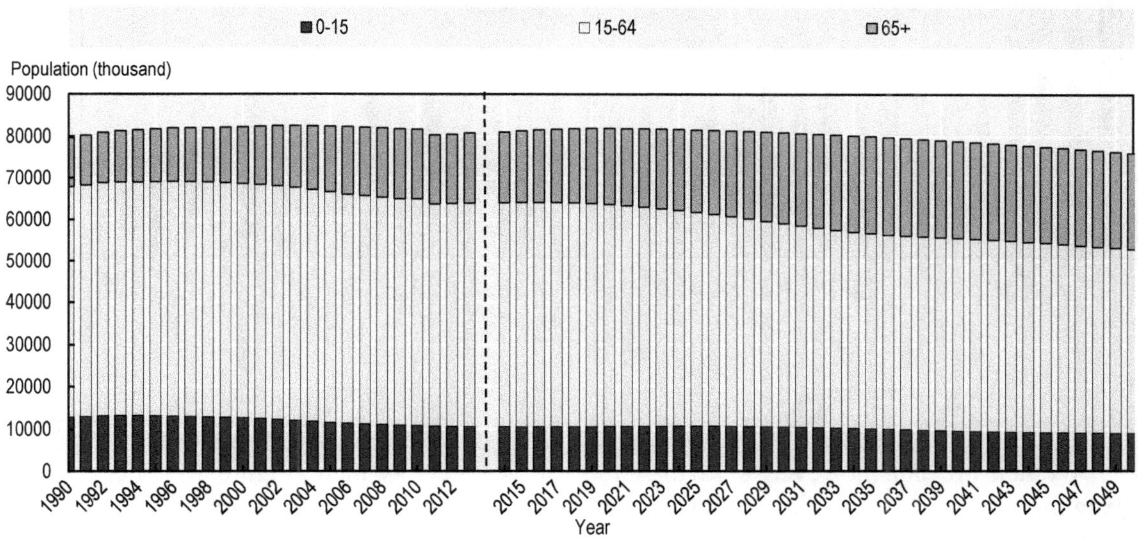

Note: Projections for 2014-50 by Destatis (2015c). The specific projection used is Variant 2 "Continued trend based on higher immigration": total fertility rate nearly constant at 1.4 children per woman with net migration declining from 500 000 in 2014 and 2015 to 200 000 in 2021 and constant thereafter.

Source: Destatis (2015c) and Destatis, https://www.destatis.de/EN/FactsFigures/SocietyState/Population.

3. Inequality and inefficiency in the labour market: German women work, but mothers are often trapped in part-time jobs

German women have made considerable inroads into the labour market in the past decade. Dual-earner households are now commonplace – 64% of German couple families with children under 15 are now dual-earner families (OECD, 2016a). However, most of them are really "one-and-a-half" earner families, with men working long hours and their partners working relatively short part-time hours (Chapter 4). In the OECD, only the Netherlands has a lower percentage of dual-earner families where both partners work full-time. Indeed, most of Germany's female employment gains over the past decade have come through part-time work.

German women are well educated but under-represented in lucrative STEM fields

Education is one important avenue through which women can improve their opportunities in the labour market and secure their families' income and well-being in later years. In the population as a whole, more men than women have completed higher education. But among the younger cohorts the opposite is true: in 2013, 32.1% of 25-to-34 year-old German women had higher-education degrees, compared to 27.9% of their male peers (Figure 2.6).

Figure 2.6. In Germany as in most OECD countries, young women are more likely to complete higher education than young men

Proportion (%) of the population who have attained higher education levels by sex, 25-to-34 year-olds, 2013

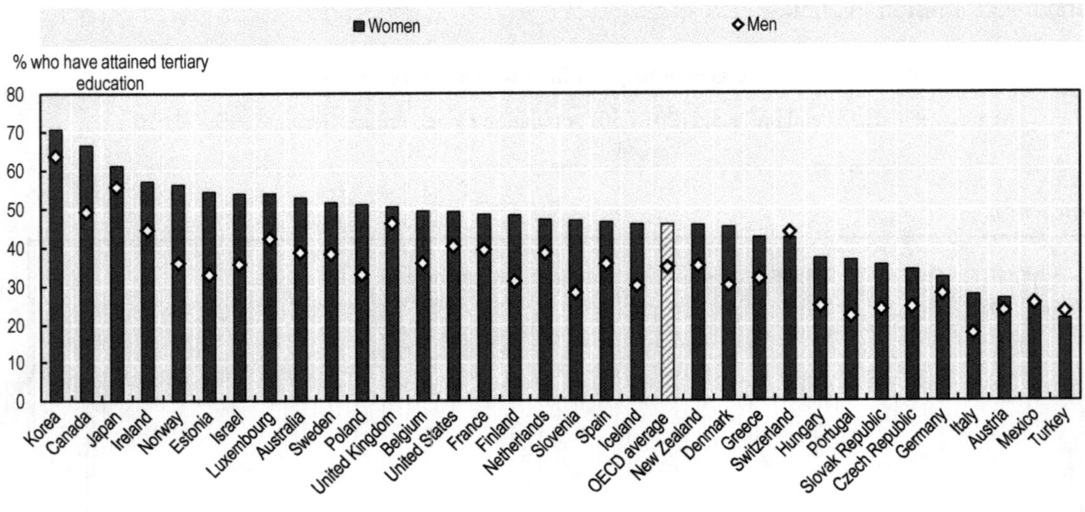

Source: OECD Gender Data Portal, http://www.oecd.org/statistics/datalab/gender-data-portal.htm.

Women are not, however, studying the same subjects as men (Figure 2.7). For example, despite the wage advantages to working in fields related to science, technology, engineering and mathematics (STEM), many German women decide against pursuing higher education in engineering and science. In 2012, they made up fewer than half of all university graduates in the fields of computing (16.7%), engineering and manufacturing (22.1%), physical sciences (41.9%), and general sciences (43.8%). Yet they have made great strides in mathematics and statistics: in 2012, nearly 60% of graduates in those subjects were women, compared to just 42.1% in 2000. At the same time, women continue to dominate, as they long have, in degree courses related to education and health and welfare.

Figure 2.7. German women are under-represented in science, technology and engineering, but not mathematics

Female share of tertiary education graduates by field of study, Germany, 2000 and 2012

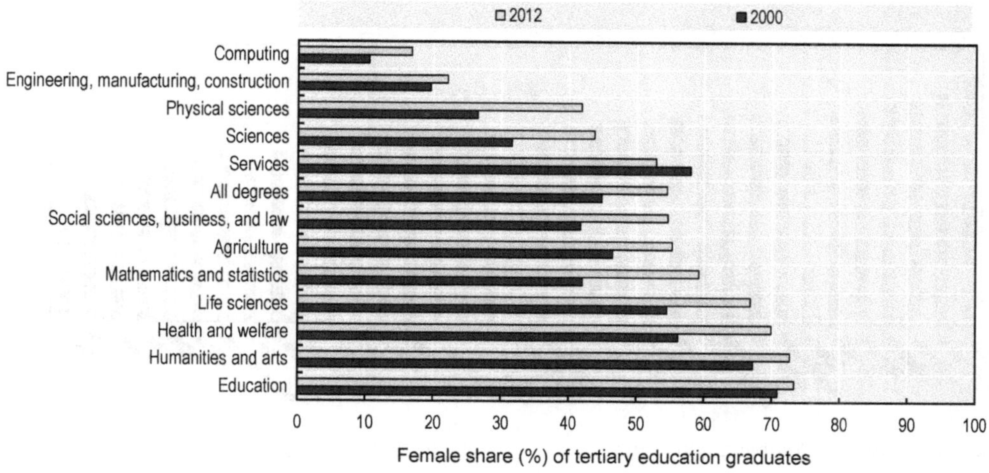

Source: OECD Gender Data Portal, http://www.oecd.org/gender/data/.

The under-representation of women in STEM-related fields of study in Germany cannot be attributed to less ability. In 2012, German 15-year-old girls scored better than their male classmates in the OECD Programme of International Student Assessment (PISA) literacy test, as well as them in the PISA science test, and only marginally less well in the mathematics test. In Germany and, indeed, throughout the OECD, there is a mismatch between girls' performances in STEM subjects at school and their later under-representation in STEM-related careers.

Increasing the number of female students who take STEM subjects at school could help steer more young women into STEM jobs and improve their earnings prospects. Public initiatives to emphasise STEM skills in early education and introduce girls to mathematics and science careers could encourage more to study related subjects. And raising awareness of how educational choices affect earnings could also coax more girls into STEM subjects. (See OECD, 2015b, for a detailed discussion of issues related to the aptitudes, behaviour and confidence of boys and girls in education.)

Germany has experienced strong growth in female and maternal employment since 2000

German women have entered the labour market in large numbers over the past couple of decades. Between 2000 and 2014, employment rates among German women (15-to-64 year-olds) increased by over 11.3 percentage points, from 58.1% to 69.5% (Figure 2.8). This is well above the OECD average increase for women over the same period (4.7 percentage points). Indeed, Germany boasted the second-largest increase in female employment in the OECD, after Chile, and now has the highest female employment rate in the OECD after the Nordic countries and Switzerland (Figure 2.8).

Figure 2.8. German women's employment rates rose significantly between 2000 and 2014

Female employment rates (%), 15-to-64 year-olds, 2000 and 2014

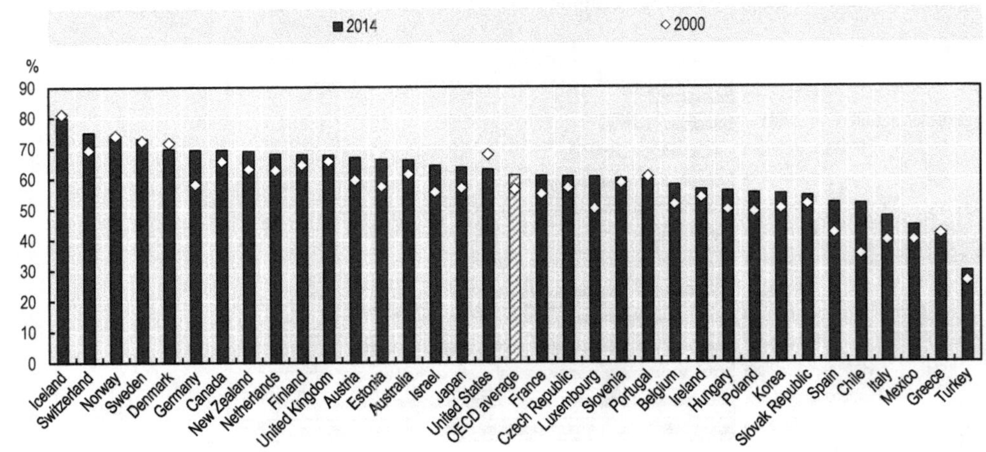

Source: *OECD Employment Database*, http://www.oecd.org/employment/emp/onlineoecdemploymentdatabase.htm.

German women also gained relative to German men (Figure 2.9). While employment rates for both German women and men have increased since 2000 – somewhat unusually for the OECD in this timeframe, as male workers in many countries experienced considerable job losses during the Great Recession – the share of women who were employed grew significantly faster. Of course, German men are still more likely to work than German women, but the gender gap in employment has fallen sharply: from 14.8 percentage points in 2000 to 8.6 percentage points in 2014.

Figure 2.9. In most OECD countries, female employment has been growing faster than male employment since 2000

Percentage point change in employment rates (15-to-64 year-olds) between 2000 and 2014, by sex

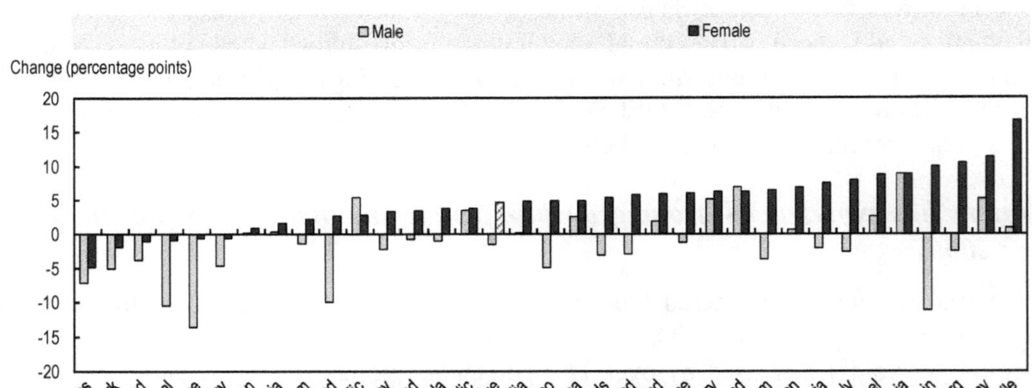

Reading note: In Germany between 2000 and 2014, the male employment rate (15-to-64 year-olds) increased by 5.2 percentage points and the female employment rate (15-to-64 year olds) increased by 11.3 percentage points.

Source: *OECD Employment Database*, http://www.oecd.org/employment/emp/onlineoecdemploymentdatabase.htm.

Much of the increase in female employment is attributable to mothers entering (or re-entering) the labour market. Between 2000 and 2013, employment among mothers with children under 18 grew by 7.8 percentage points, from 59.0% to 66.8% (BMFSFJ, 2014). Increases in employment rates were greatest among mothers of very young children – by 9 percentage points to 42.1% for mothers with children between one and two years, and by 12.9 percentage points to 55% for those with children between 2 and 3 (ibid., also see Keller and Haustein, 2013).

Women often work part-time and men frequently work long hours

German women often work part-time. About 37.5% of employed German women usually work part-time hours,[3] defined as usual working hours of less than 30 hours per week (Figure 2.10). This is a similar rate to some other OECD countries – such as Australia, Japan and the United Kingdom – but far higher than in France, Spain and Sweden, where less than 25% female employees work part-time. In these countries, female employees are more likely to be working between 30 and 39 hours per week (France) or 40 hours per week (Spain and Sweden).

Part-time work is particularly common among German mothers (Figure 2.11). In 2013, over half of all employed German mothers with children under 15 were working less than 30 hours per week, compared to just under 25% in France and less than 10% in Finland and Portugal. Only the Netherlands, where more than 70% of working mothers with children under 15 work part-time, has a higher rate.

And the frequency of part-time work among German mothers is increasing, too. Indeed, almost all of the recent gains in maternal employment have been driven by mothers entering part-time work – between 2000 and 2013, the share of employed mothers working 32 hours per week or less increased by over 11 percentage points, from 36% to 47% (BMFSFJ, 2014). Between 1996 and 2012, the share of working mothers in part-time employment in East Germany almost doubled, from 23% to 44% (Keller and Haustein, 2013).

Figure 2.10. Women work fewer hours than men throughout the OECD

Distribution of employees (all ages) by usual weekly working-hour bands, selected countries, 2014

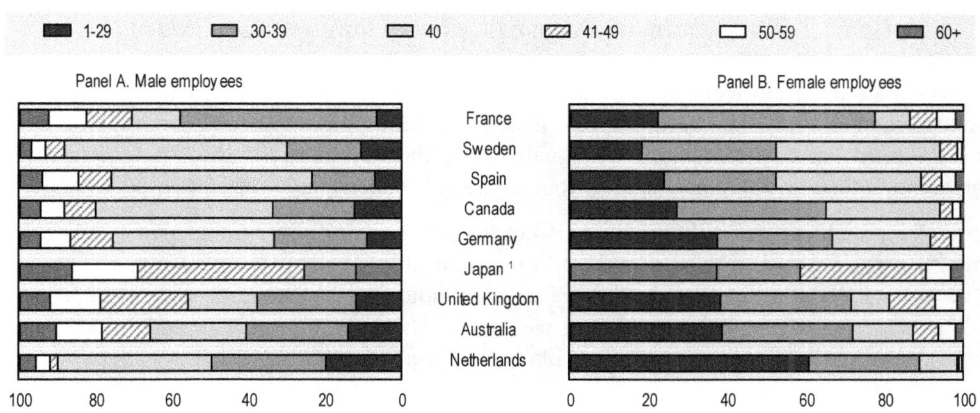

Note: Countries are ranked in ascending order by the proportion of all employees (male and female) whose usual weekly working hours are 1-29 hours.

1. For Japan, the usual weekly working-hours bands are 1-29, 30-39, 40-48, 49-59 and 60+.

Source: *OECD Employment Database*, http://www.oecd.org/employment/emp/onlineoecdemploymentdatabase.htm.

Figure 2.11. Working mothers in Germany work mainly part-time

Maternal employment rates by part-time/full-time status, mothers (15-to-64 year-olds) with at least one child aged 0-to-14, 2013 or latest available year

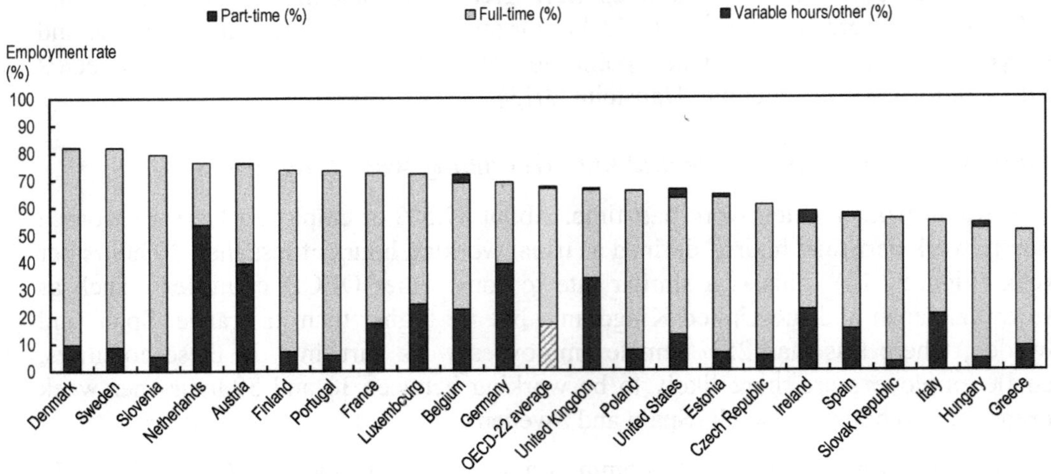

Note: For the United States, mothers (15-to-64 year-olds) with at least one child aged 0-17. Data for Denmark, Finland and Sweden refer to 2012.

1. The distinction between part-time and full-time employment is based on a common definition (usual weekly working hours of less than 30 in the main job).

Source: OECD calculations based on the European Union Labour Force Survey for European countries, and Current Population Survey (CPS) for the United States.

German men work longer hours. Less than 10% of employed German men usually work less than 30 hours per week (Figure 2.10), with part-time work particularly rare for fathers (Keller and Haustein, 2013; see Chapter 4). Instead, most employed German men usually work at least 40 hours per week, with over 13% usually working for 50 hours or more. Such long average hours complicate efforts to combine work with parenting and contribute to widespread dissatisfaction with work-life balance (see Box 2.2 on the diminishing returns to long hours).

Box 2.2. The unintended consequences of long working hours

Today's workers are driven to work longer and harder. The "time macho" culture – which denotes employees who aim to be the first and last person in the office – fosters competition in the workplace over who is (or appears to be) working the most hours. When employees finally leave their actual work site, the presence of pervasive technology can pressure them to continue working from any location and at any time of day.

Yet the payoff for such excessively long hours is not higher output or better productivity. While productivity does increase with hours worked, it does so only up to a point: a large body of research finds that productivity "maxes out" at around 40 hours per week. After five eight-hour days, it plateaus then declines as workers' anticipate adding extra hours and produce less in each one. The risk of accidents and errors increases, and miscommunication and poor decisions are more likely. Workers' health suffers, as well, which diminishes productivity.

Addressing the issue of over-long hours requires cultural shifts within organisations and policies that afford workers adequate protection. The payoffs to companies can be considerable: in addition to greater productivity and a healthier workforce, companies that embrace reasonable work hours also gain on the stock market and in competition for diverse human capital.

Box 2.2. The unintended consequences of long working hours *(cont.)*

Working more for worse work

Businesses have long sought to find the ideal working week for maximising production. At the turn of the 20th century, German entrepreneur Ernest Abbe was one of many businessmen who conducted studies into workers' performance over hours worked. He found that reducing daily shifts at his optics factory from nine to eight hours increased total production. Another well-known management pioneer, Henry Ford, experimented with various working hour combinations in the 1920s, and eventually concluded that his workers could produce more in five days than in six, and in eight-hour shifts rather than ten.

Productivity falls beyond a certain hours threshold. Modern econometric evaluations of historical and current worker data confirm what Abbe, Ford, and others learned many years ago: that workers are productive for a limited number of hours. Despite the demands of producing ammunition for World War I, British female factory workers' output peaked, on average, at the threshold of 48 hours per week. Beyond that point, the rate of output fell away (Penceval, 2014). Workers simply do not produce output at the same rate over time. Fatigue and stress reduce functionality and employees may produce less per hour if they anticipate having to stay at work longer. An oft-cited Business Roundtable study of construction workers on overtime found that, after two months, a work schedule of 60 or more hours per week cut productivity so much that delays in job completion were greater than if the same crew had worked a 40-hour week (Business Roundtable, 1980). In addition to sapping the morale of workers and making them more error-prone, difficulties in providing materials, tools, equipment, and information at the appropriate rate cause efficiency losses (Thomas and Raynar, 1997). Workplace decisions also suffer. Long hours contribute to decision fatigue: too many decisions throughout the day tires the brain and leads to deterioration in the quality of choices made.

Overtime errors, accidents, and injuries increase. Additional hours increase the risk of error, accidents, and injuries in all industries (Penceval, 2014; Dembe et al., 2005). The over-long hours and excessive workloads of engineers and technicians at the Kennedy Space Center in the United States before the space shuttle Challenger accident is just one well-documented example of how overworked employees can make tremendous mistakes (US Presidential Commission, 1986). But few industries are immune to accidents caused by overwork (Dembe et al., 2005). In the medical field, doctors, nurses, and medical interns have been found to make more errors in treating patients (Rogers et al., 2004; Flinn and Armstrong, 2011) and are more likely to be involved in motor vehicle accidents (Barger et al., 2005) after long shifts. In all industries, the ability to perform in tasks that require focus and concentration decreases as a function of time, a phenomenon known as "vigilance decrement" (Ariga and Lleras, 2010). Simply put, it is hard to concentrate for a long time.

Workplace relationships suffer. Important workplace intangibles like emotional intelligence and interpersonal communication are affected by long hours, as well. Overworked employees are more likely to be sleep-deprived (Faber et al., 2015). Sleep deprivation, in turn, reduces empathy towards others, impairs impulse control, diminishes the quality of interpersonal relationships, and makes it harder for people to cope with challenges, as they experience reduced positive thinking and lower action orientation (Killgore et al., 2008). Lack of sleep also damages judgement of human facial emotions and makes individuals more likely to interpret facial cues negatively (van der Helm et al.; 2010). Such subtle forms of miscommunication make workplace collaboration more difficult.

Overworked brains and bodies: long hours contribute to poor health

Long work hours are linked to poor physical health, which is bad both for workers and companies interested in healthy employee retention. One obvious consequence of long working hours is the greater likelihood of workplace accidents. But there are also chronic risks. A recent meta-analysis of 12 cross-national studies that looked at 22 000 participants found that working longer than eight hours a day is associated with 40% to 80% greater risk of coronary heart disease. The causal mechanisms are prolonged exposure to psychological stress, higher levels of the stress hormone cortisol, poor eating habits, and a lack of physical activity due to insufficient leisure time (Virtanen et al., 2012). Mental health suffers, too, from the stress of hours worked and sleep lost. In addition to impaired cognitive functions, overworked employees are more likely to experience major depressive episodes, as researchers found when studying the British civil service (Virtanen, 2008; Virtanen et al., 2012). People with excessive work hours are also more likely to abuse alcohol (Virtanen, 2015).

Box 2.2. The unintended consequences of long working hours *(cont.)*

Long work hours take a toll on families and partnerships that is harder to quantify. The years in which employees are expected to climb the corporate ladder coincide with parenting years, especially among women, as their fertility window is more restricted. Workers are often forced to choose between bringing up young children or putting in "face time" at the office. Evidence across countries shows that children are negatively affected by their parents' non-standard work schedules, which includes working in the evenings, at night and on weekends. Parents are more likely to be depressed, parenting quality is likely to suffer, children and parents have reduced time together, and the home environment is overall less supportive, especially in lower-income families. Children, in turn, experience a variety of effects at different ages, including behavioural problems (especially among young children and adolescents), slower cognitive development (particularly among pre-schoolers), higher body mass index, less engagement in school and extracurricular activities, and sleep problems. (For a full review of the cross-national literature, refer to Li et al., 2014.)

Long hours persist, despite evidence as to their negative effects

Given the plentiful evidence on the negative effects of long working hours, it is remarkable that so many workers across the OECD spend over 40 hours per week on the job. OECD time-series data reveal that Germany is one of about ten OECD countries in which the share of the employed population working an average of over 40 hours per week has increased since 2000. (Other discussions of trends in long working hours include Gray et al., 2004, on Australia; and Cha and Weeden, 2014, on the United States.) Employers and workers both play a part in perpetuating long hours. In many businesses, long working hours have become a part of organisational culture and a way for employees to show that they are loyal, "ideal" workers (Cha and Weeden, 2014; Sharone, 2004). As for lower-income employees, working additional hours may simply be a financial necessity. Fear of job loss is another factor.

Employers, in turn, have been slow to realise that additional time in the office does not usually mean more value added. Some research suggests that the wage premium for long hours is actually on the rise (Cha and Weeden, 2014). Leaders and managers in organisations who have probably sacrificed their time to reach their current rank may have difficulty accepting that work can be done in fewer hours. Some workplaces may actually penalise "non-compliers" – those employees who opt for flexible hours and family leave – by denying them promotion, lowering their visibility to superiors, or excluding them from important projects. In-office "face time" remains an important metric of employee evaluation, even if it is no measure of output (Elsbach and Cable, 2012).

In one consulting firm, for example, researchers found that men pretended to work 60- to 80-hour weeks by strategically timing when to send emails, scheduling phone calls at odd hours, and discreetly taking family leave without formal permission. In contrast, female workers were far more likely to make use of formally reduced hours and were consequently marginalised within the firm (Reid, 2015).

Although it might be harder to quantify diminished productivity among knowledge workers than manual labourers, many of the same negative effects emerge: long hours contribute to stress, sleep deprivation, disagreements with colleagues, and mistakes on the job. Even software engineers argue that programming errors are more likely to occur (and take longer to fix) after long hours, despite the tech industry's glorification of seemingly endless workdays (Robinson, 2005).

What can be done?

Public policies can help prevent overwork. Working-hour legislation and the legal right to request flexible working arrangements have historically helped protect workers. However, real change needs to occur in organisational culture and practice. There is a lot that companies can do to prevent long hours. The overarching goal is to adjust workplace culture so that managers prioritise tasks, time management, and efficient output rather than time in the office. Leaders must recognise that working long hours is not necessary for high-quality work and may even prevent it.

Few parents share paid work equally

Ideally, equal sharing in families should empower partners to share labour market work equitably while ensuring an adequate household income and allowing time for each other. Yet, few families anywhere manage to share paid work equally (Figure 2.12, striped bars). Denmark has, at 30.1%, the highest proportion of couples where both partners work reduced full-time hours (defined as between 30 and 39 hours of paid work per week). In Norway, France, Finland and Belgium, between 15% and 26% of couple families choose the dual reduced full-time model. In Germany, however, both partners in only 1.2% of couples work between 30 and 39 hours. Such low rates are, in fact, widespread in Europe – the share of couple families working dual reduced full-time hours is lower than 5% in 17 out of 26 countries.

The most common working arrangement in German couple families is the father working full-time and the mother working short part-time hours, or not at all. About 34.8% of German couple families have a father who works 40 or more hours per week and a mother who works 29 hours per week or less (Figure 2.12, white bars), while about 23.9% have a father working 40 or more hours and a mother who is inactive or unemployed (grey bars). In Eastern European countries, as in Sweden and Portugal, the most common set-up is both parents working full-time (dark blue bars, and Chapter 4).

The Netherlands – which has a long tradition of part-time work, especially among women (Chapter 4) – boasts the highest share, at 18.1%, of couple families where the father works between 30 and 39 hours and the mother between 1 and 29. In Germany, the share of families practicing this "reduced full-time hours plus small part-time" model is 5.3%.

Figure 2.12. Few families share paid work equally with both partners working reduced full-time hours

Proportion (%) of couples (female partner aged 25 to 45 with at least one child) practicing four different working time arrangements

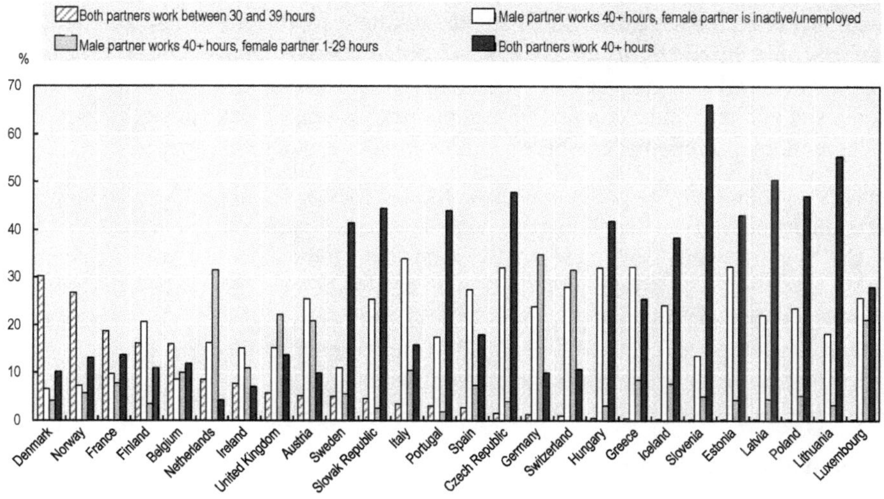

Note: Countries are sorted in descending order according to the proportion of couples with both partners working between 30 and 39 hours.

Source: OECD calculations based on the European Union Statistics on Income and Living Conditions (EU SILC) survey, 2012.

Box 2.3. Bargaining in households: A theoretical debate

How do families decide how to split paid and unpaid work? Who chooses who does what and who gets what? Why should policy makers care about men and women having equal opportunities to participate in paid work?

Motivated by Becker's seminal theory of the division of labour in the family (Becker, 1981 and 1985), scholars have debated intra-household bargaining for decades. In Becker's rational choice model, the family is viewed as a single entity with common preferences. All family members work together to maximise the well-being of the family unit, and to achieve maximum returns, Becker argues, members participate in a strict "sexual division of labour" – one partner (typically the man) specialises in paid labour, while the other (typically the woman) specialises in unpaid housework. While these roles could be reversed, women typically specialise in household labour because of a temporary comparative (biological) advantage in caregiving around child birth. These initial comparative advantages then turn into long-lasting behaviours because people tend to get better at skills the more they use them. Early socialisation also reinforces gendered roles, Becker argues, because parents seek to prepare their children for responsibilities which, they assume, will benefit them in the marriage market.

While Becker's theory may appear old-fashioned, it does hold considerable predictive power: in all OECD countries, men spend more time in paid work and women more time on housework and child care. Yet, this division of labour is neither strict nor fixed, as "common preferences" models like Becker's would suggest – rather, divisions of labour vary across couples and have blurred with time (Bianchi et al., 2000; Coltrane, 2000; Sullivan, 2000; Lachance-Grzela and Bouchard, 2010).

In response to the shortcomings of "common preferences" models, economists have developed various alternative theories around how men and women divide paid and unpaid work. "Bargaining" models attempt to account for other factors, such as power differentials within the family and the possible effects of the threat of divorce (see Lundberg and Pollak, 1996, for an overview of this literature). These models assume that partners still work together up to a point, but also compete and negotiate over roles and resources based on their relative bargaining power. Men's higher earnings, together with other resources such as education, often afford them greater say in decisions and allow them to opt out of less desirable tasks like housework, even if it is not efficient for the family. Women, who are generally more dependent on the income of male partners, have less choice.

Bargaining models help illustrate how women's participation in paid work affects behaviours at home. For instance, women often decrease their housework as their earnings increase, at least up to the point where both partners contribute equally to income (Lachance-Grzela and Bouchard, 2010). Bargaining models would suggest that this is because the earnings from paid work help women negotiate over unpaid labour. But the bargaining power associated with increased female earnings has additional implications for women and families. For example, women tend to spend income differently to men, and it is also now almost conventional wisdom that children do better when their mothers control a larger share of household resources, even if much of this evidence comes from development economics (Lundberg and Pollak, 1996). Supporting women's paid work, bargaining models would say, would provide them more discretion over where and how family resources are spent.

The debate remains relevant today as policy makers consider whether – and how – to level the playing field for women in paid and unpaid work. Given that young women's levels of educational attainment now match or outpace men's in most OECD countries and that, increasingly, men and women partner with someone with a similar socioeconomic status, losses may be substantial if women stay at home. The OECD has conducted extensive research into how women's paid employment positively affects macro-level outcomes like economic growth, socio-economic equality, and fertility rates (OECD; 2012, 2015a). But bargaining theory suggests the stakes are just as high at home for individual women, their partners, and their children.

The gender wage gap lingers

German women still earn less than German men, even when looking only at employees working full-time. Germany has a gender wage gap that is slightly wider than the OECD average, though the gap has narrowed since the year 2000. In 2013, female full-time workers earned nearly 13.4% less than their male peers (Figure 2.13). The gap varies across income deciles, with differences between low-income male and female workers amongst the greatest in the OECD: in 2012, low-income (bottom decile) German women earned 15.6% less than bottom decile German men. This disparity is greater than the OECD average gender wage gap for the poorest workers (10.5%), and far higher than in some OECD countries (e.g. Hungary, Luxembourg, New Zealand and Norway) where gender gaps in the bottom decile earnings are smaller than 2% (*OECD Employment Database*, 2015).

Figure 2.13. The gender wage gap persists but has narrowed since 2000 in most OECD countries, including Germany

Gender gap[1] in median earnings of full-time employees, 2000, 2006, and 2013 or closest available year

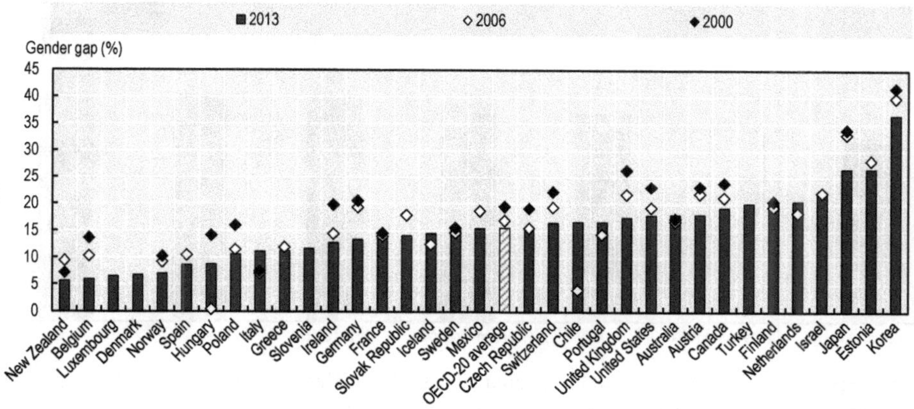

Note: For 2013, data for Estonia, Luxembourg, the Netherlands, Slovenia and Turkey refer to 2010, for Israel to 2011, and for France, Italy, Poland, Spain, Sweden and Switzerland to 2012.

1. The gender wage gap is unadjusted and calculated as the difference between the median earnings of men and women relative to men's median earnings. Estimates of earnings used in the calculations refer to the gross earnings of full-time wage and salary workers. However, the definition may slightly vary from one country to another.

Source: *OECD Employment Database*, http://www.oecd.org/employment/emp/onlineoecdemploymentdatabase.htm.

Women lag behind in entrepreneurship

German women are less likely to be entrepreneurs than German men. In 2013, only 2.5% of working women in Germany were self-employed, compared to 6.7% of working men. Although women are actually more likely to be self-employed in Germany than in many other OECD countries, female self-employment rates were higher, at over 3%, in Hungary, Korea, New Zealand, Portugal, Spain and Switzerland, and reach as high as 4% in Greece and Italy (OECD, 2016b).

After starting their own business, German female entrepreneurs are also likely to earn much less than their male counterparts – nearly 43% less in 2011 (Figure 2.14). And although self-employed women earn less than self-employed men everywhere, the disparity in Germany is significantly wider than the OECD average of 36.1%.

The earnings gap between male and female entrepreneurs can be ascribed chiefly to the lower capitalisation of female-run companies, the choice of sector, a lack of managerial experience, and the shorter hours female entrepreneurs devote to their businesses, as they are more likely than men to combine paid work with family care commitments. In Germany, the lower earnings of female entrepreneurs may be another consequence of insufficient public child care support for working mothers.

Governments across the OECD have sought to promote female entrepreneurship by fostering gender-neutral legal frameworks for business, ensuring gender-equal access to finance, and pairing funding schemes with support such as financial literacy training, business training, mentoring, and increased access to professional financial and legal advice. It is also important that governments and educational institutions provide women with more information on the process and benefits of running a business (OECD, 2014a).

Figure 2.14. Female entrepreneurs often earn a lot less than male entrepreneurs

Gender earnings gap[1] in self-employment income, selected OECD countries, 2006 and 2011

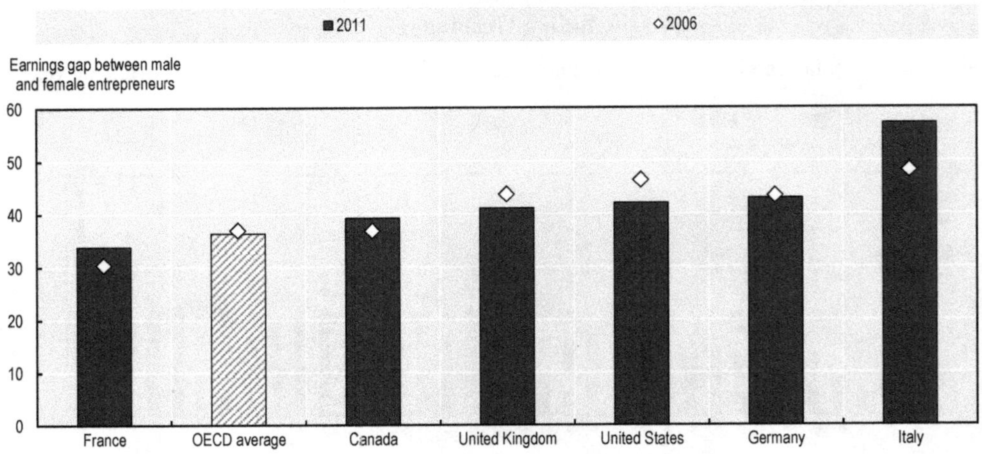

1. The "gender earnings gap" is unadjusted and calculated as the difference between male and female average self-employment incomes divided by the male average self-employment income.

Source: OECD Gender Data Portal, https://www.oecd.org/gender/data/.

4. Inequality in unpaid work: Women still do the lion's share of work at home

While German women have increasingly participated in the labour market over the past 15 years, they continue to spend a good deal of time on housework and child care. Compared to other OECD countries, Germany remains a mid-range performer when it comes to the gendered division of unpaid household labour. Women still continue to carry out the bulk – about 65% – of all unpaid labour in the home, which includes child care.

In no OECD country do men do more unpaid work than women. Time use surveys conducted by a number of OECD countries illustrate where Germany stands on the sharing of housework (Figure 2.15). The Nordic countries, of course, perform far better than their peers. In Norway, for example, women do around 210 minutes of unpaid labour a day, compared to men's 160. Korea, Japan, Mexico, and Turkey bring up the rear, with Korean women, for instance, doing about 230 minutes of unpaid labour per day and men only 45.

The hours that German women spent on unpaid work fell slightly between 2001-02 and 2012-13, although this was almost entirely offset by an increase in the amount of time spent on paid work (Figure 2.16). In Germany, as in many other countries, mothers spend considerably more time than fathers on child care and housework, even when both parents are in full-time employment (Chapter 5 discusses time use among partners in households in detail).

Figure 2.15. Women continue to do more unpaid labour than men throughout the OECD

Gender distribution of time spent on child care and other unpaid work, 15-to-64 year-olds, latest available year

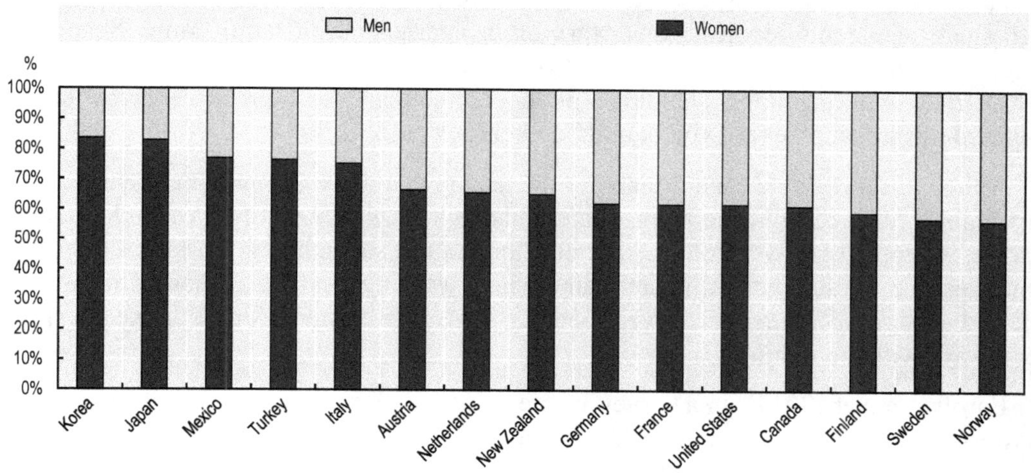

Note: Reference years are as follows: Austria, 2008-09; Canada, 2010; Finland, 2009-10; France, 2009; Germany, 2001-02; Italy, 2008-09; Japan, 2011; Korea, 2009; Mexico, 2009; Netherlands, 2005-06; New Zealand, 2009-10; Norway, 2010; Sweden, 2010; Turkey, 2006; and the United States, 2014.

Source: OECD Gender Data Portal, https://www.oecd.org/gender/data/.

Figure 2.16. German women continue to do more housework and child care than German men

Average time spent on paid and unpaid work activities for men and women (30-to-44 year-olds) in hours per day, Germany, 2001/02 and 2012/13

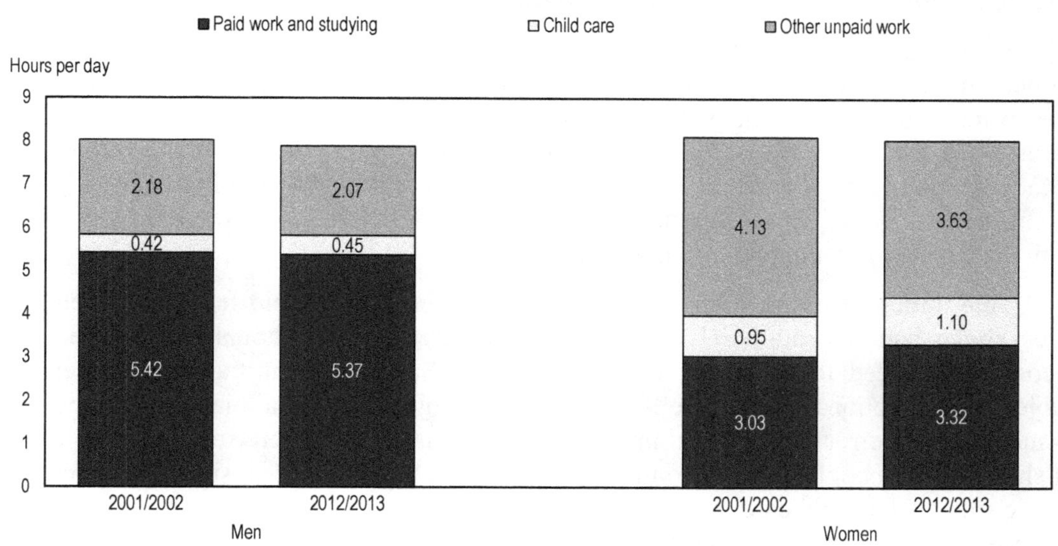

Note: "Paid work and studying" includes time spent on all activities related to paid employment (including travel) and all activities related to personal education (including time spent both at an educational institutional and at home, and any related travel time). "Child care" includes time spent on activities oriented primarily towards a child, including physical care, assistance with education and learning, reading to and playing with the child, and accompanying the child to appointments. "Other unpaid work" includes all other unpaid activities relating to the household (such as cooking, cleaning, shopping, caring for adult household members, looking after pets and animals, gardening, and home and vehicle maintenance). It excludes time spent on voluntary work outside of the home. All three categories exclude time spent on personal leisure activities.

Source: Destatis (2015b).

5. Germans feel the pinch of work-life conflict

Families in Germany feel caught between work and home life, with a relatively high share of parents reporting that work often interferes with family time. Surveys suggest that most mothers and fathers of young children would prefer their spouse to reduce their working hours, although public opinion has become more favourably disposed towards mothers of young children being in paid work.

Although survey data cannot pinpoint the factors that drive German preferences for part-time or reduced full-time work, some – like culture, social institutions, and labour markets – probably play a role. Culturally, the stigma surrounding working mothers continues to exert some effect in Germany, where working mothers are sometimes still referred to as *Rabenmutter* (or "raven mothers", a derogatory term for mothers who are not always with their child).

Eurobarometer (2014), in a survey where respondents were allowed to select three answers, found that Germans considered the four most important areas of action in boosting the number of women in paid work outside the home were:

- equal pay between men and women (47%),
- more flexible working arrangements (40%),
- measures to enable women to combine a job with housework and parenting (40%),
- more accessible child care support (39%).

Over one-third of Germans say that work often interferes with family life

German parents, together with their Belgian and French peers, are more likely than parents in most other European countries to report that work interferes with the time they want to devote to their partner or family (Figure 2.17). In Germany, 30.8% of parents feel that work often or constantly interferes with family time, while a further 35.5% say that work sometimes interferes. By contrast, in Norway and Portugal, only 15.2% and 11.8% of parents, respectively, state that work often or always interferes with the time they would prefer to devote to the family.

While attitude surveys offer important insights into how people feel about their lives above and beyond purely quantitative measures such as hours worked and income, they need to be interpreted with caution. Surveys on attitudes and other subjective perceptions (such as well-being) may be subject to cultural bias (understood as measurement error) and cultural impact (where culture plays a more substantive role in shaping how people experience their lives). Certain policy stances, such as greater public support for child care, may also raise people's expectations as to their work-life balance. A large body of literature confirms the impact of culture on subjective measures of well-being (see Exton et al., 2015 for an overview), while a recent study finds that culture may account for 20% of unexplained country-specific variance in such measures (ibid.).

A detailed attitude survey comparing Germany and France paints a more nuanced, albeit partly contradictory, picture of public opinion (Allensbach Institut für Demoskopie, 2015). It finds that, while German perceptions of the family have increasingly converged with those of the French in the past few years, differences remain, mostly with regard to work-life conflict. In 2013, 48% of German parents with at least one child under 14 years old said that they, or their partner, felt that they have had to cut back on their education and/or careers for their children, as opposed to only 12% of French respondents. Generally, German parents also report more stress than French parents (48% vs. 26%). And, while more 16-to-49 year-old respondents found their fellow Germans to be child-friendly in 2013 (33%) than in 2007 (25%), considerably more French parents – over 80% – said so in both years.

On the other hand German opinions have converged to French ones in other areas: the ideal size of family for German respondents increased from on average 1.8 children in 2007 to 2.2 in 2013, bringing it closer to the French ideal of 2.4 children in both years. Similarly, fears of the financial restrictions of parenthood amongst childless 16-to-49 year-olds declined from 68% to 53% in Germany, while in France they dropped from 46% to 41%.

Figure 2.17. German parents are more likely than most of their peers in Europe to report work-life conflict

Distribution of responses to the statement "How often do you find that your job prevents you from giving the time you want to your partner or family?" by those with at least one child, 2010

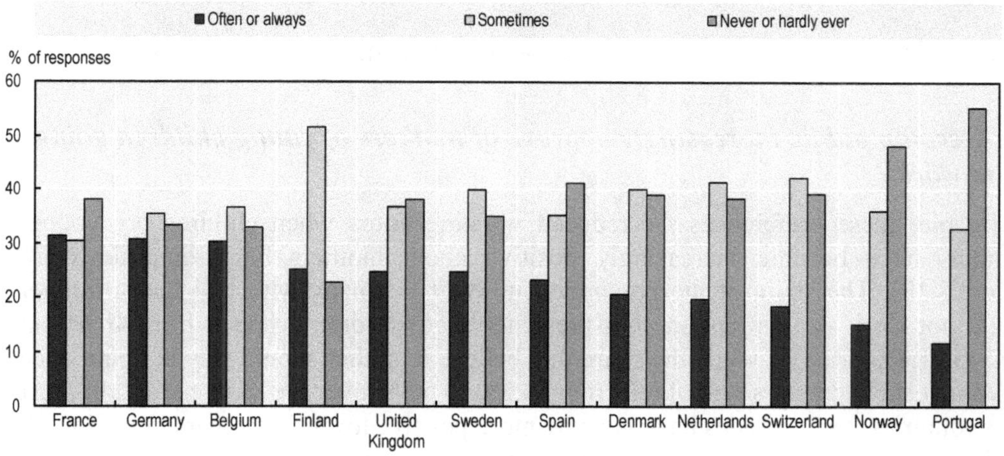

Source: OECD calculations based on the European Social Survey, Round 5 (2010), http://www.europeansocialsurvey.org/.

Germans with young children generally prefer their partner to work fewer hours outside the home (Figure 2.18). German fathers work longer hours than most other Europeans, with their female partners wishing that they worked around five hours less per week. They also would themselves like to reduce their working hours (BMFSFJ, 2014). German men would also prefer their partners to work fewer hours, even though they work, on average, only 24.2 hours per week. (See Chapter 4 for a more detailed discussion of German fathers' relatively long – and German mothers' relatively short – working hours.)

Younger Germans today have different perceptions of parenthood than their elders. 54% of 18-to-34 year-old male respondents consider a family model with both parents working full-time and sharing family responsibilities as an option for themselves, compared to 41% of 50-to-56 year-olds (BMFSFJ, 2015). These shifting perceptions are also evidenced in young parents' wishes with regard to their paid working hours: one-third of those with children under three would like to see both partners working about 30 hours per week and sharing family responsibilities (BMFSFJ, 2014).

Figure 2.18. Fathers and mothers of young children would prefer their partners to work fewer hours

Cross-national responses to survey questions on partners' average working hours, and partners' preferred working hours, 2010

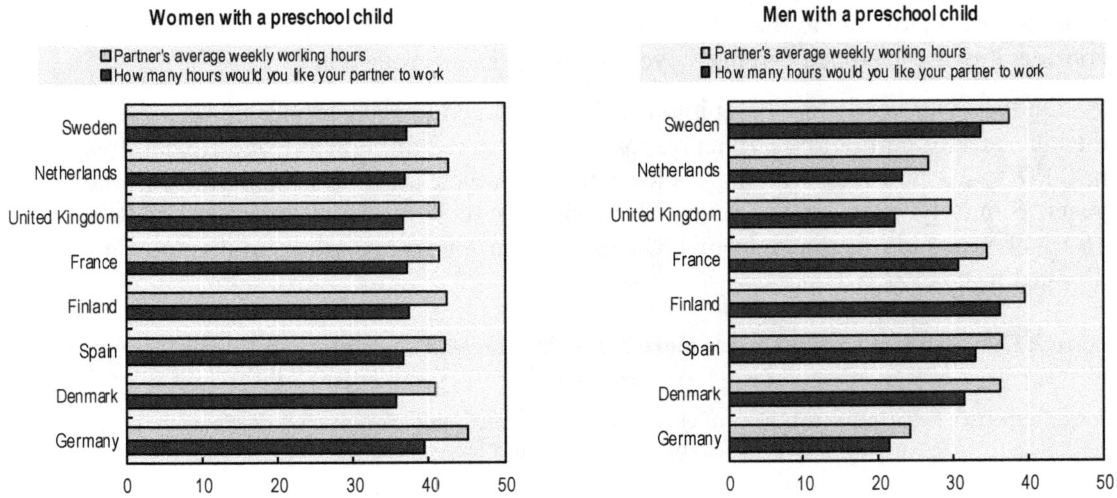

Source: OECD calculations based on the European Social Survey, Round 5 (2010), http://www.europeansocialsurvey.org/.

The German public increasingly approve of mothers of young children going out to work

Despite these preferences for reduced working hours when children are young, Germans have become increasingly positive about mothers being in paid work (Figure 2.19). The share of the population in West Germany who feel that a mother should not work at all when she has pre-school-age children dropped from 46.6% in 2002 to 21.8% in 2012, while the share that believe a mother should stay at home once the youngest child enters school fell from 14.3% to 6.8% over the same period. In most other countries, too, attitudes have become more positive towards mothers in paid work – only in Japan and Austria do traditional attitudes prevail.

There is still resistance to mothers working full-time, however, at least in West Germany. Only 4% of the West German population believe that mothers of pre-school-age children should work full-time, up slightly from 2.9% in 2002 (Figure 2.19, Panel A). The acceptance of full-time working mothers increases slightly once when children start school (Panel B), but most of the population in West Germany still believe that mothers should be working only part-time, if at all.

Respondents in East Germany are far more likely to be supportive of working mothers and full-time working mothers in particular (Figure 2.19, Panel A). In East Germany, 54.3% of people think that mothers of young children should work part-time, and 29.8% that they should work full-time – a higher share than in Sweden.

Figure 2.19. Opinions towards working mothers have improved slightly over time

Panel A. Distribution of responses to the question "Do you think that women should work outside the home full-time, part-time or not at all when there is a child under school age?", 2002 and 2012

Panel B. Distribution of responses to the question "Do you think that women should work outside the home full-time, part-time or not at all after the youngest child starts school?", 2002 and 2012

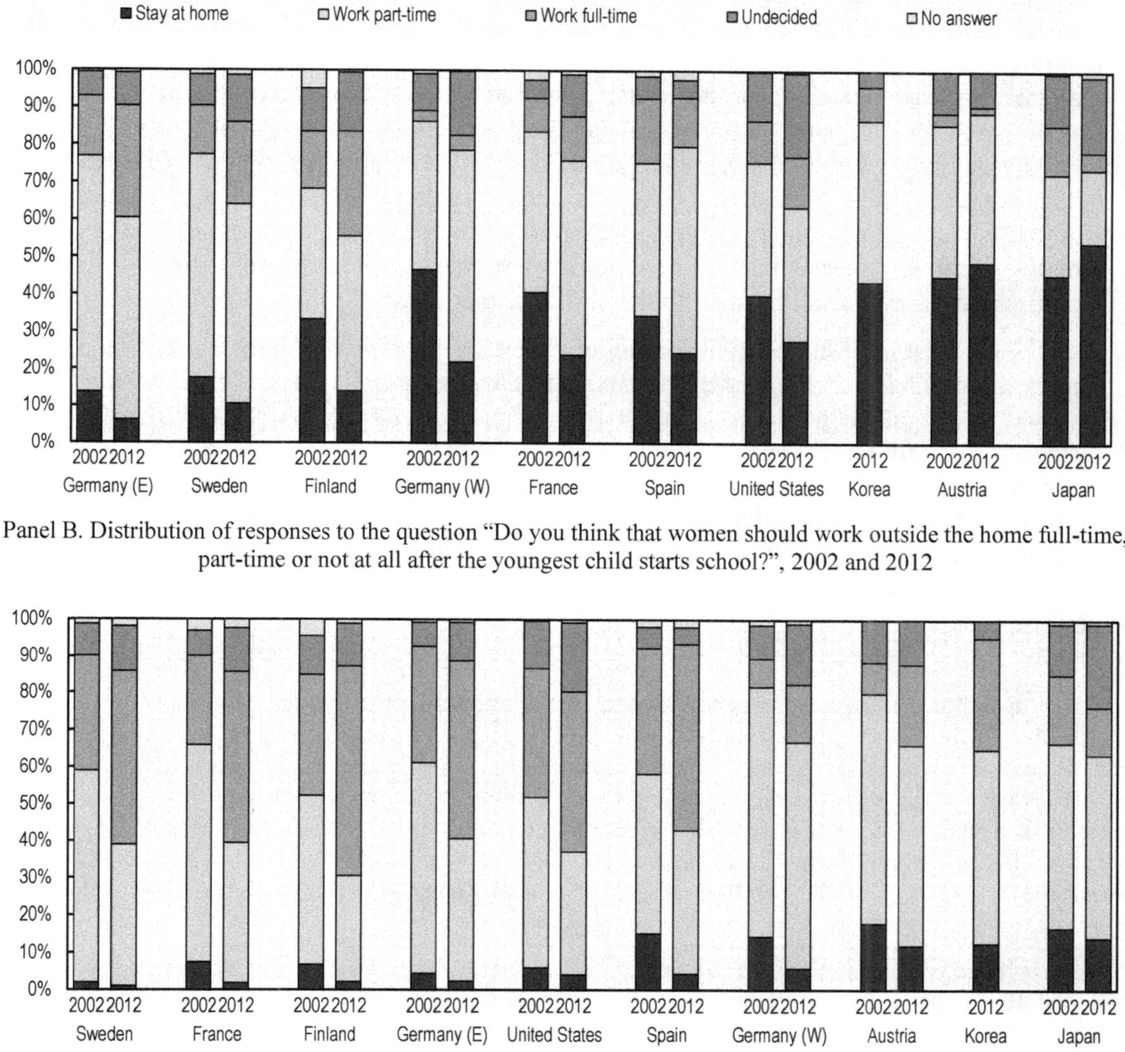

Source: OECD calculations based on the International Social Survey Programme (ISSP) 2002 and 2012, http://www.issp.org/index.php.

The time around child birth is a critical moment for sharing between parents. The German public generally believes that paid child birth-related leave policies (maternity, paternity and parental leave) should be available. In fact, only 7.3% of all German respondents are not in favour of such policies, the lowest proportion among surveyed populations, with the exception of Sweden with 5.1% (ISSP, 2012).[4]

Furthermore, most Germans who support the idea of paid leave believe that both parents should make use of leave (see Figure 1.1), with about 40% saying that mothers and fathers should share it equally. Indeed, in 2012, 40.4% of East Germans and 43.3% of West Germans in favour of paid parental leave thought that, if both parents worked full-time before the birth of the child, they should share paid leave time equally. Only in Sweden did more respondents – 61% – support equally shared paid parental leave.

6. Can Germany's labour force afford equal partnership?

The size of the German labour force is set to decrease sharply over the next few decades. The population is ageing and the working-age population is expected to decline considerably (see Figure 2.5). Moreover, shifts in the age distribution of the working-age population mean that workers themselves are becoming older. Because older workers are less likely to be in the labour force and, if they are, tend to work shorter hours, overall participation rates and average working hours are set to decline, too. The gathering force of these changes will put considerable pressure on German labour supply. OECD projections, based on current rates of labour market entry and exit and current population dynamics, suggest that the size of the full-time equivalent labour force in Germany – that is, the number of workers in the economy adjusted for working hours – could fall from around 38 million in 2015 to 32 million in 2040.

Any discussion of more equal sharing of paid work in Germany must consider the impact it could have on the size of the labour force. For example, "equal sharing" that involves an overall reduction in labour participation and working hours – through, for instance, reduced male working hours and stable female hours – would intensify pressures on the size of the German labour force. On the other hand, any redistribution of paid and unpaid work that leads to an overall increase in labour supply – by facilitating increases in the time women spend in paid work, for example – could help offset looming labour shortages and, as a result, strengthen Germany economic performance.

Box 2.4. Family policies and attitudes: A chicken-and-egg relationship

Attitudes towards maternal employment and gender roles in families have changed considerably over the last few decades. Among younger adults, in particular, the male breadwinner model is losing support in favour of greater maternal labour force participation. At the same time, family policies have been changing, with many countries strengthening overall support for families by, for example, expanding the provision of early child education and care (ECEC). About one-third of OECD countries have introduced parental leave policies that reserve at least two months paid leave for the father (OECD, 2016a).

Ferragina and Seeleib-Kaiser (2014) highlight that the drivers of policy change have changed across time. In the 1980s and 1990s social democratic and women's organisations were the main forces behind family policy reform. Since the 2000s, public opinion has increasingly backed a "modernised" family with working mothers. This broader support has been essential for policy reform (also see Morgan, 2013).

Societal attitudes and social policies interact and affect each other. Pfau-Effinger (2004 and 2005), Kremer (2006), Morgan (2013), Ferragina and Seeleib-Keiser (2014), and Mischke (2014) argue that attitudes towards family models and gender roles in the family context interact simultaneously with cultural norms and values, socio-economic factors (e.g. labour market attributes and low fertility rates), and the design of family policies themselves (e.g. policies supporting the single-earner or dual-earner family model).

Müller and Blome (2013) quantitatively analyse the effect of attitudes towards maternal employment in the years from 1990 to 1999 on work-life policy reforms between 1993 and 2007 in 11 European countries. They find a positive relationship between beliefs on maternal employment and policies implemented. In countries where attitudes were more supportive of maternal employment, work-care policies were more likely to support dual-earner families. Weckström (2014) also found a strong correlation between attitudes towards mothers in work and prevailing child care policies in several countries. However, while the recent expansion of ECEC has been important in supporting mothers in paid work, they do not *per se* foster more equal sharing between partners. Instead, they mainly liberate woman so that they have some time for paid work, but without increasing fathers' involvement in child care (Daly, 2011; Ciccia and Bleijenbergh, 2014).

Cross-country evidence points to what more equal partnership in Germany might look like in terms of levels and patterns of paid work. OECD time use data, for example, suggest that gender differences in paid and unpaid work are narrowest in Canada, France, the Nordic countries and the United States (Chapters 4 and 5). Although patterns of paid work do vary across these countries, female labour force participation rates tend to be higher and average female working hours longer than in Germany, while male working hours are generally a little shorter than in Germany (Figure 2.20). In Denmark and Norway, for example, female participation rates are relatively high (at around 84%) and working hours fairly long (around 34 hours per week). Average male hours, by contrast, are short – 37 to 38 hours per week (Figure 2.20). Finland, France and the United States, for their part, take a slightly different approach. Men's average working hours are long, at over 40 hours per week, but so, too, are women's – between 35 and 38 hours per week, depending on the country. As for Sweden, it lies somewhere in the middle: female participation rates and working hours are high at 88% and 36 hours per week, respectively, while male working hours are slightly shorter than in Germany at just under 40 hours per week.

Figure 2.20. Female labour participation rates and working hours tend to be higher, and male working hours a little lower, in countries with more equal divisions of paid and unpaid work than Germany

Labour force participation rates and average usual weekly working hours,[1] 25-to-54 year-olds, by sex, selected countries, 2014

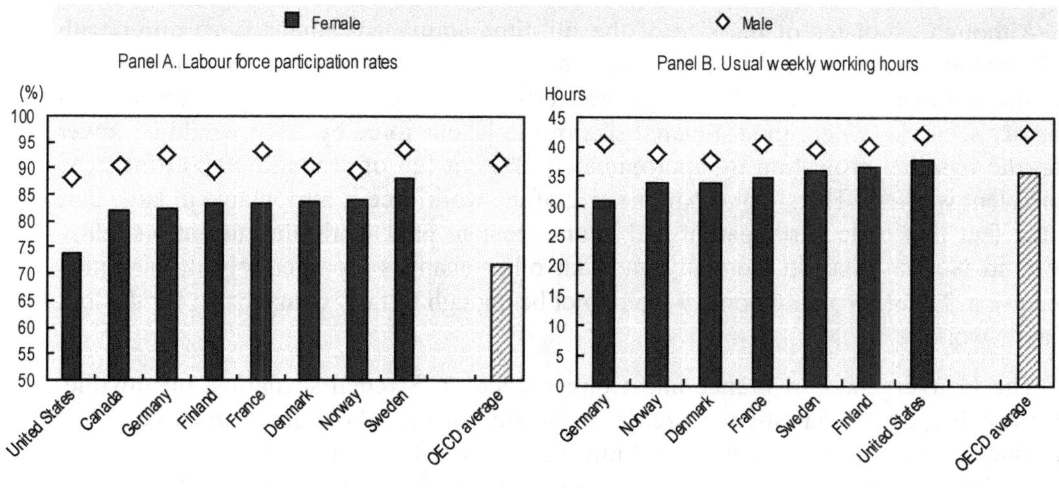

1. Data on average usual weekly working hours for the United States refer to dependent employees only. Data for Canada are missing.

Source: *OECD Employment Database*, http://www.oecd.org/employment/emp/onlineoecdemploymentdatabase.htm.

Figure 2.21 simulates what potentially could happen to the size of the labour force if Germany adopted patterns of paid work similar to those in countries with more gender-equal divisions of work. It shows projections for the size of the German full-time equivalent labour force (15-to-74 year-olds) under standard (baseline) conditions, and in alternative scenarios where male and female participation rates and working hours among workers of "prime age" (25-to-54 year-olds) have converged by 2040 with those currently practiced in three more "gender-egalitarian" countries – France, Norway and Sweden (see Annex 2.A1 for technical details):

- *The Convergence on France scenario.* As male participation rates and average working hours in France are not too dissimilar to Germany's (Figure 2.21), patterns of male paid work would not need to change much. Convergence on France would, however, call for a small increase in women's participation rates and a considerable increase in their usual weekly working hours.
- *The Convergence on Norway scenario.* As female working hours are currently fairly long and male working hours fairly short in Norway relative to Germany (Figure 2.20), this would involve a fairly large increase in female usual weekly working hours and some decrease in male working hours. It would also involve a decrease in male participation and a small increase in female participation.
- *The Convergence on Sweden scenario.* This would involve a decrease in male average usual weekly working hours in Germany, and large increases in both female participation rates and female weekly working hours (Figure 2.20).

To illustrate the potentially achievable labour supply gains from changes in patterns of paid work, Figure 2.21 also shows estimates from a fifth scenario, Convergence on Male Patterns, where female patterns of paid work would move towards and eventually mirror German men's. This scenario assumes that male labour force participation rates and usual weekly working hours remain at the baseline throughout. Female participation rates and hours, meanwhile, gradually approach the male baseline before full convergence in 2040 (see Annex 2.A1).

Although estimates of the size of the full-time equivalent labour force differ with each scenario, none predicts a labour force that is substantially smaller than the standard baseline estimate (Figure 2.21). The lowest estimate comes from the Convergence on Norway scenario, where the estimated size of the labour force by 2040 would be lower than the baseline projection by approximately 2% – a fall of around 620 000 full-time equivalent workers. The slight dip in the size of the workforce is attributable in large part to the fact that male participation and hours spent in paid work are currently slightly lower in Norway than in Germany and that other changes – particularly the assumed increase in female working hours – would not be enough to fully compensate for the loss of male workers.

The Convergence on France and Convergence on Sweden scenarios, meanwhile, both involve a potential slight increase in the size of the labour force, relative to the baseline projection. Converging on France's patterns of paid work by 2040 would boost the size of the full-time equivalent labour force by about 3.8% (around 1.2 million full-time equivalent workers). Converging on Sweden's patterns would lead to a slightly larger increase, of around 4.43% (1.4 million full-time equivalent workers). And in the latter scenario, the gender gap in labour force participation would be reduced by 30%, which exceeds the target set at the Brisbane 2014 G20 leaders' summit to reduce the gap in labour force participation rates between men and women in G20 countries by 25 % by 2025 (OECD, ILO, IMF and World Bank, 2014).

Neither increase would be sufficient to fully offset the projected decline in the size of the German labour force – in both, the projected size of the labour force in 2040 remains at least 4.5 million full-ime equivalent workers short of the 2012 labour force. Indeed, the overall decline is only just fully addressed in the Convergence on Male Patterns scenario which assumes that, by 2040, female patterns of paid work will be identical to the male baseline. Nevertheless, estimates from both the Swedish and

French convergence scenarios suggest that moving towards the paid work practices of countries with more equal sharing could help temper the projected shrinking of the German labour force. In fact, emulating Swedish-style patterns of paid work could halt the decline by as much around 22%.

Figure 2.21. Shifting towards patterns of paid work similar to those in countries with more gender-equitable divisions of paid and unpaid work would (at worst) do little damage to the size of the German labour force

Projected size of the total full-time equivalent labour force (15-to-74 year-olds) under different scenarios, 2012-40

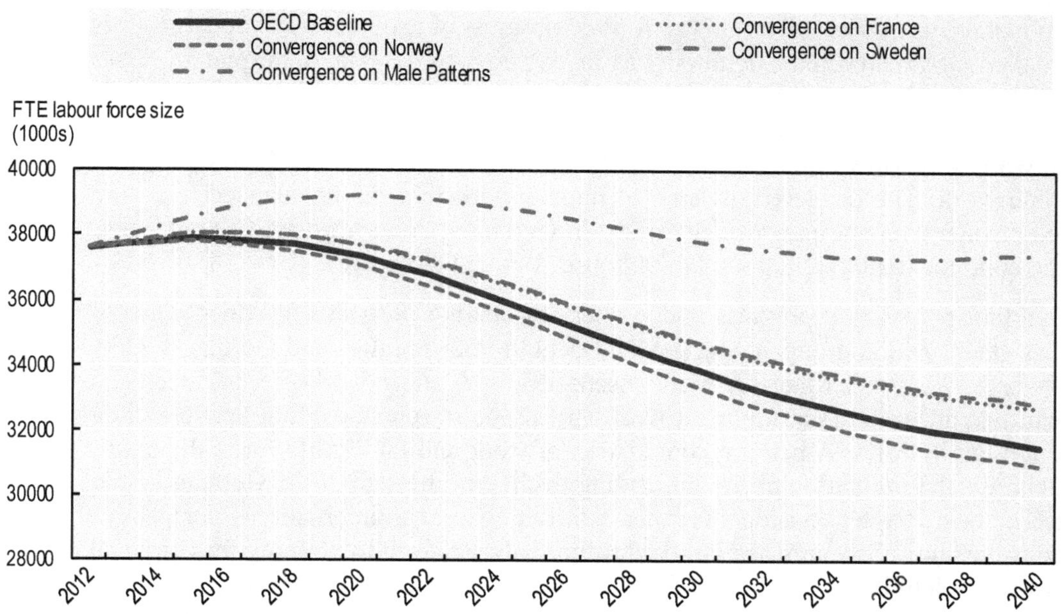

Source: OECD estimates based on OECD population data, population projections from Destatis (2015c), and the *OECD Employment Database*, www.oecd.org/employment/emp/onlineoecdemploymentdatabase.htm.

Given that the size of the labour force is a central determinant of gross domestic product (GDP), transitioning to patterns of paid work similar to those in France and, in particular, Sweden would help expand the labour force and so boost German economic performance. OECD estimates suggest that, despite the likely decline in the size of the labour force, GDP per capita in Germany is expected to grow at a respectable average annual rate of around 1.38% per year between 2012 and 2040 (OECD, 2014b). However, simulations based on a modified version of the OECD's long-term growth models (see Annex 2.A1) suggest that shifting towards French- or Swedish-style patterns of paid work could potentially add 0.10 to 0.11 percentage points to that average annual rate – equivalent to an increase of between USD 1 300 to USD 1 500 in GDP per capita by 2040.

7. Concluding remarks

German families have been changing over the past few decades. Couple families remain common, but an increasing number of children now grow up with unmarried cohabitating parents. Women are also having more children now than they were twenty years ago, but fertility rates remain well below both the OECD average and the population replacement rate.

The ways in which German families organise paid work have been changing, too. Germans have become more accepting of mothers going out to work, particularly once children start school but also, to a lesser degree, when they are very young. These shifts in attitudes have been accompanied by large increases in the share of German mothers in paid work. Germany now has a maternal employment rate that is higher than the average for OECD countries, and a female employment rate that is the highest in the OECD outside of the Nordic countries and Switzerland.

Still, there is plenty of room for further progress. Favourable attitudes towards maternal employment often extend only as far as part-time work and, despite increases in the frequency of female employment, the "main-earner model" continues to dominate in Germany, albeit in a modified form – German men work long full-time hours, while German women (and especially German mothers) are likely to be in short part-time work. The gendered division of unpaid work remains unbalanced too, with limited change over the past decade or so. In Germany, as in most OECD countries, women continue to do the lion's share of housework and childcare.

Building on existing progress and further rearranging the ways in which German families share paid and unpaid work would benefit both families and German society as a whole. Many Germans remain unsatisfied with their work-life balance, and German parents are among the most likely in Europe to report conflict between their work and family roles. A better reconciliation of work and family life for both parents is crucial for the mitigation of the impending decline in the size of the German labour force. The next chapter considers German family policy in an international perspective and considers how Germany can build on recent policy reform to promote further equal partnership in families.

Notes

1. "Parent", "mother" or "father" refers to the mother or father residing in a household where at least one child under 18 lives together with a couple (married or cohabitating) identified as his/her parents.

2. The TFR is defined as the number of children an average woman would give birth to at the end of her childbearing years. Allowing for mortality during infancy and childhood, and holding net migration constant, the population is replaced at a TFR of around 2.1 children per woman.

3. Unless otherwise specified, the distinction between part-time and full-time employment used in this section is based on a common definition (usual weekly working hours of less than 30 in the main job). Exact rates of part-time and full-time employment may differ from those presented later in Chapter 4, where the distinction between part-time and full-time employment is self-defined by survey respondents.

4. In countries with no or short parental leave, such as the United States, higher proportions of respondents do not favour such schemes.

References

Ariga, A. and A. Lleras (2011), "Brief and Rare Mental 'Breaks' Keep You Focused: Deactivation and Reactivation of Task Goals Pre-empt Vigilance Decrements", *Cognition*, Vol. 118, No. 3, pp. 439-443.

Barger, L. et al. (2005), "Extended Work Shifts and the Risk of Motor Vehicle Crashes Among Interns", *New England Journal of Medicine*, Vol. 352, No. 2, pp. 125-134.

Becker, G. (1985), "Human Capital, Effort, and the Sexual Division of Labor", *Journal of Labor Economics*, University of Chicago Press, Vol. 3, No. 1, pp. S33-S58.

Becker, G. (1981), *A Treatise on the Family,* Harvard University Press, Cambridge.

Bianchi, S.M. et al. (2000), "Is Anyone Doing the Housework? Trends in the Gender Division of Household Labor", *Social forces*, Vol. 79, No. 1, pp. 191-228.

BMFSFJ – Federal Ministry for Family Affairs, Senior Citizens, Women and Youth (2015), "Dossier Väter und Familie – erste Bilanz einer neuen Dynamik", Bundesministerium für Familie, Senioren, Frauen und Jugend, Berlin.

BMFSFJ (2014), "Family Report 2014 – Benefits, Effects, Trends", Bundesministerium für Familie, Senioren, Frauen und Jugend, Berlin.

Business Roundtable (1980), "Scheduled Overtime Effect on Construction Projects: A Construction Industry Cost-effectiveness Project Report", A Construction Industry Cost Effectiveness Project Report, monograph, Business Roundtable, New York.

Coltrane, S. (2000), "Research on Household Labor: Modeling and Measuring the Social Embeddedness of Routine Family Work", *Journal of Marriage and Family*, Vol. 62, No. 4, pp. 1208-1233.

Destatis – German Statistical Office (2016), "Scheidungen – Maßzahlen zu Ehescheidungen 2000 bis 2014", Wiesbaden, http://www.destatis.de/DE/ZahlenFakten/GesellschaftStaat/Bevoelkerung/Ehescheidungen/Tabellen/MasszahlenEhescheidungen.html.

Destatis (2015a), "Bevölkerung und Erwerbstätigkeit: Haushalte und Familien. Ergebnisse des Mikrozensus, 2014", Statistisches Bundesamt, Wiesbaden.

Destatis (2015b), "Zeitverwendungserhebung: Aktivitäten in Stunden und Minuten für ausgewählte Personengruppen", Statistisches Bundesamt, Wiesbaden.

Destatis (2015c), "Bevölkerung Deutschlands bis 2060: 13. koordinierte Bevölkerungsvorausberechnung", Statistisches Bundesamt, Wiesbaden.

Elsbach, K. and D. Cable (2012), "Why Showing your Face at the Office Matters", *MIT Sloan Management Review: Research Highlight*, Summer.

Eurobarometer (2014), "Gender Equality Module", European Commission.

Exton, C., C. Smith and D. Vandendriessche (2015), "Comparing Happiness across the World : Does Culture Matter?", *OECD Statistics Working Papers*, No. 2015/04, OECD Publishing, Paris, http://dx.doi.org/10.1787/5jrqppzd9bs2-en.

Faber, N., J. Hausser, and N. Kerr (2015), "Sleep Deprivation Impairs and Caffeine Enhances my Performance, But Not Always our Performance: How Acting in a Group Can Change the Effects of Impairments and Enhancements", *Personality and Social Psychology Review,* advance online publication, http://dx.doi.org/10.1177/1088868315609487.

Flinn, F. and C. Armstrong (2011), "Junior Doctors' Extended Work Hours and the Effects on their Performance: The Irish Case", *International Journal for Quality in Health Care,* Vol. 23, No. 2, pp. 210-217.

Helm, E. van der, N. Gujar, and M. Walker (2010), "Sleep Deprivation Impairs the Accurate Recognition of Human Emotions", *Sleep*, Vol. 33, No. 3, pp. 335-342.

Allensbach Institut für Demoskopie (2015), "Familienbilder in Deutschland und Frankreich – Vergleich der Ergebnisse von Repräsentativbefragungen der Bevölkerung im Alter von 16 bis 49 Jahren in beiden Ländern", Allensbach.

ISSP – International Social Survey Programme (2012), "Family and Changing Gender Roles IV", ZA No. 5900, online tabulation tool, http://zacat.gesis.org/webview/index.jsp?object=http://zacat.gesis.org/obj/fStudy/ZA5900.

Johansson, Å. et al. (2013), "Long-Term Growth Scenarios", *OECD Economics Department Working Papers*, No. 1000, OECD Publishing, Paris, http://dx.doi.org/10.1787/5k4ddxpr2fmr-en.

Killgore, W. et al. (2008), "Sleep Deprivation Reduces Perceived Emotional Intelligence and Constructive Thinking Skills", *Sleep Medicine*, Vol. 9, No. 5, pp. 517-526.

Lachance-Grzela, M., and G. Bouchard (2010), "Why Do Women Do the Lion's Share of Housework? A Decade of Research", *Sex Roles*, Vol. 63, No. 11-12, pp. 767-780.

Li, J. et al. (2014), "Parents' Non-standard Work Schedules and Child Well-being: A Critical Review of the Literature", *Journal of Primary Prevention*, Vol. 35, No. 10, pp. 53-73.

Lück, D. (2015), "Vaterleitbilder: Ernährer und Erzieher?", *Familienleitbilder in Deutschland*, Bundesinstitut für Bevölkerungsforschung.

Lundberg, S. and R. Pollak (1996), "Bargaining and Distribution in Marriage", *Journal of Economic Perspectives*, Vol. 10, No. 4, pp. 139-158.

OECD (2016a), *The OECD Family Database*, OECD Publishing, Paris, http://www.oecd.org/els/family/database.htm.

OECD (2016b), "OECD Gender Data Portal", OECD Publishing, Paris, https://www.oecd.org/gender/data/.

OECD (2015a), *In It Together: Why Less Inequality Benefits All*, OECD Publishing, Paris, http://dx.doi.org/10.1787/9789264235120-en.

OECD (2015b), *The ABC of Gender Equality in Education: Aptitude, Behaviour, and Confidence*, PISA, OECD Publishing, Paris, http://dx.doi.org/10.1787/9789264229945-en.

OECD (2014a), *Enhancing Women's Economic Empowerment, through Entrepreneurship and Business leadership in OECD Countries*, OECD, Paris, http://www.oecd.org/gender/Enhancing%20Women%20Economic%20Empowerment_Fin_1_Oct_2014.pdf.

OECD (2014b), *OECD Economic Outlook*, OECD Publishing, Paris, http://dx.doi.org/10.1787/eco_outlook-v2014-1-en.

OECD (2012), *Closing the Gender Gap: Act Now*, OECD Publishing, Paris, http://dx.doi.org/10.1787/9789264179370-en.

OECD, ILO, IMF and World Bank (2014), "Achieving Stronger Growth by Promoting a More Gender-balanced Economy", Report prepared for the G20 Labour and Employment Ministerial Meeting, Melbourne, Australia, 10-11 September, www.oecd.org/g20/topics/employment-and-social-policy/ILO-IMF-OECD-WBG-Achieving-stronger-growth-by-promoting-a-more-gender-balanced-economy-G20.pdf.

Pencavel, J. (2014), "The Productivity of Working Hours", *IZA Discussion Paper*, No. 8129, Bonn.

Robinson, E. (2005), "Why Crunch Mode Doesn't Work: Six Lessons", International Game Developers Association.

Rogers, A. et al. (2004), "The Working Hours of Hospital Staff Nurses and Patient Safety", *Health Affairs*, Vol. 23, No. 4, pp. 202-212.

Sharone, O. (2004), "Engineering Overwork: Bell-curve Management at a High-tech Firm", in C.F. Epstein and A.L. Kalleberg (eds.), *Fighting for Time: Shifting Boundaries of Work and Social Life*, Russell Sage Foundation, New York.

Sullivan, O. (2000), "The Division of Domestic Labour: Twenty Years of Change?", *Sociology*, Vol. 34, No. 3, pp. 437-456.

Thomas, R. and K. Raynar (1997), "Scheduled Overtime and Labor Productivity: Quantitative Analysis", *Journal of Construction and Engineering Management*, Vol. 123, No. 2, pp. 181-88.

US Presidential Commission on the Space Shuttle Challenger Accident (1986), "Report to the President".

Annex 2.A1

Estimating the effects of changes in male and female patterns of paid work on the German labour force and German GDP per capita

To illustrate the potential effects of equal sharing and changes in patterns of paid work on German labour supply and economic performance, this report estimates both the projected size of the German full-time equivalent labour force (15-to-74 year-olds) and projected German gross domestic product (GDP) per capita in five hypothetical labour market scenarios. Each scenario assumes different trajectories for male and female labour force participation rates and male and female usual weekly working hours between 2012 and 2040 (Table 2.A1.1 summarises what the male, female and aggregate labour force participation rates and average usual weekly working hours would be in 2040 under each scenario). The scenarios are:

- *The "Baseline" scenario.* The labour force participation rates of German men and women of all ages are estimated using the OECD's dynamic age-cohort model. It projects participation rates (by gender and by five-year age group) based on current (i.e. 2003-12) rates of labour market entry and exit. Average usual weekly working hours for each gender and five-year age group are held constant at their 2012 values.

  Under the Baseline scenario, overall male and female labour force participation rates (15-to-74 year-olds) are projected to decline by about 2.3 percentage points and 0.7 percentage points, respectively, by 2040. Total average usual weekly working hours (15-to-74 year-olds) are projected to decline slightly, too – by about 0.3 hours per week in both cases – entirely on account of shifts in the age-distribution of the working population.

- *The Convergence on France scenario.* This scenario assumes that the labour force participation rates of German men and women aged 25 to 54 and their usual weekly working hours will, by 2014, converge linearly for each five-year age group with the rates and hours observed in France in 2012. To avoid any complication that might stem from differences in educational systems and pension or retirement systems, participation rates and usual weekly working hours of 15-to-24 year-olds and the over-55s follow the standard baseline projection.

  With respect to the baseline, convergence with France's labour participation rates and working hours by 2040 would lead to a fall of about 0.4 percentage points in the overall labour force participation rate (15-to-74 year-olds) and an increase of 1.6 hours per week in overall average usual weekly working hours (15-to-74 year-olds).

- *The Convergence on Norway scenario.* This scenario assumes that the labour force participation rates of German men and women aged 25 to 54 and their usual weekly working hours will, by 2040, converge linearly for each five-year age group with the rates and hours observed in Norway in 2012. Again, to avoid any complication due to differences in educational systems and pension or retirement systems, the participation rates and usual weekly working hours of 15-to-24 year-olds and the over-55s are kept at the baseline.

  Relative to the baseline, convergence with Norway's labour participation rates and working hours by 2040 would lead to a fall of about 1.2 percentage points in Germany's overall labour force participation rate (15-to-74 year-olds), and no net change in overall average usual weekly working hours (15-to-74 year-olds).

- *The Convergence on Sweden scenario.* This scenario assumes that the labour force participation rates of 25-to-54 year-old German men and women and their usual weekly working hours will, by 2040, converge linearly for each five-year age bracket with the rates and hours in Sweden in 2012. Once more, the participation rates and usual weekly working hours of 15-to-24 year-olds and the over-55s remain at the baseline.

  Relative to the baseline, convergence with Sweden's employment rates and working hours potentially yields a small increase of about 0.6 percentage points in Germany's overall labour force participation rate (15-to-74 year-olds), and an increase of about 1.2 hours per week in overall average usual weekly working hours (15-to-74 year-olds).

- *The Convergence on German Male Patterns scenario.* For German men of all ages, this scenario takes the baseline projection for the labour force participation rates and usual weekly working hours. It assumes that the labour force participation rates and usual weekly working hours of German women of all ages will, by 2040 and for each five-year age group, converge with the respective baseline male rates and hours. In other words, by 2040, female patterns of paid work in each five-year age group will be identical to those of the male baseline projection.

  With respect to the baseline, the convergence of German women's patterns of paid work on the male baseline would, by 2040, yield a substantial increase of about 3.8 percentage points in the overall labour force participation rate (15-to-74 year-olds) and a very large increase of about 4.3 hours per week in male and female average usual weekly working hours (15-to-74 year-olds).

Table 2.A1.1. Summary of the effects of assumed changes in male and female patterns of paid work on overall labour force participation rates and overall average usual weekly working hours in Germany

Overall labour force participation rates (15-to-74 year-olds) and overall average usual weekly working hours (15-to-74 year-olds) in 2012 (observed) and in 2040 (projected) under each of the hypothetical scenarios, Germany[1]

		Overall labour force participation rates (%) (15-74 year olds)			Overall average usual weekly working hours (15-74 year olds)		
Year	Scenario	Total	Male	Female	Total	Male	Female
2012	-	67.07	72.52	61.63	35.60	39.90	30.55
2040	Baseline	65.17	69.26	60.95	35.30	39.61	30.25
	Convergence on France	64.81	69.46	60.01	36.86	39.95	33.16
	Convergence on Norway	63.92	67.42	60.30	35.28	37.92	32.24
	Convergence on Sweden	65.80	69.43	62.05	36.46	38.77	33.80
	Convergence on German Male Patterns	69.02	69.26	68.77	39.59	39.61	39.56

Source: OECD estimates based on OECD population data, population projections from Destatis (2015c), and the *OECD Employment Database*, www.oecd.org/employment/emp/onlineoecdemploymentdatabase.htm.

Estimates of the size of the German full-time equivalent (FTE) labour force (15-74 year-olds) under each of these scenarios were produced using the OECD's in-house labour force projection model, with the projected size of the labour force adjusted according to the assumptions made about both labour force participation rates and usual weekly working hours in the given scenario. In each case the headcount labour force (by gender and five-year age group) was calculated first using population projections from Destatis (2015c) and the assumed labour force participation rates, with this headcount value then transformed (by gender and five-year age group) into the full-time equivalent using the assumed values for average usual weekly working hours. In this instance "full-time" refers to usual weekly working hours equal to 40 hours per week, so the FTE labour force was calculated as the headcount labour force multiplied by usual weekly working hours for the relevant group, divided by 40.

Estimates of German GDP per capita under each of the scenarios, meanwhile, were produced using a modified version of the long-term growth models presented by the OECD in the *OECD Economic Outlook No. 95* (see Johansson et al., 2013 for technical details). These growth models estimate GDP based on a standard Cobb-Douglas production function, with the usual long-term growth determinants – i.e. physical capital, human capital, potential employment, and labour efficiency. Potential GDP across the projection period (here, 2012 to 2040) is estimated by projecting trends and changes in the various input components, with projections of the components themselves based on both long-term dynamics within the given country and on convergence patterns between countries (see OECD, 2014b; and Johansson et al., 2013 for details on the measures, data and assumptions used to project the individual components).

Changes to and potential growth in German GDP per capita in each scenario were estimated by adjusting projections from these long-term growth models according to the assumed change (relative to the baseline) in the overall labour force participation rate – which, as a determinant of growth, enters the model as a sub-component of potential employment – and the assumed change (relative to the baseline) in overall average usual weekly working hours – which, in growth accounting terms, enters the model as part of labour efficiency. No change is assumed in the Baseline scenario, so the estimates of GDP per capita in this scenario are identical to those in the *OECD*

Economic Outlook No. 95. In each case changes and developments in all other production factors – such as physical capital and human capital and the remaining sub-components of potential employment and labour efficiency – were held steady at the baseline.

It should be pointed out that the projections used in these scenarios are simply mechanical. In other words, they assume that any changes in labour force participation rates or weekly working hours do not interact with, or have any indirect effects on, other labour inputs or any other production factors, including physical or human capital. It is possible, for example, that changes in labour force participation rates and weekly working hours among "prime age" (25-to-54 year old) women could lead to changes in participation and/or hours among older workers if, for instance, grandparents or older friends and relatives are used as substitute carers for children. If any such indirect effects occur, the impact of changes in patterns of paid work on the overall labour supply may differ from those estimated here. It should also be noted that the estimates of GDP per capita in the different scenarios do not factor in any possible effects of changes in patterns of paid work on household production. Again, to the extent that changes in male or female labour supply lead to changes in household production or to shifts between measured and unmeasured economic activity, the estimates shown here may not fully capture the effects of a change in patterns of paid work on economic output. With these limitations in mind, the projections presented both in Figure 2.21 and Table 2.A1.2 should be read only as estimates or approximations of the impact of changes in patterns of paid work on overall labour supply or on GDP per capita. Nonetheless, they continue to provide an indication of the possible or potential effects the stem from changes in the sharing of paid work between men and women.

Table 2.A1.2 shows the resulting estimates of German GDP per capita in 2040 plus the average annual rate of growth in German GDP per capita over the period 2012-40 under each of the hypothetical scenarios. The results in the table include:

- None of the scenarios project an average annual rate of growth in GDP per capita that is substantially lower than the baseline average annual rate. The lowest estimated average annual rate comes from the Convergence on Norway scenario, where GDP per capita is projected to grow at an average rate of 1.34% per year over the years between 2013 and 2040 – very slightly lower than the baseline average annual rate of growth (1.38%).

- Both the Convergence on France and Convergence on Sweden scenarios project an average annual rate of growth in GDP per capita that is higher than in the Baseline scenario, reflecting the relative increase in the size of the labour force in the French and Swedish scenarios. Under the Convergence on France scenario, GDP per capita is estimated to grow at an average annual rate of 1.48% per year, about 0.10 percentage points higher than the Baseline scenario. Estimated annual growth in GDP per capita in the Convergence on Sweden scenario is very slightly higher still, at an average of 1.49% per year. These enhanced rates of growth would, by 2040 and relative to the baseline, translate into potential increases in annual GDP per capita of around USD 1 300 and USD 1 500 (PPP 2005), respectively.

- The estimated average annual rate of growth in GDP per capita in the Convergence on German Male Patterns scenario is considerably higher than that projected in the Baseline scenario. It projects that GDP per capita will grow at an average annual rate of around 1.80%, about 0.4 percentage points higher than the Baseline scenario estimate. By 2040 and relative to the baseline, that growth rate would translate into an increase in annual GDP per capita of around USD 6 300 (PPP 2005). However, as Table 2.A1.2 shows, the scenario requires a substantial increase in female labour participation and an even higher increase in female average usual weekly working hours.

Table 2.A1.2. Summary of the potential effects of assumed changes in male and female patterns of paid work on GDP per capita and growth in GDP per capita in Germany

Projected GDP per capita (USD PPP 2005) in 2040 and average annual growth (%) in GDP per capita over the period 2013-40 under the various hypothetical scenarios, Germany[1]

Scenario	Projected GDP per capita (USD 2005 PPP), 2040	Projected average annual growth (%) in GDP per capita, 2013-2040
Baseline	51489.94	1.38%
Convergence on France	52798.07	1.48%
Convergence on Norway	50811.20	1.34%
Convergence on Sweden	52950.84	1.49%
Convergence on German Male Patterns	57740.19	1.80%

1. German GDP per capita (USD PPP 2005) in 2012 was USD 35 039.33

Source: OECD estimates based on OECD (2014), *OECD Economic Outlook No. 95* (Edition 2014/1), *OECD Economic Outlook: Statistics and Projections Databases*; OECD estimates based on OECD population data, population projections from Destatis (2015c), and the *OECD Employment Database*, www.oecd.org/employment/emp/onlineoecdemploymentdatabase.htm.

Chapter 3

Policies to support equal partnerships in families in Germany

This chapter considers ways in which Germany may continue to promote equal partnerships in families. The chapter first introduces the issues and sets out the main findings, before examining policies in OECD countries that foster equal partnership in families and discussing how those policies differ in their approach and tools. Section 3 looks at how financial incentive structures embodied in tax/benefit systems may encourage both parents to work. Parental leave is a critical component of policies to reconcile work and family life and the main subject of the next section, which considers how reform in Germany has changed father's and mother's leave taking behaviour. Section 5 analyses the implications of a potential family working-time model. Such a scheme could foster gender equality, involve fathers more in child care and housework, and enable mothers to work full-time or longer part-time hours. The next section discusses the provision of early childhood education and care services and out-of-school-hours care. Finally, the chapter considers how stakeholders can (and have) come together to offer flexible working-time arrangements that help balance paid work with family commitments.

The statistical data for Israel are supplied by and under the responsibility of the relevant Israeli authorities. The use of such data by the OECD is without prejudice to the status of the Golan Heights, East Jerusalem and Israeli settlements in the West Bank under the terms of international law.

1. Introduction and main findings

Across the OECD, public policies seek to support parents in achieving their desired work-life balance. There are many underlying, often interrelated, reasons for doing so. They include fighting child poverty, supporting family well-being, encouraging self-sufficiency, promoting parental labour force participation, and generally promoting gender equality and inclusive growth. However, the focus on the underlying motivations varies by country and over time, which contributes to differences in support systems across the OECD. This chapter assesses recent developments in family policies in Germany, and estimates how they might affect gender equality and economic growth in Germany in the future.

Section 2 takes an international overview of policies that affect equal partnerships in families and explores cross-national differences in the use and design of policy tools. Section 3 evaluates the financial incentives for parents to work set by tax-benefit systems. Section 4 assesses parental leave arrangements and discusses ways in which German fathers may devote more time to parenting from the outset. Section 5 discusses how a "family working-time model" could, operating on certain assumptions, encourage more equal sharing amongst parents after parental leave is over and how it may help macroeconomic outcomes like increasing Germany's labour supply and promoting economic growth. Section 6 analyses the expansion of early childhood education and care and out-of-school-hours support in Germany, while Section 7 reviews how flexible work arrangements may help parents balance paid work and unpaid household labour. The evidence in this chapter seeks to help strengthen Germany's resolve to continue its ongoing progress towards a more balanced reconciliation of work and family for mothers and fathers.

Main findings

Consistent public policies and a continuum of support help parents to combine work and family commitments as children grow up:

- Reforms in the mid-2000s ushered in a change in the German policy approach that saw a greater focus on public investment in families with children in the early years of childhood. Overall spending per child during the early years has moved closer to Swedish levels.
- Tax-benefit policies in around one-third of OECD countries encourage the equal sharing of paid work. Many countries' tax-benefit systems are more or less neutral towards couples who share paid work.
- The German tax-benefit system, by contrast, discourages couples from sharing paid work equally. The joint income tax system, free co-insurance of spouses, and the cap on social security contributions in Germany, ensure that the tax burden on household labour increases strongly when a second person takes up employment unless s/he engages in a tax free minijob with income of up to EUR 450 per month.
- Financial incentives to work for second earners in couple families could be improved in different ways, as for example through a separate tax-free allowance for second earners, or assessing health contribution on basis of the number of adults who are insured, with compensation for low-income families. Other in-

work benefits could also encourage secondary earners in low-income families to contribute more to the household income.

- Parental leave is as important for children as for their fathers and mothers. Reserving part of parental leave exclusively for fathers and generally encouraging more equally shared parenting through parental leave provisions, encourages young couples to continue sharing equally when they become parents and can help prevent reversion to traditional gender roles. The greater involvement of fathers not only supports mothers in their returns to the labour market, but also contributes to better father-child relationships.
- The 2007 reform of the parental leave system in Germany was in line with international best practice and a great step towards a more gender-balanced division of paid and unpaid work. It significantly increased the likelihood of mothers resuming work earlier than prior to the reform and markedly increased fathers' uptake of parental leave.
- *ElterngeldPlus* denotes the reform introduced in 2015. It seeks to encourage both parents to work part-time work and take parental leave. It offers financial incentive to both partners in couple families to engage in paid work for 25 to 30 hours per week for at least four months. The impact of the reform should be closely monitored to determine whether it indeed contributes to greater uptake of leave by fathers for longer periods.
- Germany has enshrined the statutory the right to reduce working hours for family reasons. It should now also introduce the legal entitlement to resume full-time work – or another level of working hours that fits changing family circumstances – within a specified timeframe.
- The family working-time model extends the *ElterngeldPlus* concept. It is a possible way forward in German policy to strike a work-life balance for families with (very) young children. One family working-time model under discussion proposes offering coupled parents an income supplement when both switch to "vollzeitnah", i.e. reduced full-time working hours, when children are young. Because the assumed increase in female working hours would almost entirely cancel out the assumed fall in male hours, "vollzeitnah" would do little or no harm to the projected German labour supply. As it is easier to move in to full-time work from a 30-hour week than from a part-time job with short hours, "vollzeitnah" could also help mothers work longer hours on a long-term basis when their children grow up. When mothers share more fully with their partners and work longer, women's career development and earnings both benefit.
- Affordable early childhood education and care (ECEC) and adequate out-of-school-hours (OSH) care are important to working families. Germany's recent expansion of child care for the under-3s and flexible OSH services are policy measures that are essential to the effort to give mothers the support they need if they are to achieve parity with fathers in paid work. Recent expansion in public investment in child care has been a positive step forward. Germany must go further, however, if it is to match the provision of support services for young children in countries such as Denmark and Sweden.
- Compared to its investment in ECEC, progress in OSH-care supports in Germany has to catch up: greater investment and broader access to OSH-care supports for

primary-school age children is needed. Child care issues do not stop when children enter primary school, and full-time workers in Germany need to arrange care before and/or after school hours. Public policy in Germany should invest more in OSH-care supports that help parents with school age children to combine full-time work with family life, also during school holidays.

- Flexible work arrangements are increasingly widespread and attractive to both employers and employees. About 90% of companies in Germany report offering employees flexible working-hour arrangements, and as workers have some say in their work schedules, flexitime helps them reconcile working hours with family time.
- The German authorities should further extend the co-operation with social partners and other stakeholders to make workplace practices more conducive to family life. Continue to promote a range of family-friendly workplace measures as in the scope of the "Neue Vereinbarkeit Memorandum", including reducing the number of hours in a typical full-time workday, encouraging fathers' leave taking, facilitating remote work, and allowing flexible work schedules.
- The German authorities are encouraged to continue with their work raising awareness of the benefits of equal partnerships in families, through public information campaigns, promotion of role models, high-visibility events, and other means of communication. Maintain support to initiatives aimed at fostering and sharing best practices at the local level such as the local alliances for families ("Lokale Bündnisse für Familie") taking into account the peculiarities of *Länder* and the role of municipalities.

2. Families benefit from gender-equal family policies

There is a wide range of social policies that seek to support families while encouraging equal sharing, fostering greater paternal involvement in parenting and promoting the empowerment of mothers. This section takes stock of policy options in OECD countries, discusses the strengths and weaknesses of various family benefits, and reviews differences in levels of public spending throughout childhood, with a particular focus on Germany.

A range of social policies seek to support families and promote equal partnerships

In many ways, families form the cornerstone of social protection. They care for their members, protect against economic loss and hardship, and play a key role in the nurturing and development of children. Governments around the world recognise the importance of families, children, men, and women in society, but approaches to family policies differ markedly across countries and over time. There are a variety of factors driving these differences – different underlying policy objectives, countries' histories, political institutions, levels of inequality, economic development, and labour market structures, to name but a few.

Across the OECD, family policies are generally geared towards "providing parents with support to give them more choice in their work and family decisions" (Adema, 2011). Measures which facilitate that choice can encompass a variety of "family-friendly" policy objectives:

- support the labour force participation of parents with children, including very young children,
- promote conditions which help adults have the number of children they desire at the time of their choosing,
- combat poverty among families with children,
- promote child well-being and development throughout the early life course,
- enhance gender equality at home and in the workplace.

Family policies do not generally target the form of coupled-parent relationships (be it cohabitation or marriage). However, because coupled parents' relationships play an important role in child development, some countries support marriage and parental counselling services. In others, like Japan and Korea, birth rates are closely tied to marriage rates, and policy initiatives to sustain the birth rate often include measures to promote marriage. One such example is the Third Plan for Ageing Society and Population in Korea that spans the years 2016 to 2020 (Government of the Republic of Korea, 2015).

Family policy objectives are interrelated. For example, supporting parents in reconciling work and family life obviously requires promoting the labour force participation of parents, and especially mothers, who are less well represented in the labour force than fathers and women without children. Policies to help balance work and family life also make it easier for parents to choose to have children despite work commitments. Increased parental employment is good for the whole family, too (Chapter 2):

- it boosts incomes (Warren and Tyagi, 2003; OECD, 2014, 2015a), which furthers children's well-being and development (Lundberg and Pollak, 1996),
- mothers who work set children a good example (McGinn et al., 2015),
- mothers' involvement in the labour market affords protection against poverty in the event of divorce, widowhood, or their partner losing his job.

Family policies to promote work-life balance are just as important for fathers as they are for mothers: children and fathers both benefit from more time with each other (Chapter 5).

Family policy objectives also feed into wider socio-economic objectives. Increasing the number of working parents can help boost economic growth, increase tax revenue to sustain social protection systems (Krebs and Scheffel, 2016), and cushion the impact of demographic change and declining working-age populations (Chapter 6).

Improving gender equality is an important policy objective across the OECD, and incorporating it into budget procedures and outlooks can help cement its role in policy development (Box 3.1). Governments increasingly recognise that there is a strong economic case for gender equality (OECD, 2012a). Much of their equality action focuses on equality between men and women in employment and paid work, and the gender gaps related to employment and pay (Chapter 2) are among the most widely used indicators of gender equality. Employment- and pay-related gender equality is, together with other outcomes, closely tied to social policies, as governments have a key role to play in giving women and families greater choice in their working and personal lives.

Policy makers increasingly recognise that gender equality in unpaid work matters, too. Women in all OECD countries devote more time to unpaid child care and housework than their male partners (also see Bittman et al., 2003, and Bertrand et al., 2015, for the relationship between earnings and unpaid work in couples). As a result, they may struggle to enter the labour force and – for those who are employed – to advance professionally. Conversely, long working hours may rob fathers of time with the family even though their relationships with their children and partners are stronger when they are more involved in parenting.

Box 3.1. Gender-responsive budgeting

Gender-responsive budgeting (GRB) aims to bring gender considerations into all aspects of the budgetary cycle. GRB seeks to:

- identify gender issues and how funds are allocated to women,
- assess how policies may improve gender equality.

GRB can be a valuable tool in implementing "share-friendly" policies as it tries to determine how men and women benefit from certain policies and what the associated costs are. The public provision of child care, for example, may involve substantial public investment. GRB attempts to estimate its benefits both for families and for the economy as a whole, since it enables mothers to participate – or participate more – in the labour market and gain greater economic independence.

Several OECD and non-OECD countries have introduced some form of gender budgeting over the past decade (OECD, 2010 and 2011a). Some have given it a legal basis (e.g. Austria, Belgium, Korea, Mexico and Spain). Others have opted for a more flexible approach. One is Norway, which has issued guidelines to ministries for gender-sensitive analyses of their budgets.

GRB is still in its early stages in many OECD countries. About half of them "always" require GRB at all levels of government. Others do so in some cases – 47% at central government level (e.g. Belgium, Finland, France, Israel, Korea, Mexico, Norway and Spain), 42% at regional level (e.g. France, Germany, Korea, Mexico, Spain and Switzerland), and 52% at local levels (e.g. the Czech Republic, Finland, Germany, Israel, Mexico, Korea, Spain and Switzerland, see OECD, 2011b).

In Germany, the federal government commissioned a study on the feasibility of GRB at federal level in 2007 (BMFSFJ, 2007), it has not implemented GRB, or any elements thereof, nationally. Berlin is one of the few *Länder* to have introduced GRB (it did so in 2003-04) and, at the local level, Freiburg and Munich are examples of cities that have undertaken a step-wise introduction of GRB (with Freiburg completing implementation in 2015).

Recent family policy developments in Germany aim for equal sharing in families

Since the mid-2000s Germany policy has moved to reflect the range of aforementioned "family-friendly" policy objectives. German family policy reform has been geared towards improving the work/life balance of families, simultaneously improving child well-being and extending opportunities for parents to pursue their labour market aspirations and have as many children as they would like at the time of their choosing. A better work/life balance policy also underpins families' economic strength and supports family member's individual financial self-sufficiency in retirement, or in case of divorce/separation of parents. Family-friendly policy objectives are actively pursued through the development of measures that provide families with supports "in cash, in kind and in time" (BMFSFJ, 2006), as illustrated by parental leave reform and the drive towards greater public investment in ECEC supports. These reforms reflect changes in attitudes amongst Germans towards organising work and family life (Chapter 2), and evidence-based as supported by a range of policy evaluations (ZEW and FFP, 2013; Prognos, 2014; Bechara et al., 2015).

German family policy objectives have recently been further refined to provide parents and children more time with each other also by promoting a more equal sharing of responsibilities in work and family life, so-called "Partnerschaftlichkeit" (BMFSFJ, 2015a). This involves a range of measures and initiatives that encourage equal partnership at home and at work. This included 2015 parental leave reform that facilitates both parents to take leave on a part-time basis and provides a partnership bonus for at least four months when both parents work around 25-30 hours per week. This reform is part of a more general policy drive to make working conditions in companies more conducive to family life in co-operation with employers, unions and other stakeholders. Public policy also continues to improve ECEC capacity, but considerable policy challenges remain including for example, regarding out-of-school-hours (OSH) care support and providing both parents with equally strong financial incentives to work (or work more) through the tax-benefit system.

Family benefit spending varies significantly across countries

Although OECD countries support families through the provision of family benefits, there is considerable variation in how much they spend on such benefits. In 2013, OECD average expenditure was 2.5% of GDP – ranging from just over 1.1% of GDP in the United States to around 4% in Denmark, France, Ireland and the United Kingdom (Figure 3.1). As for Germany, the figure was 3.2% of GDP, up from 3% in 2001.

The country where public expenditure on family benefits was highest was France, but as the financial crisis unfolded in 2007-08, it also mounted sharply as a proportion of GDP in Iceland, Ireland and the United Kingdom. The rise was related to:

- declining, and subsequently weak, GDP growth (the numerator in international comparisons of spending on family benefits),
- a simultaneous increase in real (i.e. inflation-adjusted) public spending on family benefits, as benefits are income-tested in many countries (OECD, 2012b).

In the United Kingdom, for example, the rise in the number of low-income families increased both the take-up of benefits (both child and working tax credits) and the number of claimants with maximum entitlements. Furthermore, since the crisis it has become harder for single parents to find jobs, which requires sustained public spending on income support programmes.

Figure 3.1. Public spending on family benefits in cash, in kind and through tax measures in selected OECD countries

Public expenditure on cash benefits for families, services and in-kind benefits for families, and tax breaks for families,[1] as a percentage of GDP, 2011 and 2013[2]

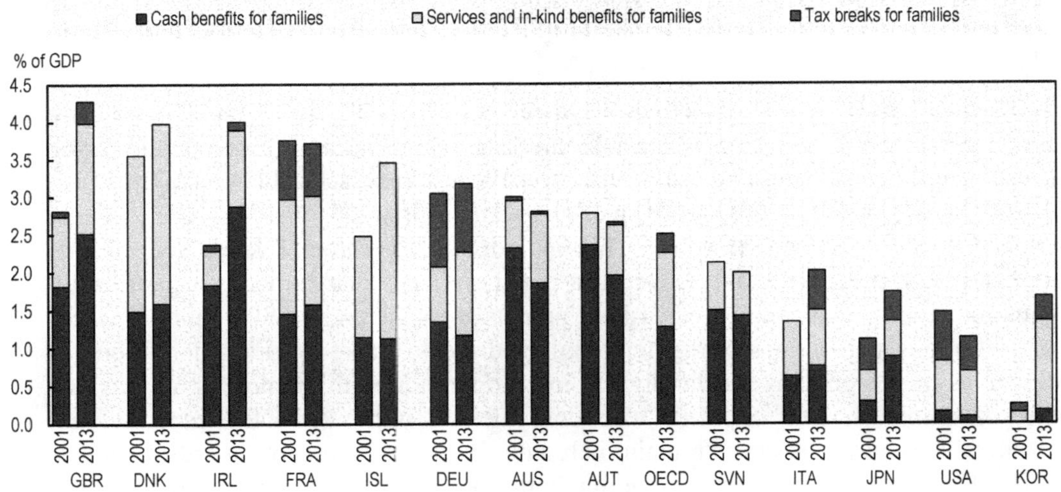

1. Family benefits include: cash benefits such as family allowances and child benefits; income support payments during maternity, paternity and parental leave; home-care payments; income support for single parents; other cash benefits like birth grants or working-family payments. In-kind benefits (or services) include day-care and home-help services and other benefits in kind. Fiscal measures include child tax credits, tax advantages for formal child care and other tax breaks which financially support families with children. Only public support that is exclusively for families (e.g. child payments and allowances, parental leave benefits and child care support) is included in the figure. Spending in other social policy areas such as health and housing support also assists families, but not exclusively, and is therefore not considered. Spending on family services (including child care) may not be fully comprehensive as such services are often provided and/or co-financed by local governments, and all relevant data may not be available.

2. Data refer to preliminary estimates. Data for European countries have been estimated using the trends in available Eurostat ESSPROS data. Data for non-European countries have been estimated using social expenditure outlook aggregated data. Tax breaks for families have been estimated from on the ratio in the previous year.

Source: *OECD Social Expenditure Database*, http://www.oecd.org/els/social/expenditure.

There is also wide variation in the prevalence of different forms of family support, such as cash benefit, family services and fiscal support (Adema et al., 2014). Cash payments – like family allowances, child benefits, working-family payments, birth grants and income support payments during child-related leave (see the notes to Figure 3.1) – account for the bulk of family support. They are worth about 1.25% of GDP on average around the OECD in 2013. Austria and Australia transfer around 2% of GDP to families in cash payments, with the figure rising to between 2.5% to 3% of GDP in the United Kingdom and Ireland. By contrast, public spending on family cash benefits in Korea and the United States is much smaller.

Family-favourable tax treatment may be built into the standard tax system or provided through allowances or credits related to the number of children. Fiscal relief to stimulate the use of child care services may also be included in family benefit spending packages, while tax breaks for families are a widely used family support tool in France and Germany, where they account for 0.7% and 0.9% of GDP, respectively.

The different emphases in underlying policy objectives can help explain cross-national differences in whether governments invest in financial (cash and/or fiscal) or in-kind family support. For example, rather than financial support – which may often weaken the financial incentive to work and reduce female employment numbers and/or hours – countries like Denmark and Sweden have chosen to develop systems of universally accessible child care and out-of-school-hours care (see "The expansion of ECEC in other OECD countries" in Section 6). They have fostered growth in female full-time employment. In Denmark, Iceland, Sweden and France, public spending on family services (including child care, day care services, and a suite of family social services) amounted to over 2% of GDP in 2013 – twice as high as the OECD average (Figure 3.1). Figure 3.1 also shows that, over time, the share of spending on family services has increased in Germany, which will be discussed further below.

In addition to these family benefits, spending on education is an important component of family-related public spending. It accounts for 5.3% of GDP on average across the OECD and 4.3% in Germany (OECD, 2015b). It is compulsory throughout the OECD for children to attend primary and secondary schooling, generally from 5 or 6 years old until the age of 16.

Public spending is important throughout childhood

In most countries, public investment (birth-grants and income support during leave) falls away shortly after children are born, before generally starting to pick up again when they are aged 3 years old and in ECEC facilities in most OECD countries (Figure 3.2). Sweden has historically been (and continues to be) a relatively high spender in public investment in children, in part because public opinion considers maternal employment to be the norm (Chapter 2) and there is not such a large decline in spending after a child's first year. Swedish policy aims to provide a continuum of support to parents with young children so they can combine work and family commitments. In Sweden, public spending on children is highest when children enter primary school, as, at that age, many also attend public OSH care facilities (see below). However, spending is generally maintained at a high level until the end of secondary school.[1]

Since the 2007 parental leave reform ushered in a new policy approach (discussed in more detail in Sections 4 and 6), Germany has continued to concentrate a greater share of its public spending on income support during the first year of a child's life (Figure 3.2). Its overall level of spending per child during the early years has risen and moved closer to Swedish levels.

As the age-spending profiles show, public investment in children in Germany and Sweden is above the OECD average throughout the early life course and, apart from the period immediately after child birth in Germany, is largely concentrated on the years of compulsory schooling, particularly the teenage years. The age-spending profile of the United States is even more pronounced because of its lack of investment in the early years: it is the only OECD country without a national paid maternity leave scheme, although a few states, such California, provide paid leave before and after child birth for fathers and mothers (Adema et al., 2015).

The lack of support for children and their families during early childhood is inefficient from a financial perspective. Investment in children should start early, as spending in the early years yields the highest returns, particularly if it is maintained throughout childhood. Early investment is acknowledged to have high social rates of return and help prevent more costly interventions later in life (OECD, 2009 and 2011c; Heckman and Masterov, 2007; Heckman et al., 2010).

Figure 3.2. Public investment in children often dips after a good start

Public spending by age of child in Germany, Sweden, the United States and the OECD (average) in PPP per capita (USD)[1]

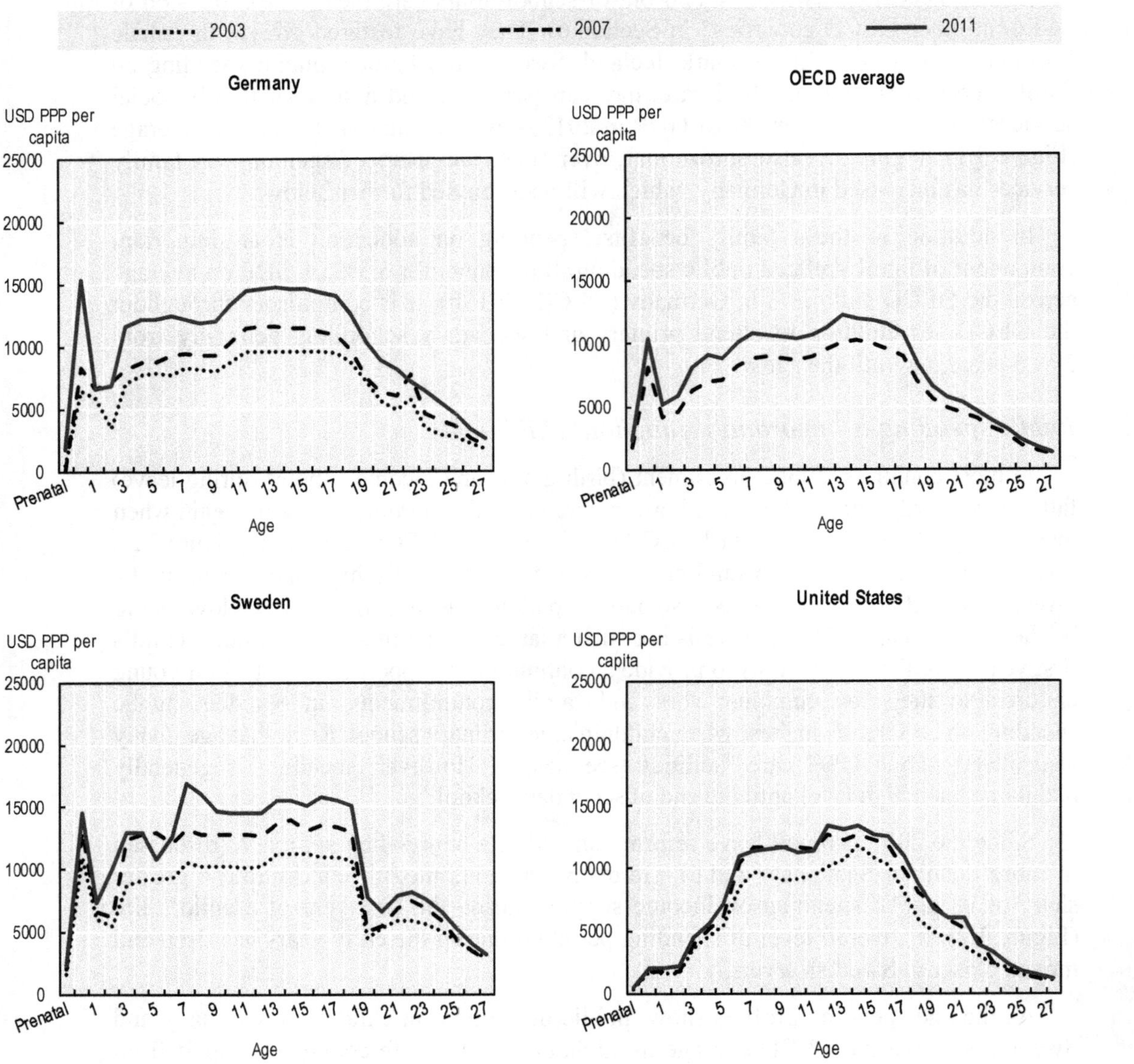

1. The indicator is calculated with the Age-Spending Profiles methodology used in OECD (2011c), *Doing Better for Families*.

Source: *OECD Family Database*, http://www.oecd.org/els/family/database.htm.

Spending early on children also contributes to equity. The family environment plays a key role in a range of child outcomes and it is important that public services should seek to account for "market failures" (e.g. parents under-investing in their children). OECD (2015a) showed that high income inequality reduces the capacity of the poorest 40% of the population to invest in their own skills and education and in those of their children. Investing early in children helps contain inequality between rich and poor with positive short and long-term consequences.

3. Financial incentives to encourage both parents to work

A key element in any family policy is how the institutional tax and benefit arrangements interact to provide both parents with equally strong financial incentives to engage in paid work (OECD, 2013a). Although tax-benefit rules are not, in general, explicitly gender-specific, certain aspects of tax-benefit systems may be more relevant to either men or women, so exacerbating the unequal distribution of paid work and earnings. In many couple families, for example, the man is the main earner with his female partner frequently earning considerably less (Chapter 2 and OECD, 2015c, for the latest data on earnings broken down by gender).

Drawing on the OECD's tax-benefit models, Figure 3.3 illustrates to what extent tax-benefit systems give couples financial incentive to share paid work equally at a given income level, i.e. 133% of the average wage (see Annex 3.A1 for the underlying methodology and Figure 3.A1.1 for results when household incomes is 200% of the average wage).[2] Figure 3.3 compares, on one hand, the net transfers to government of a dual-earner couple with two children where both partners earn 67% of the average wage with, on the other hand, the net transfers of a single-earner couple with two children and the same household earnings. If the dual-earner couple's net transfers to government (what the couple pays in taxes and social security contributions less the benefits received) are lower than the single-earner couple's, the tax-benefit system encourages sharing and gives the second earner financial incentive to take up work. If the net transfers are higher than the single-earner couple's, the opposite holds and the second partner has no financial incentive to take up work. If net transfers to government are broadly the same in both scenarios, the tax-benefit system is said to be broadly neutral towards sharing (and the blue diamonds overlap with the white triangles in Figure 3.3).

In about two-thirds of OECD countries it pays for a couple-family to be dual earners. Across the OECD, such families pay the government net transfers of about 17.6% on average while – at a gross income of 133% of the average wage – single-earner couple families transfer 21.5%. Across the OECD, a household where both partners contribute equally enjoys, on average, a 5.4% higher net income than a single-earner couple family (see the indicator on proportional gains and losses at the bottom of Figure 3.3).

In one-third of the OECD countries, it makes little difference to net transfers paid by households earning 133% of the average wage whether one or two earners contribute to household income. In France and Germany, by contrast, single-earner couples pay less tax than dual earners. The overall effect of tax-benefit systems on financial incentives to share paid work varies across the income ranges and associated levels of taxation. However, the findings in Figure 3.3 are also true of Germany and most other OECD countries when household income is double average earnings (as Figure 3.A1.1 confirms). It cannot be said of France and Germany, therefore, that their tax-benefit systems act as financial incentives for couple families to equally share paid work (discounting any other obstacles to sharing that might differ in the two countries).

Figure 3.3. In most OECD countries, dual-earner couples are better off than single-earner couples

Net transfers[1] to government as a proportion (%) of gross household earnings and the proportional difference in household net income for an equal dual-earner couple with both partners earning 67% of the average wage[2] and a single-earner couple with 133% of the average wage, families with two children (age 4 and 6)

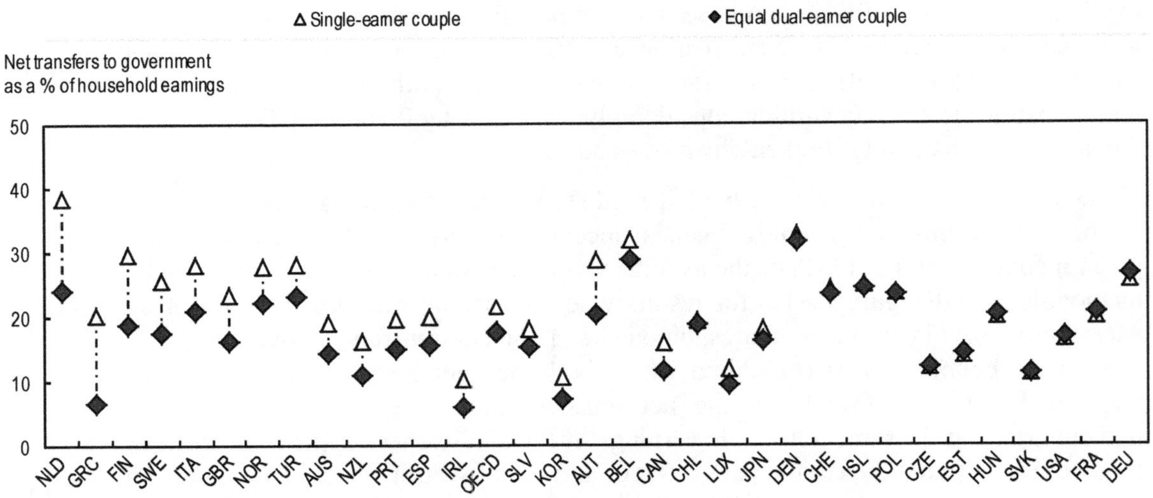

Gain or loss of net income due to equal sharing relative to net income of single-earner couple (%):

24 17 16 11 10 9 8 7 7 7 6 6 5 5 4 4 3 3 3 3 3 2 2 1 1 1 0 0 0 0 0 0 -1

Note: Countries are ranked in ascending order of the differences in net income of dual-earner and single-earner couple households as percentages of the net income of single-earner couples – see values listed at bottom of figure.

1. "Net transfers" refers to what households pay the government in taxes and contributions minus the benefits received. The white dot refers to a household where the primary earner has work income of 133% of the average wage. The dark dot refers to a household where both partners earn 67% of the average wage, so that household income adds up to 134%.

2. Refer to OECD (2016a) for a definition of average wage (AW).

Source: OECD, "Tax and Benefit Systems: OECD Indicators", http://www.oecd.org/els/soc/benefits-and-wages.htm.

What makes a share-friendly tax-benefit system

To what extent tax-benefit systems promote equally shared paid work is determined largely by the design of the following three policy settings (OECD, 2015d; OECD, 2015e; OECD, 2016a; Rastrigina and Verashchagina, 2015; Immervoll et al., 2009):

1. Personal income tax

   In individually based personal income tax systems, like those of Finland and Sweden, both partners are taxed on their individual gross earnings. If progressive tax systems tax higher incomes at higher rates than lower incomes, then progressivity in an individualised system means that:

   – if the highest (or primary) earner in the family earns additional income, that income is taxed at a higher rate than if the second earner increases their earnings by the same amount;

   – as long as one partner earns more than the other, the family will have a higher disposable income if the primary earner shares work more equally with the secondary earner.[3]

In all, individually based income tax systems with progressive tax rates encourage the equal sharing of paid work.

Countries with largely flat-rate income tax systems (e.g. Estonia and Hungary) are mostly neutral towards how couples share paid work. As the tax rate is no higher for higher incomes, it does not affect the family's disposable income whether one partner earns all income alone or whether both partners do.

"Joint income tax systems" discourage equally shared paid work. In joint tax systems like Germany's, or family-based regimes, such as France's *quotient familial*, partners' earnings are pooled and assessed at the same marginal rate. As the tax rate is based on partners' joint income, it is irrelevant how much each partner contributes. Under a progressive tax schedule in a joint system, second earners are effectively taxed at higher marginal rates than if they were taxed individually because the primary earner's income already covers the lower brackets (taxed at lower rates). The higher the principal earner's income, the higher the tax rate on the secondary earner's income – hence less financial incentive for the secondary earner to contribute to the family income. In addition, if the tax allowance for dependent children can be shifted from the secondary to the primary earner (and can be used even if the secondary earner does not contribute to family income), second earners (usually mothers) have further financial disincentive to increase their working hours beyond tax-exempt thresholds and, for example, to work in other than casual jobs such as *minijobs*.

2. Social security systems

Social security contribution rates that are proportional to an individual's gross earnings treat equally shared paid work neutrally – examples are the systems in Finland, Greece, Italy, Norway and Sweden. Progressive rates, as in France at most earnings levels, either encourage partners to share paid work equally (with the second, lower, earner paying lower contributions than the higher-earning partner) or they treat partners' relative earnings levels neutrally.

Lower contribution rates at low earnings give non-working partners in couple families financial incentive to enter the labour market and/or increase their working hours and work income (as in Belgium, Israel and Germany). On the other hand, secondary earners have strong financial incentive to limit their working hours and, by the same token, their earnings in order to avoid paying the full rate – if exemptions from social security contributions are in place and/or contribution rates across low earnings levels are gradually increased. In Germany, for example, contribution rates from income earned in so-called *midijobs* – casual jobs paid between EUR 450 and EUR 850 per month – gradually increase to the full rate (Box 3.3).

By contrast, social security contribution caps at higher income levels (as in Austria and Germany) discourage couples from sharing paid work when one partner earns above the ceiling – EUR 6 200 per month in former West Germany and EUR 5 400 in former East Germany in 2016. In that event, if the higher-earning partner were to increase their earnings, they would not have to pay any more social security contributions. By contrast, if their partner, who earns less than the income ceiling, increases their gross earnings, then the household tax burden, which includes social security contributions, will increase.

3. Benefits

Like universal child benefits or earnings-related benefits (such as income support during parental leave), other welfare benefits, too, can be means-tested at the individual and/or the household level. If an inactive partner or partner with limited paid working hours in a low-income household enters work or increases their working hours, the household may lose its entitlement to certain benefits in part or in full. Second earners in low-income households may not therefore have much financial incentive to increase their working hours, although that would depend on the rate at which benefits are withdrawn.

At low levels of income, in-work benefits can incentivise women to join the labour market or increase their hours (OECD, 2015d). For example, in Finland and the Netherlands, where in-work benefit entitlements are based on an individual's income, secondary earners in the lowest income decile have financial incentives to work part-time. Other in-work benefits are contingent on working at least a certain amount of hours, which gives women incentive to work more than short part-time hours – at least 38 hours in every fortnight in Ireland, for example.

When in-work benefits are applied to household earnings, and earnings assessments therefore include the partner's income, they afford little or no incentive to the partners of full-time earners to enter the labour market or increase their hours if they work part-time. For example, in the United States, the earned income tax credit (EITC) is assessed on family income. If a secondary earner in a family with two children in 2014 increased their earnings by so much that the yearly family income was higher than USD 49 186, the family no longer qualified for the tax credit.

France and Germany both have joint tax systems with progressive tax rates. Yet the German benefit system includes elements that worsen the disincentive effects of its income splitting (OECD, 2016b):

- The design of so-called *minijobs* and *midijobs*[4] (see Box 3.3) further discourages secondary earners from increasing their working hours. *Minijobs* are mainly held by women: in 2014, they occupied 77.1% of all *minijobs* and 11.6% of women are employed in *minijobs* (Destatis, 2016a).
- The free co-insurance of the spouse of a partner who is insured in the national health security system further deters mothers from entering the labour market and sharing paid work more equally (OECD, 2016a).
- In married couples where the one partner (typically the husband) earns an income above the social security ceiling – and thus pays no contributions on income above the ceiling – the second partner (typically the wives) have less incentive to work (more) other than in *minijobs*, widely exempted from social security contributions.

Financial incentives to work and contribute (more) to household income for second earners in couple families in Germany could be improved in different ways (see Box 3.2 and OECD, 2016b). For example, granting a separate (non-transferable) tax-free allowance to the second earner would lower tax on the additional income. Health insurance contributions could be based on the size of family and low-income households could receive government transfers to cover all or part of the contributions they are not able to pay for themselves (OECD, 2016b). In Switzerland, for example, adults pay a compulsory lump-sum contribution to national health insurance, while low-income households receive a transfer from the government to cover all or part of national health contributions, depending on income.

Box 3.1. Income tax splitting in Germany and the constitution

There are two articles in the German constitution that affect the design of family taxation:

- Article 6 grants "special protection" to marriage and families, which is generally taken to mean that married taxpayers pay less, or no more, tax than unmarried taxpayers with similar incomes (Bach et al., 2011).
- Articles 20 and 28 oblige the legislator to build social considerations into the design and implementation of laws based on the notion of the *Sozialstaatsprinzip* (welfare state principle). Income tax laws therefore grant each adult individual a basic tax allowance (*Grundfreibetrag*), worth EUR 8 652 in 2016, deemed equivalent to a minimum subsistence income.

The German constitution does not explicitly refer to the system of joint taxation in its current form (*Ehegattensplitting*, or income tax splitting). Other tax systems can be compatible with the constitution (see Spangenberg, 2005; Prognos, 2014; and Bach et al., 2011, for different reform scenarios), as long as they comply with both the *Grundfreibetrag* requirement and do not disadvantage married couples.

In 2015, Germany introduced a national minimum wage which may eventually change partnered mothers' financial incentives to take up paid work and affect their labour market behaviour. Prior to the advent of the minimum wage, most studies anticipated that it would have a considerable effect on the jobs and wages of the marginally employed, which included *minijobbers*, most of whom were female partners. To date, however, there is little cause-effect evidence of the minimum wage having an impact on employment and wages in different types of job and among groups such as working mothers (BMWi, 2015; Bossler and Gerner, 2016; IAB, 2016). The first descriptive evidence, though, shows that, since 2015, less people (mainly students and retired) have had *minijobs* as their main job (IAB, 2016; IAQ, 2016a) and that some of the marginally employed have moved into standard employment contracts (IAB, 2016a). In contrast, the number of people in *minijobs* as a secondary job has not fallen since 2015 (IAQ, 2016b).

Box 3.2. Does the German tax-benefit system encourage sharing? Evidence from an in-depth evaluation

In 2009 the German Ministry for Family Affairs, Senior Citizens, Women and Youth and the Ministry of Finance commissioned a comprehensive evaluation of family-related policies in Germany. It analysed a wide range of measures – child benefits and allowances, parental leave, tax-splitting advantages for married couples, tax allowances for single parents, child care supports, higher unemployment benefits for claimants with families, and reduced rates for parents' contributions to compulsory long-term care insurance. All policies were assessed against the following yardsticks:

- the reconciliation of work and family life,
- children's well-being,
- families' economic stability and how different family types benefit from different policies,
- the extent to which they supported parents' desire to have children.

Box 3.2. Does the German tax-benefit system encourage sharing? Evidence from an in-depth evaluation *(cont.)*

One part of the analysis evaluated the effects of the tax-benefit system using a population-based microsimulation model and applying 2010 benefit rules to data in the German Socioeconomic Panel (ZEW and FFP, 2013). As well as modelling the interactions of the tax-benefit system, the analysis also considered how individual policies affected labour market participation and public finances by hypothetically abolishing a specified policy and comparing the resulting outcomes with the actual situation. Finally, it simulated the effect of policy practices from other countries on the German tax-benefit system.

The evaluation found that two components of the German tax-benefit system particularly discourages shared paid work:

- The tax-splitting system is not conducive to more equal sharing and does not contribute to the economic independence of the second earner (often the woman). Introducing the French *quotient familial* practice would – all else being equal – hardly increase the German labour supply at all, even if Germany adopted other elements of the French child benefit system. Introducing individual taxation, as in Sweden, would lead to a marked rise in the labour market participation of mothers, a slight fall in fathers' participation, and, therefore, more equal sharing of paid work. This result was corroborated by Eichhorst et al. (2012), in a microsimulation study that also considered labour demand. It found that individual taxation would lead to a more equal distribution of paid work between partners, especially those partners with medium to high levels of educational attainment.
- Free national health insurance for the spouse of a primary earner, and other exemptions from social security contributions, can trap secondary earners in marginal employment or non-employment. In Germany, *minijobbers* (who earn up to EUR 450 per month) are exempted from social security contributions (and old age pension at the employee's request), while contribution rates for people who work in *midijobs* (paid between EUR 450 and EUR 850 per month) pay gradually incremented contribution rates. Over EUR 850, they would pay the standard rate.

Although *minijobs* and *midijobs* are part of the tax-benefit system, the evaluation did not consider them, as they are not a specifically family-related policy. Yet, more than half of all *minijobbers* (often women) have a partner who is in full-time employment. Eichhorst et al. also found that scrapping *minijobs* and *midijobs* in the current tax-splitting system, with its free national health insurance for spouses of primary earners, would not dramatically affect the labour supply – many partnered women would stop working while others would increase their working hours, particularly in households where secondary earner have completed only secondary education, as higher-education graduates are rarely in *mini-* or *midijobs*. However, Eichhorst et al. do show that there would be significant increase in the labour supply of mothers if scrapping *minijobs* and *midijobs* also entailed the introduction of individual taxation.

4. Parental leave policies can change fathers' parenting behaviour and help mothers resume work more quickly

OECD countries have policies that entitle parents to periods of (paid) leave before and after the birth of a child – maternity, paternity and/or parental leave. While maternity benefits have long been common across the OECD, paid father-specific leave is a more recent development. Paid father-specific leave did not exist in OECD countries in the 1970s, with only Spain, Luxembourg and Belgium providing any kind of paid entitlement for fathers – one day, two days, and three days, respectively. However, in 1990, Denmark and Sweden introduced father-specific paid leave, since when 17 more countries have followed suit. (For an overview of parental leave arrangements in OECD countries, see Adema et al., 2015, and on recent reforms in Germany, see section below.)

Apart from the United States, all OECD countries operated nationwide paid maternity leave programmes of 12 weeks or more in 2014. And in two-thirds of countries, mothers often also make use of paid parental leave entitlements. Adding up paid maternity leave and parental leave yields an OECD-wide average duration of just over one year of paid leave entitlements that mothers can use (Figure 3.4, Panel A).

To increase fathers' take-up of leave and foster better sharing of caring (Chapter 5), many OECD countries have introduced father-specific paid leave periods. They include any period of employment-protected paternity leave, parental leave that is reserved exclusively for fathers ("daddy quotas"), or sharable parental leave that is effectively "reserved" for fathers, as it must be used by the main leave taker's partner (usually the father) if the family is to qualify for bonus weeks. (Figure 3.4, Panel B includes only non-transferable fathers' entitlements.)

Entitlements to paid parental leave are family-based in the OECD, leaving it up to the parents in couple families to decide how they would like to share leave. Not only do mothers frequently earn less than fathers, they earn less the more children they have, as career breaks for child birth and parenting drive wages down. So it costs households less in the short term if mothers take up available leave.

The design of parental leave rules can significantly influence the likelihood of mothers resuming work and the number of hours they work. Comparison of the proportion of German mothers who worked before and after the parental leave reform in 2007 reveals that the – already low – share of mothers with very young children who worked dwindled still further between 2006 and 2014 (Figure 3.5). Nevertheless, mothers whose youngest child was 1 or 2 years old were more likely to work in 2014 and a greater share of mothers worked 15 hours or more. Kluve and Schmitz (2014) confirm the descriptive evidence and show that the 2007 reform increased the likelihood of mothers – particularly the highly-educated – resuming work within five years of child birth and working longer hours. The benefit system introduced in 2007 was more generous than the one that it superseded, so initially cost more. However, with parents (mostly women) returning to work sooner and in greater numbers, much of the additional cost – up to 25% – is estimated to be offset by increases in tax receipts and falls in public expenditure associated with inactivity within the first five years after the child's birth (Bechara et al., 2015).

Figure 3.4. Paid leave available to fathers has increased over the past 15 years, while leave available to mothers has remained fairly constant

Panel A. Length of paid maternity and parental leave available to mothers in weeks, 2000 and 2014

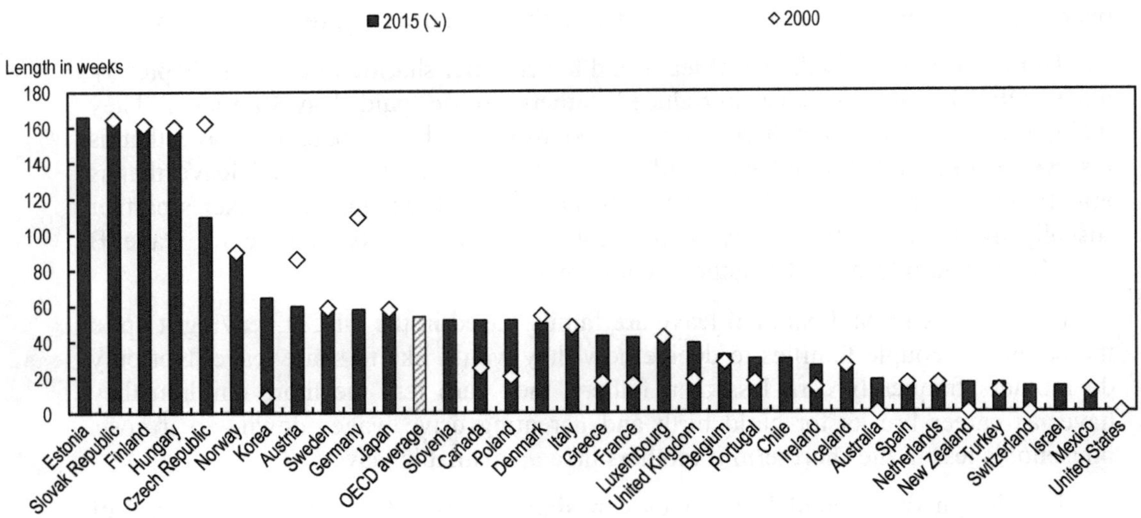

Panel B. Length of paid paternity and parental leave reserved for fathers in weeks, 2000 and 2014

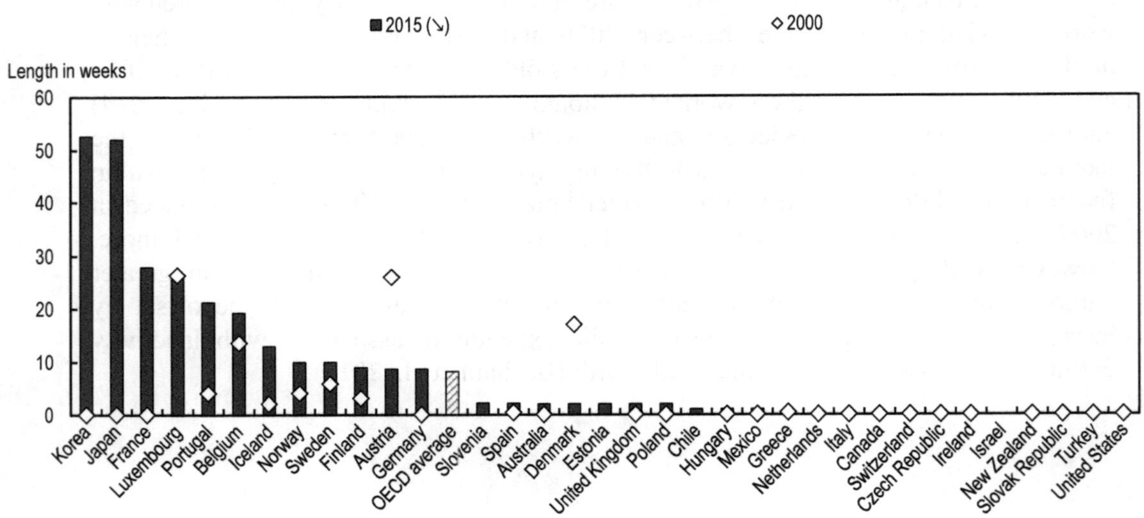

Panel A: Information refers to weeks of paid maternity leave and any weeks of paid parental leave and paid home care leave (e.g., sometimes under different names, such as "child-care leave" or "child-raising leave") that are available to mothers.

Panel B: Information refers to entitlements to paternity leave, "father quotas", or periods of parental leave that can be used only by the father and cannot be transferred to the mother, together with any weeks of sharable leave that must be taken by the father in order for the family to qualify for "bonus" weeks of parental leave.

Source: *OECD Family Database*, www.oecd.org/els/family/database.htm.

Figure 3.5. Young mothers in Germany have resumed paid work more quickly in recent years

Share of mothers working different hours, by youngest child's age, in percentage[1]

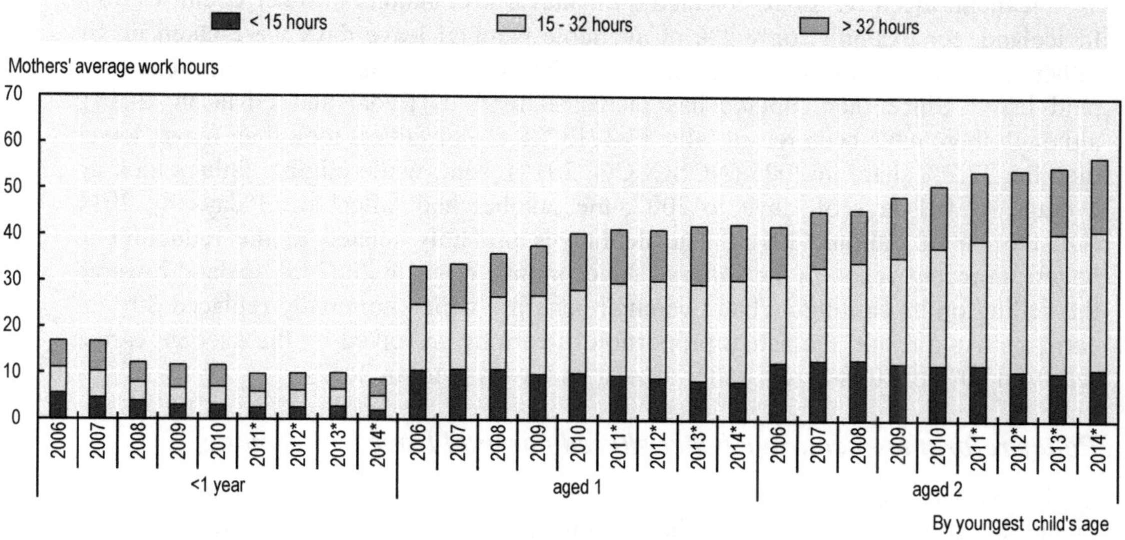

1. Hours worked refer to the total number of hours usually worked in a week, including regular overtime hours.

* Extrapolated from population forecast in the 2011 census.

Source: BMFSFJ (2014).

In most OECD countries, father-specific entitlements tend to be far shorter than maternity and parental leave. On average, OECD countries offer nine weeks of paid paternal leave, although nine provide no paternal leave at all, and ten offer two weeks or less, generally paid in full (Figure 3.4, Panel B). However, there are a growing number of countries with provisions for longer paternal leave, with nine of them allotting fathers three months or more. In North America, the Canadian province of Québec has introduced a five-week period of paid leave exclusively for fathers in its parental leave scheme. After recent reforms, individual paid leave entitlements in the two East Asian OECD countries – Japan and Korea – are now as long as 12 months. Japanese fathers are paid around 58% of average earnings, equivalent to 30.4 weeks of leave on full pay – by far the most generous father-specific scheme in the OECD (OECD, 2015f). However, fewer than 5% of Japanese and Korean fathers use their paid leave entitlements – possibly because few Japanese and Korean fathers are aware of them. However, it is also likely that they fear for their career prospects should they take months of parental leave.

There are different reasons for urging fathers to use parental leave – to change gender stereotypes, foster gender equality between men and women at home and give children the chance to spend time with both parents (Chapter 5). Fathers' leave helps women in the workforce, too: if men and women are equally likely to take leave, employers are less likely to discriminate against women of childbearing age at the time of hiring. Sweden was the first OECD country to introduce paid parental leave in 1974. It took the form of a shareable leave period of six months (Chronholm, 2007). In 1995, it introduced a one-month leave period exclusively for fathers, which it subsequently extended to two, then three, months. Over the years, the proportion of parental leave days taken by fathers has gradually risen – from 5% in 1980 to 10% in 1995 and 24% in 2012.

Financial incentive share changed the behaviour of fathers in other countries, too. In Iceland, for example, only 3% of available parental leave days were taken up by fathers prior to the introduction in 2001 of a three-month father-specific entitlement to paid leave. Since then, uptake has increased tenfold (Eydal and Gíslason, 2014), although there have been recent falls: in 2013, 28.5% of fathers took their leave, lower than the 32.7% share in 2005 (NOSOSCO, 2015). And, while eligible fathers took an average of 101 days of leave in 2007, the number had fallen to 73 days by 2014 (Directorate of Labour, 2015). The decline is probably related to the reduction in benefit in recent years. In the wake of the economic crisis in 2007/08, Iceland lowered the ceiling on its earnings-related parental benefit – which nominally replaced 80% of earnings. As a result, the actual proportion of earnings received by the average earner fell from 80% in 2008 to just under 60% at its lowest point in 2012.

Policy reform to encourage better shared parental leave in Germany

In Germany, too, an overhaul of the parental leave system has contributed to a rise in the share of fathers claiming the parental leave allowance to just over 34% for fathers whose child was born in 2014 (Destatis, 2016b). Shared leave is on the rise in Germany, a trend that should contribute to better father-child relationships (Chapter 5) and greater female participation labour force. See Dustmann and Schönberg, 2012; Geyer et al., 2015; and Kluve and Schmitz, 2014, on the effects of the 2007 parental leave reform.

In 1986 West Germany introduced *Erziehungsgeld*, an eight-month-long parental leave scheme that followed the 14 weeks of maternity leave. In the first six months, parents received a flat rate of DEM 600, followed by a means-tested benefit in the last two months. Between 1986 and 2007, the periods of payment and employment protection were extended – in 1990, paid parental leave was lengthened to 16 months and, in 1992, parents were given the option of taking employment-protected parental leave for up to three years after the birth of their child (Dustmann and Schönberg, 2012; Kamerman and Kahn, 1991; Merz, 2004).

The year 2007 ushered in a radical parental allowance reform, *Elterngeld*, that introduced an earnings-related benefit with floors and ceilings that superseded the flat rate, means-tested *Erziehungsgeld*. The parental leave benefit was set at 67% of the parent's net average earnings during the 12 months preceding child birth, with a ceiling of EUR 1 800 per month and a floor of EUR 300. The first 12 months were paid and, if partners (usually the father) used at least two months of parental leave, it was topped up with another two months – 14 months in all. It was, in fact, possible to extend parental leave to up to 24+4 months (if each parent took at least four months), with a proportional reduction in the monthly payment rate. Unpaid employment-protected leave was available for a maximum of 36 months (Moss and Korintus, 2008).

Figure 3.6. Fathers' take-up of parental leave increased in Germany

Share of children born 2008 through 2014, as a percentage, whose fathers received parental leave benefit

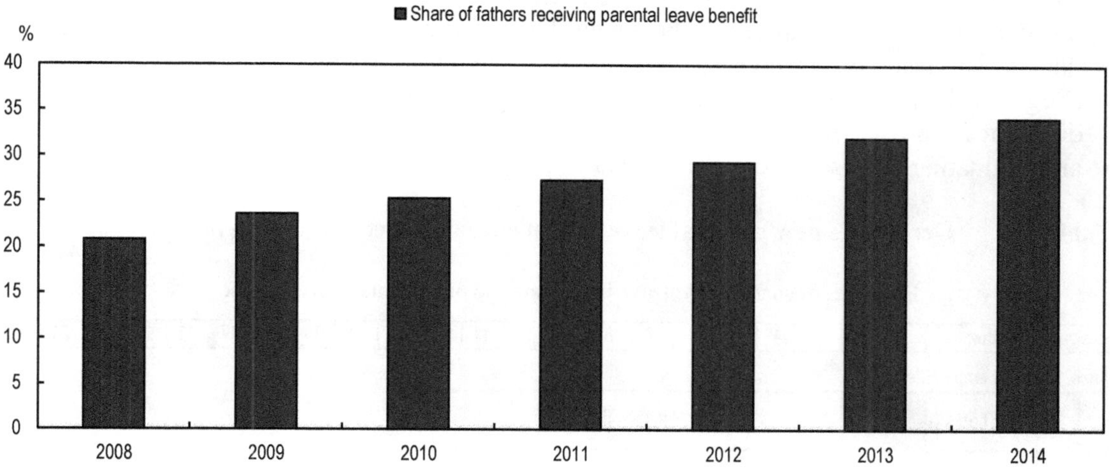

Source: Destatis (2016), "Öffentliche Sozialleistungen - Statistik zum Elterngeld, Beendete Leistungsbezüge für in den Jahren 2008 bis 2012 geborene Kinder", https://www.destatis.de/DE/ZahlenFakten/GesellschaftStaat/Soziales/Soziales.html.

To encourage sharing, the 2007 reform gave second partners – in practice, the father – financial incentives to take parental leave, too. The share of children whose fathers took up parental leave benefit rose steadily, from 20.8% in 2008 to 34.2% in 2014 (Figure 3.6). And while there is no fully comparable data available for the years before the 2007 reform, data do show that, in 2006, only 3.5% of fathers received the child-raising allowance (Destatis, 2012).

The 2007 reform was unkind, however, to couples where both partners worked part-time (up to 30 hours per week). They received only a partial parental allowance (*Teilelterngeld*), while each month that they worked counted towards the benefit as if they had not worked at all and taken full benefit (see Example 1 in Table 3.1). Working part-time thus reduced the remaining benefit eligibility period by 50% (the *doppelter Anspruchsverbrauch*, or double shortfall effect) and parents returning to work on equal part-time bases received smaller benefits than those where one partner stayed home entirely.

The 2015 reform of the parental leave system – *ElterngeldPlus* – resolved the "part-time" shortcoming. It introduced financial incentives that encouraged parents to share paid work equally by doubling the duration of the benefit for parents who worked part-time (see Examples 2a and 2b in Table 3.1). As before, the benefit replaces the forgone earnings of parents who work part-time – as in the usual parental leave scheme. Additionally, when both partners in a couple work 25 to 30 hours per week for at least four months during or after the period of receipt of the usual *Elterngeld* or *ElterngeldPlus* allowance, they are rewarded with *Partnerschaftsbonus*, a partnership bonus. It is equivalent to four additional months of *ElterngeldPlus*. The 2015 reform is also very flexible as to how and when parents may use the benefit entitlement and the three year employment protection period.

The Swedish parental leave scheme and its emphasis on more gender-equal sharing of parental leave have inspired many other countries to include incentives for fathers (such as the so-called "daddy months") in their parental leave systems. Sweden's parental leave also offers a gender bonus to reward equally shared leave, whereby parents receive a tax-free bonus of about EUR 5 for every day that they use parental leave equally up to a maximum of about EUR 1 485 (Duvander et al., 2014). Yet, Sweden's experience with gender bonus has been chequered – take-up has been limited due to a lack of awareness and it is scheduled to be scrapped in 2017 (Regeringskansliet, 2016). While the design of the Swedish *jämställdhetsbonus* is very different from *ElterngeldPlus*, it underlines the importance of consistently monitoring and evaluating such schemes, and of ensuring that parents are well aware of the rules.

Table 3.1. Germany's new parental leave system encourages equal sharing between partners

Examples of sharing paid leave in the new and old parental leave scheme

<table>
<tr><th colspan="2">Child age in months:</th><th>1</th><th>2</th><th>3</th><th>4</th><th>5</th><th>6</th><th>7</th><th>8</th><th>9</th><th>10</th><th>11</th><th>12</th><th>13</th><th>14</th><th>15</th><th>16</th><th>17</th><th>18</th><th>19</th><th>20</th><th>21</th><th>22</th></tr>
<tr><td colspan="24">Example 1: Old scheme ("Elterngeld")</td></tr>
<tr><td rowspan="2">Parent 1:</td><td>Work hours:</td><td colspan="2">0</td><td colspan="10">part-time (<30 hours)</td><td colspan="10"></td></tr>
<tr><td>Benefit:</td><td colspan="2">PLB</td><td colspan="10">topping up part-time earning as up to a threshold</td><td colspan="10"></td></tr>
<tr><td rowspan="2">Parent 2:</td><td>Work hours:</td><td colspan="2">0</td><td colspan="10">part-time (<30 hours)</td><td colspan="10"></td></tr>
<tr><td>Benefit:</td><td colspan="2">PLB (partner months)</td><td colspan="10">none</td><td colspan="10"></td></tr>
<tr><td colspan="24">Example 2a: New scheme ("Elterngeld" and "Elterngeld Plus")</td></tr>
<tr><td rowspan="2">Parent 1:</td><td>Work hours:</td><td colspan="2">0</td><td colspan="10">part-time (<30 hours)</td><td colspan="4">part-time (25 to 30 hours)</td><td colspan="6"></td></tr>
<tr><td>Benefit:</td><td colspan="2">PLB</td><td colspan="10">PLB plus</td><td colspan="4">PLB plus (bonus)</td><td colspan="6"></td></tr>
<tr><td rowspan="2">Parent 2:</td><td>Work hours:</td><td colspan="2">0</td><td colspan="10">part-time (<30 hours)</td><td colspan="4">part-time (25 to 30 hours)</td><td colspan="6"></td></tr>
<tr><td>Benefit:</td><td colspan="2">PLB (partner months)</td><td colspan="10">PLB plus</td><td colspan="4">PLB plus (bonus)</td><td colspan="6"></td></tr>
<tr><td colspan="24">Example 2b: New scheme ("Elterngeld" and "Elterngeld Plus")</td></tr>
<tr><td rowspan="2">Parent 1:</td><td>Work hours:</td><td colspan="6">0</td><td colspan="12">part-time (<30 hours)</td><td colspan="4">PLB plus (bonus)</td></tr>
<tr><td>Benefit:</td><td colspan="6">PLB</td><td colspan="12">PLB plus</td><td colspan="4">PLB plus (bonus)</td></tr>
<tr><td rowspan="2">Parent 2:</td><td>Work hours:</td><td colspan="2">0</td><td colspan="16">full-time</td><td colspan="4">part-time (25 to 30 hours)</td></tr>
<tr><td>Benefit:</td><td colspan="2">PLB (partner months)</td><td colspan="16">none</td><td colspan="4">PLB plus (bonus)</td></tr>
</table>

Note: PLB is short for "parental leave benefit" as paid since 2007 (*Elterngeld*). "Partner months" are the additional two months of parental leave benefit paid to couples where both parents take parental leave. "PLB plus" refers to the new *ElterngeldPlus* scheme parental leave benefit plus possible bonus. "Bonus" refers to the additional months of parental leave benefit parents are entitled to if they both work part-time between 25 and 30 hours.

Source: Based on www.familien-wegweiser.de/ElterngeldrechnerPlaner/rechner.xhtml?cid=1.

In August 2013, a home care allowance (*Betreuungsgeld*) of EUR 100 per month (raised to EUR 150 in August 2014) was introduced. Parents could claim it if they do not use public child care for their 2- or 3-year-old child after the expiry of the parental leave benefit. Critics of the policy feared that parents from poorer socio-economic backgrounds might claim the home care allowance, their children would not benefit from ECEC, and mothers would have less incentive to resume work. A first study into parents' intentions to claim the home care allowance lent some credence to those concerns: parents who were less well educated and/or those whose first language was not German were less inclined than German-speaking or more highly educated parents to send their children to ECEC "because" of the home care allowance (Fuchs-Rechlin et al., 2014). In July 2015, the Constitutional Court ruled that the policy did not fall within the federal government's remit and the federal home care allowance was abolished, leaving room for the *Länder* to develop their own initiatives.

5. Policies towards a flexible "family working-time model"

Parental leave policies that allow parents to share paid work and child care responsibilities more equally can serve as a stepping stone to a better reconciliation of work and family life as children grow up. *ElterngeldPlus*, introduced in 2015, encourages parents to simultaneously reduce their paid working hours for a certain period in order to spend time with children and allow each other to pursue his or her career.

If the parents of young children in Germany are to share responsibilities more equitably, fathers need to do more unpaid work (which includes parenting) and mothers should work longer paid hours (see Chapters 4 and 5 for a detailed discussion). If it were to become mainstream practice for both parents to work reduced hours, at least during children's early years, mothers might be able to increase their working hours and fathers' their parenting time. And if it became as common for fathers as for mothers to work part-time, employers might come to consider fathers as likely as mothers to work shorter hours when children are young. Less stigma would then attach to men working part-time and they would not be so heavily penalised for doing so (OECD, 2015a).

One proposal that touches upon the idea of equally shared part-time working, and has recently been publicly debated in Germany, is that of *Familienarbeitszeit*, or family working time. It involves income support for couples with children where both partners work *vollzeitnah* – i.e. "reduced full-time working hours" – in order to balance breadwinning and parenting responsibilities more equally between partners (BMFSFJ, 2014). The income support supplement would be tax-financed and single parent families would also be eligible.

Müller et al. (2013, 2015) develop and simulate different *Familienarbeitszeit* scenarios according to:

- how the income supplement is calculated – whether it is dependent on net income or a lump-sum benefit,
- the number of hours that both parents would have to work in order to qualify for family working-time benefit – exactly 32 hours or between 28 and 32 hours per week.

The income-dependent benefit assumes a 65% net replacement rate for middle and higher incomes and is proportionally higher for lower incomes as it is capped at EUR 360 per month. The lump-sum benefit, by contrast, offers a benefit of EUR 250 per parent. The authors assume that parents claim the benefit for children aged 1 to 3 years old as income support once they have used up their parental leave benefit.

Between 2010 and 2012, both partners worked between 30 and 35 hours per week in less than 1% of couples and between 25 and 35 hours in less than 2% of couple partners (also see Chapter 4). If couples where both partners worked 32 hours per week were alone eligible for the family working-time benefit, both the income-dependent and the lump-sum benefit would prompt 2.5% of couples to choose the family working-time model, according to the simulations by Müller et al. The simulated scenarios estimate the net fiscal cost at between EUR 220 million per annum (for a lump-sum benefit for 32 working hours) and EUR 350 million euros (for an income-dependent benefit with more flexible working hours). The simulations do not factor in possible behavioural changes which could, in the long run, translate into higher take-up among working families. There would be more eligible families and take-up would increase if:

- there were no or less child care restrictions,
- the tax system were more conducive to sharing,
- couples could choose working hours more flexibly.

A provision for flexible working hours that allowed employees to reduce their working hours every few years to anywhere between around 32 and 40 hours per week (like the currently discussed *Wahlarbeitszeitgesetz* scheme in Germany; FES, 2015) would further widen parental options – if parents could also increase their working hours again within a certain time on reduced hours (see "The right to adjust working hours" in Section 7).

How would a family working-time scheme affect the German labour force?

Chapter 2 showed how the German labour force is expected to shrink over the next few decades, perhaps by as much as 6 million full-time equivalent workers by 2040. A family working-time model that operated on the assumptions above could sizeably increase the length of working hours for a number of German employees (see Annex Figure 3.A2.1).

OECD estimates based on data from the 2012 European Union Labour Force Survey and the eligibility criteria set out by Müller et al. suggest that, as of 2012, up to about 1.7 million German employees, around 4.3% of all those in employment, could claim family working-time benefit should they – and, where relevant, their partner – choose to work the required hours (Annex 3.A2). Potential male claimants would number around 815 000 employees – of whom just under 800 000 are in dual-earner couples and about 15 000 are single fathers. As for possibly eligible claimants among female employees, there are 910 000, of whom about 800 000 are in dual-earner couples and about 105 000 are single mothers. Average usual working hours among these potentially eligible employees are, at 32.9 hours per week, not far off the 28-32 hour corridor proposed in some family working-time scenarios. However, they vary sharply between the sexes: the average working week among potentially eligible men is just below 41.7 hours, while among potentially eligible women it is 24.9 hours.

Despite the considerable change in working hours for the men and women involved, the adoption of a family working-time model in line with the assumptions of Müller et al. would have an almost negligible effect on the projected size of the German labour force.[5] The reason would be that any drop in the male labour supply attributable to a family working-time scheme would be almost entirely offset by a simultaneous increase in the female supply of labour (Annex 3.A2). In other words, because the assumed rise in female working hours almost entirely cancels out the assumed drop in male hours, the implementation of a family working-time scheme would do little or no harm to the projected German labour supply. If, however, both parents increased their working hours to full-time when their youngest child entered kindergarten, the gains would be substantial (Chapter 2).

6. Rolling out a comprehensive early childhood education and care policy and supporting parents as children grow older

Parenthood is a time at which it is critical that couples should share paid and unpaid work and that an adequate, affordable provision of ECEC should enable them to work and have families. Between 2000 and 2011, average OECD-wide ECEC expenditure rose from 0.5% to 0.7% of GDP (Figure 3.7). With the exceptions of Slovenia and the United States, it climbed in all countries, in fact. Most of the Nordic countries increased their (already high) ECEC spending between 2000 and 2011, while France's relatively high ECEC expenditure grew at roughly the same pace as GDP between 2000 and 2013.

Figure 3.7. Germany is investing more in early childhood education

Public expenditure on early childhood education and care as a percentage of GDP, 2000, 2011 and 2013 where available

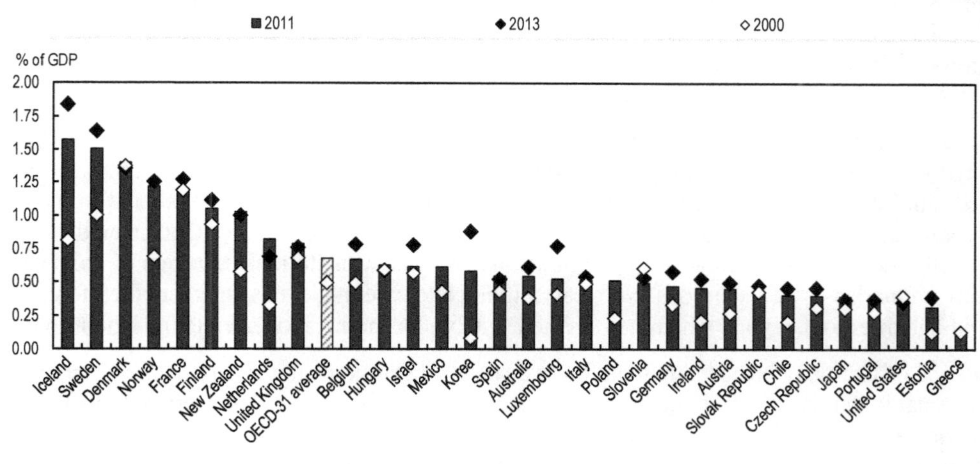

Note: In some countries local governments play a key role in financing and providing child care services. Such spending is comprehensively recorded in Nordic countries, but in some other (often federal) countries it may not be fully captured by the OECD social expenditure data.

Data for 2013 are preliminary and might be subject to change.

Source: OECD Social Expenditure Database, http://www.oecd.org/social/expenditure.htm.

ECEC expenditure in Germany was below the OECD average in 2000, at 0.3% of GDP, spending had increased considerably by 2011, and preliminary data for 2013 point to a continued expansion (Figures 3.7). Traditionally, ECEC in West Germany began with kindergarten from the age of 3 upwards (OECD, 2015f, and Box 3.3). With the expansion of ECEC, child care enrolment rates among the under 3s climbed from low levels in 2006 (13.6% vs. the 28.1% OECD average) to make up considerable ground on the OECD by 2013 – 29.3% versus 32.9%. The latest data for the first quarter of 2015 show a further rise, to 32.5%, in German enrolment rates (Destatis, 2015a).

Box 3.3. Path-dependence of work and care policies across different countries

In a broad analysis of how history and institutions evolve, Saxonberg (2014) explores the paths of family policies in four post-communist Eastern and Central European countries that were once part of the Austro-Hungarian Empire: the Czech Republic, Hungary, Poland and the Slovak Republic. Saxonberg pinpoints four critical moments that shaped those countries' institutions and opinions about when (and if) women should return to the labour market:

- Under the Austro-Hungarian Empire, the Imperial School Act of 1872 established a two-tier ECEC model with nurseries for children under 3 years of age and kindergarten for older children.
- Early in communist rule, responsibility for kindergartens was assigned to ministries of education as kindergartens were considered to serve primarily educational goals.
- In the 1950s nurseries became the remit of ministries of health as care for the under 3s was considered a health matter.
- Later, under communist rule, governments extended maternity leave until a child was 3 years old in order to avoid costly investment in problem-ridden, ill-reputed nurseries. At the time nurseries were overcrowded, abetting the spread of disease among nursery-age children. They were concerned solely with physical care, disregarding children's psychological or learning needs.

Such developments led to a norm of "threeness" according to Saxonberg: mothers stayed home during the child's first three years. They went back to work once their child had started attending kindergarten, which led to high enrolment rates in kindergarten, but very low ones in nurseries. Interestingly, the basic family policy schemes have changed little in the recent past, even after the fall of communism. Indeed, countries introduced paternal leave mainly upon pressure from the European Union and, except for Hungary, the cut support for nurseries so producing further obstacles to the resumption of work among mothers with children under 3 years of age.

Saxonberg contrasts the experience of post-communist countries with the experience of Germany, Sweden, and the United Kingdom. Sweden has historically encouraged women to work and could rely on a traditionally unified, highly regarded child care system of nurseries with no minimum age requirements. Women's influence in non-government groups and policy making was pivotal to the enactment of legislation that created parental leave exclusively for fathers. The United Kingdom, by contrast, has a weaker institutional tradition of child care policies and relies mostly on market-driven solutions. No clear unified child care model has emerged, therefore, and there is no specific child-age threshold beyond which it is deemed suitable for mothers to return to the labour market.

The experience of Germany has been marked by two sets of institutions: the traditionally conservative welfare state in West Germany and the family policies marked under communist rule in East Germany. In West Germany kindergarten started at the age of 3 years old, a norm that was much less firmly established than in Eastern Europe. In West Germany, paid parental leave was not limited exclusively to the child's first three years. The result was low female labour force participation. In the GDR, by contrast, women enjoyed an income-replacement parental leave benefit for one year, while nurseries were expanded and child care infrastructure improved. The policies resulted in considerably higher female labour force participation. With reunification, West German policy makers had to contend with pressure to maintain East Germany's ECEC infrastructure and support its traditionally higher female labour market attachment, which helped pave the way for the radical parental leave reform of 2007.

The expansion of early childhood education and care in Germany

In the years leading up to the 2007 reforms of ECEC and parental leave, societal attitudes in Germany had become increasingly more favourable towards maternal employment and the participation of very young children in ECEC (Chapter 2 and Blome, 2012). The changing family policy discourse was driven not only by changes in attitudes, but also by persistently low fertility rates and the desire to keep highly educated women in the labour force. Traditionally greater ECEC-supported female labour market involvement in East Germany also challenged the more traditional family policies of West Germany (Morgan, 2013; Blome, 2012; Seeleib-Kaiser and Toivonen 2011; Ahrens, 2010; Rüling 2010; Henninger et al., 2008; Korthouwer, 2008).

In 2007 – the same year in which the new parental leave system was introduced – the federal, regional and local governments decided that, by 2013, 35% of under-3s should have a public ECEC place in order to support parents' return to work after parental leave benefit was over (also see below on the experiences of Sweden, France and Korea). Since August 2013, children aged 1 year or older have been legally entitled to an ECEC place. The number of guaranteed preschool ECEC hours varies widely across the *Länder* (regional governments) with, for example, four hours per day in Berlin and ten hours per day in Saxony-Anhalt (BertelsmannStiftung, 2015a). Federal, regional and local governments (*Kommunen*) project a further expansion of ECEC, aiming to provide 810 000 ECEC places for the under-3s by 2018, compared to 662 701 in 2014 and 286 905 in 2006 (Destatis, 2015a).

In Germany, the *Länder* and *Kommunen* are primarily responsible for operating and expanding the ECEC infrastructure for children under 3 years old. The federal government supports the expansion of ECEC, with subsidies earmarked for co-financing ECEC projects run by regional and local jurisdictions (BMFSFJ, 2015a). In 2015, federal backing focused particularly on high-quality all-day care (the *Kita Plus* programme). Yet the bulk of ECEC costs remain the responsibility of local jurisdictions which, in 2010, shouldered over two-thirds of all expenditure, while the regional governments covered most of the rest (ESSPROSS, 2010).

The supply of and demand for ECEC has increased in recent years, with the gap between the two actually narrowing between 2012 and 2014 for children over 1 year old. The cost of child care for German parents is below the OECD average (see below on child care costs in international comparison), while, in all age groups, supply continues to fall short of demand – in 2014, 32.3% of under-3s years were offered a place, while 41.5% of parents requested one (BMFSFJ, 2015a). Parents are also making increasing use of longer child care hours per week: in 2006 only a quarter of children between 3 and 6 years old were enrolled full-time (at least seven continuous hours per day) in ECEC, while the figure in 2013 was 42% (DIPF, 2014: 55). Clearly, then, German parents have benefitted from a major expansion in ECEC for young children in recent years. At the same time, the growing demand for ECEC and more flexible ECEC services indicate that both parents wish to work and that further progress is needed.

The expansion of ECEC in other OECD countries: Sweden, France and Korea

A number of OECD countries have developed extensive ECEC systems over the years, although their timing, pace and methods have differed. Three countries – Sweden, France and Korea – are examples of extensive systems that were developed at different times and in different ways. Sweden was one of the earliest countries in the OECD to develop a comprehensive ECEC system. France, too, has a long history of broadly based ECEC for slightly older children (the 3-to-5s) and more recently expanded services for the very young. Korea, on the contrary, has no ECEC tradition, though it embarked upon a rapid expansion of centre-based care in the early 2000s.

Sweden

In 1965, only about 3% of children up to the age of 6 used public child care and preschool services in Sweden. However, rapid expansion throughout the 1970s and early 1980s had increased the provision to roughly 50% by as early as 1985 (Figure 3.8, Panel A). Sustained public investment has seen growth in enrolment continue steadily and almost year-on-year ever since. In 2013, about 76% of all Swedish children under 7 years old used public ECEC services, a proportion that climbs to roughly 87% if the under 1s – most of whom are cared for at home by parents on parental leave – are discounted.

The expansion of ECEC in Sweden has built largely on publicly subsidised and, for the most part, publicly run centre-based services and collective care arrangements. Home-based family day care services are available, but their use has declined since the mid-1980s – in 2013, they accounted for only around 2% of children aged 0 to 5 (OECD, 2005, 2015g). Instead, the large majority of young children attend day care institutions with care provided in groups of around 17 on average (SCB, 2015; Skolverket, 2015; OECD, 2015g). Even from a very young age, day care institutions focus heavily on child development and early learning outcomes – indeed, although initially developed with the express aim of facilitating parental employment (Kamerman and Moss, 2009), ECEC in Sweden has since become an integral part of the education system with its own curriculum and educational targets. However, Sweden's comprehensive, public, centre-based system is relatively expensive (OECD, 2005). In 2013 public expenditure on ECEC services in Sweden was 1.64% of GDP, the second highest level of spending on ECEC in the OECD after Iceland (see Figure 3.7 and OECD, 2015h).

France

France has a similarly long tradition of extensive ECEC provision, particularly for slightly older children. For those aged between 3 and 5 years old, services have historically been (and continue to be) dominated by the comprehensive *école maternelle* (preschool) system – public, centre-based services that, like the Swedish preschools, are considered a core part of the national educational system. Even as early as 1960-61 the *école maternelle* system catered to around 63.3% of children aged between 3 and 5, although considerable expansion during the 1960s and 1970s saw coverage widen to roughly 97% by 1980-81 (Bouysse et al., 2011). Since 1989, all 3-to-5 year-olds have been entitled to a place in the local *école maternelle*, with participation steady at (or effectively at) 100% ever since (ibid.).

ECEC services for very young children, however, are more fragmented and decentralised, with much of the recent expansion of provision for the under-3s based on individual or private care arrangements such as those offered by *assistantes maternelles* (registered child-minders) or "home carers" (child-minders who work in the child's home). Particularly since the 1990s, French ECEC policy with regard to children under 3 years old has placed less emphasis on direct provision and more on flexibility and parental choice – primarily through various demand-side subsidies and measures to help parents meet the costs of private arrangements. Since 2004, for example, parents who use *assistantes maternelles* or home carers have been entitled to financial assistance through the Young Child Care Service (PAJE), a supplementary provision that itself builds upon earlier forms of support for parents.[6]

The result has been a considerable increase in the availability of individual or private care arrangements for very young children: between 1995 and 2010, for example, the number of children looked after by *assistantes maternelles* more than doubled. Indeed, despite falls in other areas of the ECEC provision, the rise in individual or private ECEC has driven the considerable rise in the overall provision, including the number of places available to 2-year-olds in preschool (Figure 3.8, Panel B).

Government policy seeks to boost ECEC by 275 000 child care places over the 2013-17 period. In practice, however, expansion has so far been on a much more restricted scale: only 31% of places planned for 2013 and 7% of those planned for 2014 had been made available. It is likely that cutbacks in financial support to families contributed to the reduced demand for child care places in 2013-14 (Haut Conseil de la Famille, 2015).

Korea

ECEC provision in Korea is, for the most part, a relatively recent development. As recently as 2002, only around 30% of Korea children aged between 0 to 6 years old used child care or preschool facilities. However, rapid growth in the 2000s and early 2010s saw that rate rise sharply (Figure 3.8, Panel A). Between 2002 and 2012, ECEC participation rates among the 0-to-6s grew at an average rate of 3.5 percentage points per year, with the proportion using child care or preschool more than doubling over the same period. Although growth has slowed slightly in the past couple of years, more than 66% of children under age 6 were enrolled in some form of child care or preschool service in 2014.

Like Sweden, the rapid growth of ECEC provision in Korea has been built almost entirely on the use of centre-based collective care arrangements. In large part, it has been driven by the scale of public financial assistance for parents using centre-based child care. Indeed, Korea has long subsidised such costs for children from very low-income households. From 2004 onwards, however, it loosened the income criteria for the subsidy and raised the centre-based ECEC subsidy itself. In 2013, it scrapped the means test for the subsidy altogether, effectively creating a universal programme of public assistance for centre-based care, regardless of income level.

As in Sweden, other forms of publicly backed care are available. In 2007, for example, the government introduced a subsidised "personal care service", offering parents the option of individual child care in the home. The personal care service is generally a part-time provision, but a full-time service for children aged 0 to 2 years old is available. However, the service is used by only a minority of children – less than 1% in 2014.

Figure 3.8. Several OECD countries have developed extensive ECEC systems, though at different times and in different ways

Trends in participation in formal child care or pre-primary education for children aged 0 to 6 in Korea and Sweden and the availability of formal child care places for children aged 0 to 2 in France[1]

Panel A. Proportion of children aged 0-6 in formal child care or pre-primary education, Korea and Sweden, 1965-2014

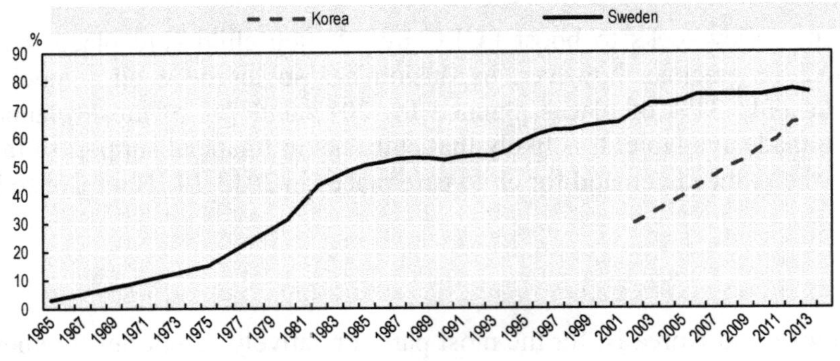

Panel B. Number of places in formal child care per 100 children aged 0-2 by type of care arrangement, France, 1995-2010

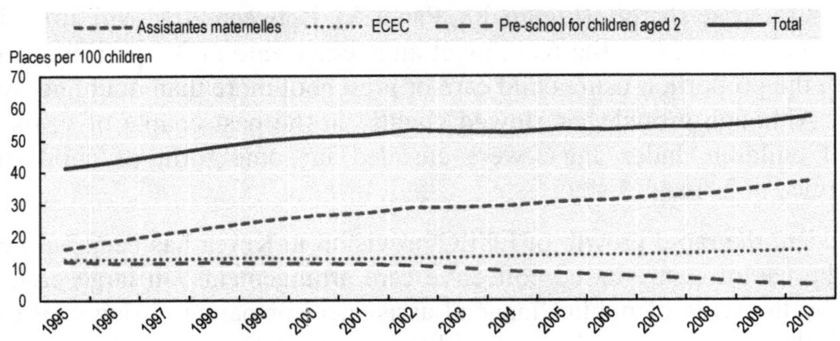

1. For Korea, data are based on the Korean calendar-year age system. The data shown in the chart cover all children aged 0-5 (where age 0 includes those not yet born) on 1st January of the given year, and thus cover all children aged 0-5, plus any children who have turned 6 by the time of the survey. For Sweden, data include all children enrolled in day care institutions and municipal family day care. Data for the years 1966-69, 1971-74, 1976-1978 and 1981 are missing and are imputed through linear interpolation. Data for France on the number of places in formal child care cover places offered by *assistantes maternelles* (registered preschool home teachers], EAJEs (part-subsidised preschool establishments), and the early schooling provision (*scolarisation précoce*) (see Vanovermeir, 2012 for details). With the exception of *scolarisation précoce*, some of preschool child care places may, on occasion, be used by a child aged 3 or over.

Source: For Korea, Korean Ministry of Health and Welfare and Ministry of Education; for France, Vanovermeir, S. (2012) and the Department of Research, Surveys, Evaluation and Statistics (DREES), http://drees.social-sante.gouv.fr/etudes-et-statistiques/; for Sweden, Swedish authorities for 1965, 1970, 1975, 1980 and 1982-2002, from 2003 onwards, Nordic Social Statistical Committee (NOSOSCO), http://nowbase.org/.

Child care costs in international comparison

Parents of young children often have trouble not only finding a place in child care, but paying for it. The OECD Tax-Benefit Models incorporate child care costs. They can, for example, calculate the net child care costs of full-time care for two children aged 2 and 3 in a typical child care facility. Out-of-pocket costs or net costs to parents are determined by child care fees minus cash benefits, rebates and tax concessions, as well as other relevant benefits.

Figure 3.9 shows out-of-pocket child care costs for a married couple where both spouses work full-time, one earning the full average wage (AW) and the partner 50% of

AW. For such dual-earner couples, the average out-of-pocket expenses across the OECD for two children in full-time care are around 17% of AW. However, centre-based formal care is most expensive in English-speaking countries (save Australia), where net costs are above 40% of the average wage. In Germany, the net child care costs for such a dual-earning family type are 11.2% of average wage – well below the OECD average.[7] While child care costs matter to German parents, the main disincentive for second earners remains the joint income tax system (OECD, 2007b, 2015e, 2016a; Rastrigina and Verashchagina, 2015).

Schröder et al. (2015) use survey data to show that poorer families throughout Germany face higher out-of-pocket child care costs than richer families for children of all ages, particularly younger ones. At the same time, well-off parents are often ready to pay more for child care (Camehl et al., 2015), so raising the issue of how child care rebates can be better designed for low-income families.

Figure 3.9. Out-of-pocket centre-based child care costs in Germany are below the OECD average

Net full-time child care costs for dual-earner family with full-time earnings of 150% of the average wage, 2012

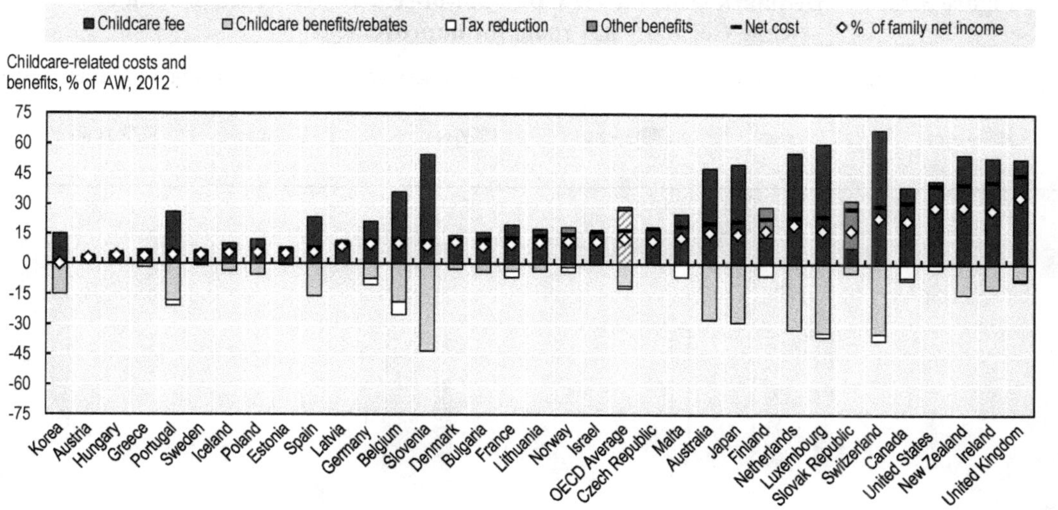

Reading note: Data refer to the situation for a two-child (age 2 and 3) full-time dual-earner family with the first earner on 100% of national average earnings and the second on 50% of average national earnings (i.e. household earnings at 150% of the national average earnings). In Germany (Hamburg), the gross full-time child care fee charged to such a family is equal to 21.5% of the national average wage (blue bars). They are entitled to child care benefits/rebates (including fee reductions) equal to 7.2% of the national average wage (light grey bars), and a tax reduction equal to 3.2% of the national average wage (light blue bars). This produces a net (out-of-pocket) full-time child care cost equal to 11.2% of national average earnings (black line), or 9.7% of the family's overall net income (white diamond).

See OECD (2016a) for information on the average wage (AW).

In a number of countries, available information on child care costs relates to a particular region or municipality – e.g. Canada (Ontario), Germany (Hamburg), Japan (Tokyo), the United Kingdom (England) and the United States (Michigan).

The results on net child care costs as a percentage of net family income account for tax reductions, child benefits and "other benefits". Although they are not primarily child care-related (e.g. family or housing benefits), they affect the net household income position.

See OECD Tax and Benefit Systems: OECD Indicators (www.oecd.org/els/soc/benefits-and-wages.htm) for more detail on the policies included and assumptions made when calculating the net full-time child care costs.

Source: OECD, "Tax and Benefit Systems: OECD Indicators", http://www.oecd.org/els/soc/benefits-and-wages.htm.

Supporting working parents of school-age children: after school hours care and all-day schools

Of course, child care issues do not stop when children enter primary school. Indeed, they may actually become more of a constraint when parents work full-time and/or irregular hours and have to arrange care before and/or after school hours and during school holidays. Public policy can help them combine full-time work with caring for school-age children by offering OSH care support and all-day schooling.

Denmark and Sweden run the most comprehensive OSH care systems in the OECD (Figure 3.10), with children attending activities before and after school, often in the school premises. In Germany OSH provisions vary from one local authority to another – games, homework, educational and sports activities, etc. Local authorities determine how much they fund and how much families pay. In recent years the share of children enrolled in OSH care has increased in recent years (DIPF, 2014, p. 79)[8] and co-operations between different stakeholders have deepened (also see examples below).

Figure 3.10. Denmark leads the OECD in out-of-school hours care provision, while Germany has room for improvement

Percentage of children aged 6 to 11 enrolled in out-of-school-hours care services by age, 2014 (or latest available year)[1]

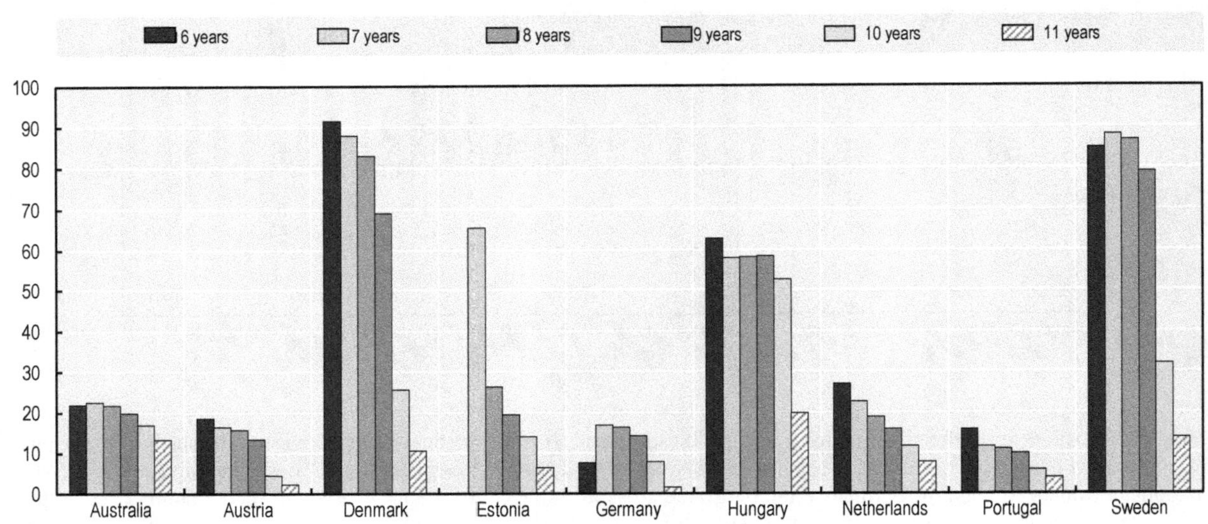

1. Data refer to 2014 for Germany; 2011 for Australia, Austria, Germany, Portugal, Sweden; 2009 for Denmark, Hungary and Netherlands, 2007 for Estonia.

Source: OECD Family Database, http://www.oecd.org/els/family/database.htm; OECD calculations for Germany based on Destatis data.

While Germany offers comparatively little OSH care, it is expanding its provision and increasing the number of all-day schools. The services offered vary widely across the *Länder*, which are in charge of education, and *Kommunen*, which are responsible for OSH care. Any school offering education and care, including lunch, on at least three days of the week for at least seven hours is considered an all-day school (Bertelsmann Stiftung, 2015a). Hours, staffing and the quality of the learning environment in all-day schools vary widely from one *Land* to another (Klemm and Zorn, 2016). Between 2005 and 2013 the number of children in all-day primary schools increased by nearly 170% (Bertelsmann Stiftung, 2015b). While in 2005 only

7.9% of children were enrolled in all-day primary schools, 24.2% of primary school-aged children attended such schools in 2013. All-day schools are more common in secondary education and, in 2011, 30.6% of all students went to all-day schools in Germany (Klemm, 2013). However, many more parents – 70% – would actually like to see their children attending an all-day school (ibid.). And 61% of parents [with child(ren) under 18] also consider all-day schools to be beneficial for child development (Allensbach Institut für Demoskopie, 2013).

Yet the opening hours of all-day schools still pose challenges to working parents. In 2013-14, most all-day primary schools offered seven or eight hours of education and care a day, with parents having to pick up their children by 4 p.m. and possibly having to leave work early to do so. Moreover, many all-day schools do not offer full-time care every day of the week – often there is no such provision one afternoon of the week, typically Friday – and schools generally close during school holidays (Bertelsmann Stiftung, 2015a). OSH care is usually more flexible, offering longer, later hours than all-day schools. Parents may drop their children off in an OSH facility before school starts and pick them up after 4 or 5 p.m. On average, children under 11 years enrolled in OSH care in Germany attend OSH care for five hours per day (ibid.). Combined with the usual school day, OSH care typically provides primary school children with more hours of education and care than in most all-day primary schools (ibid.).

On average, French parents work more paid hours than their German peers (Chapter 2), so make wide use of OHS care, child minders, relatives and a mix thereof. The preschool and primary school day usually starts at 8.30 a.m. and finishes at 4.30 p.m. except on Wednesdays, when it ends at midday. After school hours, children have access to OSH care services provided and run by municipalities and which vary widely as a result. In 2010, two-thirds of preschool children went home directly after school, 16% were picked up by a child-minder or relative, and 18% stayed at school where OSH care services were provided (ONPE, 2012). A slightly higher proportion (70%) of primary school children go home straight after school, while 14% are picked up by a non-parent. One-quarter of primary school children use OSH services to do their homework and play games (which include sport), and the remaining 6% are cared for at home by a child minder or relative. Many families mix home-based child care with other services, particularly on Wednesday afternoons when 59% of primary school children are at least partly looked after by parents in the afternoon, 11% by their grandparents, and 3% by another person. Yet 40% of primary school children are also involved in activities provided by the local authorities and associations (Sautory et al., 2011).

Parents everywhere are in special need of support during the school holidays. Swedish municipalities keep their *fritidshem*, or OSH centres, open, with many of them using the services of external providers which offer music and sports activities. In October 2014 (thus during the term and not during school holidays), 83.2% of children aged 6 to 9 years old and 20.7% of 10-to-12 year-olds were enrolled in such centres (Skolverket, 2016). If during school holidays there is not enough demand for the local centre to stay open during the holidays, parents are offered a spot at another near-by facility. Fees are income-dependent and affordable: in Stockholm, for example, the maximum fee charged in 2015 was SEK 858 (about EUR 92) per month (City of Stockholm, 2016).

In Germany, child care for school children during school holidays is a particular concern of German parents, with 54% wishing it were better (BMFSFJ, 2014). The services offered vary widely from one local authority to another. While many dual-earner families have to find their own (possibly costly) solutions, there have been some innovative local initiatives in recent years. The "Lokale Bündnisse für Familie" (the Local Alliance for Families) is a local stakeholder scheme that serves as an information platform for best practices (see "Recent policy initiatives in Germany bring together various stakeholders" below). In Dienheim (Rhineland-Palatine), for example, the Local Alliance for Families proposes activities from 8 a.m. to 4 p.m. during school holidays. In another initiative, companies in Hanau fund holiday programmes with a wide range of activities for the children of employees from the participating companies.

7. Time for work and the family: policies and stakeholder agreements to promote flexible work schedules

The right to adjust working hours

Workplace organisation issues are usually resolved through employer-employee negotiations, but policy has moved in recent years to try to support working parents through flexible workplace arrangements. Workers are now entitled to adjust their working hours or ask their employer to do so. Employers may deny requests for compelling business reasons, but must explain refusals. Table 3.2 presents employees' statutory rights to flexible working arrangements for family reasons in selected OECD countries.

Work schedule flexibility should work in both directions. Parents should not only be able to reduce their working hours, they should also know that they may resume full-time working hours when their children grow up. A few countries have complemented the right to work part-time with the entitlement to return to full-time work and/or automatically revert to previous hours after a certain specified period (Table 3.2). While such provisions are an important first step, they are often applicable only for a few years. In Germany, for example, parents have long benefitted from the right to part-time work during the child's first three years. Since the 2015 reform of parental leave (*ElterngeldPlus*), German parents may use that right more flexibly and opt to use a third year between their child's third and eighth year.

Some countries have enacted a general entitlement to work longer and shorter hours, thus allowing parents to adjust their paid working hours more easily as their children get older. In the Netherlands, for example, an employee in companies with ten or more employees who has been working for at least a year for that company has the right to request that his/her working hours be lengthened or shortened (Eurofund, 2015a). Employees must request the change at least four months before they wish it to take effect. The employer can turn down the request only for important business reasons, such as being unable to find a replacement (if the request is for shorter hours) or there not being enough work (if the request is for longer hours). In the United Kingdom, all employees (regardless of company size) may request flexible working hours after 26 weeks of employment (Eurofund, 2015b). The request can be refused based on serious business grounds only.

Table 3.2. Statutory rights to flexible work arrangements for family reasons, selected countries

	Work arrangements around childbirth		Right to request reduced working hours or part-time work (acceptable grounds for refusing requests: N = none; SB = serious business grounds; AG = any grounds)				
	Work shift for medical reason during pregnancy and after childbirth	Working time arrangement for nursing and breastfeeding	Part-time work or changes to working hours for family reasons: To care for a child	Part-time work or changes to working hours for family reasons: To care for an adult	Automatic reversion to previous hours	Part-time employees as a proportion (%) of total employees (2014)[1]	Female part-time employees as a proportion (%) of total female employees (2014)[1]
Australia	Yes	-	SB	SB	No	24.5	37.1
Austria	Yes	Yes	N	N	Yes	20.4	34.7
Belgium	Yes	Yes	N[2,3]	N[3]	Yes	19.1	31.6
Canada	Yes[4]	-	-	-	-	18.4	25.5
Denmark	Yes	-	AG[2]	-	Yes	20.2	25.7
Finland	-	-	SB[2]	AG	Yes	12.2	15.8
France	Yes	Yes	N[2,6]	SB[6]	Yes	14.3	22.3
Germany	Yes	Yes	SB[2]	N[5]	Yes	22.6	37.6
Netherlands	Yes	Yes	N[2,6]	SB[6]	Yes	39.7	61.7
New Zealand	Yes	Yes	SB[6]	SB[6]	No[7]	20.6	30.8
Norway	-	Yes	SB[2]	SB	Yes	19	27.8
Sweden	Yes	Yes	N[2]	-	Yes	13.5	17.5
United Kingdom	Yes	-	SB[6]	SB[6]	No[7]	23.4	36.4
United States	-	Yes	AG	N	Yes	13	17.9

1. Common definition of part-time employment (30 hours per week in the main job). For the United States, data refer to dependent employees only.

2. A right to (request) reduced working hours or part-time work to care for a child is incorporated in the statutory entitlement to parental leave. In some countries (e.g. Finland, Norway, Sweden), parents may request part-time work to care for a child on grounds other than the statutory entitlement and/or after the expiry of the parental leave period. In other countries (e.g. Belgium, France, the Netherlands) employees also have more general statutory entitlements in addition to reduced working hours.

3. Under the Time Credit system, companies must approve requests unless they employ fewer than ten employees or more than 5% of the total workforce are currently already using the Time Credit system.

4. Only the federal jurisdictions and the provinces of Quebec and Manitoba have specific provisions.

5. Under *Familienpflegezeit*, employees in firms with more than 25 employees are legally entitled to work part-time (minimum 15 hours per week) for up to 24 months and/or to take full-time leave for up to six months to care for a dependent relative. Employees in firms with 16 to 25 employees are legal entitled to part-time work or full-time leave for up to six months. Firms with fewer employees can refuse requests on any grounds.

6. In France, the Netherlands, New Zealand, and the United Kingdom, employees have a general statutory right to request reduced working hours or part-time work which they can use, among other reasons, to care for a child or an adult. In France, employees may request transfers from full-time to part-time work and from part-time to full-time work, which the employer can refuse on serious business grounds or if no suitable position is available. In the Netherlands, employees have a general entitlement to request longer or shorter working hours, which the employer can refuse only on serious business grounds. Employees may submit such requests only if they work in a company with a workforce of more than 10, and if they have worked at least 12 months in the company. In New Zealand, all employees may request a change in their hours, days or place of work, either temporarily or permanently. Employers must consider the request but can refuse on business grounds or if it conflicts with a collective agreement. In the United Kingdom, employees have the right to request changes to their hours, days or place of work, which the employer must consider and can refuse only on serious business grounds (limited to employees who have worked for the same employer for at least 26 weeks).

7. In New Zealand and the United Kingdom, changes to working hours and/or other work arrangements granted under the entitlement to request flexible working result in a permanent change in the contract, unless the employee and employer agree at the time of request that the change is for a set and specified period of time.

8. Many countries require employees to meet additional criteria for requesting part-time work or changes to working hours (e.g. length of service or size of firm), see OECD (2015f).

Source: *OECD Family Database*, www.oecd.org/els/family/database.htm; ILO Working Conditions Laws Database, www.ilo.org/dyn/travail/travmain.home; Moss (2015).

Recent policy initiatives in Germany bring together various stakeholders

However, as employers' and employees' are the crucial stakeholders in workplace relations, legislation generally goes further than merely formalising standard principles and seeks to generate change in workplace practices. In Germany, a wide range of recent policy initiatives address the numerous obstacles in the way of more equal sharing in working families. They complement the recent drive in public policy to expand child care services and parental leave reform.

In 2011, the federal government, the Confederation of German Trade Unions (DGB), the German Chamber of Commerce (DIHK) and the German Confederation of Skilled Crafts (ZDH) signed the "Charter on Family-Oriented Working Hours" calling on all "stakeholders to actively pursue the opportunities of family-oriented work hours and innovative working-hour models in the best interest of the German economy". The signatory stakeholders and the employers' association (BDA) followed up the charter in 2015 with the "Neue Vereinbarkeit Memorandum" (New Reconciliation Memorandum) on ways to balance work and family life. The memorandum sought to:

- identify where there had been progress in the work-life balance – e.g. a higher profile for the issue, better child care infrastructure, greater awareness of flexible working hours in companies, and higher levels of maternal employment;
- identify challenges – e.g. raising awareness of family responsibilities in companies, caring for adult family members, encouraging fathers to engage in unpaid work, supporting mothers' returns to the labour market after child birth, and encouraging mothers to work longer paid hours;
- draw up guidelines to help employees and employers successfully balance work and life throughout the life cycle.

The memorandum calls for equal sharing to become a mainstream work-life model among young men and women. Its guidelines appeal to employers to offer "flexitime" arrangements as part of the "Arbeitgeberattraktivität 2020" attractive workplace branding exercise and to promote *vollzeitnah*, the reduced full-time working-hours model (generally accepted to be around 28-30 hours). They also emphasise that equal sharing involves fathers as much as mothers and call for the provision of affordable high-quality child care.

Box 3.4. Initiatives to develop family-friendly workplaces in Germany

The new reconciliation memorandum was developed within the context of the company network known as "Erfolgsfaktor Familie" (Family as Success Factor) and co-funded by the European Social Fund. It shares information and best practices among family-friendly companies and other stakeholders, and holds competitions and events to raise awareness of family-friendly workplace issues. The network connects more than 1 200 companies (www.erfolgsfaktor-familie.de/).

In addition there are about 650 local networks, the "Lokale Bündnisse für Familie" (the Local Alliances for the Family). They bring together stakeholders (employers, unions, local authorities, foundations, churches, employment agencies, universities, child care providers, etc.) that exchange information on family-related services like the local child care provision or training for employees in caring for family members.

Since 1999, companies in Germany have been able to apply for certification as a family-friendly employer (*Audit Berufundfamilie*), along the lines of an initiative in Austria (OECD, 2002). The independent Hertie Foundation audits companies – assessing their processes, identifying their goals, and, where necessary, suggests new workplace arrangements – then certifies them "family-friendly" if they meet criteria. Large firms make the widest use of such audits – 42% of companies with more than 1 000 employees are certified. However, the process is considered too time-consuming by most small companies with less than 20 employees, only 8% of which are certified (DIHK, 2012).

As regards the current expansion of child care, the federal government also sponsors company-run child care services as part of the programme, "Betriebliche Kinderbetreuung" (Company-run Childcare). The companies involved receive subsidies towards the operating costs of newly created child care facilities. Joint ventures of smaller and medium-sized companies and collaborative ventures with non-profit and private providers are also eligible for funding. The subsidy is awarded for up to two years to facilitate the initial set-up, but thereafter the costs are borne by employers and possibly by employees who use the service.

Flexible working-time arrangements in companies

To help employees in general and working parents in particular strike a better work-life balance, stakeholders in many countries have introduced a range of measures to foster a wider range of flexible working-time arrangements (FWTAs). Although FTWAs can take diverse forms, they are typically:

- reduced working hours or part-time work,
- staggered work schedules,
- time banking schemes, e.g. overtime that can be taken as time off.[9]

FWTAs are increasingly widespread and attractive to both employers and employees. For workers, the reasons are obvious – the ability to exert some control over their work schedule helps them better balance working hours with family time. Flexitime arrangements have been found to reduce stress and family-work conflicts, such as missed deadlines due to family responsibilities (Halpern, 2005).

For employers, the benefits of flexible work arrangements are still being debated and the availability of flexitime varies according to a firm's size and sector. Research has found that FWTAs are an asset in helping to recruiting skilled workers (Bloom et al., 2009) and fostering a family-friendly public image (den Dulk et al., 2013). Greater employee freedom in scheduling work is also associated with higher job satisfaction, greater loyalty and motivation, and lower absenteeism (Baltes et al., 1999). Flexitime arrangements are also good for greater female labour force participation, as they make it possible to parent well while engaging in paid work. And the presence of female managers, in turn, increases the likelihood that employers will provide flexible working arrangements (Bloom et al., 2009).

In the private sector, too, there are some bottom-line payoffs to FWTAs. Firms with family-friendly practices have been found to have better overall management practices (ibid.) and experience higher stock valuations after family-work initiatives are announced (Arthur and Cook, 2004). Large organisations are more likely to offer FWTAs than small or medium-sized organisations, as it can be costlier for smaller business to rearrange tasks among workers. This, of course, is a challenge in countries with large numbers of small and medium-sized enterprises like Germany (Goodstein, 1994; Ingram and Simons, 1995). Across European countries 80% of large companies offer flexitime, compared to 71% of medium firms and 64% of small firms (European Company Survey, 2015).

The use of FWTAs has increased over time in the OECD area,[10] but there is still considerable variation from one country to another. Despite the large number of small or medium-sized companies German companies do quite well in the provision of flexible working time (Figure 3.11). Over 90% of organisations in Austria, Denmark Finland, Germany and Sweden report that they offer staggered working hours and/or time banking. By contrast, only 60% of companies in Greece do so. The proportion of employees entitled to FWTAs also varies across countries, and not all firms offer their employees flexitime. Again, Germany does well in this regard: 78% of German firms allow all employees to build up overtime credits for days off, a greater share than in most European companies surveyed.

Figure 3.11. Germany is among the five countries where the most companies offer flexible working-time arrangements

Panel A. Share of organisations offering staggered work hours and/or time banking, select European countries, 2013

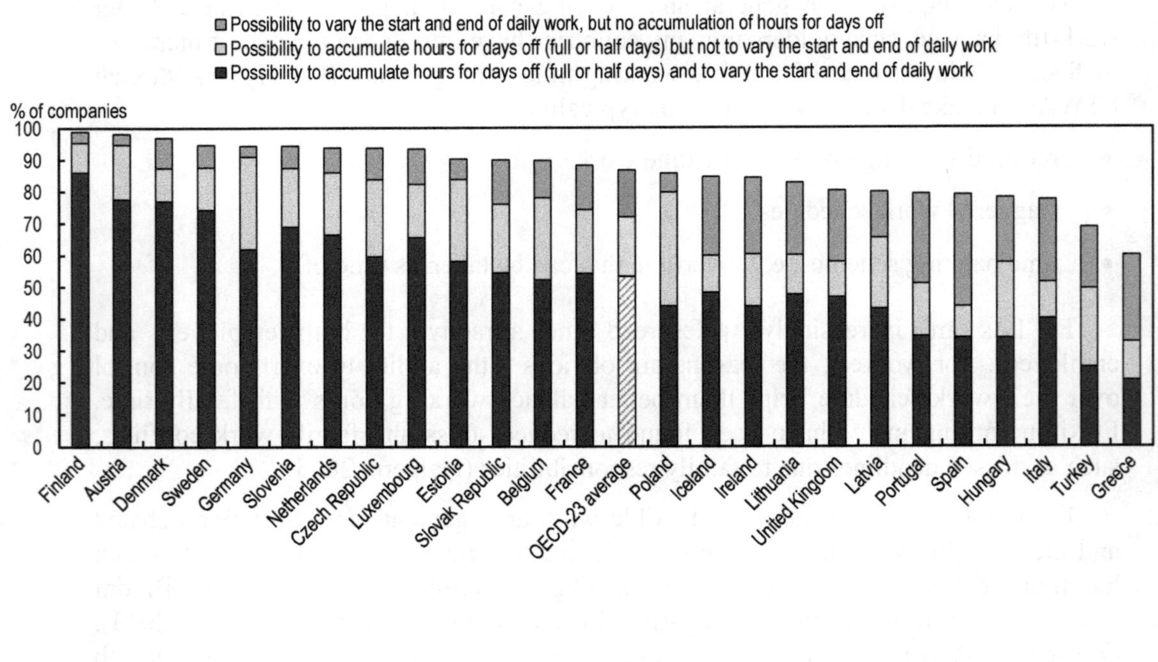

Figure 3.11. Germany is among the five countries where the most companies offer flexible working-time arrangements *(cont.)*

Panel B. Proportion of companies reporting that all, or only some, employees are eligible to use overtime hours towards days off, select European countries, 2013

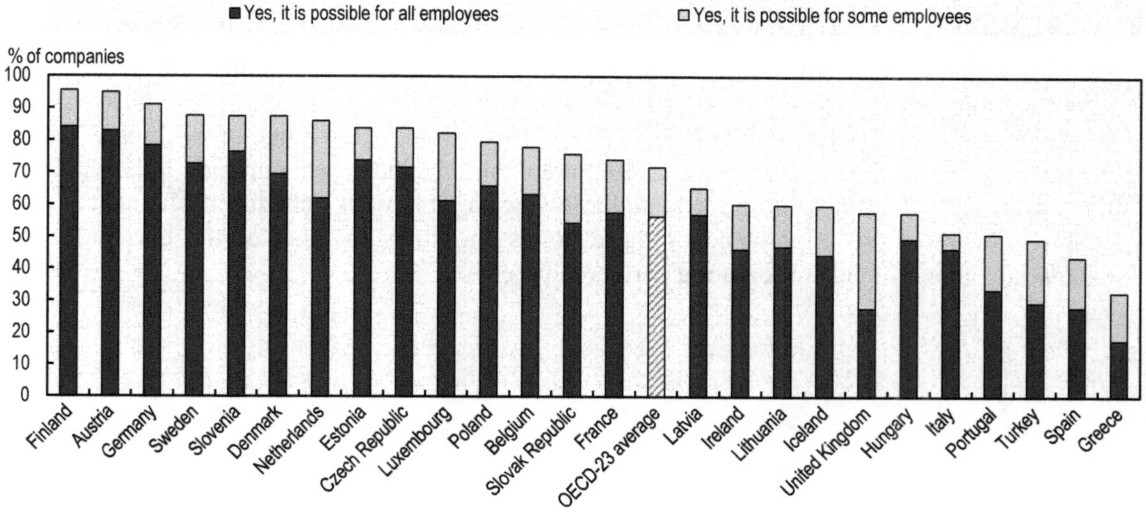

Source: OECD calculations from the 2013 European Company Survey.

8. Concluding remarks

Germany has made great strides in reforming policies that support working families and promote equal partnership among partnered parents. In the past, labour market institutions, public policies, and social norms reinforced traditional gender roles, especially in West Germany, but social policy reforms over the last decade have increased opportunities for parents. The new German family policy approach aims to provide parents and children with more time together by fostering a more equal partnership in the sharing of work and family life responsibilities ("Partnerschaftlichkeit").

Parental leave reform in 2007 (Ëlterngeld") significantly increased the probability of mothers' return to work after the expiry of the benefit. In line with international best practice, the 2007 reform also led to an increase in the number of fathers taking leave. The 2015 parental leave reform ("ElterngeldPlus") facilitates combining part-time work and leave-taking and incentivises better leave-sharing among partners in the household. Building on these experiences, German policy can continue to develop family-policy supports including options for parents with young children to work reduced full-time hours for a specific period of time, such as currently debated in Germany under the notion of the "family working time model". Such a policy could help many fathers to invest more time in their children at a young age. In contrast to long-term short part-time hours, working reduced full-time hours on a temporary basis is likely to have positive effects on women's earnings and career opportunities.

Affordable quality ECEC and OSH-care services are a key ingredient of a successful public policy model aimed at reconciling the work and family life of both parents. Since the mid-2000s, Germany has considerably increased its investment in ECEC services to the benefit of both children and their parents. However, ECEC participation rates are still below the OECD average and more investment is needed to increase capacity and to meet parents' needs more flexibly. Furthermore, public policy in Germany should invest more in OSH-care supports that help parents with school-age children to combine full-time work with family life during the school year and over school holidays.

Finally, labour market institutions, workplace cultures and access to flexible working arrangements are key to aligning working conditions with family life. It is important to extend the cooperation with social partners and other stakeholders to make workplace practices more conducive to family life and promote the range of workplace measures as in the "Neue Vereinbarkeit Memorandum", including encouraging fathers' leave-taking, facilitating remote work, and allowing flexible work schedules. The next chapter illustrates the importance of these policy measures in view of the current unequal division of paid work among partnered parents.

Notes

1. There are differences between Nordic countries' family policies, For example, the duration of paid parental and home care leave differs considerably: from around 1 year in Denmark and Iceland to up to 3 years in Finland and Norway. But regardless of child-related leave lasts, family policy in the Nordic countries aims to leave no gap in support between the expiry of parental leave and the start of formal child care (or preschool).

2. The OECD Tax-Benefit Models calculate tax burdens, benefit entitlements and net incomes for a range of different labour market and household situations that take into account each country's rules and how the different elements in its tax-benefit systems interact (see Annex 3.A1). The overall effect of tax-benefit systems on the financial incentive to share paid work varies across income ranges and associated levels of taxation. However, the results presented in Figure 3.A1.1 also hold true for household income that is double average earnings in most countries (see els/family/database.htm for further information and data).

3. In various countries (e.g. Denmark, Iceland and the Netherlands), individual tax systems include "joint elements" such as tax relief and tax credits that are transferable between partners.

4. *Minijobs* are casual, tax-exempt jobs where wages do not exceed EUR 450. *Midijob* are also casual jobs, paid between EUR 450 and EUR 850, where workers pay gradually higher contributions.

5. Annex 3.A2 provides estimates of the projected size of the full-time equivalent labour force (15-74 year-olds) under an alternative scenario. In the scenario, all employees potentially eligible for the family working-time benefit adopt, by 2025, usual weekly working hours of 32 hours per week, the upper limit of the 28-32 hour flexible family working week. The projected full-time equivalent labour force is very slightly smaller under the family working-time scenario than under the baseline. But even by 2025 – when average usual hours among eligible employees are assumed to reach 32 hours per week – the difference in the size of the labour force is only about 37 000 full-time equivalent workers, a fall of only around 0.1%.

6. The Young Child Care Service (PAJE) is a supplementary provision that itself builds upon earlier forms of support for parents who use individual arrangements such as the *Aide à la famille pour l'emploi d'une assistante maternelle agréée* (Allowance for the Employment of a Registered Child Minder – AFEAMA) and *Allocation de garde d'enfant à Domicile* (Home Childcare Allowance – AGED).

7. For country-specific information on tax-benefit systems and child care costs, see the OECD webpage, "Benefits and Wages: Country specific information", at http://www.oecd.org/els/soc/benefits-and-wages-country-specific-information.htm.

8. As OSH care and all-day school cannot be clearly discerned in the data, some double-counting may occur.

9. Remote work, or telecommuting, is also a flexible work arrangement, but data are not included in the surveys referenced here.

10. Companies increasingly report that they recognise the importance of the work-family balance. A survey of German companies found that the share of those that support or plan to support parents through child care rose from 25% to 50% from 2007 to 2012. Furthermore, in 2013, 80.7% of German firms considered family-friendliness important, up from 46.5% in 2003 (DIHK-Unternehmensbarometers, 2012).

References

Adema, W. (2012), "Setting the Scene: The Mix of Family Policy Objectives and Packages Across the OECD", *Children and Youth Services Review*, Vol. 34, Elsevier, pp. 487-498.

Adema, W., C. Clarke and V. Frey (2015), "Paid Parental Leave: Lessons from OECD Countries and Selected U.S. States", *OECD Social, Employment and Migration Working Papers*, No. 172, OECD Publishing, Paris, http://dx.doi.org/10.1787/5jrqgvqqb4vb-en.

Adema, W., P. Fron and M. Ladaique (2014), "How Much Do OECD Countries Spend on Social Protection and How Redistributive Are their Tax/benefit Systems?", *International Social Security Review*, Vol. 67, No. 1/2014, pp. 1-25.

Adema, W., P. Fron and M. Ladaique (2011), "Is the European Welfare State Really More Expensive", *OECD Social, Employment and Migration Working Papers*, No. 124, OECD Publishing, Paris, http://dx.doi.org/10.1787/5kg2d2d4pbf0-en.

Ahrens, R. (2010), "Sustainability in German Family Policy and Politics", GPS, Vol. 6, No. 3, pp. 195-229.

Allensbach Institut für Demoskopie (2015), *Weichenstellungen für die Aufgabenteilung in Familie und Beruf*, Research report on a representative survey of parents commissioned by the German Ministry of Family, Seniors and Youth, Allensbach.

Allensbach Institut für Demoskopie (2013), *Monitor Familienleben 2013 – Einstellungen der Bevölkerung zur Familienpolitik und zur Familie*, Allensbach.

Bach, S. et al. (2011), "Reform des Ehegattensplittings: Nur eine reine Individualbesteuerung erhöht die Erwerbsanreize deutlich", *DIW Wochenbericht*, No. 41.

Baltes, B. et al. (1999), "Flexible and Compressed Workweek Schedules: Aa Meta-Analysis of their Effects on Work-Related Criteria", *Journal of Applied Psychology*, Vol. 84, No. 4, pp. 496-513.

Bechara, P., J. Kluve and M. Tamm (2015), *Fiskalische Refinanzierungseffekte des Elterngeldes*, report commissioned by the German Ministry for Families, Seniors, Women and Youth, Essen.

Bergman, S. (2004), "Collective Organizing and Claim Making on Child Care in Norden: Blurring the Boundaries between the Inside and the Outside", *Social Politics*, Vol. 11, No. 2, pp. 217-246.

BertelsmannStiftung (2015a), "Trends der FBBE in Deutschland – zentrale Ergebnisse des Länderreports 2015".

BertelsmannStiftung (2015b), "Trends der FBBE in Deutschland – Ländermonitor 2015, Tabellen", http://www.laendermonitor.de/typo3conf/ext/jp_downloadslm/pi1/download.php?datei=fileadmin/contents/downloads/2015/tabellen_laendermonitor_2015.pdf&ftype=pdf.

Bertrand, M., E. Kamenica and J. Pan (2015), "Gender Identity and Relative Income within Households", *Quarterly Journal of Economics*, Oxford University Press, Vol. 130, No. 2, pp. 571-614.

BiB – Federal Institute for Population Research (2015), "Familienleitbilder- Muss alles perfekt sein? Leitbilder zur Elternschaft in Deutschland", Bundesinstitut für Bevölkerungsforschung, Wiesbaden.

Bittman, M. et al. (2003), "When Does Gender Trump Money? Bargaining and Time in Household Work", *American Journal of Sociology*, Vol. 109, No. 1, pp. 186-214.

Blome, A. (2012), "Why (Not) Now? The Politics of Work/care Policy Reforms in Germany and Italy at the Turn of the Century", Dissertation, Humboldt University Berlin.

Blome, A. and K. Müller (2013), "Beliefs and Policy Change: Do Politics Respond to People's Attitudes? The case of work/care policies", mimeo.

Bloom, N., T. Kretschmer and J. Van Reenen (2009), "Determinants and Consequences of Family-friendly Workplace Practices – An International Study". LSE/Stanford mimeo.

BMFSFJ (2015a), "Fünfter Bericht zur Evaluation des Kinderförderungsgesetzes", German Ministry of Family, Seniors, Women and Youth, Berlin.

BMFSFJ (2015b), "Dossier Väter und Familie – erste Bilanz einer neuen Dynamik", German Ministry of Family, Seniors, Women and Youth, Berlin.

BMFSFJ (2014), "Family Report 2014 – Benefits, Effects, Trends", German Ministry of Family, Seniors, Women and Youth, Berlin.

BMFSFJ (2007), "Machbarkeitsstudie Gender Budgeting auf Bundesebene", German Ministry of Family, Seniors, Women and Youth, Berlin.

BMFSFJ (2006), "Familie zwischen Flexibilität und Verlässlichkeit – Perspektiven für eine lebenslaufbezogene Familienpolitik. Siebter Familienbericht", German Ministry of Family, Seniors, Women and Youth, Berlin.

BMWi (2015), "Mindestlohn: Bisher keine Nebenwirkungen! ", *Monthly Report*, German Federal Ministry for Economic Affairs and Energy, pp. 13-18, December.

Bossler, M.a nd H. Gerner (2016), "Employment Effects of the New German Minimum Wage – Evidence from Establishment-level Micro Data", *IAB-Discussion Paper*, No. 10/2016, Nürnberg.

Bouysse, V., P. Claus and C. Szymankiewicz (2011), *L'école maternelle : Rapport à monsieur le ministre de l'Éducation nationale, de la Jeunesse et de la Vie associative,* Inspection générale de l'administration de l'éducation nationale, Rapport N° 2011-108, ttp://media.education.gouv.fr/file/2011/54/5/2011-108-IGEN-IGAENR_215545.pdf.

Camehl, G. et al. (2015), "Höhere Qualität und geringere Kosten von Kindertageseinrichtungen - zufriedenere Eltern? ", *DIW Wochenbericht*, No. 46, pp. 1105-1113.

Ciccia, R. and I. Bleijenbergh (2014), "After the Male Breadwinner Model? Childcare Services and the Division of Labor in European Countries", *Social Politics*, Vol. 21, No. 1.

City of Stockholm (2016), *Fritidshem, avgifter*, Stockholms stad, Stockholm, http://www.stockholm.se/ForskolaSkola/FritidshemFritidsklubb/Avgifter-for-fritidsverksamhet/.

Daly, M. (2011), "What Adult Worker Model? A Critical Look at Recent Social Policy Reform in Europe from a Gender and Family Perspective", *Social Politics*, Vol. 18, No. 1.

Destatis – German Statistical Office (2016a), "Atypische Beschäftigung – Erwerbstätige1 in unterschiedlichen Erwerbsformen nach soziodemografischen Merkmalen und Wirtschaftsabschnitten 2014 in 1 000", Wiesbaden, https://www.destatis.de/DE/ZahlenFakten/GesamtwirtschaftUmwelt/Arbeitsmarkt/Erwerbstaetigkeit/TabellenArbeitskraefteerhebung/AtypischeBeschaeftigung.html.

Destatis (2016b), "Öffentliche Sozialleistungen – Statistik zum Elterngeld, Beendete Leistungsbezüge für in den Jahren 2008 bis 2012 geborene Kinder", https://www.destatis.de/DE/ZahlenFakten/GesellschaftStaat/Soziales/Soziales.html.

Destatis (2015a), "Kinder und tätige Personen in Tageseinrichtungen und in öffentlich geförderter Kindertagespflege am 01.03.2015 – Bundes- und Länderergebnisse", Wiesbaden.

Destatis (2015b), "Bevölkerung Deutschlands bis 2060: 13. koordinierte Bevölkerungsvorausberechnung", Statistisches Bundesamt, Wiesbaden.

Destatis (2012), "Elterngeld – wer, wie lange und wie viel?", *Press release*, 27 June 2012, Wiesbaden, https://www.destatis.de/DE/PresseService/Presse/Pressekonferenzen/2012/Elterngeld/statement_egeler_elterngeld_PDF.pdf?__blob=publicationFile.

DIHK – Chamber of Industry and Commerce (2012), "Vereinbarkeit von Familie und Beruf: Vom 'Gedöns' zum Schlüssel gegen den Fachkräftemangel", Ergebnisse des IHK-Unternehmensbarometers, Deutsche Industrie- und Handelskammer, pp. 1-12.

DIPF – German Institute for International Educational Research (2014), *Bildungsbericht 2014*, Report commissioned by the Conference of the German Ministers for Culture of the Länder, Deutsches Institut für Internationale Pädagogische Forschung.

Directorate of Labour (2015), "Data provided by the permanent delegation of Iceland to the OECD".

Dulk, L. den et al. (2013), "National Context in Work-life Research: A Multi-level Cross-national Analysis of the Adoption of Workplace Work-life Arrangements in Europe", *European Management Journal*, Vol. 31, No. 5, pp. 478-494.

Dustmann, C. and U. Schönberg (2012), "Expansions in Maternity Leave Coverage and Children's Long-Term Outcomes", *American Economic Journal – Applied*, Vol. 4, No. 3, pp. 190-224.

Duvander, A., L. Haas and C. Hwang (2014), "Country Note – Sweden" ,in *10th International Review of Leave Policies and Related Research 2014*, London, http://www.leavenetwork.org/fileadmin/Leavenetwork/Annual_reviews/2014_annual_review_korr.pdf.

Eichhorst, W. et al. (2012), *Geringfügige Beschäftigung: Situation und Gestaltungsoptionen*, Study commissioned by the Bertelsmannstiftung, Gütersloh.

Eurofund (2015a), "Working Life Country Profiles – The Netherlands", EurWORK European Observatory of Working Life, Dublin, http://www.eurofound.europa.eu/observatories/eurwork/comparative-information/national-contributions/netherlands/netherlands-working-life-country-profile.

Eurofund (2015b), "Working Life Country Profiles – United Kingdom", EurWORK European Observatory of Working Life, Dublin, http://www.eurofound.europa.eu/observatories/eurwork/comparative-information/national-contributions/united-kingdom/united-kingdom-working-life-country-profile.

Eurofound (2015c), *Third European Company Survey – Overview report: Workplace practices – Patterns, performance and well-being*, Publications Office of the European Union, Luxembourg.

European Company Survey on Reconciliation of Work and Family Life (2010), *Final Report*.

Eurostat (2010), "European System of Integrated Social Protection Statistics (ESSPROS)".

Evertsson, M. (2014), "Gender Ideology and the Sharing of Housework and Child Care in Sweden", *Journal of Family Issues*, Vol. 35, pp. 927-949.

Ferragina, E. and M. Seeleib-Kaiser (2014), "Determinants of a Silent (R)evolution: Understanding the Expansion of Family Policy in Rich OECD Countries", *Social Politics,* Vol. 22, No. 1.

Förster, M.F. and G. Verbist (2012), "Money or Kindergarten? Distributive Effects of Cash Versus In-Kind Family Transfers for Young Children", *OECD Social, Employment and Migration Working Papers*, No. 135, OECD Publishing, Paris, http://dx.doi.org/10.1787/5k92vxbgpmnt-en.

Friedrich-Ebert-Stiftung (FES) (2015), *Arbeit – Leben – Fortschritt: Progressive Ideen für die Arbeitswelt von morgen*, Bonn.

Fuchs-Rechlin, K. et al. (2014), *Kommunale Bedarfserhebungen – Der regionalspezifische Betreuungsbedarf U3 und seine Bedingungsfaktoren*, Report for the Ministry of Family, Seniors, Women and Youth, Dortmund.

Geyer, J., P. Haan and K. Wrohlich (2015), "The Effects of Family Policy on Maternal Labor Supply: Combining Evidence from a Structural Model and a Quasi-experimental Approach", *Labour Economics*, Vol. 36, pp. 84-98.

Goodstein, J.D. (1994), "Institutional Pressure and Strategic Responsiveness: Employer Involvement in Work-family Issues", *Academy of Management Journal*, Vol. 37, pp. 350-382.

Government of the Republic of Korea (2015), "2016-2020 Plan for Ageing Society and Population", Korea.

Grunow, D. and N. Baur (2014), "The Association between Norms and Actions – The Case of Men's Participation in Housework", *Comparative Population Studies*, Vol. 39, No. 3, pp. 521-558.

Halpern, D (2005). "How Time-flexible Work Policies Can Reduce Stress, Improve Health, and Save Money", *Stress and Health*, Vol. 21, pp. 157-168.

Häusermann, S. (2006), "Changing Coalitions in Social Policy Reforms: The Politics of New Social Needs and Demands", *Journal of European Social Policy*, Vol. 16, No. 1, pp. 5-21.

Haut Conseil de la Famille (2015), "Point sur l'évolution de l'accueil des jeunes enfants", *Notes et avis*, http://www.hcf-famille.fr/spip.php?rubrique11.

Heckman, J. and D. Masterov (2007), "The Productivity Argument for Investing in Young Children", *NBER Working Paper*, No. 13016, Cambridge, United States.

Heckman J. et al. (2010), "A New Cost-benefit and Rate of Return Analysis for the Perry Preschool Program: A Summary", *IZA Discussion Paper*, No. 17, Bonn.

Henninger, A. and A. von Wahl (2010), "Das Umspielen von Veto-Spielern. Wie eine konservative Familienministerin den Familialismus des deutschen Wohlfahrtsstaates unterminiert", in C. Egle and R. Zohlnhöfer (eds.), *Die zweite Große Koalition. Eine Bilanz der Regierung Merkel 2005-2009*, VS Verlag, Wiesbaden, pp. 361-379.

Henninger, A., C. Wimbauer and R. Dombrowski (2008), "Demography as a Push toward Gender Equality? Current Reforms of German Family Policy", *Social Politics*, Vol. 15, No. 3, pp. 287-314.

Holst, E., A. Busch-Heizmann and A. Wieber (2015), "Führungskräfte-Monitor 2015: Update 2001 – 2013-2015", *DIW Berlin – Politikberatung kompakt*, No. 100.

IAB – Institut für Arbeitsmarkt- und Berufsforschung (2016), *Arbeitsmarktspiegel: Entwicklungen nach Einführung des Mindestlohns (Ausgabe 1)*, Institut für Arbeitsmarkt-und Berufsforschung (IAB), Nürnberg.

IAQ – Institut für Qualifikation und Arbeit (2016a), *Geringfügig Hauptbeschäftigte, 2003-2015 – Absolut und Altersstruktur in %,* Duisburg-Essen, http://www.sozialpolitik-aktuell.de/tl_files/sozialpolitik-aktuell/_Politikfelder/Arbeitsmarkt/Datensammlung/PDF-Dateien/abbIV67a.pdf.

IAQ (2016b), *Trotz Mindestlohn: Ungebrochener Anstieg der geringfügigen Nebenbeschäftigung,* Duisburg-Essen, http://www.sozialpolitik-aktuell.de/tl_files/sozialpolitik-aktuell/_Politikfelder/Arbeitsmarkt/Datensammlung/PDF-Dateien/abbIV67b_Grafik_Monat_04_2016.pdf.

Immervoll, H. et al. (2009), "An Evaluation of the Tax-Transfer Treatment of Married Couples in European Countries", *OECD Social, Employment and Migration Working Papers*, No. 76, OECD Publishing, Paris, http://dx.doi.org/10.1787/227200406151.

Ingram, P. and T. Simons (1995), "Institutional and Resource Dependence Determinants of Responsiveness to Work-family Issues", *Academy of Management Journal*, Vol. 38, pp. 1466-1482.

Kamerman, S. and A. Kahn (1991), "Child Care, Parental Leave and the Under 3s: Policy Innovation in Europe", Auburn House, New York.

Kamerman, S.B. and P. Moss (eds.) (2009), *The Politics of Parental Leave Policy: Children, Parenting, Gender and the Labour Market*, The Policy Press, Bristol.

Kearney, A.T. (2015), "Vereinbarkeit wagen! Ergebnisse der dritten 361°A.T. Kearney-Familienstudie".

Klemm, K. (2013), *Ganztagsschulen in Deutschland – eine bildungsstatistische Analyse*, Report commissioned by the Bertelsmann Foundation.

Klemm, K. and D. Zorn (2016), *Die landesseitige Ausstattung gebundener Ganztagsschulen mit personellen Ressourcen, Ein Bundesländervergleich*, Report commissioned by the Bertelsmann Foundation.

Kluve, J. and S. Schmitz (2014), "Mittelfristige Effekte der Elterngeldreform in Ost- und Westdeutschland", *Vierteljahrshefte zur Wirtschaftsforschung*, Vol. 83, No. 4, pp. 163-81.

Korthouwer, G. (2010), "Party Politics as We Knew It? Failure to Dominate Government, Intraparty Dynamics and Welfare Reforms in Continental Europe", Amsterdam Institute for Social Science Research (AISSR).

Krebs, T. and M. Scheffel (2016), "Structural Reform in Germany", *IMF Working Paper*, No. 16/96.

Kremer, M. (2006), "The Politics of Ideals of Care: Danish and Flemish Child Care Policy Compared", *Social Politics*, Vol. 13, No. 2, pp. 261-285.

Leitner, S. (2010), "Germany Outpaces Austria in Childcare Policy: The Historical Contingencies of 'Conservative' Childcare Policy", *Journal of European Social Policy*, Vol. 20, No. 5, pp. 456-467.

Lundberg, S. and R. Pollak (1996), "Bargaining and Distribution in Marriage", *Journal of Economic Perspectives*, Vol. 10, No. 4, pp. 139-158.

McGinn, K., M. Ruiz Castro and E. Long Lingo (2015), "Mum's the Word! Cross-national Effects of Maternal Employment on Gender Inequalities at Work and at Home", *Harvard Business School Working Paper*, No. 15-094.

Merz, M. (2004), "Women's Hours of Market Work in Germany: The Role of Parental Leave", *IZA Discussion Paper*, No. 1288, Bonn.

Mischke, M. (2014), "Public Attitudes toward Family Policies in Europe. Linking Institutional Context and Public Opinion", Springer VS, Wiesbaden.

Morgan, K. (2013), "Path Shifting of the Welfare State: Electoral Competition and the Expansion of Work-Family Policies in Western Europe", *World Politics*, Vol. 65, No. 1, pp. 73-115.

Moss, P. (2015), *International Leave Policies and Related Research 2015*, http://www.leavenetwork.org/lp_and_r_reports.

Moss, P. and M. Korintus (eds.) (2008), "International Review of Leave Policies and Related Research", Department for Business Enterprise and Regulatory Reform, *Employment Relations Research*, Series No. 100.

Müller, K., M. Neumann and K. Wrohlich (2015a), "Familienarbeitszeit Reloaded: Vereinfachung durch pauschalierte Leistung und Flexibilisierung durch Arbeitszeitkorridor", *DIW Berlin – Politikberatung kompakt*, No. 105.

Müller, K., M. Neumann and K. Wrohlich (2015b), "Labor Supply Under Participation and Hours Constraints", mimeo, DIW Berlin (forthcoming).

Müller, K., M. Neumann and K. Wrohlich (2013), "Familienarbeitszeit – Wirkungen und Kosten einer Lohnersatzleistung bei reduzierter Vollzeitbeschäftigung", Friedrich-EbertStiftung, Forum Politik und Gesellschaft, Berlin.

NOSOSCO – Nordic Social Statistical Committee (2015), *Social Protection in Nordic Countries 2012/2013*, Nordic Social Statistical Committee, Denmark.

OECD (2016a), *Taxing Wages 2016*, OECD Publishing, Paris, http://dx.doi.org/10.1787/tax_wages-2016-en.

OECD (2016b), *OECD Economic Surveys: Germany 2016*, OECD Publishing, Paris, http://dx.doi.org/10.1787/eco_surveys-deu-2016-en.

OECD (2015a), *In It Together: Why Less Inequality Benefits All*, OECD Publishing, Paris, http://dx.doi.org/10.1787/9789264235120-en.

OECD (2015b), *Education at a Glance 2015: OECD Indicators*, OECD Publishing, Paris, http://dx.doi.org/10.1787/eag-2015-e.n

OECD (2015c), *OECD Employment Outlook 2015*, OECD Publishing, Paris, http://dx.doi.org/10.1787/empl_outlook-2015-en.

OECD (2015d), "Gender Wage Gaps and Work Incentives", Report commissioned by the European Union.

OECD (2015e), "Can Mothers Afford to Work", Report commissioned by the European Union, mimeo.

OECD (2015f), *OECD Family Database*, OECD, Paris, http://www.oecd.org/social/family/database.htm.

OECD (2015g), *Starting Strong IV: Monitoring Quality in Early Childhood Education and Care*, OECD Publishing, Paris, http://dx.doi.org/10.1787/9789264233515-en.

OECD (2015h), *OECD Social Expenditure Database (SOCX)*, OECD, Paris, www.oecd.org/social/expenditure.htm.

OECD (2014), *Society at a Glance 2014: OECD Social Indicators*, OECD Publishing, Paris, http://dx.doi.org/10.1787/soc_glance-2014-en.

OECD (2013a), "Recommendation of the Council on Gender Equality in Education, Employment, and Entrepreneurship", Document adopted at the Meeting of the OECD Council at Ministerial Level, 29 may 2013, http://www.oecd.org/gender/C-MIN(2013)5-ENG.pdf.

OECD (2013b), *PISA 2012 Results: Excellence through Equity: Giving Every Student the Chance to Succeed,* OECD Publishing, Paris, http://dx.doi.org/10.1787/9789264201132-en.

OECD (2012a), *Closing the Gender Gap: Act Now*, OECD Publishing, Paris, http://dx.doi.org/10.1787/9789264179370-en.

OECD (2012b), "Social Spending during the Crisis – Social Expenditure (SOCX) Data Update 2012", http://www.oecd.org/els/soc/OECD2012SocialSpendingDuringTheCrisis8pages.pdf.

OECD (2011a), "Findings from the Gender Equality Module of the 2011 Paris Declaration Monitoring Survey", OECD Publishing, Paris, available at www.oecd.org/dac/gender.

OECD (2011b), "Survey on National Gender Frameworks, Gender Public Policies and Leadership", Developed by the MENA-OECD Governance Programme, OECD Publishing, Paris.

OECD (2011c), *Doing Better for Families*, OECD Publishing, Paris, http://dx.doi.org/10.1787/9789264098732-en.

OECD (2011b), *Help Wanted? Providing and Paying for Long-Term Care*, OECD Health Policy Studies, OECD Publishing, Paris, http://dx.doi.org/10.1787/9789264097759-en.

OECD (2010), "Progress in Public Management in the Middle East and North Africa. Case Studies on Policy Reform", OECD Publishing, Paris, http://dx.doi.org/10.1787/9789264082076-en.

OECD (2009), *Doing Better for Children*, OECD Publishing, Paris, http://dx.doi.org/10.1787/empl_outlook-2010-en.

OECD (2007a), *Babies and Bosses – Reconciling Work and Family Life: A Synthesis of Findings for OECD Countries*, OECD Publishing, Paris, http://dx.doi.org/10.1787/9789264032477-en.

OECD (2007b), "Can Parents Afford to Work? Childcare Costs, Tax-Benefit Policies and Work Incentives", Chapter 4 of Benefits and Wages: OECD Indicators, OECD Publishing, Paris, http://dx.doi.org/10.1787/ben_wages-2007-en.

OECD (2005), *Babies and Bosses – Reconciling Work and Family Life (Vol. 4): Canada, Finland, Sweden and the United Kingdom*, OECD Publishing, Paris, http://dx.doi.org/10.1787/9789264009295-en.

OECD (2002), *Babies and Bosses – Reconciling Work and Family Life (Vol. 2), Austria, Ireland and Japan*, OECD Publishing, Paris, http://dx.doi.org/10.1787/9789264104204-en.

Oliver, R. and M. Mätzke (2014), "Childcare Expansion in Conservative Welfare States: Policy Legacies and the Politics of Decentralized Implementation in Germany and Italy", *Social Politics*, Vol. 21, No. 2.

ONPE – Observatoire National de la Petite Enfance (2012), *L'accueil du jeune enfant en 2012*, France.

Pfau-Effinger, B. (2004), "Development of Culture, Welfare State and Women's Employment in Europe", Ashgate, Aldershot.

Poortman, A. and T. Van der Lippe (2009), "Attitudes toward Housework and Child Care and the Gendered Division of Labor", *Journal of Marriage and Family*, Vol. 71, No. 3, pp. 526-541.

Prognos (2014), *Gesamtevaluation der ehe- und familienbezogenen Maßnahmen und Leistungen in Deutschland – Endbericht*, report commissioned by the German Ministries of Finance and Families, Seniors, Women and Youth, Berlin.

Rastrigina, O. and A. Verashchagina (2015), "Secondary Earners and Fiscal Policies in Europe", Report to the European Commission, Directorate-General Justice and Consumers.

Regeringskansliet (2016), *Slopad jämställdhetsbonus*, Socialdepartementet, Stockholm.

Rüling, A. (2010), "Re-framing of Childcare in Germany and England: From a Private Responsibility to an Economic Necessity", *German Policy Studies*, Vol. 6, No. 2, pp. 153-186.

Sautory O., V. Biausque and J. Vidalenc (2011), "Le temps périscolaire et les contraintes professionelles des parents", *INSEE Première*, No. 1370, Paris.

Saxonberg, S. (2014), *Gendering Family Policies in Post-Communist Europe – A Historical-Institutional Analysis*, Palgrave Macmillan.

SCB – Statistics Sweden (2014), "Statistisk årsbok för Sverige 2014", SCB, Stockholm.

Schober, P. (2011), "The Parenthood Effect on Gender Inequality. Explaining the Change in Paid and Domestic Work When British Couples Become Parents", *European Sociological Review*, Vol. 29, No. 1, pp. 74-85.

Schröder, C., K. Spieß and J. Storck (2015), "Private Bildungsausgaben für Kinder: Einkommensschwache Familien sind relativ stärker belastet?", *DIW Wochenbericht*, No. 8, pp. 158-169.

Seeleib-Kaiser, M. and T. Toivonen (2011), "Between Reforms and Birth Rates: Germany, Japan, and Family Policy Discourse", *Social Politics: International Studies in Gender, State & Society*, Vol. 18, No. 3, pp. 331-360.

Skolverket (2016), *Elever och grupper i fritidshem 14 oktober 2014,* Swedish National Agency for Education, Stockholm, http://www.skolverket.se/statistik-och-utvardering/statistik-i-tabeller/fritidshem/elever-och-grupper.

Skolverket (2015), *Statistik om förskolan,* Swedish National Agency for Education, Stockholm, http://www.skolverket.se/statistik-och-utvardering/statistik-i-tabeller/forskola.

Spangenberg, U. (2005), "Neuorientierung der Ehebesteuerung: Ehegattensplitting und Lohnsteuerverfahren", *Hans-Böckler-Stiftung Working Paper*, No. 106.

Stadt Freiburg (2008), "Gender Budgeting", developed by Geschäftsstelle Gleichstellung of the City of Freiburg.

Weckström, S. (2014), "Defamilialisation Policies and Attitudes and Behaviour among Mothers in Twelve European Countries. Do Results for Denmark, Finland and Sweden Differ from the Others?", *Finnish Yearbook of Population Research*, XLIX, pp. 5-29.

ZEW – Zentrum für Europäische Wirtschaftsforschung and FFP – Forschungszentrum Familienbewusste Personalpolitik (2013), *Evaluation zentraler ehe- und familienbezogener Leistungen in Deutschland*, report commissioned by Prognos AG, Mannheim.

Annex 3.A1

Tax-benefit models: Methodology and limitations

OECD tax-benefit models calculate tax burdens, benefit entitlements and net incomes for a range of different labour market and household situations. They simulate assessments of different families' tax liabilities and benefit entitlements using a detailed representation of relevant policy rules and parameters (including tax rates, benefit eligibility criteria, and any rules determining the interaction of relevant policy areas, such as whether some benefits are taxable or not). On the tax side, simulated payments include income taxes and mandatory contributions to public or private social insurance schemes. On the benefit side, calculations account for all cash transfers that are typically available to able-bodied working-age individuals and their families: unemployment benefits, social assistance, housing benefits for rented accommodation, other minimum-income benefits, family benefits, and in-work transfers.

The tax-benefit models are regularly used to produce a range of indicators for policy monitoring and analysis. They include work-incentive measures (e.g. marginal effective tax rates) and indicators of income adequacy (e.g. the net income of benefit recipients or low-wage workers relative to commonly used poverty thresholds). Further information on the OECD's tax-benefit models can be found at http://www.oecd.org/els/soc/benefits-and-wages.htm.

For the present analysis, a number of specific methodological choices have or have not been made. The most important choices are:

- Calculated net incomes are shown for the period of reference (thus for 2013). They do not, therefore, account for any longer-term income gains resulting, for example, from improved future career opportunities or the build-up of pension. Such longer-term considerations, as well as the intrinsic and non-monetary benefits of employment, can lead individuals to work even if employment brings little or no short-term economic advantage.
- At the same time, work-related costs, such as commuting, or the opportunity costs of time spent at work (rather than parenting at home or enjoying leisure time, for example) are not taken into account in the calculations reported here.
- The availability of child care and child care costs are not considered here.
- For simplicity, the discussion refers to married couples, although many countries treat registered partnerships on the same footing as married couples for tax and benefit purposes.

Whether the model-based current-period gains from work under- or overstate family's perceptions of gains depends on household attributes and individual preferences.

Figure 3.A1.1. Net transfers to government in different couple-family earnings combinations at 200% of the average wage

Net transfers to government as a percentage of gross household earnings and the proportional difference in household net income for a dual-earner couple with both earning 100% of the average wage and a single-earner couple with 200% of the average wage, families with two children (aged 4 and 6)

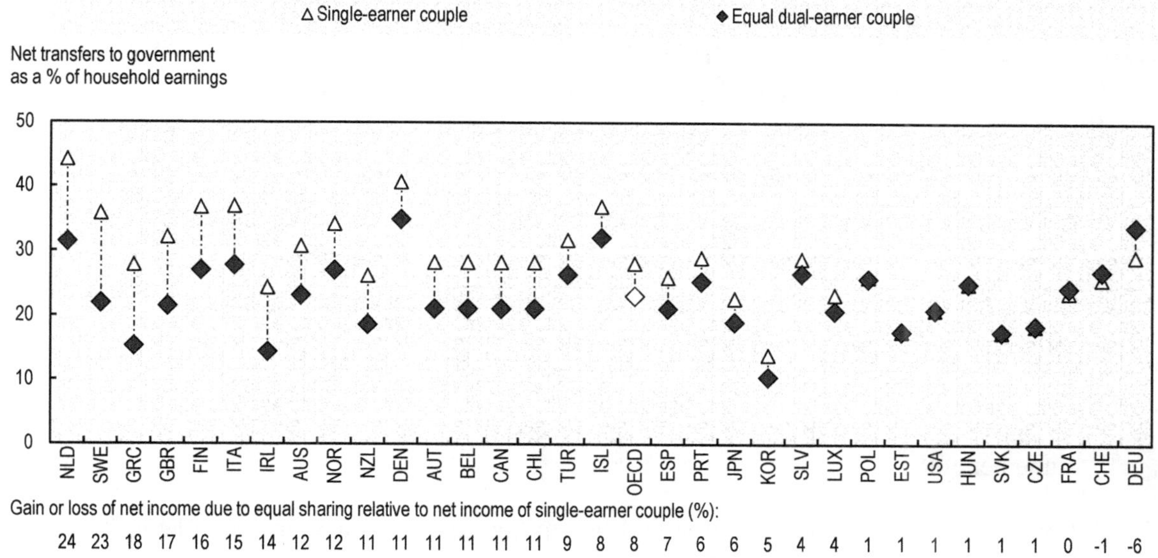

1. Countries are ranked in ascending order of the differences in net income of dual-earner and single-earner couple households as percentages of the net income of single-earner couples – see values listed at bottom of figure.

2. "Net transfers" refers to what households pay the government in taxes and contributions minus the benefits received. The white triangle refers to a household where the primary earner has work income of 133% of the average wage. The dark diamond refers to a household where both partners earn 67% of the average wage, so that household income adds up to 134%.

3. Refer to OECD (2016a) for a definition of the average wage (AW).

Source: OECD, "Tax and Benefit Systems: OECD Indicators", www.oecd.org/els/soc/benefits-and-wages.htm.

Annex 3.A2

Estimating the effects of a hypothetical "family-working time" scheme on the size of the German labour force

To examine the potential impact of a hypothetical "family working-time scheme" on German labour supply, research produced for this report estimated:

- the number of employees in Germany who may, on certain assumptions, be eligible for the family working-time benefit;
- the effect on the size of the German labour force if all the potentially eligible employees adopted the working hours necessary to claim the family working-time benefit.

The number of employees who would be entitled to family working-time benefit was estimated using data from the 2012 European Union Labour Force Survey (EU LFS) and the policy parameters and assumptions proposed by Müller et al. (2013, 2015). Estimates were specifically based on the following two entitlement criteria:

- Eligibility for the benefit is limited to employed parents who either live in a dual-earner couple or are a single parent.
- The benefit can be claimed for a duration of up to three years per child.

For the sake of simplicity, the following two assumptions were also made:

- All potentially eligible employees and, where relevant, their partners choose to adopt the hours required to be eligible for the benefit.
- All potentially eligible employees choose to use their entire three-year entitlement immediately on expiry of paid parental leave. In other words, they use the benefit in its entirety when the child in question is between 1 and 3 years old. In effect, and assuming that no individuals have more than one child aged between 1 and 3 years at any one time, this further limits eligibility only to individuals with a child aged between 1 and 3 years old.

Because the EU LFS questions households, the assessment of the employees who met all the required criteria was based entirely on the age of the children and the employment status of the partners who were recorded as living in the same household. The eligible population was estimated as the number of individuals who:

a) were employed;

b) lived in a household with a youngest child aged between 1 and 3 years;

c) either lived in the same household as an employed partner (i.e. were a part of a dual-earner couple) or did not have a partner living in the same household (i.e. were considered a single parent).

Table 3.A2.1 shows, by gender and broad age group, the resulting estimates of potentially eligible employees and their actual average usual weekly working hours. Given the assumptions, a total of just over 1 722 000 individuals were estimated as potentially eligible for the family working-time benefit: men accounted for around 814 000 of them, and women just under 908 000. Almost all the potentially eligible employees were aged between 25 and 54 years old, with only around 48 000 in the 15-to-24 year-old age group and less than 4 000 in the 55-to-64 year-old bracket. Among the potentially eligible employees, the men were actually working 41.7 average usual working hours per week and the women 24.9.

Table 3.A2.1. Summary of the number of German employees potentially eligible for the family working-time benefit and average working hours among those potentially eligible employees

Estimated number of employees (15-to-64 year-olds) potentially eligible for the family working-time benefit as proposed by Müller et al. (2015) and average usual weekly working hours of those potentially eligible employees, by gender and broad age group, 2012

	Men		Women	
Age group	Number of potentially eligible employees	Average usual weekly working hours	Number of potentially eligible employees	Average usual weekly working hours
15-24	9227	39.6	38796	27.0
25-54	801563	41.7	868877	24.8
55-64	3138	41.3	512	26.6
Total	813928	41.7	908185	24.9

Note: Eligibility for the proposed family working-time benefit is based on the criteria set out by Müller et al. (2013, 2015) – i.e. eligibility is restricted to employed parents living either in a dual-earner couple or as a single parent, with the entitlement lasting for three years per child and assumed to be taken when the child is between 12 and 48 months old. The numbers shown in the table reflect the number of people who: a) are employed; b) live in a household with a youngest child aged between 1 and 3 years old; and c) either live in the same household as an employed partner (i.e. are a part of a dual-earner couple) or do not have a partner living in the same household (i.e. are considered a single parent).

Source: OECD estimates based on the 2012 European Union Labour Force Survey.

The potential impact on the projected size of the German full-time equivalent (FTE) labour force (15-to-74 year-olds) of these employees adopting family working-time hours was estimated using the OECD's in-house labour force projection model. It is a dynamic model that projects (by gender and five-year age group) the size of the labour force over a given time frame, based on given assumptions about trends and changes in labour force participation rates and working hours. The size of the labour force was estimated according to two different scenarios:

- *The Baseline scenario*. The labour force participation rates of German men and women of all ages were estimated using a dynamic age-cohort model that projects participation rates by gender and by five-year age group based on current (2003-12) rates of labour market entry and exit. The average usual weekly working hours of each gender and five-year age group were held constant at their 2012 values.

- The *Baseline with family-working-time scenario.* As in the baseline scenario, the labour force participation rates of men and women of all ages were estimated using a dynamic age-cohort model that projects participation rates by gender and by five-year age group based on current (2003-12) rates of labour market entry and exit. Average usual weekly working hours, however, were adjusted by gender and five-year age group on the assumption that, by 2025 and with linear adjustment, any and all employees who were potentially eligible for the family working-time benefit would adopt usual weekly working hours equal to 32 hours per week, the upper limit of the family working-time corridor proposed by Müller et al. (2015). Because estimates of the number of workers likely to be eligible for the family working-time benefit in future years were not available, it was assumed that (for each gender and five-year age group) the proportion of potentially eligible employees remained constant at 2012 levels across the entire projection period.

For both scenarios the headcount labour force was calculated first using population projections from Destatis (2015b) and the assumed labour force participation rates (identical in both scenarios). The headcount was then converted (by gender and five-year age group) into the full-time equivalent using the assumed values for average usual weekly working hours. "Full-time" in this instance refers to usual weekly working hours equal to 40 hours per week, so the FTE labour force was calculated as the headcount labour force multiplied by the usual weekly working hours of the relevant group, divided by 40. Figure 3.A2.1 shows the resulting estimates for the projected size of the German full-time equivalent labour force (15-74 year-olds).

Estimates of the size of the labour force produced under the Baseline with family working-time scenario are merely mechanical adjustments insofar as they assume any change in weekly working hours driven by family working time does not interact with, or have any indirect effect on, labour participation rates or working hours among those who are not eligible for the benefit. It is possible that a family working-time policy could have effects that go beyond the working hours of those immediately eligible if, for example, it encouraged changes in working hours among those who had previously used the benefit but were no longer eligible. To the extent that any family working time would, or could, have any such indirect effect, the actual impact of a family working-time policy on German labour supply may differ from the effects estimated under the baseline with family working-time scenario.

Figure 3.A2.1. Under certain assumptions, a family working-time model would do little or no damage to the size of the German labour force

Projected size of the total full-time equivalent labour force (15-to-74 year-olds) under different scenarios, 2012-40[1]

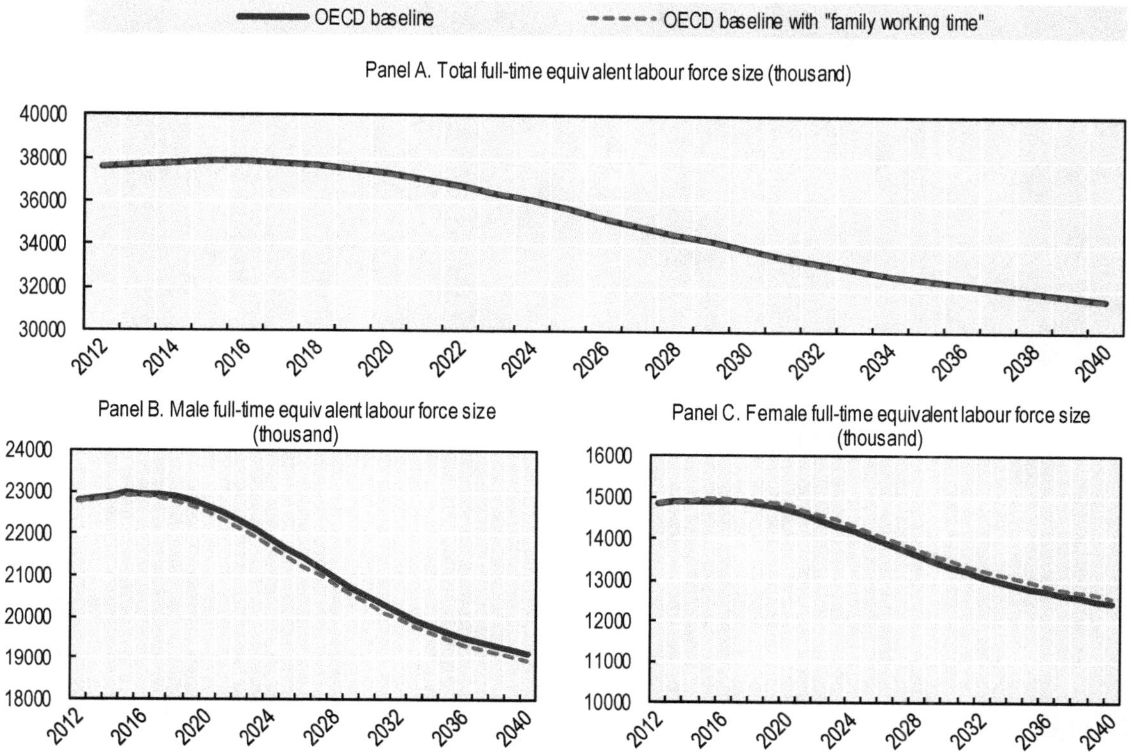

1. Projections of the number of workers that are likely to be eligible for the family working-time benefit in future years are not available. The projection here assumes that the proportion who are potentially eligible remains constant at 2012 levels across the projection period. It also assumes that the adoption of family working-time hours does not have any indirect effect either on labour participation rates or on working hours among who that are not eligible for the benefit.

Source: OECD estimates based on the OECD population data, population projections from Destatis (2015c), the *OECD Employment Database*, http://www.oecd.org/employment/emp/onlineoecdemploymentdatabase.htm, and the 2012 European Union Labour Force Survey.

Chapter 4

Earning and working unequally: Partnered parents in paid work

This chapter focuses on gender inequality in paid work. The chapter looks first at the working weeks of men and women of different ages across the OECD. It then focuses on German parents to find that German women are more likely to work part-time and shorter part-time hours than in OECD countries. And when they do work full-time, their hours – and those of their male partners – are quite long. As a rule, though, German mothers in employment work short part-time hours, while fathers work long full-time hours. On average German mothers and fathers do not share paid work equally. As a result, mothers contribute less than fathers to household income. Accordingly, the wide gaps in earnings and working hours are the main subject of the next section. The last section analyses why some mothers work part-time and some full-time. It factors into its analysis mothers' levels of educational attainment, the number of children they have, how old they are, and the earnings and working hours of their partners. The chapter calls for policies that support the work-life balance and sustain birth rates, female employment, and more equally shared paid work.

The statistical data for Israel are supplied by and under the responsibility of the relevant Israeli authorities. The use of such data by the OECD is without prejudice to the status of the Golan Heights, East Jerusalem and Israeli settlements in the West Bank under the terms of international law.

1. Introduction and main findings

The equal access of fathers and mothers to paid work, working hours, and earnings is central to promoting equal partnerships in families. While working fathers and mothers are good role models for boys and girls (Chapter 2), parents who share paid work more equally find it easier to share more equally sharing at home and have more time with each other and for the family. A more equal sharing of paid work also enables both partners to pursue their individual labour market aspirations, enhancing their self-sufficiency, and reducing the risk of poverty in the event of divorce or in old age, when the other partner passes away. Equality of access to paid work also fosters fairer decision making in couples and contributes to overall family well-being.

However, mothers OECD-wide struggle to contribute equally to household income. In Germany, as in other OECD countries, few parents[1] share paid work equally and full-time employees, be they men or women, often work longer than 40 hours per week.[2] Such long hours complicate mothers' efforts to combine full-time work with parenting, an issue that is exacerbated in Germany by the relatively short days in pre-, primary and secondary school (Chapter 3). In part for that reason, German mothers who work part-time work shorter hours than in other countries and they face difficulties to revert to full-time work as their children get older. As for their male partners, their long hours curtails the time that they spend with their families and the amount of unpaid work that they do at home. All these factors contribute to a relatively wide gender gap in working hours and earnings among German couples with children. There need to be institutional changes in the provision of care for young and school-aged children, cultural changes and changes in the labour market, if German women are to have the opportunity to increase their working hours and/or participate in full-time work.

The chapter starts with a descriptive look at men's and women's paid work arrangements across the OECD. It finds that German women are more likely to work part-time than women in most other OECD countries, and that Germany has large within-couple gaps in working hours and earnings. The final section explores why some mothers works full-time and some part-time, using a regression analysis of the contributory factors and focusing on mothers' education, the number and ages of their children, and the earnings and working hours of their partners.

Main findings

- The average gender gap in working hours and earnings from (self-)employment within couples with at least one child is high in Germany in comparison to all other European countries and the United States. In Germany the gap in working hours and earnings opens up as women become mothers and often reduce working hours or become inactive on the labour market.
- Few parents share working hours equally across OECD countries. Work arrangements with both partners working reduced full-time working hours (here defined as between 30 and 39 hours/week) are most prevalent in Denmark, Norway, France and Finland. In Germany the main earner model with the man working full-time and the woman working part-time (1 to 29 hours per week) is the most common arrangement among couples with children. In most Eastern

European countries, both parents working full-time is the prevailing pattern for couples with children.

- Part-time work for partnered mothers in Germany but also in Austria and Switzerland means fewer hours in paid employment than in other countries. A German part-time employed partnered mother works about 20 hours per week on average, while a partnered mother in part-time work in Nordic countries or France often averages 30 hours per week. The main reason for part-time working partnered mothers in Germany to not work full-time is housework and care responsibilities at home.
- For full-time (40 hours or more per week) working mothers, weekly working hours are highest in Austria, Switzerland and Germany while they are relatively low in France and the Nordic countries. By contrast, the majority of partnered mothers work between 35 and 39 hours in Denmark, Finland, France and Norway. In Iceland and Sweden as well as in the United States, most partnered mothers work between 40 and 44 hours per week.
- German partnered fathers also have relatively long weekly working hours compared to their peers in other OECD countries. By comparison, in most Nordic countries fathers have relatively short weekly working hours.
- In some European countries – particular those where many women work part-time on a long-term basis – mothers are less likely to work full-time if their partner has relative high earnings. In these countries many mothers appear to reduce working hours once the household can afford it.
- Unequal sharing has long-run implications for career progression and self-sufficiency and contributes to significant gender wage gaps and, in the long run, to gender pension gaps across the OECD.

2. Coupled parents' working-hour patterns vary across the OECD

Across the OECD, women are less likely to be in paid work than men, and female employment rates are on average 12 percentage points below men's (Figure 4.1). Compared to women elsewhere in the OECD, German women have made considerable progress in entering the labour market over the past decade and Germany now has the highest female employment rate in the OECD after the Nordics and Switzerland (Chapter 2). Between 2000 and 2014, employment rates among 15-to-64 year-old German women increased by over 11 percentage points, from 58.1% to 69.5%. Germany boasted the second-largest increase in female employment in the OECD over that period, second only to Chile.

However, examination of working hours reveals starker gender differences. The OECD-wide gender gap in full-time employment rates was 22.4 percentage points in 2013, with the gap in Germany slightly wider at 24.6 percentage points (Figure 4.1). The implication is that, more than elsewhere in the OECD, German women work short paid hours per week.

In line with the general trend across the OECD (Chapter 2), dual-earner households have become commonplace in Germany: they account for 64% of German families with children under the age of 14. However, in keeping with the high incidence of part-time work among German women, most dual-earning families are in fact "one-and-a-half" or "one-and-a-quarter" earners, with men working long full-time hours and their female partners short part-time hours and, therefore, contributing relatively little to household income.

Figure 4.1. German gender gaps in employment are narrower than the OECD average, but not when working hours are taken into consideration

Gender gaps in employment rates and full-time equivalent employment rates,[1] 15-to-64 year-olds, 2014

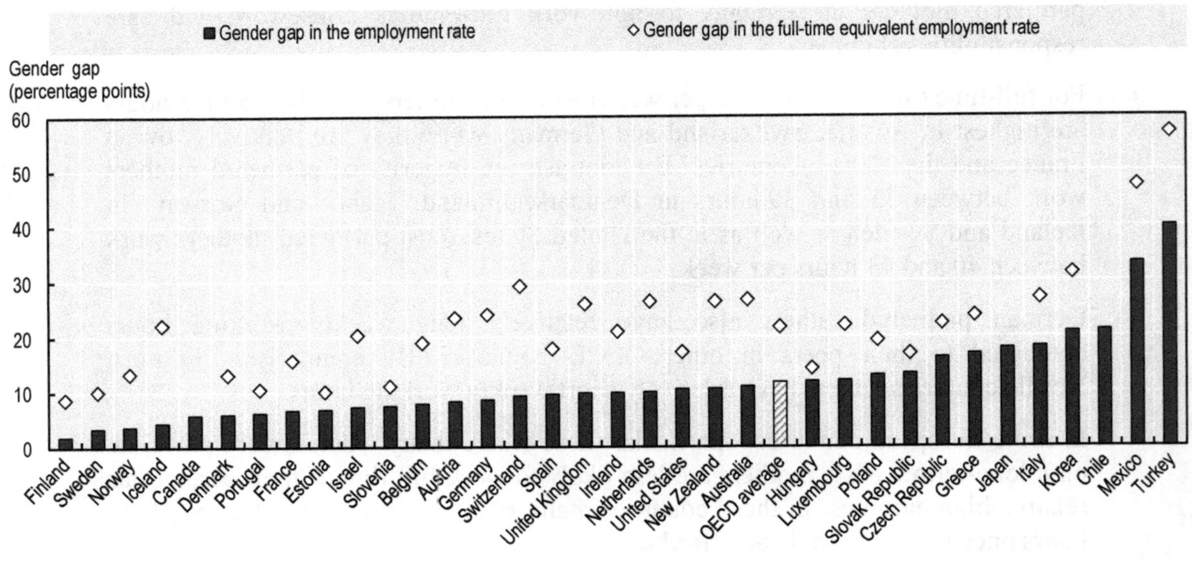

1. The full-time equivalent employment rate is calculated as the employment rate among 15-to-64 year-olds multiplied by the average usual hours worked per week per person in employment (both dependent and self-employment) and divided by 40. For the United States, the full-time equivalent is calculated from usual working hours for dependent employees only. For Korea, data reflect actual rather than usual weekly working hours.

Source: OECD Employment Database, http://www.oecd.org/employment/emp/onlineoecdemploymentdatabase.htm.

German women are more likely to work part-time than women elsewhere

In Germany, reduced weekly working hours are common among women, regardless of their age. Most men work full-time. Some other European countries show similar patterns but, in most of them, the gender gap in working hours is much narrower. In all European countries – except, to a certain extent, the Netherlands (see Box 5.3 in Chapter 5) – and in the United States, working full-time is the norm among men of all ages. When it comes to women, though, the picture is much more mixed, as examination of the variety of working arrangements for men and women in selected OECD countries.

Broadly speaking, European countries can be divided into four groups according to women's employment arrangements:[3]

1. *Women in long-term part-time work.* Countries in which women work far fewer hours per week than men, regardless of their age, chiefly because they work in part-time jobs.

   Countries are Austria, Belgium, Germany, Ireland, Luxembourg, the Netherlands, Switzerland and the United Kingdom.[4]

2. *Polarised female labour force participation.* Countries in which women either work full-time or are inactive, regardless of their age.

   Countries are Italy, Greece, Spain, Portugal, Lithuania, Poland and Slovenia.[5]

3. *Women in short-term inactivity.* Countries in which women resume full-time work after a period of inactivity.

   Countries are the Czech Republic, Estonia, Finland, Hungary, Latvia and the Slovak Republic.[6]

4. *Narrow gender gap in working hours.* Countries with a persistent but relatively narrow gender gap in working hours.

   Countries are Denmark, France, Iceland, Norway and Sweden.[7]

Figures 4.2 and 4.3 illustrate the labour force patterns of men and women at different ages in the four country groups, taking one country as an example of each group.

Germany is clearly part of Country Group 1, "Women in long-term part-time work", with a high proportion of women working part-time, especially from the age of 30 on. The share of German women working part-time increases across age-group and remains substantial in the oldest age brackets. The gender gap in working hours for the active working-age population (Figure 4.3, left-hand panel) and the whole population (Figure 4.3, right-hand panel) confirm this pattern. Even though Figures 4.2 and 4.3 take a cross-sectional perspective and consider women of different ages only in a given year, the implication is that once women in Germany work part-time they do not resume full-time employment. Indeed, they appear to be stuck in a "part-time trap".

Italy exemplifies Country Group 2, "polarised female labour force participation", where women either work full-time or not at all (inactive or unemployed) and part-time work is less widespread than in Country Group 1 (Figure 4.2). Inactivity is widespread, particularly among older women, suggesting that once they are out of employment it is difficult to return to work. Figure 4.3 shows a correspondingly wide gender gap in working hours across all ages in the overall working-age population (right-hand panel). However, as women who participate in the labour market mostly work full-time, the working hours gender gap in the active population is narrower than in Country Group 1. Inactivity is somewhat less widespread among women aged 40 and over in the second group's Eastern European countries (Lithuania, Poland and Slovenia) than in the Southern European ones (Portugal, Spain and Greece). Unemployment is nevertheless high in those countries and seems frequently to result in early retirement.

The Czech Republic belongs to Country Group 3, "women in short-term inactivity", where the age profile suggests that women resume full-time work after a period of inactivity. Figure 4.2 shows high rates of inactivity only among younger women, while most of those aged 40 and over work full-time. As a consequence, the gender gap in working hours is narrow in all age brackets in the active population (Figure 4.3, left-hand panel). As for the population of working age, the gender gap in working hours is significantly narrower among older age groups, as many women have switched from inactivity to full-time work (Figure 4.3, right-hand panel).

Figure 4.2. Women rather than men adapt their working hours over the life course

Distribution of the population by self-defined labour market status, by gender and five-year age group, four example countries, 2012

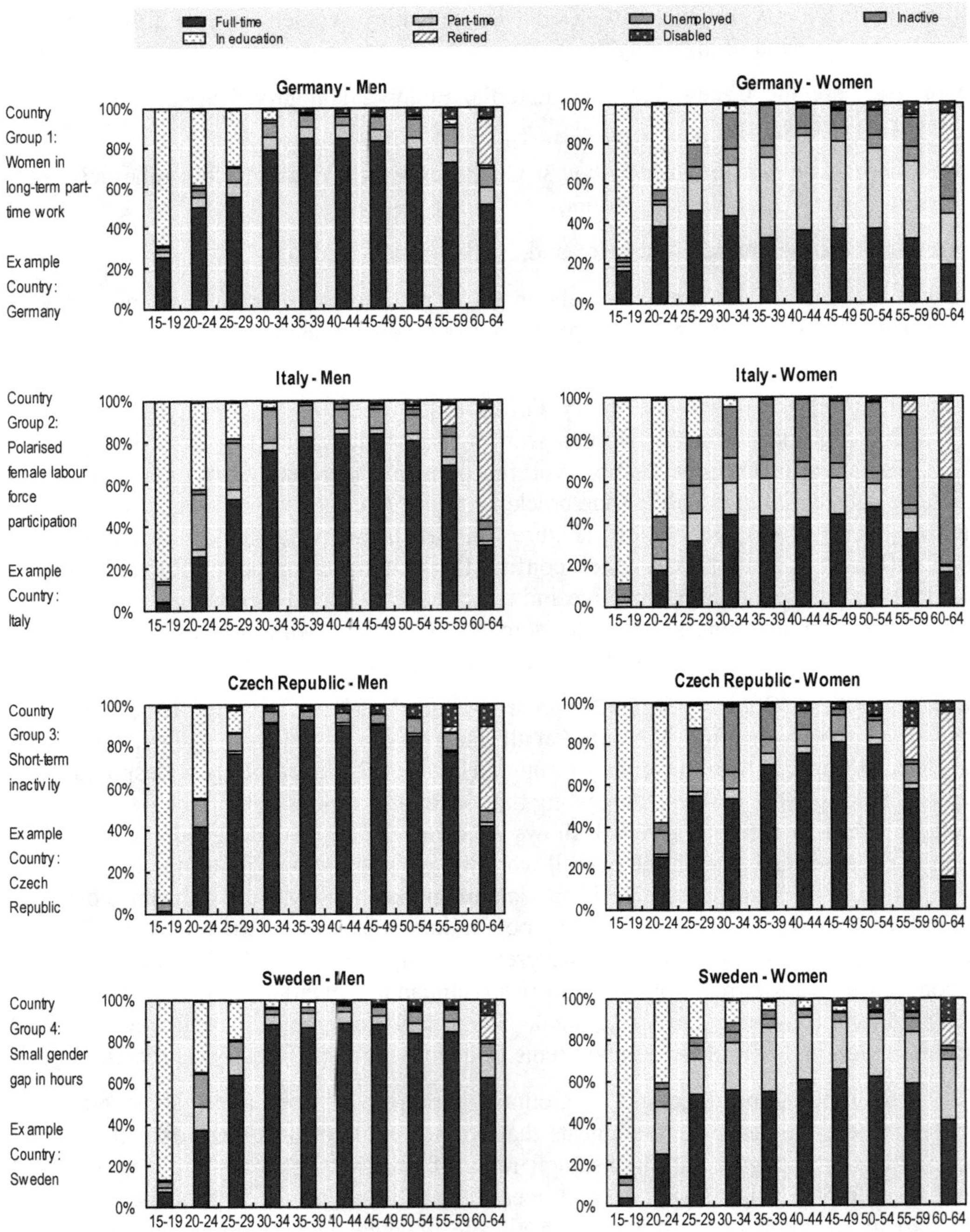

Note: The distinction between part-time and full-time employment is self-defined, i.e. based on the respondent's own perception of whether they are in part-time or full-time employment. "Part-time" and "full-time" therefore include the self-employed.

Country Group 1: Austria, Belgium, Germany, Ireland, Luxembourg, the Netherlands, the United Kingdom and Switzerland. Country Group 2: Italy, Greece, Spain, Portugal, Lithuania, Poland and Slovenia. Country Group 3: the Czech Republic, Estonia, Finland, Hungary, Latvia and the Slovak Republic. Country Group 4: France, Iceland, Norway and Sweden.

Source: OECD calculations based on European Union Statistics on Income and Living Conditions (EU SILC) 2012.

Figure 4.3. Countries with women in long-term part-time work (e.g. Germany) and polarised female labour force behaviour (e.g. Italy) have wider gender gaps in working hours

Average usual weekly working hours among the active working-age population and total working-age population, by sex and five-year age groups, in four example countries, 2012

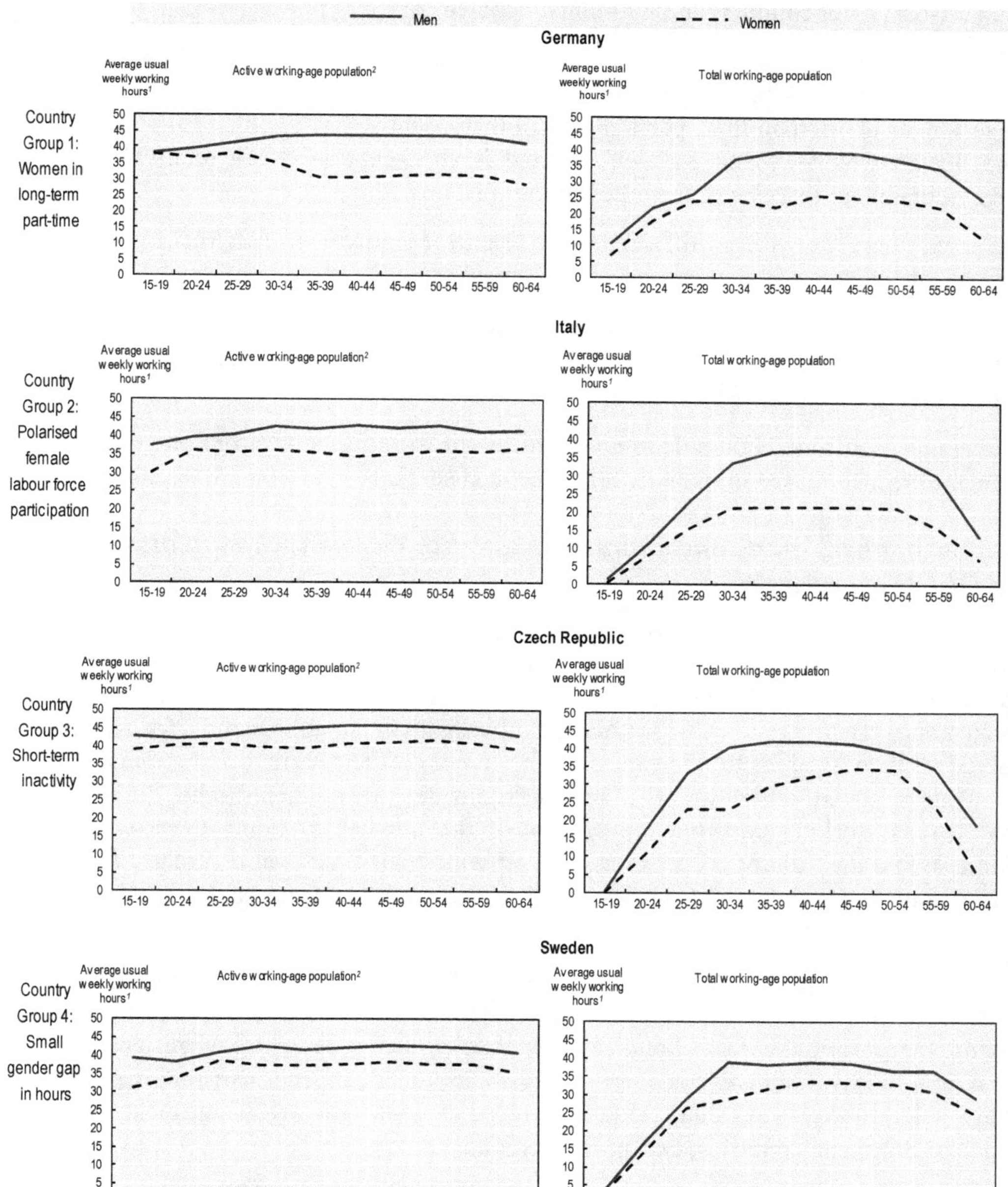

Note: Country Group 1: Austria, Belgium, Germany, Ireland, Luxembourg, the Netherlands, Switzerland and the United Kingdom. Country Group 2: Italy, Greece, Spain, Portugal, Lithuania, Poland and Slovenia. Country Group 3: the Czech Republic, Estonia, Finland, Hungary, Latvia and the Slovak Republic. Country Group 4: France, Iceland, Norway and Sweden.

1. Usual working hours of the (self-)employed. Data refer to total hours worked in all jobs.

2. "Active working-age population" denotes 15 to 64 year-olds of working age who are in employment or self-employment. "Total working-age population" encompasses all 15 to 64 year-olds of working age.

Source: OECD calculations based on European Union Statistics on Income and Living Conditions (EU SILC) 2012.

Sweden represents Country Group 4, "narrow gender gap in hours", where both full-time and part-time work are frequent (Figure 4.2). Figure 4.3 points to a relatively narrow working-hours gender gap that is broadly uniform in all age groups in the active and total working-age population. Finland is not part of this country group as part-time work is not common among Finnish women.

The relatively narrow gender gap in working hours in the Country Group 4 is driven by women working longer and men shorter hours. Female part-time workers average longer hours than their peers in most other countries, while men in Denmark, France, Iceland, Norway and Sweden (Iceland is an exception) work relatively low average hours in comparison to the other country groups.

In sum, there are sharp differences in female employment patterns from one OECD country to another. There are two main reasons:

- whether women can and/or whether they choose or not to return to full-time work after a period of low or no work, as illustrated by the widely varying working hours of women aged 45 and over;
- average "part-time" hours denote very different working hours from one country to another (discussed in more detail in the next section).

Partnered mothers' part-time hours are shorter in Germany than in most other OECD countries

Throughout Europe, women work fewer hours than men, often for family reasons (European Commission, 2006). In most countries, partnered women with at least one child living in the same household are most at "risk" of being inactive or working reduced hours (Bettio et al., 2013). Accordingly, analysis in this section focuses on partnered women aged 25 to 45 years old who live with their partner and at least one child. Unless stated otherwise, the analysis considers respondents who described themselves as working part-time, regardless of the number of hours they reported working. While the volume of hours associated with "part-time" varies greatly across countries and sectors within countries, the self-declared part-time status is taken to mean working fewer hours than the "typical" worker with a standard contract.

Part-time working mothers in Sweden, Denmark and France work the most hours at around 30 per week on average (Figure 4.4). In Mexico, Canada, Ireland and Germany they work the least hours at less than 20 per week. In Switzerland and Austria, too, the working week is short (less than 23 hours). Indeed, part-time working mothers seldom do more than 25 hours of paid work per week in most other continental European countries, except for Belgium.

As for part-time working fathers (partnered with a woman aged 25-45 with at least one child), they work longer hours on average than part-time working mothers (see Annex Figure 4.A1.1). While in Belgium, Denmark, France and Sweden, they work over 30 hours per week, their hours are shortest in Canada, Mexico and the Slovak Republic – less than 20 hours. With just short of 28 hours per week, German fathers are middle-ranking (also see Figures 4.A1.4 and 4.A1.5 on the overall average working hours of mothers and fathers in the annex).

There is cross-national variation in how part-time working mothers schedule their working hours across the week. In German-speaking countries mothers often work half a day throughout the week, while the part-time work of mothers in the Nordic countries and France – over 25 hours a week on average – is more akin to reduced full-time, with mothers either working only on certain days or reduced daily hours. In France, for example, it is common for part-time workers to work four days out of five, with the mothers of young children taking Wednesdays off – as primary schools were, until recently, closed on Wednesdays (Pailhé and Solaz, 2009). In Sweden, where the working day starts relatively early, flexible working schemes allow parents to leave work in the afternoon to pick up their children (OECD, 2007).

Figure 4.4. German mothers work relatively short part-time hours

Average usual weekly hours of partnered mothers working part-time, aged 25 to 45, with at least one child, 2012

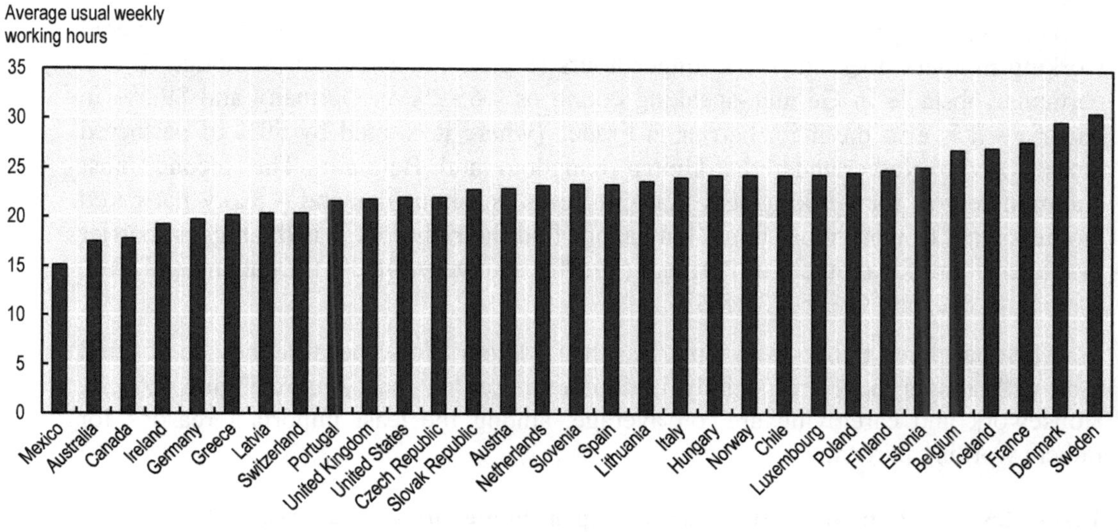

Note: Usual working hours of the (self-)employed for European countries, actual hours worked for Chile and Mexico. Data refer to total hours worked in all jobs, except for Chile where only hours worked in the main job are considered.

The distinction between part-time and full-time employment is self-defined – i.e. based on respondents' own perceptions of whether they are in part-time or full-time employment. Part-time status based on weekly working hours below 30 for Australia, Canada and Mexico.

Data for Australia refer to 2014, for Canada to 2011, for Chile to 2013, for Mexico to 2014, and for the United States to 2014.

Source: OECD calculations based on the Household, Income and Labour Dynamics in Australia (HILDA) Survey 2014 for Australia, the Survey of Labour and Income Dynamics (SLID) 2011 for Canada, the *Encuesta de Caracterización Socioeconómica Nacional* (CASEN) 2013 for Chile, European Union Statistics on Income and Living Conditions (EU SILC) 2012 for European countries, the *Encuesta Nacional de Ingresos y Gastos de los Hogares* (ENIGH) 2014 for Mexico, the Current Population Survey (CPS) 2014 for the United States.

In German-speaking countries, by contrast, restricted opening hours in schools, kindergartens and day-care centres compel part-time working women to work half-days only (see Chapter 3 on policies, and OECD, 2007). Despite efforts to invest more in all-day schools and all-day child care facilities, most primary and secondary schools in Germany are still closed in the afternoon (Horemans and Marx, 2013). Parents (generally mothers) are expected to organise study and recreation activities for their children in the afternoon, as otherwise children are home alone.

While the German public has shown growing acceptance of working mothers and institutional support has increased for young families in recent years (Chapters 2 and 3), social stigma still attaches to full-time working mothers (pejoratively dubbed

Rabenmutter, "raven" mothers), while children who stay home alone in the afternoon are called Schlüsselkinder, "latchkey kids". Interestingly, in France mothers who do not work are sometimes termed *mère poule*, literally the "mother hen", meaning their "only" occupation is raising children (Fagnani, 2004).

On average across European countries less than 10% of partnered mothers who work less than 30 hours per week do so because they do not want to work longer hours (Figure 4.5., Panel A). And, while 30.8% of Swedish mothers working less than 30 hours per week would not want to work longer hours, the share working less than 30 hours per week out of all (self-)employed mothers is relatively small at 7.52% to begin with (Figure 4.5, Panel B).

However, unpaid work at home is the main reason why one in two partnered working mothers does not work longer hours (Figure 4.5, Panel A). Although, it is a particular obstacle in German-speaking countries – 65.2% in Germany and 89.5% in Austria – it is also the main barrier in France (where it is cited by 59% of partnered mothers), the Netherlands, the United Kingdom and Belgium. The second most common reason for working less than 30 hours is labour demand – many partnered mothers want to work more hours but cannot find the right job. It is the biggest barrier to longer hours for mothers in Portugal (73.8%), Hungary (48.3%), Denmark (44.9%), Latvia (42.8%) and Greece (39.8%).

Most partnered fathers who work less than 30 hours do so because they do not find jobs with longer hours, especially in Southern Europe (see Annex Figure 4.A1.2). Housework and caregiving are, on average, among the least important reasons for fathers working part-time.

Figure 4.5. In most countries family responsibilities are the main reason for mothers working part-time

Panel A. Main reasons (in percentages) for partnered women aged 25-45, with at least one child, working less than 30 hours/week

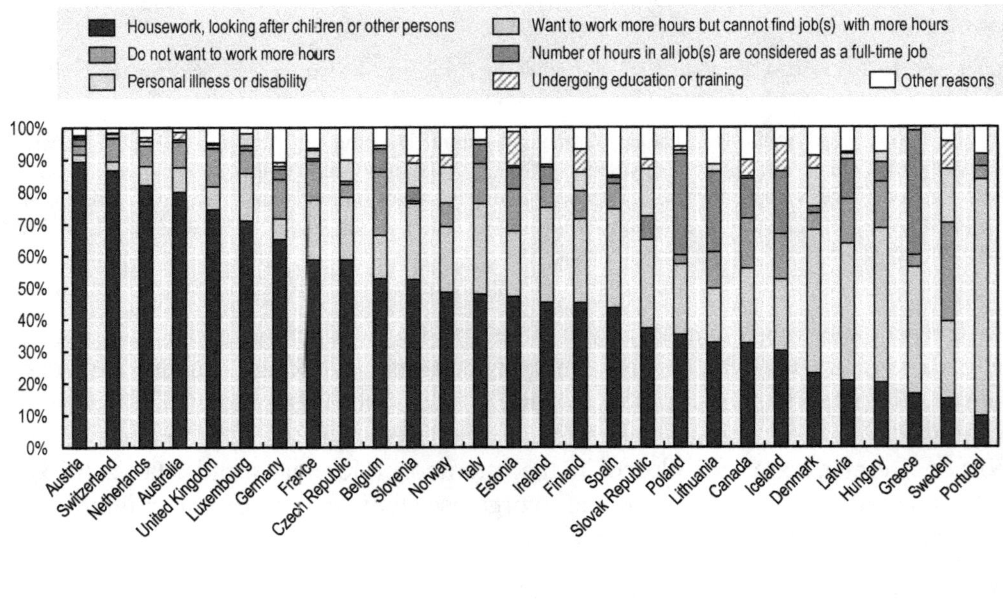

Figure 4.5. In most countries family responsibilities are the main reason for mothers working part-time *(cont.)*

Panel B. Share (in percentages) of mothers working fewer than 30 hours/week out of all working partnered mothers (partnered, aged 25 to 45, with at least one child)

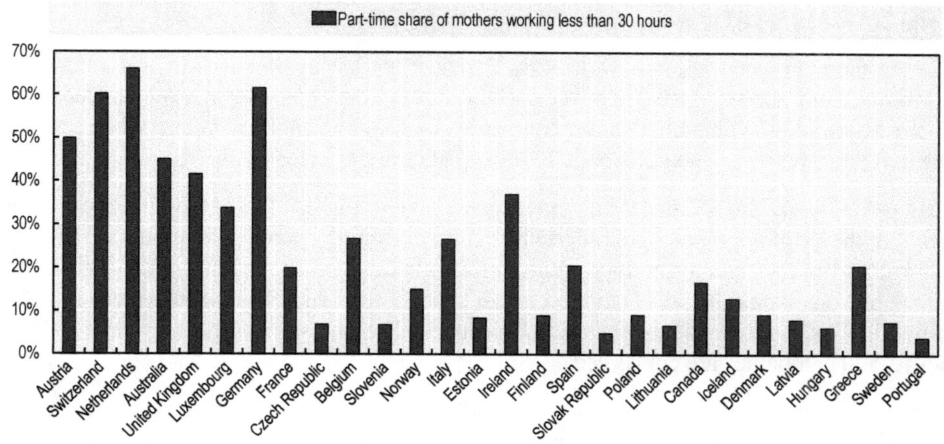

Note: Usual working hours of the (self-)employed for European countries. Data refer to total hours worked in all jobs, except for Chile where only hours worked in the main job are considered.

Source: OECD calculations based on the Household, Income and Labour Dynamics in Australia (HILDA) Survey 2014 for Australia, the Survey of Labour and Income Dynamics (SLID) 2011 for Canada, European Union Statistics on Income and Living Conditions (EU SILC) 2012 for European countries.

Part-time working mothers run the risk of getting caught in the so-called "part-time trap", which limits their career prospects, also after their children leave home (Lestrade, 2013). Having to leave the office early every day rules many part-time working women out of senior decision-making positions (Box 4.1), while leaving in late afternoon or being absent one day per week is generally less damaging to career advancement. As part-time jobs are concentrated in low-skilled jobs, women who reduce their working hours are likely to downgrade occupationally, while switching employer is particularly detrimental (see Connolly and Gregory, 2010 on the experience in the United Kingdom). The longer part-time work lasts, the less likely it is that women will resume a full-time position, and many never manage to recover their previous career trajectory (ibid.).

Part-time work and marginal employment are also detrimental to mothers' and, by the same token, families' incomes. In Germany, women make up the bulk of workers in marginal employment like *minijobs* and *midijobs* – flexitime casual jobs which provide limited levels of social security, income and career options. Evidence from the United Kingdom (Connolly and Gregory, 2010) and Austria shows that part-time work is often poorly paid (at hourly rates) compared to the equivalent full-time employment. In Austria, for example, part-time workers earn 31% less than full-time workers in equivalent employment (Bergmann et al., 2010). And in many European countries part-time employees are significantly more exposed than full-time workers to the risk of poverty, particularly women and those who have no choice but part-time work (Horemans and Marx, 2013). Indeed, the shorter the weekly working hours are, the greater the risk of poverty is. The driving factors are insecure, low income, poor career prospects, and meagre chances of returning to full-time work.

Box 4.1. The recent introduction of (binding) gender quotas in Germany

Women are still underrepresented in top corporate jobs throughout the OECD area (OECD, 2012a). And Germany lags far behind, with women occupying only 6.1% of seats on the boards of directors in Forbes Global 500 companies in 2013, compared to the OECD-wide average of 18%.

In May 2015, Germany enacted a law to foster gender parity in the private and public sectors. Since January 2016, women must account for 30% of seats in the supervisory (non-executive) boardrooms of stock-listed *and* so-called "co-determined" companies, large companies of 2 000 or more workers, where employees appoint half the members of the supervisory board. About 200 companies are affected by the requirement.

Companies that are *either* stock-listed *or* co-determined have to publish their own numerical objectives for the share of women that they will appoint to their supervisory and managing boards and in their top management ranks. Although the law does not stipulate a statutory minimum female quota, a firm cannot set a goal where the share of women in senior positions would be less than the current share if that share has already reached 30%. Companies have to report publicly on progress in reaching their objectives. They must meet them by June 2017, then draw up new ones. About 3 500 companies are concerned.

On the supervisory boards of state-owned companies where the federal government can appoint all board members, the gender quota of 30% has to be met from 2016 onwards and, from 2018, the target is 50%. If the federal government can appoint three or more but not all members of the board, the 30% (then 50%) quota applies to newly appointed members only. In the public service, targeted shares of male and female staff at the different levels of management have to be set out in a gender equality plan (the *Gleichstellungsplan*) that also describes the concrete measures for achieving those aims and for better reconciling work and family life.

Legally entitling part-time employees to revert to full-time hours within a specified timeframe would be a valuable policy lever in helping parents (mainly mothers) to avoid getting "locked" into part-time employment (Chapter 3). In Germany, parental leave provisions grant each parent the right to resume, during the child's first three years, their previous working hours. A recent reform has further enabled parents of children born after June 2016 to make even more flexible use of the job protection provision: With the employer's consent, they can use 12 months of the 36 month employment-protection period any time between the child's third and eighth birthday. But, beyond the provisions of parental leave (*Elternzeit*) and family care leave (*Pflegezeit* and *Familienpflegezeit*), employees in Germany are not legally entitled to resume full-time work once their reduced working hours have been approved by their employer (see Chapter 3 for an international comparison of legal provisions).

Full-time hours of German parents are relatively long

While German mothers work comparatively short part-time hours, the opposite is true of those in full-time work, a further incentive for them to work part-time. On average, full-time working mothers in Germany put in nearly 42 hours per week, outstripped only by Swiss and Austrian mothers with about 44 hours per week (Figure 4.6). In Norway, Denmark and France, by contrast, full-time working mothers work, on average, less than 40 hours per week.

Full-time working fathers in Germany also work relatively long hours at just above 45 hours (see Annex Figure 4.A1.1) – above the European average, but less than other European countries such as Austria, Switzerland and Poland. Fathers in Norway, Denmark, Sweden, and Finland, for their part, work fewer hours than the European average but still more than 40 hours per week. Relatively low regular weekly working hours in full-time jobs are thus common among both women and men in Denmark,

Sweden, Norway, and Finland. The similar hours worked by mothers and fathers in full-time employment in the Nordic countries may have important implications for mothers' career opportunities: leaving work early in the afternoon may be less detrimental to their careers when their male colleagues are as likely to do the same.

Figure 4.6. The hours worked by German mothers in full-time jobs are relatively long

Average usual working week of partnered mothers who work full-time, aged 25-45, with at least one child, 2012

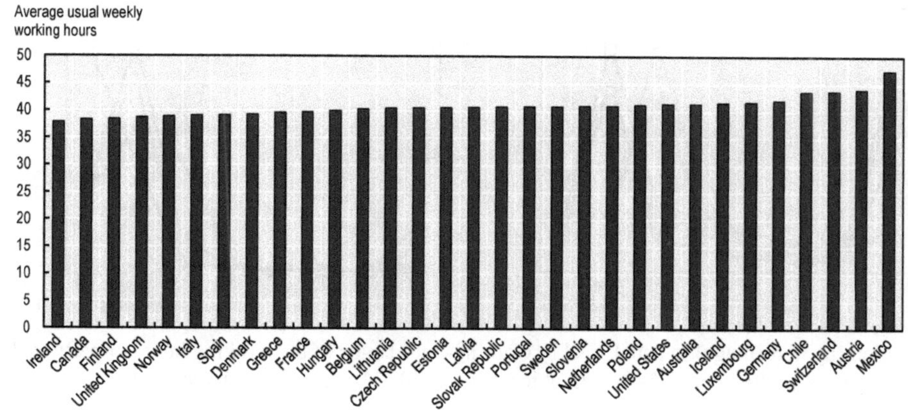

Note: Usual working hours of the (self-)employed for European countries, actual hours worked for Chile and Mexico. Data refer to total hours worked in all jobs, except for Chile where only hours worked in the main job are considered.

The distinction between part-time and full-time employment is self-defined – i.e. based on respondents' own perceptions of whether they are in part-time or full-time employment. Part-time status based on weekly working hours below 30 for Canada and Mexico.

Data for Australia refer to 2014, for Canada to 2011, for Chile to 2013, for Mexico to 2014, and for the United States to 2014.

Source: OECD calculations based on the Household, Income and Labour Dynamics in Australia (HILDA) Survey 2014 for Australia, the Survey of Labour and Income Dynamics (SLID) 2011 for Canada, the *Encuesta de Caracterización Socioeconómica Nacional* (CASEN) 2013 for Chile, European Union Statistics on Income and Living Conditions (EU SILC) 2012 for European countries, the *Encuesta Nacional de Ingresos y Gastos de los Hogares* (ENIGH) 2014 for Mexico, the Current Population Survey (CPS) 2014 for the United States.

German mothers and fathers' working hours are mirror images

The low average gender gap in weekly working hours in Nordic countries and France is related to the relatively long weekly working hours of part-time working women and relatively low average weekly working hours of full-time working fathers and mothers. Figure 4.7 shows the distribution of partnered fathers and mothers across eight tranches of working hours, contrasting the Nordic countries, France and the United States (Panel A) with the German-speaking countries (Panel B).

It is relatively common that partnered mothers work between 30 and 39 hours per week in France, Finland, Norway and, to some extent, Sweden. Most partnered mothers in the first three countries work between 35 and 39 hours, while in Sweden, Iceland and the United States, their working week lies between 40 and 44 hours. Partnered fathers in those countries mostly work 39 hours or more and between 35 and 39 hours per week in Norway and France. The distribution of Swedish and American fathers' working hours is similar to that of mothers, with the great bulk putting in between 40 and 44 hours per week. In Iceland, France and Sweden, a non-negligible share of partnered fathers work over 45 hours per week.

Figure 4.7. Partnered mothers are less likely to work full-time in German-speaking countries than in selected OECD countries

Panel A. Distribution (by percentage) in usual weekly working-hour bands of the working hours of partnered mothers and fathers – female partner aged 25-45 with at least one child – Finland, France, Iceland, Norway, Sweden and the United States, 2012

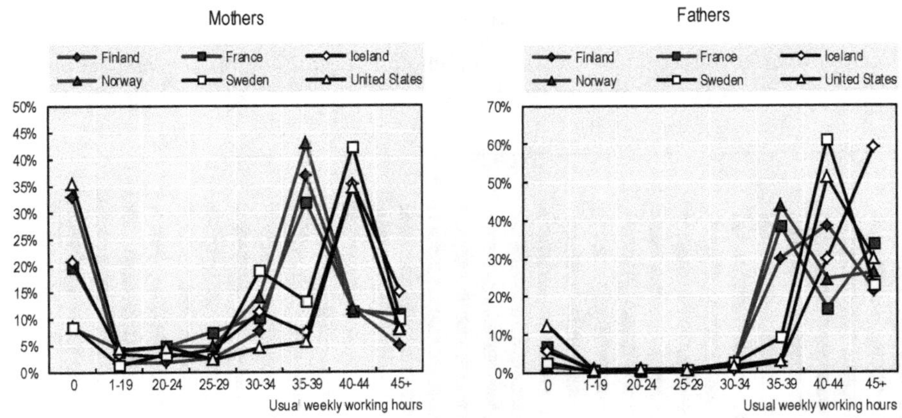

Panel B. Distribution (by percentage) in usual weekly working-hour bands of the working hours of partnered mothers and fathers – female partner aged 25-45 with at least one child – Austria, Germany and Switzerland, 2012

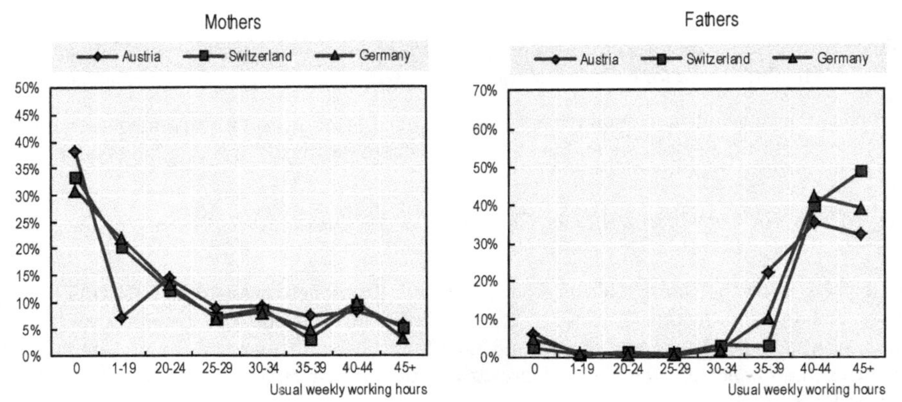

Note: Usual working hours of the (self-)employed for European countries. Data refer to total hours worked in all jobs. Data for the United States refer to 2014.

Source: OECD calculations based on European Union Statistics on Income and Living Conditions (EU SILC) 2012 for European countries, Current Population Survey (CPS) 2014 for the United States.

The distribution of French partnered fathers' working weeks appears bimodal, the most common lying between 35 and 39 hours, and the second most widespread 45 hours or more. Although, the legal full-time working week is 35 hours in France, company managers (*cadres*) often are paid on a task-oriented basis, so often work over 35 hours. Disparities in working hours in France are therefore likely to stem more from the definition of regular full-time working hours between occupations and the public and private sectors than from workers choosing between full-time and part-time.

The distribution of mothers' and fathers' working hours in German-speaking countries (Panel B) differs markedly from the countries discussed above. Partnered mothers' distribution is nearly the mirror image of partnered fathers' in Germany, Austria and Switzerland. Working weeks of fewer than 40 hours is unusual among fathers and the proportion of those doing more than 44 hours is much greater than in

France, the United States and the Nordics – the one exception is Iceland, where most men work over 45 hours per week, as in Switzerland.

Few parents share paid work equally across OECD countries

Ideally, equal sharing in families should also empower partners to provide an adequate household income and spend time with each other. Yet, across Europe, the within-couple gap in working hours – the male partner's hours less the female partner's hours in couples where the male partner works – is generally sizable (Figure 4.8). With German mothers so frequently working less than 30 hours per week and fathers putting in long hours, the within-couple hours gap in Germany is amongst the widest at over 25 hours per week, together with Austria and Switzerland. Gaps are wide, too, in Southern Mediterranean countries, because so many women are inactive. As for Sweden, Norway and Denmark, they boast the narrowest gaps in working hours within couples (below ten hours per week). Eastern European countries also tend to have below average within-couple gaps.

Within-couple gaps in working hours are narrowest either when both partners work 40 hours or when both work approximately 38 hours per week (data not shown here). The hours gap obviously is widest in families where women do not work at all and their male partners tend to work more than 40 hours per week. Nor do mothers necessarily step up their paid work to offset reductions in their partners' hours: if the father does not work, the mother still works only some 19 hours per week on average – which may, in part, be related to assortative mating that brings together partners with the same socioeconomic background (as in university and college students).

Figure 4.8. German-speaking countries have large within-couple gender gaps in working hours

Average within-couple gender gap in usual weekly working hours (couples with a female partner aged 25 to 45 and at least one child), 2012

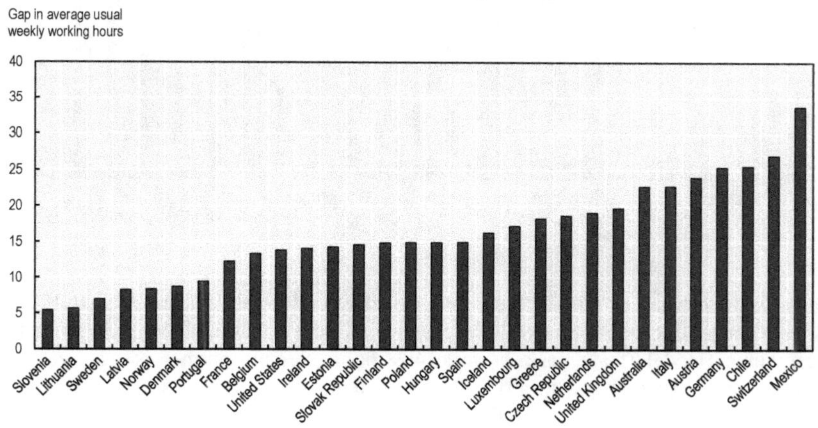

Note: Usual working hours of the (self-)employed for European countries, actual hours worked for Chile and Mexico. Data refer to total hours worked in all jobs, except for Chile where only hours worked in the main job are considered.

Data refer to the average absolute gap in usual weekly working hours between the male member and the female member of a couple (male partner's usual weekly working hours – female partner's usual weekly working hours). Jobless couples where neither partner works (inactive or unemployed) are excluded. Data for both partners not available in the public use version of SLID for Canada.

Data refer for Australia to 2014, for Chile to 2013, for Mexico to 2014, and for the United States to 2014.

Source: OECD calculations based on the Household, Income and Labour Dynamics in Australia (HILDA) Survey 2014 for Australia, the *Encuesta de Caracterización Socioeconómica Nacional* (CASEN) 2013 for Chile, European Union Statistics on Income and Living Conditions (EU SILC) 2012 for European countries, the *Encuesta Nacional de Ingresos y Gastos de los Hogares* (ENIGH) 2014 for Mexico, the Current Population Survey (CPS) 2014 for the United States.

Couples with children can choose from a variety of work arrangements, five of the most common being (Figure 4.9):

- "dual-full-time-earner model", where both partners work over 40 hours,
- "male-breadwinner model", where the male partner works over 40 hours and the female partner is inactive or unemployed,
- "main-breadwinner model", where the male partner works over 40 hours and the female partner 1 to 29 hours,
- "dual-reduced full-time model", where both partners work 30 to 39 hours;
- "reduced-full-time-plus-part-time model", where the male partner works 30 to 39 and the female partner 1 to 29 hours per week.

Figure 4.9. Few families share market work equally with both partners working between 30 and 39 hours per week

Percentage of couples (female partner aged 25-45 with at least one child) practicing five different working-time arrangements, 2012

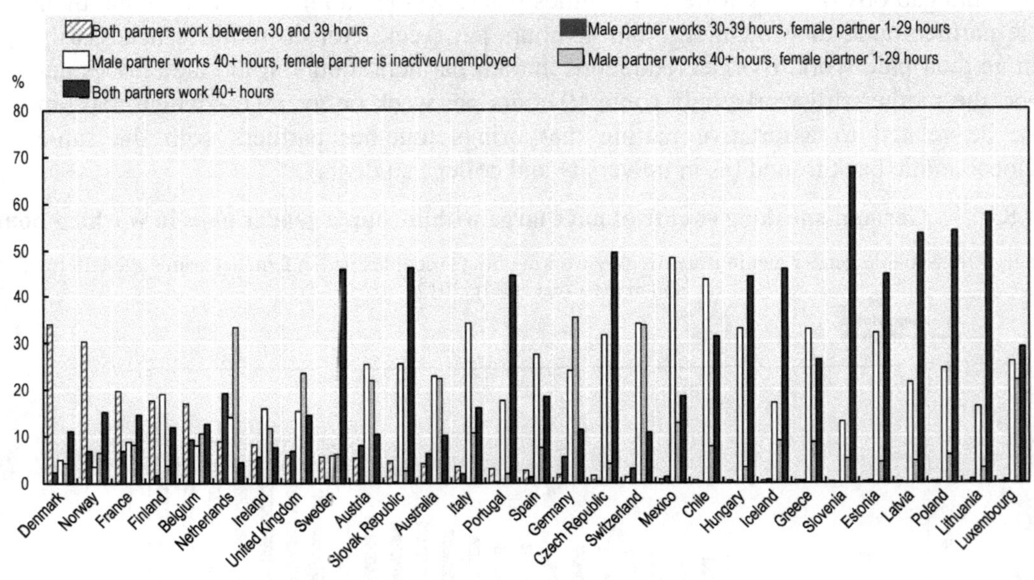

Reading note: In Germany out of married or cohabitating couples where the female partner is aged 25-45 and with at least one child, 1.8% couples work dual reduced full-time (both partners work between 30 and 39 hours, striped bars), 24% follow the traditional male breadwinner model (male partner works 40+ hours, female partner is inactive, white bars), 35.4% practice the main breadwinner model (male partner works 40+ hours, female partner works 1-29 hours, grey bars). In 11.3% of couples both partners work full-time (40+ hours, dark blue bars) and in 5.8% of couples the male partner works 30-39 hours and the female partner works 1-29 hours (dotted bars).

Usual working hours of the (self-)employed for European countries, actual hours worked for Chile and Mexico. Data refer to total hours worked in all jobs, except for Chile where only hours worked in the main job are considered.

"Inactive/unemployed" based on self-declared labour market status. Data for both partners not available in the public use version of SLID for Canada.

Data for Australia refer to 2014, for Chile to 2013, and for Mexico to 2014.

Source: OECD calculations based on the Household, Income and Labour Dynamics in Australia (HILDA) Survey 2014 for Australia, the *Encuesta de Caracterización Socioeconómica Nacional* (CASEN) 2013 for Chile, European Union Statistics on Income and Living Conditions (EU SILC) 2012 for European countries, the *Encuesta Nacional de Ingresos y Gastos de los Hogares* (ENIGH) 2014 for Mexico, the Current Population Survey (CPS) 2014 for the United States.

At 33.9%, Denmark has the highest proportion of couples where both partners work "reduced full-time hours". In Norway, France, Finland and Belgium, between 17% and 30% of couple families practice the dual-reduced full-time model. In Germany, partners in only 1.8% of couples both work between 30 and 39 hours, a low rate common in many other European countries. Indeed, in 16 out of 26 European countries the share of dual reduced full-time couple families is lower than 5%.

The greatest share, 19.22%, of couple families with the father working between 30 and 39 hours and the mother between 1 and 29 is to be found in the Netherlands – which has legally enshrined flexitime and has a long tradition of part-time work, especially among women (Chapter 2). In Germany, 5.8% of families practice such a "reduced-full-time-plus-part-time model".

Dual full-time work is the most common working arrangement in families in Eastern European countries such as Lithuania, Slovenia, the Czech Republic, Hungary and Latvia. The male breadwinner model is the most widely practiced by couples in most Southern European countries, with the exception of Portugal, where both partners usually work over 40 hours per week.

Sweden boasts a high share of couples where the man works over 40 hours per week and the woman working 30 to 39 hours (results not shown here). The combination is also widespread in Norway, France, Finland, Denmark and Belgium. In those countries, the proportion of couples where the male partner works 30 to 39 hours per week and the woman over 40 is also higher than in other European countries (results not shown).

In German families, the most likely work arrangement is the father working full-time and the mother less than 29 hours per week or not at all. The "main-breadwinner model" is, at 34.8% (Figure 4.9, grey bars) the most common in German couple families, followed by the traditional "male-breadwinner model" where the mother is inactive or unemployed (23.9%, white bars).

A more detailed comparison of paid work arrangements in France and Germany reveals that paid work is considerably less "polarised" in French couples (Figure 4.10) In Germany, the combination of full-time working father and non-working or part-time working mother predominates. In France, the combination of two full-time earners is much more common with couples most likely choosing dual reduced full-time, or one partner working full-time and the other partner working between 30 and 39 hours. The third most common practice in France is the "dual full-time earner model". The distribution of work arrangements in which the male partner does not work is much the same in both countries.

Figure 4.10. Within-couple gender gaps in working hours are greater in Germany than in France

Distribution of within-couple usual weekly working-hour combinations among couples with a female partner aged 25-45 and at least one child, 2012

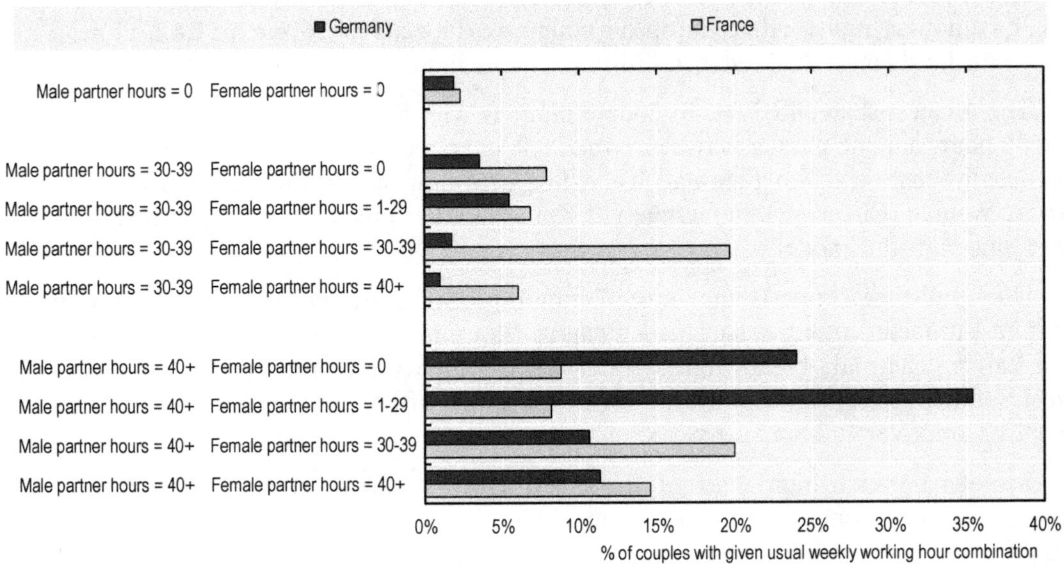

Reading note: Data refer to couples with a female partner aged 25 to 45 and at least one child, only. In Germany, 24% of such couples have a male partner working full-time (40+ hours per week) and a female partner not working (0 hour per week). In France, 8.2% of such couples have a male partner working full-time (40+ hours per week) and a female partner not working (0 hour per week).

Usual working hours of the (self-)employed for European countries, actual hours worked for Chile and Mexico. Data refer to total hours worked in all jobs.

Data show only the combinations that represent over 1% of the selected couples.

Source: OECD calculations based on European Union Statistics on Income and Living Conditions (EU SILC) 2012.

3. Mothers contribute less than fathers to household earnings in couple families across the OECD

Mothers' average contribution to households' overall earnings from employment and self-employment is lowest in German-speaking countries, followed by Southern Mediterranean countries (Figure 4.11). While German mothers contribute only one-quarter of household income from their earnings on average, they contribute over 35% in France, Sweden and Denmark.

Figure 4.11. Mothers in couples earn lower shares of household earnings in German-speaking countries

Average within-couple female share of earnings, couples with a female partner aged 25-45 and at least one child, income reference year 2011

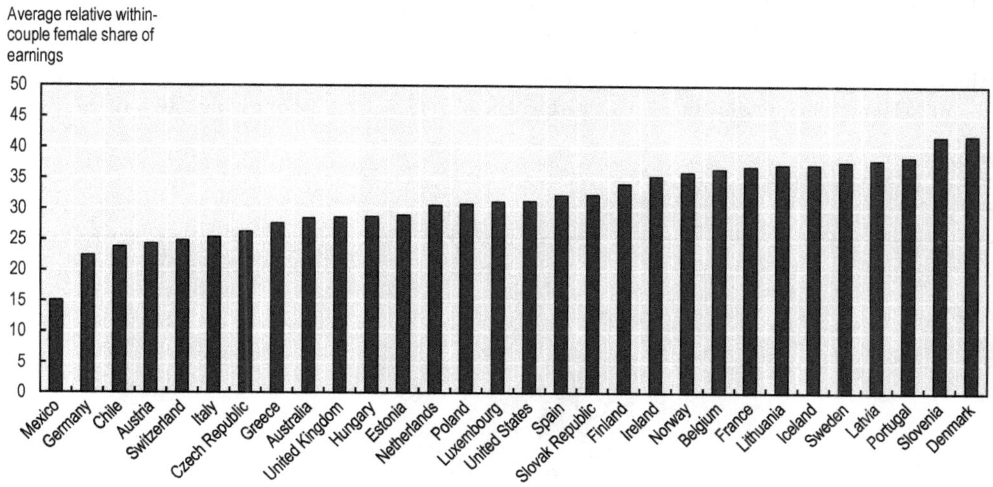

Reading note: Data refer only to couples with a female partner aged 25-45 and at least one child. In Germany, the average female share of total earnings within such couples is 22.4%, while in Denmark the average female share of total earnings within such couples is 42%.

Usual working hours of the (self-)employed for European countries, actual hours worked for Chile and Mexico. Data refer to total hours worked in all jobs, except for Chile where only hours worked in the main job are considered.

Data refer to the average female share of a couple's total earnings (female partner's earnings divided by male partner's earnings plus female partner's earnings). Jobless couples where neither partner works (inactive or unemployed) are excluded. Data for both partners not available in the public use version of SLID for Canada.

Data for Australia refer to 2014, for Chile to 2013, for Mexico to 2014, and for the United States to 2014. The income reference year is 2011 for European countries, 2010 for Canada, 2013 for Chile and 2014 for Mexico and the United States.

Source: OECD calculations based on the Household, Income and Labour Dynamics in Australia (HILDA) Survey 2014 for Australia, the *Encuesta de Caracterización Socioeconómica Nacional* (CASEN) 2013 for Chile, European Union Statistics on Income and Living Conditions (EU SILC) 2012 for European countries, the *Encuesta Nacional de Ingresos y Gastos de los Hogares* (ENIGH) 2014 for Mexico, the Current Population Survey (CPS) 2014 for the United States.

Figure 4.12 illustrates a strong, significantly negative correlation between the average contribution of mothers to earnings and the average within-couple working-hour gender gaps. The wide disparities in working hours between partners, as observed in German-speaking countries, thus translate into mothers' limited contributions to household earnings. Low within-couple gaps in working hours, by contrast, coincide with relatively narrower earnings gaps between partners in Slovenia, Latvia, Lithuania and Portugal, where dual full-time employment (over 40 hours per week) is the dominant pattern. Gaps in hours and earnings are also comparatively narrow in France and almost all Nordic countries, where it is relatively common that both partners put in 30 to 39 hours per week.

While mothers work shorter hours than fathers, women and part-time workers are also more likely to be paid less per hour than full-time working men. Many countries' ranking in the within-couple earnings gender gap pretty much matches their ranking in the average gender gap in hourly gross earnings among all employees (Eurostat, 2016). In countries with a comparatively wide gender pay gap (like the German-speaking countries) mothers' contribute relatively less to household earnings. Slovenia and Belgium, by contrast, are among the countries with the lowest gender gap in both couples' working hours and hourly wages.

Figure 4.12. Mothers work least and contribute least to household earnings in German-speaking countries

Average within-couple gender gap in usual weekly working hours, and average relative within-couple female share of earnings for couples with a female partner aged 25-45 and at least one child, 2011/12

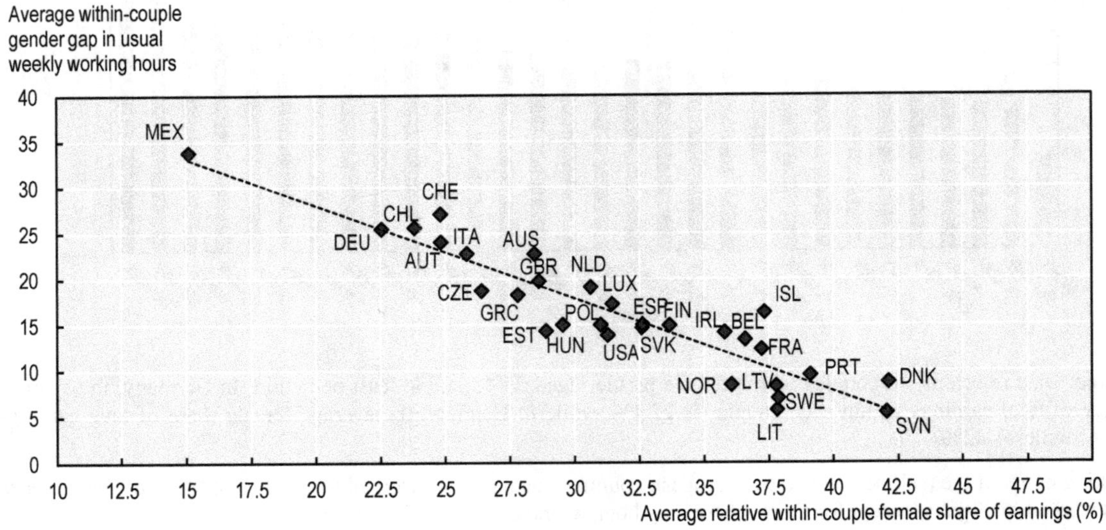

Note: Usual working hours of the (self-)employed for European countries, actual hours worked for Chile and Mexico. Data refer to total hours worked in all jobs, except for Chile where only hours worked in the main job are considered.

Jobless couples where neither partner works (inactive or unemployed) are excluded.

Data refer to the average female share of a couple's total earnings (female partner's earnings divided by male partner's earnings plus female partner's earnings). Data for both partners not available in the public use version of SLID for Canada.

Data refer to the average absolute gap in usual weekly working hours between the male member and the female member of a couple (male partner's usual weekly working hours – female partner's usual weekly working hours). Data for both partners not available in the public use version of SLID for Canada.

Data for Australia refer to 2014, for Chile to 2013, for Mexico to 2014, and for the United States to 2014. The income reference year is 2011 for European countries, 2010 for Canada, 2013 for Chile and 2014 for Mexico and the United States.

Source: OECD calculations based on the Household, Income and Labour Dynamics in Australia (HILDA) Survey 2014 for Australia, the *Encuesta de Caracterización Socioeconómica Nacional* (CASEN) 2013 for Chile, European Union Statistics on Income and Living Conditions (EU SILC) 2012 for European countries, the *Encuesta Nacional de Ingresos y Gastos de los Hogares* (ENIGH) 2014 for Mexico, the Current Population Survey (CPS) 2014 for the United States.

Mothers' contribution to household earnings is also larger in couples where the father belongs to the country's lowest earnings tercile (Figure 4.14, right-hand panel). Women's education, however, can lessen the earnings gap with their partners, as the mothers' relative contributions to households' overall earnings rises with their levels of educational attainment (Figure 4.14, left-hand panel). Nevertheless, the gender earnings gap has long-term consequences, including for incomes in retirement (Box 4.2).

Figure 4.13. Mothers' contribution to household earnings increases with educational attainment and decreases with partner earnings

Average relative within-couple female share of earnings by female partner's educational attainment level and by male partner's earnings level, couples with a female partner aged 25-45 and at least one child, pooled data across selected 26 EU countries, 2012

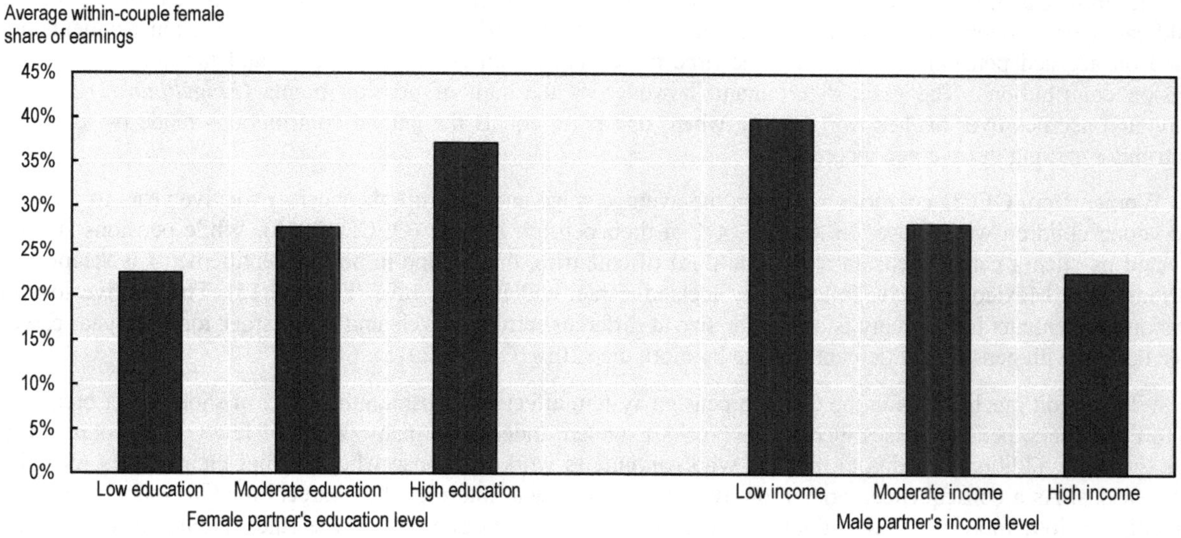

Note: Data refer to the average female share of a couple's total earnings (female partner's earnings divided by male partner's earnings plus female partner's earnings]. Jobless couples where neither partner works (inactive or unemployed) are excluded.

Female partner's education levels correspond to the International Standard Classification of Education (ISCED) 1997: low education – highest level of educational attainment at ISCED 1997 Levels 0 2 (pre-primary, primary, lower secondary); moderate education – highest level of educational attainment at ISCED 1997 Levels 3 4 (upper and post-secondary), and high education – highest level of educational attainment at ISCED 1997 Levels 5 6 (tertiary education).

Male partner's income levels are determined by country-specific income terciles, and includes gross employee income as well as profits from self-employment.

Countries included are Austria, Belgium, the Czech Republic, Denmark, Estonia, Finland, France, Germany, Greece, Hungary, Iceland, Ireland, Italy, Latvia, Lithuania, Luxembourg, the Netherlands, Norway, Poland, Portugal, the Slovak Republic, Slovenia, Spain, Sweden, Switzerland and the United Kingdom.

The income reference year is 2011.

Source: OECD calculations based on European Union Statistics on Income and Living Conditions (EU SILC) 2012.

Box 4.2. Gender gaps in work become gender gaps in retirement

Labour market experience is an important factor in shaping retirement income. In Germany and elsewhere in the OECD, women generally work fewer years than men and are more likely to leave the formal labour force to care for the family. Such career breaks can lead to lower pension entitlements, contribute to lower personal savings, and heighten the risk of poverty among elderly women, particularly in the event of divorce or their partner's death.

Various factors contribute to gender gaps in old age income. Women have shorter effective working lives than men – not only in Germany, but throughout the OECD. Women aged 65 and over in 2008/9 worked, on average, 13 years less than men in the 13 OECD countries covered by the SHARELIFE survey (D'Addio, 2009 and 2015). Such disparities are echoed in old-age pensions – women's average mandatory pension benefits were 28% lower than men's in 2011 in 25 OECD countries (ibid). Even if they had the same labour market trajectory as men, gender wage gaps (OECD, 2016) entail lower old age incomes for women.

Box 4.2. Gender gaps in work become gender gaps in retirement *(cont.)*

Life events like child birth, parenting, and caring for elderly relatives affect both wage progression and the accumulation of earnings over a lifetime. Pension credits can help lessen the gap between men and women in old age and, to that end, most mandatory public earnings-related pension schemes provide special pension credits for child care (for an overview of countries' regulations see OECD, 2015, p. 88). In Germany, pension payments are based on accrued pension contributions, the time of retirement, an adjustment factor, and the current value of pension contributions. The main determinant, however, is the sum of pension points (*Entgeltpunkte*) that an individual accrues over his/her working life where one point equals the annual contributions made by a typical contributor earning the average income.

Women from OECD countries who earn the average wage and interrupt their career for five years to care for two young children would lose, on average, 4% of their pension income (OECD, 2015). While pensions are not affected by such a career break in about one-third of countries, the decline in pension entitlements is steepest in Germany and Mexico, at 11%, followed by Iceland, Israel and Italy at 10% (Figure 4.15). The relative loss in pension entitlements in Germany is of similar size at different earnings levels and even larger for a ten-year career interruption, with pension entitlements falling by more than 20% (OECD, 2015).

While credit mechanisms in the German pension system effectively cushion the effect of short career breaks of up to three years, pension losses increase as breaks lengthen. Indeed, Germany is one of few OECD countries to give the same additional credits to mothers who continue to work and those who interrupt their careers for child care reasons. As a consequence, women on average earnings who interrupt their careers for five years to care for two children lose more pension entitlements than in other OECD countries. These rules should provide strong incentives for mothers to remain in the labour market. Yet, the share of part-time women workers among people employed is 37% compared to the OECD average of 22%. Striking the right balance between length of leave from work and benefit entitlements is fundamental to ensuring that working women (and men) return to work but do not lose too much from career interruptions.

Figure 4.14. Career breaks reduce pension entitlements

Gross pension entitlements of low-, average-, and high-earning mothers who interrupt their careers for five years versus those of their peers with unbroken careers, 2014

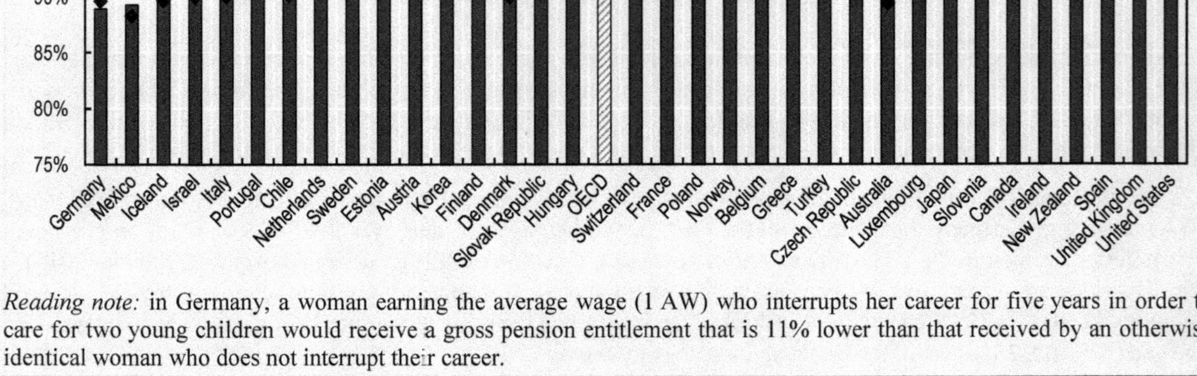

Reading note: in Germany, a woman earning the average wage (1 AW) who interrupts her career for five years in order to care for two young children would receive a gross pension entitlement that is 11% lower than that received by an otherwise identical woman who does not interrupt their career.

Box 4.2. Gender gaps in work become gender gaps in retirement *(cont.)*

Figure 4.14. Career breaks reduce pension entitlements *(cont.)*

Note to Figure 4.14 (cont.): AW stands for "average wage". The average-wage worker concept used by the OECD, in which 0.5 AW denotes half of the AW ("low earnings"), and 2 AW denotes twice the AW ("high earnings"). The models assume that, after labour market entry at the age of 20, a woman with two children aged 2 and 4 interrupts her career for up to ten years between 30 and 40 years old, then resumes full-time employment up to the national retirement age. The indicator illustrated is the ratio between the pension entitlement of that woman and the pension entitlement of a woman with two children who works a full career without interruption – which is the baseline in the figure. The pension entitlements are forward-looking and assume that the pension rules of the year 2014 will apply throughout the worker's career until she reaches the standard pension age in her country. Legislation that will be implemented gradually over the long term are also included in the modelling.

Source: OECD and G20 indicators in OECD (2015).

German pension rules for child care breaks have become more generous over time. Between 1986 and 1992, mothers accrued a maximum of 0.75 pension points for a child's first year. For mothers of children born after 1 January 1992, however, the pension points were paid for a longer period covering the child's first three years for an additional contribution of no more than EUR 42 per month (in 2012 values). In 2014, mothers of children born before 1 January 1992 became eligible for two years of pension per child and, while fathers could also claim it, it was granted mainly to mothers (Thiemann, 2015).

4. What makes mothers choose full- or part-time employment?

For fathers full-time work is the norm, and while in most countries mothers are now also in paid employment their average working hours vary considerably across countries. For example, among European countries, the proportion of mothers in full-time work varies from 8% in the Netherlands to 77% in Slovenia. In addition to country-specific factors, such as public child care support (Box 4.3), there are also individual and family-specific reasons why women choose to work full- or part-time.

Box 4.3. The determinants of female labour force participation

Recent evidence shows that female labour force participation is influenced by a number of factors, such as the rise in female educational attainment, changes in the nature of the labour market, family-friendly policies, and the tax system (Thévenon, 2013 and 2015; Cipollone et al., 2013; Kalíšková, 2015). Changes in labour markets have been powerful factors in growing female labour force participation in OECD countries, particularly the development of the services sector and the expansion of part-time work, which have enabled a greater proportion of women to work and keep working after they start to have children.

Policies which aim to help parents reconcile work and family commitments are also found to have a positive influence on female labour force participation. With national data from 18 OECD countries between 1980 and 2007, Thévenon (2013, 2015) analyses how aggregate levels of female labour force participation respond to policies that support the work-life balance. The analysis takes in variables on paid leave (public spending and duration), child care serv ices for children under the age of 3 (public spending and enrolment rates), public expenditure on other family benefits, and financial incentives to work (such as tax incentives that encourage both partners in couple families to go out to work). The results reveal, in particular, that expansions in child care service provisions significantly boost women's labour market participation and exert a greater positive influence on female employment than variations in the weeks of paid leave. Child care provision for the under 3s doubled, on average, between the mid-1990s and the late 2000s, producing an estimated 2.5 percentage point increase in the employment rates of 25-to-54 year-old women – a quarter of the total increase between 1995 and 2008.

Box 4.3. The determinants of female labour force participation *(cont.)*

The effect of child care services also differs across countries, but is most pronounced in those where support for working mothers is greatest. Accordingly, the expanded provision of child care services for the under 3s was found to have a weaker effect on female employment rates in Continental and Southern European countries, where it may have merely converted the informal into formal child care (Akunduz and Plantenga, 2015).

The effect of policies also varies according to women's levels of educational attainment. Cipollone et al. (2015) found that child care subsidies and child-friendly policies had positive impacts on the activity rates of 25 to 34 year-old women with children who were educated to medium and high levels. By contrast, there was no effect among poorly educated women.

Female employment is also responsive to financial incentives. Thévenon (2013, 2015) estimates that higher tax rates for second earners deter woman from working, although that effect is tempered in an institutional environment which is friendly to a work-life balance. The effect of financial incentives is greatest in English-speaking countries, where female employment rates appear to be reduced by increases in the duration of paid leave and/or the relative tax rates affecting second earners in couple families. This finding makes sense in countries where labour markets are flexible enough to allow workers to move in and out of the labour force, and where working hours can be adjusted to family needs and constraints like high child care costs.

Kalíšková (2015) also measured the effect of tax-benefit policies on the female labour supply in a broad sample of 26 European countries between 2005 and 2010. She estimates that a 10-percentage point increase in the "participation tax rate" – the proportion of lost earnings offset by lower taxes and higher benefits when a mother is not in paid work – reduces by 2 percentage points the likelihood of her working. The effect is more pronounced among single mothers, women in the middle of the skills distribution, and in countries that have lower rates of female employment.

Table 4.1 shows the results of an empirical analysis of the individual and family factors that influence women in choosing between full- and part-time employment. The analysis considers a sample of employed 25-to-45 year-old women with at least one child and a full-time working partner (the distinction between of full- and part-time work is self-defined), drawn from 26 European countries.

The likelihood of a mother working full-time is estimated against part-time work as a function of:

- the woman's age,
- the age of the youngest child,
- the number of children,
- the woman's marital status,
- the woman's level of educational attainment,
- the income level of the full-time employed partner,
- whether the partner works more than 44 or less than 40 hours per week in his full-time job.

Table 4.3 shows the results of the logit regression analyses of the factors above. Model 1 controls for the woman's age, the number of children and the age of youngest child, marital status, and level of education. Model 2 adds in the partner's characteristics. In both cases results are presented as "average marginal effects", that is, as the estimated change in the probability of working full-time rather than part-time resulting from a change in a given characteristic, holding all else constant. Annex Table 4.A2.1 shows for the same models the average adjusted probabilities – that is, the average probability of an employed mother with the given characteristic working full-time, having accounted for the other factors.

Table 4.1 suggest that employed mothers are more likely to work full-time as their children grow up, and are less likely to work full-time the more children they have. The probability of an employed mother (with a full-time working partner) working full-time increases significantly with the age of their youngest child – at least once the youngest child is aged 11 or above (see Model 1) – and decreases significantly with the number of children present in the household (see Model 1).

The characteristics of the mother also play a role (Table 4.1, Model 1). Being highly educated, for example, significantly increases the likelihood of an employed mother working full-time rather than part-time. On average, holding all else constant, the probability of an employed mother with a low level of educational attainment being in full-time work is 64.4% (see Annex Table A2.1). For employed mothers with a high level of educational attainment, this is 72.2% – a difference of just under 8 percentage points. Being unmarried also significantly increases the likelihood of an employed mother working full-time, although the size of the association here is only small. On average, holding all else constant, the probability of working full-time rather than part-time is only about 2 percentage points higher for unmarried mothers than for married mothers. Age has less of an effect – there is no significant difference in the probability of full-time employment across age groups, at least after controlling for other factors.

The characteristics of the partner – specifically, the earnings of the partner – have an effect too. Results from Model 2 suggest that the likelihood of an employed mother being in full-time employment falls as her partner's earnings increase – with high-earning partners significantly less likely to work full-time than those with low- or moderate-earning partners. By contrast, the partner's weekly full-time hours share no association with the probability of an employed mother being in full-time or part-time work, all else being constant.

Table 4.1. Own and partner characteristics are important for mothers' probability of full-time employment against part-time employment

Average marginal effects of logit regressions with robust standard errors, women aged 25 to 45 with at least one child and a full-time employed partner, European countries

		(1)		(2)	
		dy/dx	t-statistic	dy/dx	t-statistic
Age:	25-29	Ref.	-	Ref.	-
	30-34	0.00157	(0.13)	0.00431	(0.34)
	35-39	0.00268	(0.22)	0.00991	(0.79)
	40-45	-0.00253	(-0.19)	0.00747	(0.56)
Age of youngest child:	1-2	Ref.	-	Ref.	-
	3-5	-0.00287	(-0.34)	-0.00214	(-0.26)
	6-10	0.0135	(1.55)	0.0143	(1.63)
	11-15	0.0617***	(6.11)	0.0608***	(6.03)
	16-20	0.101***	(8.02)	0.0994***	(7.85)
	21-28	0.114***	(5.22)	0.111***	(5.07)
Number of children:	1	Ref.	-	Ref.	-
	2	-0.0409***	(-6.92)	-0.0397***	(-6.72)
	3	-0.0790***	(-9.04)	-0.0783***	(-8.97)
	4 or more	-0.0761***	(-4.78)	-0.0767***	(-4.81)
Marital status:	Married	Ref.	-	Ref.	-
	Not married	0.0231***	(3.39)	0.0206**	(3.02)
Education:	Low education (ISCED 1997 levels 0-2)	Ref.	-	Ref.	-
	Middle education (ISCED 1997 levels 3-4)	0.0106	(1.11)	0.0174	(1.80)
	High education (ISCED 1997 levels 5-6)	0.0777***	(8.02)	0.0915***	(9.24)
Partner earnings (full time):	Low earnings (1st tercile)	-	-	Ref.	-
	Middle earnings (2nd tercile)	-	-	-0.00669	(-1.07)
	High earnings (3nd tercile)	-	-	-0.0448***	(-6.86)
Partner's weekly working hours (full-time)	Less than 40h	-	-	Ref.	-
	40-44h	-	-	-0.00345	(-0.48)
	45+h	-	-	-0.00156	(-0.21)
Country fixed effects		yes	-	yes	-
Number of observations		23237	-	23237	-

Note: t statistics in parentheses: * $p<0.05$, ** $p<0.01$, *** $p<0.001$. dy/dx for factor levels is the discrete change from the base level.

Women's education levels correspond to the International Standard Classification of Education (ISCED) 1997: low education – highest level of educational attainment at ISCED 1997 Levels 0 2 (pre-primary, primary, lower secondary); moderate education – highest level of educational attainment at ISCED 1997 Levels 3 4 (upper and post-secondary), and high education – highest level of educational attainment at ISCED 1997 Levels 5 6 (tertiary education).

Male partners' earnings level are determined by country-specific earnings terciles and include gross employee income and profits from self-employment.

Countries included are Austria, Belgium, the Czech Republic, Denmark, Estonia, Finland, France, Germany, Greece, Hungary, Iceland, Ireland, Italy, Latvia, Lithuania, Luxembourg, the Netherlands, Norway, Poland, Portugal, the Slovak Republic, Slovenia, Spain, Sweden, Switzerland and the United Kingdom.

The income reference year is 2011.

Source: OECD calculations based on European Union Statistics on Income and Living Conditions (EU SILC) 2012.

Different factors are at play in different groups of countries

Of course, these factors may not have the same effect across all countries. As discussed throughout this chapter, women's employment arrangements differ considerably from country to country, and the characteristics that drive full-time employment in a country where most employed mothers work part-time may not be the same as those in a country where full-time employment is more common. Table 4.2 shows results from for Model 2 but for each of the four country groups identified earlier separately.

The results shown in Table 4.2 suggest that, while there are a number of similarities, the role played by the various factors highlighted above do sometimes differ from one country group to another. For example, while the age of the youngest child shares an association with the probability of full-time work in all four country groups, the exact timing of the relation varies. Employed mothers in Country Group 3 ("Women in short-term inactivity"), for instance, are likely to resume full-time work relatively quickly. In this country group, the probability of an employed mother working full-time increases significantly even as soon as the youngest child reaches the age of 3-5. In Country Group 2 ("Polarised female labour market behaviour"), where mothers work either full-time or not at all, the probability of working full- rather than part-time increases only when the youngest child is aged between 6 and 10 years old. And in countries where mothers often work part-time ("Women in long-term part-time work", Country Group 1), the probability of working full-time increases only when the youngest child is 11 to 15 years old, as is also the case in countries with a relatively narrow gender gap in working hours (e.g. France and the Nordics, Country Group 4).

The impact of the number of children on the probability of a mother working full-time differs too. In Eastern European countries (Country Group 3), the number of children in a household does not appear to have a significant impact on the likelihood of an employed mother working full- rather than part-time. In all other country groups, the probability of full-time employment falls as the number of children rises.

High education has a similar effect Country Group 1, Country Group 2 and Country Group 4. For mothers in these country groups, the association with education largely follows that shown for the whole sample in Table 4.1: employed mothers with a high level of educational attainment are significantly more likely to work full-time than otherwise similar employed mothers with a low level of education attainment, all else held constant. Country Group 3 again stands out. Unlike the other three country groups, the probability of an employed mother working full- or part-time does not differ across levels of education.

The effects of the partner's characteristics on the chances of an employed woman working full-time are not uniform across country groups either. In Country Groups 2, 3 and 4, the characteristics of the partner share little or no association with the probability of an employed mother working full-time. In Country Group 2, there is a negative significant association between an employed mother having a high-earning partner and the likelihood of the mother working part-time, but the marginal effect is only small. Employed mothers with a high-earning partner are only about 2 percentage points less likely to work full-time than otherwise similar mothers with a low-earning partner. Otherwise, the partner's characteristics appear to have no effect on the probability of full-time work.

However, for employed mothers in Country Group 1 ("Women in long-term part-time work"), the characteristics of the partner do seem to have a considerable effect on the probability of mothers' full-time employment. In this group, mothers are less likely to work full-time if they have a high-earning partner – about 10 percentage points less likely in fact, relative to women with a low-earning partner – and are also significantly *more* likely to work full-time if they have a partner who works very long full-time hours (45 hours per week or more). This latter finding may appear a little counter-intuitive, as mothers might be expected to reduce their working time when their partners work long hours. Then again, the results may reflect a tendency among individuals to choose partners with the same or similar characteristics (e.g. education levels) and preferences (e.g. regarding the pursuit of labour market aspirations).

Table 4.2. Partners' earnings are more important for mothers' probability of full-time against part-time employment in Country Group 1

Marginal effects of logit regressions with robust standard errors, women aged 25 to 45 with at least one child and a full-time employed partner, European countries, by country group

		Country Group 1		Country Group 2		Country Group 3		Country Group 4	
		dy/dx	t-statistic	dy/dx	t-statistic	dy/dx	t-statistic	dy/dx	t-statistic
Age:	25-29	Ref.		Ref.		Ref.		Ref.	
	30-34	-0.00882	(-0.37)	0.0253	(1.08)	0.00198	(0.09)	0.0201	(0.63)
	35-39	0.0167	(0.68)	0.0201	(0.86)	0.00669	(0.31)	0.0313	(0.96)
	40-45	-0.0249	(-0.95)	0.0307	(1.26)	0.0156	(0.69)	0.0437	(1.26)
Age of youngest child:	1-2	Ref.		Ref.		Ref.		Ref.	
	3-5	0.000590	(0.04)	0.00472	(0.33)	0.0683*	(2.17)	-0.0201	(-0.97)
	6-10	-0.0250	(-1.47)	0.0431**	(3.02)	0.106***	(3.32)	0.00162	(0.07)
	11-15	0.0671**	(3.19)	0.0430*	(2.57)	0.131***	(3.97)	0.0774**	(3.04)
	16-20	0.190***	(6.27)	0.0665***	(3.44)	0.134***	(3.94)	0.0796*	(2.34)
	21-28	0.151**	(2.61)	0.103***	(3.65)	0.157***	(4.41)	0.0105	(0.11)
Number of children:	1	Ref.		Ref.		Ref.		Ref.	
	2	-0.0740***	(-5.83)	-0.0238**	(-2.63)	0.000456	(0.05)	-0.0677***	(-4.13)
	3	-0.0898***	(-5.07)	-0.0483**	(-2.94)	-0.0150	(-1.03)	-0.174***	(-7.75)
	4 or more	-0.153***	(-4.36)	-0.00375	(-0.11)	-0.0298	(-1.18)	-0.126***	(-3.41)
Marital status:	Married	Ref.		Ref.		Ref.		Ref.	
	Not married	0.0397**	(2.59)	-0.0131	(-0.88)	0.0300**	(3.20)	0.0144	(0.95)
Education:	Low education (ISCED 1997 levels 0-2)	Ref.		Ref.		Ref.		Ref.	
	Middle education (ISCED 1997 levels 3-4)	-0.0253	(-1.34)	0.0339*	(2.44)	0.0251	(1.06)	0.0339	(1.10)
	High education (ISCED 1997 levels 5-6)	0.0802***	(3.89)	0.109***	(7.71)	0.0423	(1.75)	0.118***	(3.89)
Partner earning (full time):	Low earnings (1st tercile)	Ref.		Ref.		Ref.		Ref.	
	Middle earnings (2nd tercile)	-0.0315*	(-2.27)	-0.00300	(-0.30)	-0.00179	(-0.19)	0.0174	(1.06)
	High earnings (3nd tercile)	-0.106***	(-7.42)	-0.0215*	(-2.01)	-0.0182	(-1.78)	-0.0247	(-1.41)
Partner's weekly working hours (full-time)	Less than 40h	Ref.		Ref.		Ref.		Ref.	
	40-44h	0.0165	(1.12)	-0.0137	(-1.01)	-0.00190	(-0.14)	-0.0215	(-1.19)
	45+h	0.0496**	(3.20)	-0.0271	(-1.88)	-0.0170	(-1.20)	-0.0184	(-1.06)
Country fixed effects		yes		yes		yes		yes	
Number of observations		6417	-	7173	-	4484	-	4648	-

Note: t statistics in parentheses: * p<0.05, ** p<0.01, *** p<0.001. dy/dx for factor levels is the discrete change from the base level.

Women's education levels correspond to the International Standard Classification of Education (ISCED) 1997: low education – highest level of educational attainment at ISCED 1997 Levels 0 2 (pre-primary, primary, lower secondary); moderate education – highest level of educational attainment at ISCED 1997 Levels 3 4 (upper and post-secondary), and high education – highest level of educational attainment at ISCED 1997 Levels 5 6 (tertiary education).

Male partners' earnings level are determined by country-specific earnings terciles and include gross employee income and profits from self-employment.

Countries included are Austria, Belgium, the Czech Republic, Denmark, Estonia, Finland, France, Germany, Greece, Hungary, Iceland, Ireland, Italy, Latvia, Lithuania, Luxembourg, the Netherlands, Norway, Poland, Portugal, the Slovak Republic, Slovenia, Spain, Sweden, Switzerland and the United Kingdom.

The income reference year is 2011.

Source: OECD calculations based on European Union Statistics on Income and Living Conditions (EU SILC) 2012.

5. Concluding remarks

How couples with children share their working hours and earnings varies widely across countries. While the within-couple working-hours gap is smallest in the Nordic countries and France, it is largest in countries where fathers typically work long full-time hours and mothers work few or no hours. For European countries the analysis in this chapter has sought to show that in most countries mothers are more likely to work full-time than part-time the more educated they are, the older their children are and the fewer children they have. In some countries the earnings of their partners also shape mothers' decision to work full-time or not.

However, the analysis also finds that different practices are observed in different groups of countries. Only in the Nordics and France are women equally distributed between full-time and part-time work, and choosing between full-time and part-time does not necessarily entail a choice between two completely different regimes. In other countries, uneven distribution suggests that mothers who want to participate in the labour market are more or less obliged to work full-time – in the group of countries where female labour force participation is polarised between full- and part-time work, and a group of countries, including Germany where mothers frequently work part-time hours on a long-term, basis.

Cross-country differences suggest that national institutions, public policy, labour market changes, living costs and norms are likely to affect partnered mothers' employment choices. However, this analysis cannot separately identify how, or to what extent, economic and normative factors affect work choices, or how their effects may change over time.

Difficulties in balancing work and family life contribute both to women' relatively low full-time equivalent employment rates and low fertility rates in German-speaking, Southern and Eastern European countries, in contrast to the Nordic countries and France (Luci-Greulich and Thévenon, 2013 and 2014; Greulich et al., 2014). Policy can help parents strike a better balance between work and family life, so helping to sustain birth rates (Chapter 6), female labour force participation, and more equally shared paid work in couple families.

Notes

1. “Parent”, “mother” or “father” refers to the residential mother or father present in a household where at least one child under 18 lives together with a couple (married or cohabitating) identified as his/her parents.

2. In the remainder of this chapter “working hours” refers only to paid hours of work. See Chapter 5 for an analysis of unpaid hours of work in couples.

3. The four country groups are similar to those identified by Delacourt and Zighera (1988), Rubery et al. (1994) and Thévenon, 1999, 2009, 2011). Differences in women’s employment regimes are discussed by analysing the impact of motherhood on women’s labour market participation. The first country group comprises countries where mothers are either inactive or work part-time (Austria, West-Germany, the Netherlands and the United Kingdom). The second one consists of countries where mothers either work full-time or are inactive (polarised behaviour in Southern European countries like Greece, Italy, Portugal and Spain). Eastern European countries represent another group where women resume full-time work after a period of inactivity (Hungary, the Czech Republic and, for earlier years, Poland). In the final group of countries, children have little impact on women’s labour market participation; female employment profiles are quite stable across age groups and most working women work full-time (France, Denmark, former East-Germany, France, and Belgium for earlier years).

4. Wide gender gap in weekly working hours (active population) between the ages of 30 and 60 (around 15 hours) and high part-time rate among active women – around 50% between the ages of 30 and 60.

5. Narrow gender gap in weekly working hours (active population) between the ages of 30 and 60 (less than five hours); low rates of part-time among active women (around 10%), but high levels of inactivity among women that are relatively independent of age (between 10% and 20%); and high unemployment rates of around 10% among women (and high unemployment among men, too).

6. Narrow gender gap in weekly working hours (active population) between the ages of 30 and 60 (less than five hours); low part-time rates among active women (below 10%); levels of inactivity among women aged between 30 and 40 are relatively high (10% to 20%), but falling from the age of 40 onwards.

7. Intermediate gender gap in weekly working hours (active population) between the ages of 30 and 60 (between 5 and 10 hours) and an intermediate part-time rate among active women of between 25% and 33% between the ages of 30 and 60.

References

Akunduz, Y.E and J. Plantenga (2015), "Childcare Prices and Maternal Employment: A Meta-Analysis", *Utrecht University School of Economics Discussion Paper*, No. 15-14.

Bergmann, N., U. Papouschek and C. Sorger (2010), "Qualität von Teilzeitbeschäftigung und die Verbesserung der Position von Frauen am Arbeitsmarkt", Research report commissioned by the Austrian Ministry for Women and the Public Service, Vienna.

Bettio, F., J. Plantenga and M. Smith (eds.) (2013), *Gender and the European Labour Market*, Routledge, London.

Cipollone, A., E. Pattichini and G. Vallanti (2013), "Women Labor Market Participation in Europe: Novel Evidence on Trends and Shaping Factors", *IZA Discussion Paper*, No. 7710, Bonn, http://ftp.iza.org/dp7710.pdf.

Connolly, S. and M. Gregory (2010), "Dual Tracks: Part-time Work in Life Cycle Employment for British Women", *Journal of Population Economics*, No. 23, pp. 907-931.

D'Addio, A.C. (2015), "Explaining the Gender Pension Gap in OECD Countries: Socio-economic Determinants and Pension Rules That Matter", unpublished manuscript.

D'Addio, A.C. (2009), "Pension Entitlements of Women with Children", Chapter 12 in R. Holtzmann, E. Plamer and D. Robalino (eds.), *Nonfinancial Defined Contribution Pension Schemes in a Changing Pension World*, Vol. 2, pp. 75-111.

Delacourt, M.L. and J. Zighera (1988), "Activité féminine et composition des familles: comparaison entre pays de la Communauté économique européenne", Recherche et Prévisions, Vol. 18, No. 1, p. 37.

European Commission (2006), "The Gender Pay Gap – Origins and Policy Responses. A Comparative Review of 30 European Countries", Directorate-General for Employment, Social Affairs and Equal Opportunities, July 2006.

Eurostat (2016), "Gender Pay Gap Statistics", Statistics explained, http://ec.europa.eu/eurostat/statistics-explained/index.php/Gender_pay_gap_statistics.

Fagnani, J. (2004), "Schwestern oder entfernte Kusinen? Deutsche und französische Familienpolitik im Vergleich", in W. Neumann (ed.), *Welche Zukunft für den Sozialstaat? Reformpolitik in Frankreich und Deutschland*, pp. 205-262, Verlag für Sozialwissenschaften, Wiesbaden.

Greulich, A., O. Thévenon and M. Guergoat-Larivière (2014), "Starting or Enlarging Families? The Determinants of Low Fertility in Europe", Research report for the World Bank's Human Development Department.

Horemans, J. and I. Marx (2013), "In-work Poverty in Times of Crisis: Do Part-timers Fare Worse?", *ImPRovE Working Papers No. 13/14*, Herman Deleeck Centrum voor Sociale Politiek, Universiteit van Antwerpen.

Kalíšková, K. (2015), "Tax and Transfer Policies and the Female Labor Supply in the EU", *IZA Discussion Paper*, No. 8949, IZA, Bonn, http://ftp.iza.org/dp8949.pdf.

Lestrade, B. (2013), "Mini jobs en Allemagne, une forme de travail à temps partiel très répandue mais contestée", *Revue Française des Affaires Sociales*, No. 4, La Documentation Française.

Luci-Greulich, A. and O. Thévenon (2014), "Does Economic Development 'Cause' a Re-increase in Fertility? An Empirical Analysis for OECD Countries (1960-2007)", *European Journal of Population*, Vol. 30, No. 2, pp. 187-221.

Luci-Greulich, A. and O. Thévenon (2013), "The Impact of Family Policy Packages on Fertility Trends in Developed Countries", *European Journal of Population*, Vol. 29 No. 4, pp. 387-416.

OECD (2016), "OECD Gender Data Portal", OECD Publishing, Paris, https://www.oecd.org/gender/data/.

OECD (2015), *Pensions at a Glance 2015: OECD and G20 Indicators*, OECD Publishing, Paris, http://dx.doi.org/10.1787/pension_glance-2015-en.

OECD (2007), *Babies and Bosses – Reconciling Work and Family Life*, OECD Publishing, Paris, http://dx.doi.org/10.1787/9789264032477-en.

Pailhé, A. and A. Solaz (2009), *Entre famille et travail. Des arrangements de couples aux pratiques des employeurs*, Editions La Découverte, Paris.

Rubery, J., C. Fagan and M. Smith (1994), "Changing Patterns of Work and Working Time in the European Union and the Impact of Gender Divisions", Report for the Equal Opportunities Unit, DGV, Commission of the European Communities.

Thévenon, O. (2016), "Do 'Institutional Complementarities' Foster Female Labour Force Participation?", *Journal of Institutional Economics*, Vol. 12, No. 2, pp. 471-497, June, http://dx.doi.org/10.1017/S1744137415000399.

Thévenon, O. (2013), "Drivers of Female Labour Force Participation in the OECD", *OECD Social, Employment and Migration Working Papers*, No. 145, OECD Publishing. Paris, http://dx.doi.org/10.1787/5k46cvrgnms6-en.

Thévenon, O. (2011), "Family Policies in OECD Countries: A Comparative Analysis", *Population and Development Review*, Vol. 37, No. 1, pp. 57-87.

Thévenon, O. (2009), "Increased Women's Labour Force Participation in Europe: Progress in the Work-Life Balance or Polarization of Behaviours?", *Population* (English Edition 2002), Vol. 64, No. 2, pp. 235-272.

Thévenon, O. (1999), "La durée du travail féminin en Europe : entre flexibilité et conformité. Une comparaison des relations emploi-famille en Allemagne de l'Ouest, Espagne, France, aux Pays-Bas et Royaume-Uni", *Recherches et Prévisions*, No. 56, pp. 47-66.

Thévenon, O. and A. Luci (2012), "Reconciling Work, Family and Children's Outcomes: What Implications for Family Policies?", *Population Research and Policy Review*, Vol. 31, No. 6, pp. 855-882, December.

Thiemann, A. (2015), "Pension Wealth and Maternal Employment: Evidence from a Reform of the German Child Care Pension Benefit", *DIW Discussion Papers*, No. 1499, German Institute for Economic Research (DIW), Berlin.

Annex 4.A1

Working hours of mothers and fathers and fathers' reasons for part-time work

Figure 4.A1.1. Part-time working hours of German fathers are higher than for mothers

Average usual weekly working hours for male part-time workers (partnered, female partner aged 25 to 45, with at least one child), 2012

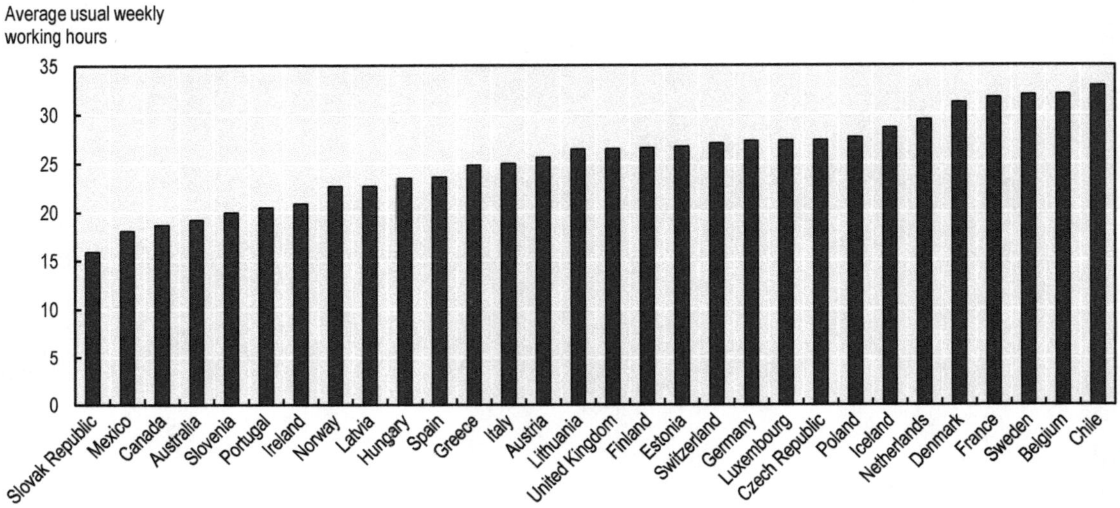

Note: Usual working hours of the (self-)employed for European countries, actual hours worked for Chile and Mexico. Data refer to total hours worked in all jobs, except for Chile where only hours worked in the main job are considered.

The distinction between part-time and full-time employment is self-defined – i.e. based on respondents' own perceptions of whether they are in part-time or full-time employment. Part-time status based on weekly working hours below 30 for Australia, Canada and Mexico.

For Canada fathers living in same household with their partner/spouse (married or common-law) and aged 25 to 50 are considered.

Data for Australia refer to 2014, Canada refer to 2011, for Chile to 2013, for Mexico to 2014, and for the United States to 2014.

Source: OECD calculations based on the Household, Income and Labour Dynamics in Australia (HILDA) Survey 2014 for Australia, the Survey of Labour and Income Dynamics (SLID) 2011 for Canada, the *Encuesta de Caracterización Socioeconómica Nacional* (CASEN) 2013 for Chile, European Union Statistics on Income and Living Conditions (EU SILC) 2012 for European countries, the *Encuesta Nacional de Ingresos y Gastos de los Hogares* (ENIGH) 2014 for Mexico, the Current Population Survey (CPS) 2014 for the United States.

Figure 4.A1.2. In most countries labour demand shortages are the main reason for fathers working part-time

Main reasons (in percentages) for partnered fathers (female partner aged 25 to 45, with at least one child), with at least one child, working less than 30 hours/week

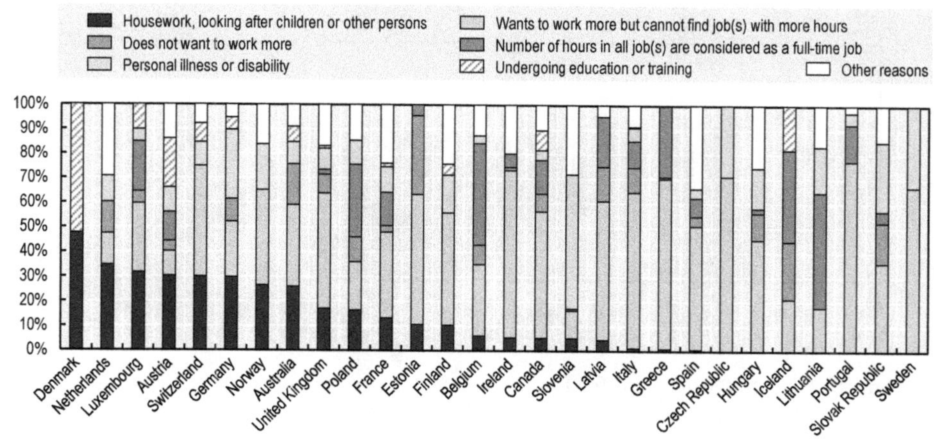

Source: OECD calculations based on the Household, Income and Labour Dynamics in Australia (HILDA) Survey 2014 for Australia, the Survey of Labour and Income Dynamics (SLID) 2011 for Canada, European Union Statistics of Income and Living Conditions (EU SILC) 2012 for European countries.

Figure 4.A1.3. Full-time working hours for German fathers are relatively high

Average usual weekly working hours for fathers (partnered, female partner aged 25 to 45, with at least one child), 2012

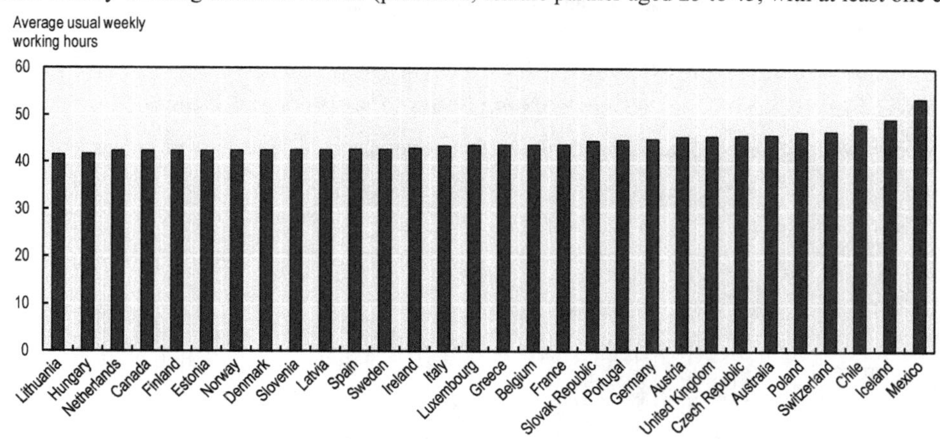

Note: Usual working hours of the (self-)employed for European countries, actual hours worked for Chile and Mexico. Data refer to total hours worked in all jobs, except for Chile where only hours worked in the main job are considered.

The distinction between part-time and full-time employment is self-defined – i.e. based on respondents' own perceptions of whether they are in part-time or full-time employment. Part-time status based on weekly working hours below 30 for Canada and Mexico.

For Canada fathers living in same household with their partner/spouse (married or common-law) and aged 25 to 50 are considered.

Data for Australia refer to 2014, for Canada to 2011, for Chile to 2013, for Mexico to 2014, and for the United States to 2014.

Source: OECD calculations based on the Household, Income and Labour Dynamics in Australia (HILDA) Survey 2014 for Australia, the Survey of Labour and Income Dynamics (SLID) 2011 for Canada, the *Encuesta de Caracterización Socioeconómica Nacional* (CASEN) 2013 for Chile, European Union Statistics on Income and Living Conditions (EU SILC) 2012 for European countries, the *Encuesta Nacional de Ingresos y Gastos de los Hogares* (ENIGH) 2014 for Mexico, the Current Population Survey (CPS) 2014 for the United States.

Figure 4.A1.4. Average working hours of (self-)employed mothers and fathers

Average usual weekly working hours of working mothers and fathers, female partner aged 25 to 45, with at least one child, 2012

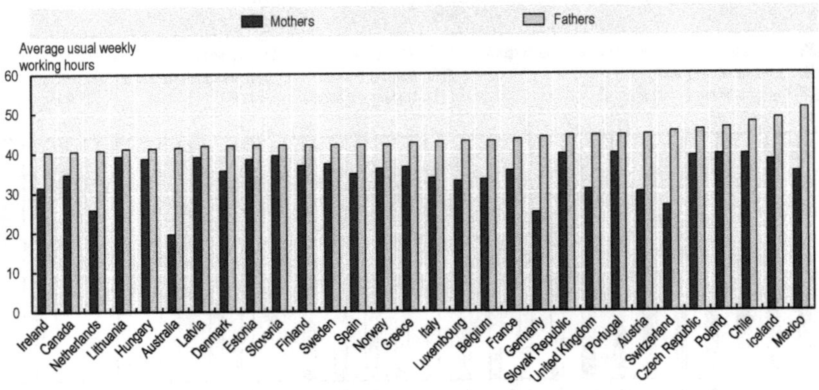

Note: Usual working hours of the (self-)employed for European countries, actual hours worked for Chile and Mexico. Data refer to total hours worked in all jobs, except for Chile where only hours worked in the main job are considered. Only work hours greater than 0 are considered.

The distinction between part-time and full-time employment is self-defined – i.e. based on respondents' own perceptions of whether they are in part-time or full-time employment. No self-defined part-time status available for Mexico, weekly working hours of below 30 hours are defined as part-time instead.

Data for Australia refer to 2014, for Canada to 2011, for Chile to 2013, and for Mexico to 2014.

Source: OECD calculations based on the Household, Income and Labour Dynamics in Australia (HILDA) Survey 2014 for Australia, the Survey of Labour and Income Dynamics (SLID) 2011 for Canada, the *Encuesta de Caracterización Socioeconómica Nacional* (CASEN) 2013 for Chile, European Union Statistics on Income and Living Conditions (EU SILC) 2012 for European countries, the *Encuesta Nacional de Ingresos y Gastos de los Hogares* (ENIGH) 2014 for Mexico.

Figure 4.A1.5. Average working hours of mothers and fathers

Average usual weekly working hours of mothers and fathers, female partner aged 25 to 45, with at least one child, 2012

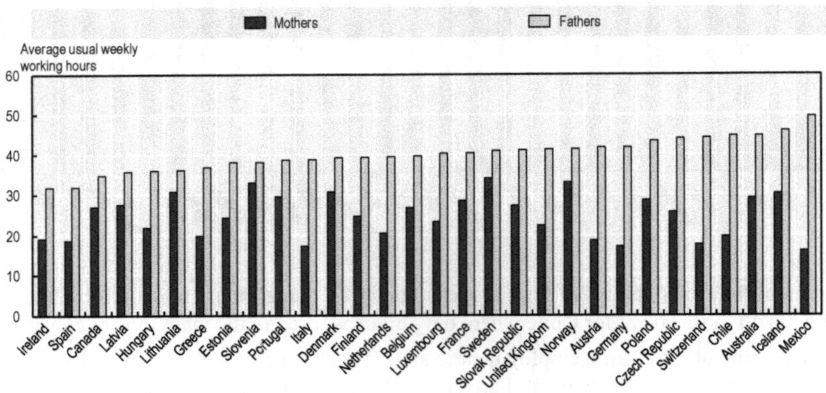

Note: Usual working hours of the (self-)employed for European countries, actual hours worked for Chile and Mexico. Data refer to total hours worked in all jobs, except for Chile where only hours worked in the main job are considered.

The distinction between part-time and full-time employment is self-defined – i.e. based on respondents' own perceptions of whether they are in part-time or full-time employment. No self-defined part-time status available for Mexico, weekly working hours of below 30 hours are defined as part-time instead.

Data for Australia refer to 2014, for Canada to 2011, for Chile to 2013 and for Mexico to 2014.

Source: OECD calculations based on the Household, Income and Labour Dynamics in Australia (HILDA) Survey 2014 for Australia, the Survey of Labour and Income Dynamics (SLID) 2011 for Canada, the *Encuesta de Caracterización Socioeconómica Nacional* (CASEN) 2013 for Chile, European Union Statistics on Income and Living Conditions (EU SILC) 2012 for European countries, the *Encuesta Nacional de Ingresos y Gastos de los Hogares* (ENIGH) 2014 for Mexico.

Annex 4.A2

Predicted probabilities of full-time employment among mothers with a dependent child

Table 4.A2.1. Predicted probabilities of full-time employment against part-time employment

Predicted probabilities of logit regressions with robust standard errors, women aged 25 to 45 with at least one child and a full-time employed partner, European countries

		(1)		(2)	
		Margin	t-statistic	Margin	t-statistic
Age:	25-29	0.684***	(58.46)	0.677***	(57.14)
	30-34	0.685***	(107.68)	0.681***	(106.32)
	35-39	0.686***	(148.23)	0.686***	(148.41)
	40-45	0.681***	(159.03)	0.684***	(159.32)
Age of youngest child:	1-2	0.659***	(94.92)	0.659***	(95.22)
	3-5	0.657***	(117.04)	0.657***	(117.54)
	6-10	0.673***	(142.90)	0.674***	(143.10)
	11-15	0.721***	(118.57)	0.720***	(118.45)
	16-20	0.761***	(80.30)	0.759***	(79.91)
	21-28	0.774***	(38.42)	0.771***	(38.22)
Number of children:	1	0.718***	(156.86)	0.717***	(156.68)
	2	0.677***	(191.24)	0.678***	(191.80)
	3	0.639***	(89.41)	0.639***	(89.43)
	4 or more	0.642***	(42.75)	0.641***	(42.54)
Marital status:	Married	0.679***	(240.75)	0.680***	(241.21)
	Not married	0.702***	(115.82)	0.700***	(115.44)
Education:	Low education (ISCED 1997 levels 0-2)	0.644***	(73.93)	0.635***	(71.77)
	Middle education (ISCED 1997 levels 3-4)	0.655***	(165.55)	0.652***	(164.13)
	High education (ISCED 1997 levels 5-6)	0.722***	(189.99)	0.726***	(189.87)
Partner earnings (full time):	Low earnings (1st tercile)			0.701***	(153.56)
	Middle earnings (2nd tercile)			0.695***	(161.18)
	High earnings (3nd tercile)			0.657***	(148.28)
Partner's weekly working hours (full-time)	Less than 40h			0.686***	(118.36)
	40-44h			0.682***	(177.46)
	45+h			0.684***	(149.76)
Number of observations		23237	-	23237	-

Note: t statistics in parentheses: * p<0.05, ** p<0.01, *** p<0.001.

Women's education levels correspond to the International Standard Classification of Education (ISCED) 1997: low education – highest level of educational attainment at ISCED 1997 Levels 0 2 (pre-primary, primary, lower secondary); moderate education – highest level of educational attainment at ISCED 1997 Levels 3 4 (upper and post-secondary), and high education – highest level of educational attainment at ISCED 1997 Levels 5 6 (tertiary education).

Male partners' earnings levels are determined by country-specific earnings terciles and include gross employee income and profits from self-employment.

Countries included are Austria, Belgium, the Czech Republic, Denmark, Estonia, Finland, France, Germany, Greece, Hungary, Iceland, Ireland, Italy, Latvia, Lithuania, Luxembourg, the Netherlands, Norway, Poland, Portugal, the Slovak Republic, Slovenia, Spain, Sweden, Switzerland and the United Kingdom.

The income reference year is 2011.

Source: OECD calculations based on European Union Statistics on Income and Living Conditions (EU SILC) 2012.

Table 4.A2.2. Predicted probabilities of full-time against part-time employment by country group

Predicted probabilities of logit regressions with robust standard errors, women aged 25 to 45 with at least one child and a full-time employed partner, European countries, by country group

		Country Group 1		Country Group 2		Country Group 3		Country Group 4	
		Margin	t-statistic	Margin	t-statistic	Margin	t-statistic	Margin	t-statistic
Age:	25-29	0.338***	(15.01)	0.807***	(36.10)	0.908***	(44.76)	0.658***	(21.63)
	30-34	0.329***	(25.82)	0.832***	(76.85)	0.910***	(85.26)	0.678***	(38.88)
	35-39	0.355***	(34.76)	0.827***	(109.55)	0.915***	(125.09)	0.689***	(56.56)
	40-45	0.313***	(32.87)	0.838***	(124.16)	0.924***	(133.55)	0.701***	(60.74)
Age of youngest child:	1-2	0.313***	(25.33)	0.803***	(68.11)	0.812***	(25.77)	0.676***	(40.08)
	3-5	0.313***	(29.06)	0.807***	(84.70)	0.880***	(73.23)	0.656***	(45.89)
	6-10	0.288***	(27.63)	0.846***	(114.36)	0.918***	(124.01)	0.678***	(52.39)
	11-15	0.380***	(26.04)	0.846***	(83.98)	0.943***	(127.92)	0.754***	(47.03)
	16-20	0.502***	(19.60)	0.869***	(65.23)	0.946***	(102.59)	0.756***	(27.70)
	21-28	0.463***	(8.36)	0.905***	(37.04)	0.969***	(68.44)	0.687***	(7.55)
Number of children:	1	0.384***	(39.03)	0.848***	(129.95)	0.921***	(121.01)	0.763***	(57.40)
	2	0.310***	(40.84)	0.824***	(137.66)	0.921***	(162.03)	0.696***	(75.96)
	3	0.294***	(20.53)	0.800***	(54.13)	0.906***	(76.67)	0.589***	(34.51)
	4 or more	0.231***	(6.89)	0.845***	(26.10)	0.891***	(38.34)	0.637***	(18.84)
Marital status:	Married	0.324***	(55.40)	0.833***	(191.60)	0.911***	(189.76)	0.686***	(86.12)
	Not married	0.364***	(25.97)	0.820***	(58.27)	0.941***	(120.60)	0.701***	(55.72)
Education:	Low education (ISCED 1997 levels 0-2)	0.309***	(17.94)	0.774***	(63.04)	0.886***	(38.47)	0.613***	(21.23)
	Middle education (ISCED 1997 levels 3-4)	0.284***	(36.08)	0.808***	(120.71)	0.911***	(146.98)	0.646***	(57.90)
	High education (ISCED 1997 levels 5-6)	0.389***	(41.20)	0.883***	(143.40)	0.928***	(148.66)	0.731***	(83.46)
Partner earning (full time):	Low earnings (1st tercile)	0.379***	(36.42)	0.840***	(117.77)	0.924***	(135.64)	0.693***	(57.15)
	Middle earnings (2nd tercile)	0.347***	(37.05)	0.837***	(116.86)	0.922***	(134.54)	0.710***	(63.72)
	High earnings (3nd tercile)	0.273***	(30.50)	0.818***	(107.66)	0.906***	(120.84)	0.668***	(56.06)
Partner's weekly working hours (full-time)	Less than 40h	0.306***	(25.95)	0.848***	(69.24)	0.923***	(79.69)	0.704***	(58.28)
	40-44h	0.323***	(38.98)	0.835***	(152.04)	0.921***	(172.49)	0.682***	(55.18)
	45+h	0.356***	(37.13)	0.821***	(106.90)	0.906***	(106.71)	0.685***	(57.89)
Number of observations		6417	-	7173	-	4484	-	4648	-

Note: t statistics in parentheses: * $p<0.05$, ** $p<0.01$, *** $p<0.001$.

Women's education levels correspond to the International Standard Classification of Education (ISCED) 1997: low education – highest level of educational attainment at ISCED 1997 Levels 0 2 (pre-primary, primary, lower secondary); moderate education – highest level of educational attainment at ISCED 1997 Levels 3 4 (upper and post-secondary), and high education – highest level of educational attainment at ISCED 1997 Levels 5 6 (tertiary education).

Male partners' earnings levels are determined by country-specific earnings terciles and include gross employee income and profits from self-employment.

Countries included are Austria, Belgium, the Czech Republic, Denmark, Estonia, Finland, France, Germany, Greece, Hungary, Iceland, Ireland, Italy, Latvia, Lithuania, Luxembourg, the Netherlands, Norway, Poland, Portugal, the Slovak Republic, Slovenia, Spain, Sweden, Switzerland and the United Kingdom.

The income reference year is 2011.

Source: OECD calculations based on European Union Statistics on Income and Living Conditions (EU SILC) 2012.

Chapter 5

How partners in couples share unpaid work

This chapter examines how equally, or unequally, couples share unpaid work – i.e. housework and parenting. The chapter uses micro data from time use surveys in 11 countries to better understand how couples share unpaid work and can do so more equally. It begins by introducing the issues to hand, then lists the chapter's main findings before looking at couples' work, both paid and unpaid. It finds that, in many but not all countries, women do more work on aggregate. It also explores how couples of different ages share unpaid work and concludes that the gender gap in unpaid work is widest in older couples. It examines couples in which both partners do paid work and finds that, in general, they share unpaid work more equally than those where only one partner works. On the whole, though, the chapter finds that women do more work, paid and unpaid, as men. Section 4 looks at the factors that affect and shape the sharing of unpaid work and observes that with parenthood couples share paid and unpaid work the traditional way. The same section also considers child care and finds that, while mothers nurture young children, the gap in parenting between fathers and mothers decreases once children start school. Indeed, a high proportion of fathers' time with their children is quality time. Section 5 gives consideration of care for other adults in the household and finds that in most countries partnered men are less likely to be involved in care than partnered women.

The statistical data for Israel are supplied by and under the responsibility of the relevant Israeli authorities. The use of such data by the OECD is without prejudice to the status of the Golan Heights, East Jerusalem and Israeli settlements in the West Bank under the terms of international law.

1. Introduction and main findings

Equal sharing in partnerships should mean that both parents do the same amount of paid and unpaid work. Yet, as the previous chapter shows, men do a lot more paid work than women on average. This chapter draws on time use data to demonstrate that, when it comes to unpaid work, women – particularly mothers – do considerably more time than men and fathers. In many countries, the gender gap in unpaid work mirrors the gender gap in paid work (OECD, 2012).

The reasons why women spend much more time on unpaid work are manifold. Some women actually prefer fewer hours of paid work and even no work at all, particularly when they have young children. However, many do want paid work and/or more paid hours. They struggle to reconcile work and family life because of constraints like access to affordable, good-quality child care facilities and flexible working-time arrangements. How partners share unpaid work is also influenced by factors closely related to the family such as its size, partners' levels of educational attainment, their relative earnings (potential), and the ways in which they are able to organise their paid working hours.

Equal sharing at home has many benefits for both partners. If men do more unpaid housework and parenting work, they free up more time for their partners in the labour market. Sharing more equally at home enables fathers to take a more active part in their children's upbringing and strengthens father-child bonding, so improving the well-being of the whole family.

This chapter analyses how couples share unpaid work. To that end, it uses micro data from harmonised time use surveys in 11 countries. It examines how couples of different ages share differently and whether couples in which both partners do paid work share unpaid work more equally than those where only one partner works (generally the man). A comparison of young couples with and without children shows how parenthood affects sharing. The last section analyses in more detail the time that parents spend caring for children and which partner cares for other adults in the household.

Main findings

- In selected OECD countries, female partners in couple families spend, on average, twice as much time on unpaid work at home as their male partners.[1] Even if both partners are in paid work on a full-time basis, they do not share unpaid work equally. Nevertheless, the unpaid work gender gap is narrower in such couples than in those where the man is the sole breadwinner.
- High-income and highly educated couples share unpaid work more equitably. Partners in such couples are also more likely both to be in full-time work.
- Of the 11 countries for which micro-data were analysed – Austria, Canada, Germany, Finland, France, Italy, Korea, Norway, South Africa, Spain and the United States – Norwegian couples are those which share paid and unpaid work most equally, even among parents with very young children. In countries with high female employment rates, more gender-equal attitudes and good-quality formal child care (e.g. Norway, Finland and France), partners in couples share more equally.
- Parenthood proves critical for sharing in couples with very young children, where parents follow more traditional gender roles compared to couples of the same age without children. Well-designed parental leave policies that explicitly encourage the father's involvement can play an important role in encouraging a couple to

sustain a more equally balanced division of paid and unpaid work throughout the time that they transition into parenthood.

- In couple families, fathers spend less time with the children than mothers do, but the gap is smaller on weekends and narrows as children grow older. Fathers spend more of their child care time in interactive parenting, also referred to as "quality time", reading to, playing with, talking to, and teaching the children. Mothers, for their part, devote a relatively larger share of their parenting time to physical care and supervision. And, while mothers spend more minutes of quality time with young children in most countries than fathers do, the gap shrinks, or even disappears, when the children are of school age.
- The literature shows that, over time and in all countries, women have gradually reduced the time they spend on unpaid work, while men still do roughly the same amount of unpaid work. While technology can help ease the unpaid workload, raising awareness of the still uneven distribution of unpaid work between men and women may help foster more equal sharing.

2. Sharing among couples

Overall men work less than women if paid and unpaid work are added together

Throughout the OECD, men do more paid work than women, while women contribute more to unpaid work (Figure 5.1). Overall, however, men work less than women. Traditionally, they are the main (or only) breadwinners, while women are mainly responsible for unpaid work, which includes housework, i.e. cleaning, cooking, caring for children and other tasks besides (Miranda, 2011). As illustrated in Chapter 4, however, many couples are now dual earners and share hours of paid work in different ways.

Figure 5.1. Women do more unpaid work than men in all countries

Female minus male total of paid and unpaid working time in minutes per day

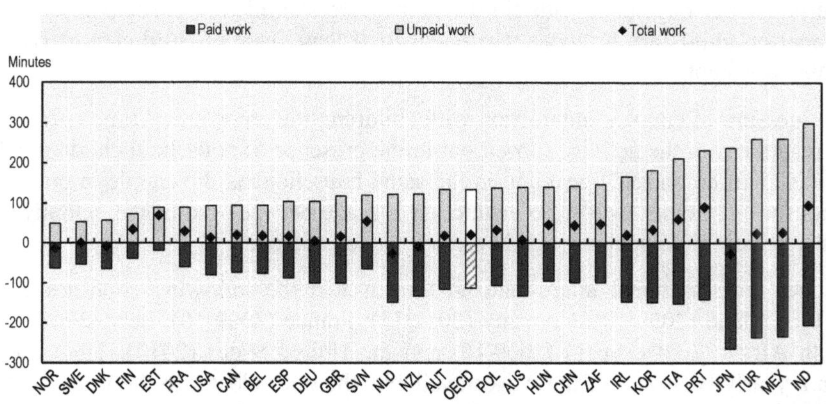

Reading note: In Germany, women do 100.73 less minutes of paid work on average per day than men (dark bars) and 105.4 more minutes of unpaid work than men (light bars). The sum total of women's paid and unpaid work is 4.31 more minutes per day on average than men's (black diamonds).

Data for Australia are for the over 15 year-olds, for Hungary 15-74 year-olds, and for Sweden 25-64 year-olds.

Reference years vary from country to country: Australia, 2006; Austria, 2008-09; Belgium, 2005; Canada, 2010; China, 2008; Denmark, 2001; Estonia, 2009-10; Finland, 2009-10; France, 2009; Germany, 2001-02; Hungary, 1999-2000; India, 1999; Italy, 2008-09; Ireland, 2005; Japan, 2011; Korea, 2009; Mexico, 2009; the Netherlands, 2005-06; New Zealand, 2009-10; Norway, 2010; Poland, 2003-04; Portugal, 1999; Slovenia, 2000-01; South Africa, 2010; Spain, 2009-10; Sweden, 2010; Turkey, 2006; the United Kingdom, 2005; the United States, 2014.

Source: OECD Gender Data Portal, http://www.oecd.org/gender/data.

Box 5.1. Time use surveys: A window into people's lives

Time use surveys are the main source of information on how individuals allot their time day-to-day. Generally, people are asked to keep a diary for one or two days of a certain week, often a week-day and a day on the weekend. In the diary, they note what they did in ten-minute time slots from a prescribed list of activities. They might also state who was with them, where they were, and what else they were doing (secondary activity). National statistics agencies and associated bodies then code the activities the respondent has written down. A fully completed diary thus accounts for a person's activities over 24 hours (or 144 times 10 minutes).

The entries in the diaries may then be grouped into broader categories of activity – such as personal care (sleeping, getting dressed, etc.), employment, education and unpaid work like housework, care and voluntary work, leisure (e.g. sports, media consumption, meeting friends) and other activities (religious activities or keeping the diary). See Miranda (2011) for a detailed outline of the applied methodology.

For the purpose of this analysis the unpaid work category was disaggregated into housework, parenting, and care for household adults. Parenting was further broken down into different sub-categories: physical care and looking after children; teaching, reading, playing and talking with them; accompanying them, and/or other/non-specified. Caring for adults living in the household and helping non-household members is recorded in all countries, but at different levels of detail. Cross-country harmonisation, particularly of information on helping non-household members is challenging, though, as some surveys offer detail on the activities that caring entails (physical care vs. support like letter-writing). Others, however, do not distinguish types of activity or who exactly benefited from the support offered.

Three main time use variables are typically extracted from time use data. In child care activities, for example, the variables are:

1. Participation rate in child care activities: the share of people that recorded a child care activity at least once over the course of the day.
2. Average minutes per day spent on child care activities: the average number of minutes spent on child care regardless of whether respondents participated at all in child care activities; the 0 minutes of those respondents not reporting any child care activity are thus also included in the average.
3. Average minutes per day spent with child care by carers/child care participants: the average time in minutes spent on child care by those that engaged at least once in child care activity during the day that the dairy was kept.

As an alternative measure of couples' interaction with children, this report uses "time spent in the presence of household children" regardless of the activity carried out in the presence of household children, where "household children" are defined as children under 18 residing in the same household as the couple in question, regardless of their biological relationship – in other words, no distinction is made between biological, adoptive and stepparents. Children who live outside their biological parents' home are not considered.

This report includes cross-sectional micro-data on time use in the following countries and years: Austria (2009); Canada (2010); Finland (2009/10); Germany (2012/13); France (2009-10); Italy (2008/09); Korea (2009); Norway (2010); South Africa (2010); Spain (2009/10) and the United States (2010). Time use surveys are not usually conducted on a yearly basis and of the waves available, the ones closest to the years 2009 and 2010 were chosen. The time use surveys are nationally representative (Annex Table 5.A.1 summarises the main features of each survey).

Despite efforts to harmonise time use surveys from one country to another, cross-national results should be interpreted with caution. For example, some countries were at different stages in the economic cycle at the time of their surveys – e.g. Spain in 2010 and Germany in 2012-13.

The gender gap in overall work for partnered men and women is widest among older couples

At different stages in their lives together, partners decide how much time to allot to paid and unpaid work and, by the same token, how to share paid and unpaid work between them. Time use data show that, in all cohorts and countries, partnered women do more work on aggregate than partnered men. The sole exceptions are the youngest cohort, 18 to 24 years old, and Norway (Figure 5.2, Panel A). In cohorts, the gender gap in overall work is widest among the over-65s everywhere except Norway. While older men often do less or no paid work at all at that age, the amount of unpaid work done by women is no lower in the oldest cohort than in younger generations.

Yet the size and shape of gender gaps[2] in paid and unpaid work are not the same from one country and cohort to another. In couple households everywhere at all ages, men do more paid work (the blue, positive bars in Figure 5.2, Panel B) whilst women do more unpaid work (white, negative bars in Panel B). On average, partnered women devote twice as much time to unpaid work as partnered men, although the imbalance varies greatly: Korean partnered men spend 19% of the time on unpaid work that Korean partnered women do, whereas in Norway the ratio is 82%.

Norway stands out on several fronts. It is the only country where, on aggregate, partnered men in all cohorts devote more time to work and where paid and unpaid work is shared most equally in all age groups. The results are confirmed by Aasve et al. (2014) who show that, in a sample of ten countries, couples in Norway share housework most equally.[3]

Among the other ten countries in Figure 5.2, three patterns seem to emerge:

1. In Finland, France and the United States partnered women devote slightly more time to aggregate work than partnered men. Yet they share paid and unpaid work more equally with their partners than in the other countries, with the exception of Norway (see Chapter 4 for further detail on the division of paid working hours between partners in couple families).
2. In Austria, Canada and Germany, men's and women's overall workloads are similar in most age groups. However, partnered women devote significantly more time than partnered men to unpaid work.
3. In Italy, Spain, Korea and South Africa the gender gap in aggregate work persists at all ages, driven largely by traditional gendered patterns in the allocation of time to paid and unpaid work.

Figure 5.2. Overall, partnered women work more than partnered men across different age groups

Panel A. Total (paid and unpaid) work done by partnered individuals, in minutes per day[1]

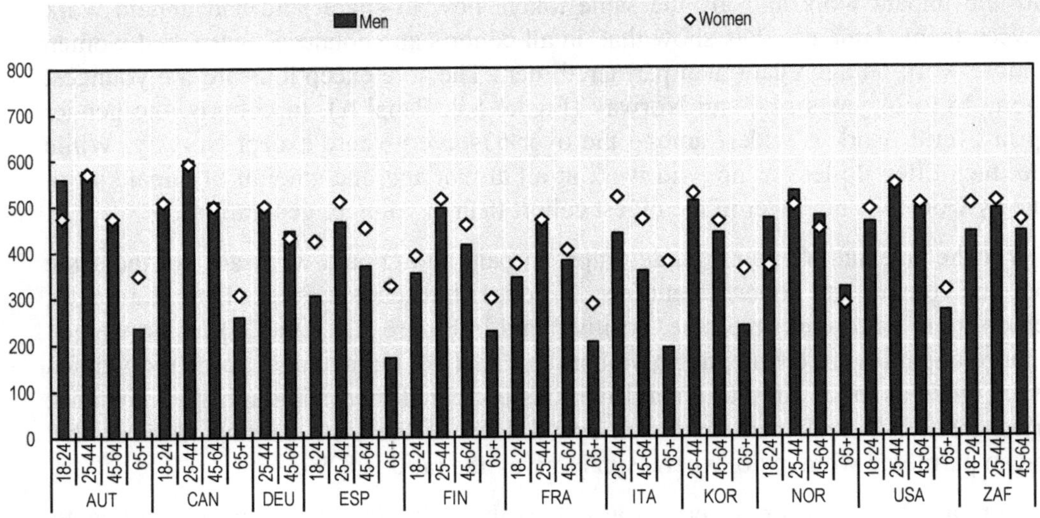

Panel B. Male-female gender gap in the paid and unpaid work of partnered people, in minutes per day[2]

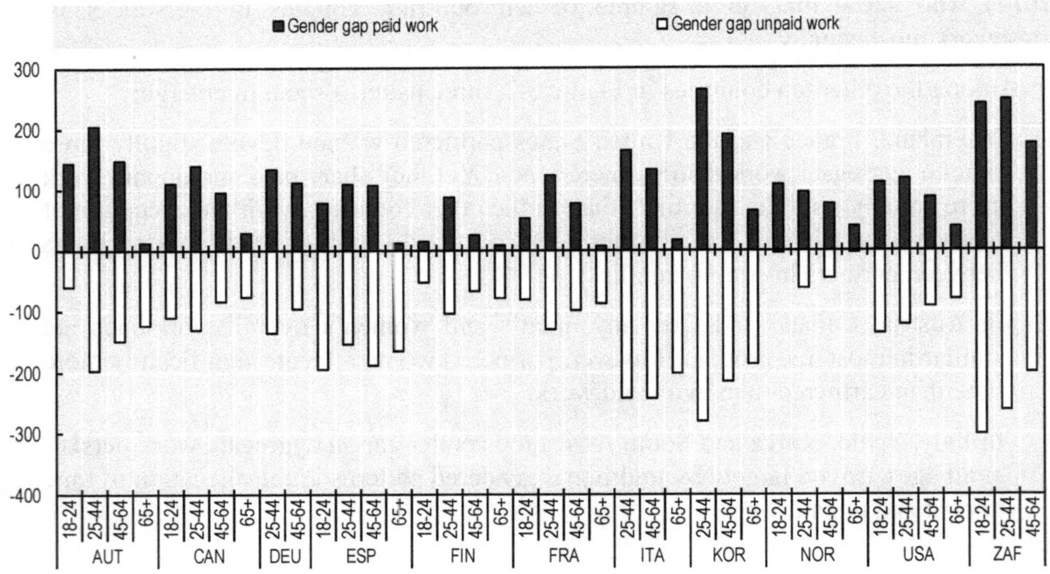

1. Time use data for partnered men and women aged 18 years or above who live in the same household as a spouse or cohabitating partner (married or not). Paid work includes time devoted to education. Too few time use diaries were kept by 18-to-24 year-old men and women living in partnership in Italy and Korea and those aged 65 or more in South Africa.

2. The gender gap in paid and unpaid work is calculated as the number of minutes per day that partnered men spend on paid and unpaid work minus the minutes per day that partnered women spend on paid and unpaid work.

Source: *OECD Time Use Database* (see Annex Table 5.A1.1 for more information); data for Germany as provided by the German Statistical Office based on the German Time Use Survey 2012-13 (Destatis, 2015).

Micro and macro level factors are associated with more equal sharing

Many factors – like partners' earnings potential, preferences and policies – may explain how couples share their overall workload and allocate time to paid and unpaid work. As outlined in Chapter 2, theoretical models of the division of paid and unpaid work in families include considerations that relate to:

- the specialised skills and comparative advantage of partners in couples,
- bargaining between partners – prompted by, for example, relative earnings and/or wishing to avoid undesirable housework,
- meeting gender norms or "doing gender".

Empirical studies associate various micro- and macro-level factors with couples sharing more equally. They are more likely to share unpaid work (more) equally, for example, if they are unmarried, have higher education qualifications, or if they come from post-communist countries (Box 5.2). Literature highlights parenthood as a critical phase, as it is a time which determines couples' future sharing patterns in paid and unpaid work (Baxter, 2008; Schober, 2013; Barnes, 2015). As Chapter 3 explains, poor public provisions (e.g. lack of child care infrastructure) and family-unfriendly workplace practices (like rigid working hours) may discourage or prevent couples from sharing throughout their lives together, while others – such as the daddy months in parental leave schemes – may encourage it.

The literature also illustrates how macro-level variables – such as gender inequality in the public sphere, societal attitudes, policies, and female employment rates – are associated with different degrees of sharing from country to country. Fuwa (2004) and Hook (2006) show that higher female employment rates are associated with men more active in unpaid work. Hook also points out that the time that single men spend on unpaid work increases with women's employment rates. She discusses gender norms or improving one's chances on the marriage market as possible explanations. Geist (2005) considered micro and macro factors simultaneously. While relative income, time availability and gender ideology shape patterns within couples, female labour force participation and the welfare regime both matter on the macro level. Men's equal gender attitudes (micro level) are important for the division of household chores particularly in countries with traditionally social-democratic regimes, such as Norway and Sweden, but less so in conservative countries like Japan, Italy and Austria (macro level). Although statistical analyses cannot establish a clear causal link between structural and institutional conditions on one hand and individual behaviour on the other, "structural effects exist in addition to the individual level process" (Geist, 2005, p. 37).

Box 5.2. What makes equal-sharers share (more) equally?

The literature has identified a number of distinguishing attributes in couple families that share (more) equally. While some studies draw on time use surveys, a large body of literature relies on surveys in which respondents (often only one partner and not both) are asked who usually performs how much of the couple's unpaid and household work. Most studies focus on housework as a traditionally female task, while some also or only focus on child care. The most commonly identified characteristics of couples who share (more) equally in the literature include:

- *Cohabitation.* Unmarried cohabitating couples share more equally than married couples (Baxter, 2005; Deding, 2006; Baxter, 2008; Dominguez-Folgueras, 2012). Married couples who first cohabitated also share more equally.
- *Partner's employment.* The more time the woman in dual-earner couples spends in paid work, the more equally such couples share housework (Gershuny et al., 2005; Grunow, 2012; Aassve et al., 2014). The pattern is driven mostly by women reducing their unpaid work, as men's unpaid work hours vary little, if at all, with women's paid work hours.
- *The relative earnings of the female partner.* Higher relative income of the female partner is associated with more equally shared household work. The relationship between relative earnings and the sharing of household work is not proportional, though, and there is evidence that in couples where the woman earns more than the man, she still does a greater share of housework (Bittman, 2003; Deding, 2006; Ponthieux et al., 2006; Procher et al., 2014; Bertrand et al., 2015; also see Box 2.3).
- *High educational attainment.* Highly educated couples exhibit less traditional norms and share housework and/or parenting more equally (Berkel and de Graaf, 1999; Davis and Greenstein, 2004; Goñi-Legaz, 2010; Sullivan, 2010; Garcia, 2014).
- *Children and parenthood.* Several studies have analysed how children and the transition into parenthood affect the sharing of unpaid household and child care work (Pfahl, 2014; Baxter, 2008; Kühhirt, 2012; Grunow et al., 2012; Schober, 2013; Schober, 2014a; Barnes, 2015). The arrival of children is found to be one of the biggest contributory factors in unequal sharing – childless couples share considerably more equally than couples with children. With parenthood many couples slip (often involuntarily) into a (more) traditional division of paid and unpaid work.
- *Post-communist countries.* Voicu et al. (2008) and Davis and Greenstein (2004) find that housework is more equally shared in the former communist countries of Eastern Europe.
- *Gender-egalitarian attitudes.* Couples with more gender-equal attitudes are more likely to share unpaid work equally (see Chapter 2).

The characteristics listed above all refer to heterosexual couples. Analyses of same-sex couples find that they do on average not fall within traditional heterosexual gender norms. Several studies, mainly in the United States, have looked at gay and lesbian couples, mostly based on surveys that ask about partners' participation in housework and parenting. Although it draws on relatively small samples and case studies, the emerging literature seems to suggest that same-sex couples, particularly lesbian couples, tend to share housework more equally than heterosexual couples (Blumstein and Schwartz, 1983; Dunne, 2000; Ciano-Boyce and Shelley-Sireci, 2002; Solomon et. al, 2005; Kurdek, 2007; Perlesz et al., 2010).

3. Sharing among couples of working age

Men in dual-earner couples do more housework than breadwinner men, but are far from equal sharers

"Equal" sharing in partnerships means that both sexes should both spend equal amounts of time on paid and unpaid work. Young parents (or parents with very young children) particularly report that they struggle to balancing work and (family) life, as they are building careers and families – the so-called "rush hour of life" (Bittman and Wajcman, 2000). Consequently, the ensuing analysis focuses on couples where the woman is of child-bearing age, 25 to 45 years old (and their partners of any age). All inactive, unemployed, employed and self-employed respondents living in partnership in the same household (married or not) are considered. Students and pensioners are excluded to restrict the analysis to the working-age population available to the labour market.

In all OECD countries, partnered women aged between 25 and 45 years old spend more time on unpaid work than partnered men – even if only men and women who work similar paid hours are compared (Figure 5.3). In Italy, for example, partnered women devote twice as much time as partnered men to unpaid work, regardless of their hours in paid work. In Canada, France, Italy and South Africa, unemployed or inactive partnered men spend less time on unpaid work than their female partners who are in paid employment and work between 30 and 34 hours.

Inactive or unemployed partnered women do more unpaid work than women in paid employment everywhere except Norway (Figure 5.3, Panel B). And while partnered women spend less time in unpaid work the more paid work they do, their unpaid work hours are not proportionally lower according to the length of their working week. In comparison to partnered women, partnered men's unpaid work hours, which are generally lower, vary far less widely with the length of their working week.

Figure 5.3. For similar hours of paid work, partnered women do more unpaid work than partnered men

Panel A. Men's unpaid work, in minutes per day, by length of working week, in hours

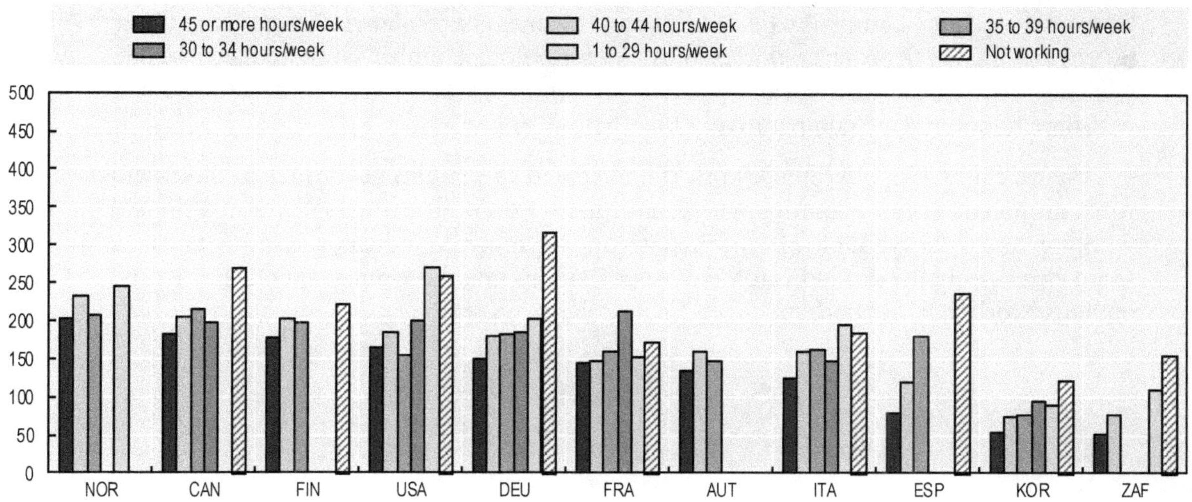

Figure 5.3. For similar hours of paid work, partnered women do more unpaid work than partnered men *(cont.)*

Panel B. Women's unpaid work, in minutes per day, by length of working week, in hours

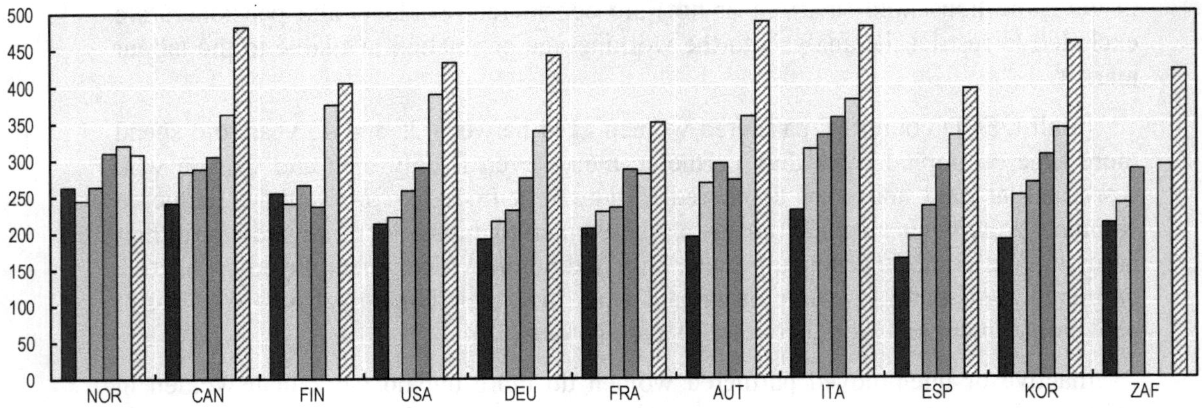

Note: Time use data for partnered men and women who live in the same household as a spouse or cohabitating partner (married or not), women's age restricted to the 25-to-45 year-old age bracket. Pensioners and students are excluded.

Missing data points for subgroups where less than 30 time use diaries were kept.

Source: *OECD Time Use Database* (see Annex Table 5.A1.1 for more information); data for Germany as provided by the German Statistical Office based on the German Time Use Survey 2012-13 (Destatis, 2015).

The time that partners devote to unpaid work is naturally determined by their own paid working hours. However, it also depends on their partner's paid working hours, as the couple has to invest at least some amount of unpaid work in the household. Chapter 4 analyses couples' paid working arrangements and shows that patterns differ by region. In the Nordic countries plus France, more couples work reduced hours, whereas men in German-speaking countries tend to work long hours and women part-time hours that are comparatively low (below 20 per week).

Figure 5.4 shows how housework is distributed in couples according to their paid work arrangements in countries where information on both partners' paid and unpaid working hours is available. If the housework asymmetry indicator is 50% partners share chores equally. An indicator above 50% shows that the woman spends more time on housework than her partner.

Figure 5.4. Even dual-earner couples with similar paid hours do not share housework equally

Percentage of housework done by the female partner, aged 25 to 45

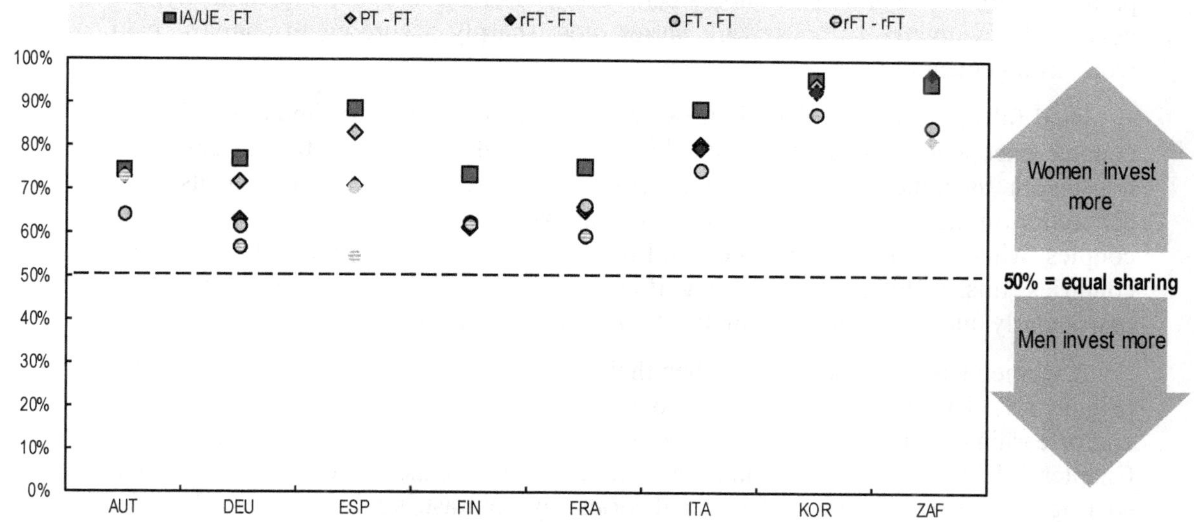

Note: The indicators are acronyms that denote first the woman's and then the man's employment status. IA/UE-FT (blue square) thus denotes a couple where she is inactive/unemployed and he works 40 hours or more – the male breadwinner couple; PT-FT (grey diamond) denotes couples where she does up to 30 hours paid work per week and he works full-time; rFT-FT (blue diamond) denotes a couple where she is in paid work for 31 to 39 hours per week and he works full-time; FT-FT (grey circle) denotes couples where both partners do 40 or more hours of paid work per week; rFT-rFT (light blue-striped circle) denotes couples where both partners usually spend between 31 and 39 hours per week at work.

No indicators are shown if less than 30 time use diaries were kept for a specific paid work arrangement. Symbols without black marker lines indicate that there were more than 30 but less than 50 diary entries for the paid work arrangement concerned – PT-FT, rFT-FT for South Africa and rFT-rFT for Austria and Spain.

The figure shows only those countries where the time use of both partners living in the same household is recorded. Female partners must be between 25 and 45 years old. Pensioners and students are excluded.

Housework comprises tasks such as cooking, cleaning, doing the laundry and gardening. It does not include shopping and care for other household members (children and adults).

Source: *OECD Time Use Database* (see Annex Table 5.A1.1 for more information); data for Germany as provided by the German Statistical Office based on the German Time Use Survey 2012-13 (Destatis, 2015).

Male-breadwinner couples (IA/UE–FT) adhere to a traditional division of all work in both the public and private spheres. Women in such couples specialise in unpaid work and their share of the total time that couples devote to housework ranges between 73% (Finland) to 95% (Korea). German male-breadwinner couples perform similarly to French and Austrian couples.

In dual-earner couples, male partners take on a bigger share of housework than in single-earner households. If the woman works reduced full-time and her partner full-time (rFT-FT), or both work full-time (FT-FT) or reduced full-time (rFT-rFT), she does a smaller share of the housework than in single-earner couples (IA/UE-FT) in European countries. In Korea and South Africa, housework is predominantly done by the woman, although male partners do a little more housework in full-time dual-earner couples.

In none of the 8 countries is the partnered woman's share of unpaid work proportionally lower in couples which work similar paid hours. While full-time dual-earner couples (FT-FT) share housework more equally, they are still far short of a fair 50-50 split. The female share of housework ranges from 88% in Korea to 62% in Germany. Housework is shared most equally in France, Spain and Germany when both partners work between 31 to 40 hours per week (rFT-rFT). In Spain and Germany, the degree of asymmetry in housework varies most sharply according to couples' paid work arrangements.

Dual full-time couples share housework more equally than part-time plus full-time couples except in France and South Africa. In all other countries the difference in housework asymmetry is significant between these two work arrangements. The difference in housework asymmetry between part-time plus full-time couples and couples where both work reduced full-time is significant in Spain. In the other countries this difference is not significant, possibly due to low case numbers (particularly among couples in which men do not work full-time).[4]

If women have a higher income than their partners, they do not do less unpaid work (Figure 5.5). The finding contradicts economic theories that consider partners' income and/or earnings potential as the decisive factor in sharing paid and unpaid work (see Chapter 2, Box 5.2 and "Micro and macro level factors are associated with more equal sharing" in Section 2 above). Gender theories, by contrast, stress the role of gender attitudes and norms. Data limitations in the time use surveys make it possible to compare the intensity of unpaid work on the basis of partners' relative incomes in only a few countries – Germany, Finland, France, Korea, Spain and South Africa. While in Finland, France, Germany and, to some extent, Spain, the gender gap in unpaid work is narrow in couples where she earns more than he does, the gap is still wide in such couples in Korea and South Africa.

The above results on the distribution of unpaid work in couples thus only partly confirm economic theories which claim that the partner with the higher earnings or greater paid workload should be doing less unpaid work. Male partners engage more in unpaid work:

- in dual-earner couples than in male-breadwinner couples (Figure 5.4),
- if the female partner earns more work income than the male partner (Figure 5.5).

However, in most of the countries analysed, men in full-time dual-earner couples are far from doing 50% of unpaid household work (taking working hours as an approximation of earnings and the paid workload). And in couples where the woman earns more than the man, women do more unpaid work on average. Neither of the two square with the predictions of economic theory, although do lend support to the "doing gender" contention that men and women seek to conform with social norms on gender, with women performing traditionally female tasks, like housework and parenting, and men doing the traditionally male thing, i.e. paid work (see "Micro and macro level factors are associated with more equal sharing" in Section 2 above).

Figure 5.5. Unpaid work is unbalanced even in couples where the woman earns the higher income

Gender gaps in unpaid work, in minutes per day, according to women's income relative to their partner's income

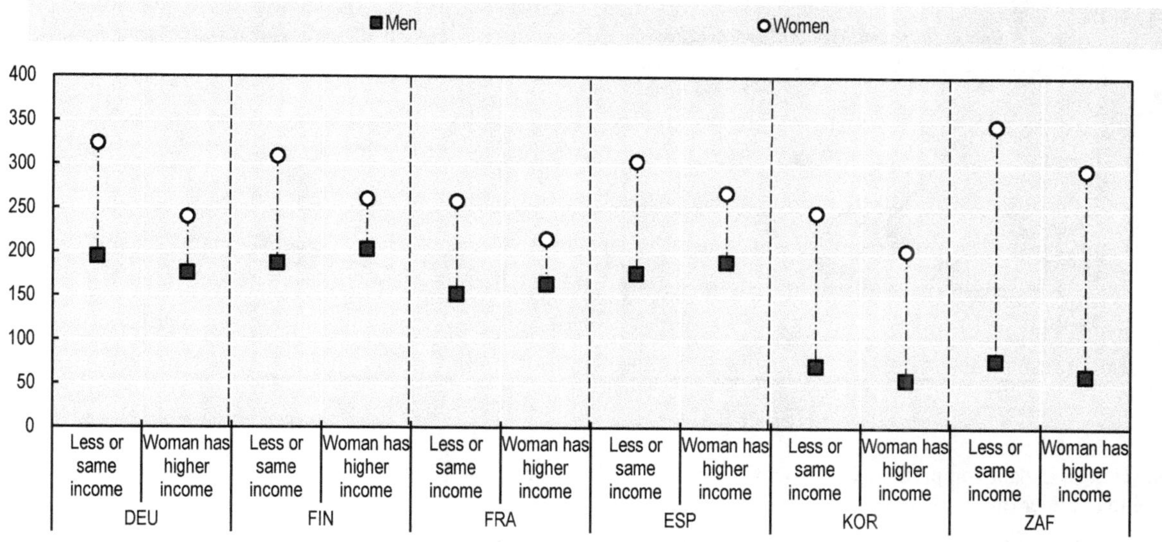

Note: Time use data for partnered men and women who live in the same household as a spouse or cohabitating partner (married or not), women's age restricted to the 25 to 45 year-old age bracket. Pensioners and students are excluded.

Income refers to respondents' monthly net income from employed or self-employed work in Germany, Spain (categorical income variable) and France (continuous variable). Income denotes respondents' individual income subject to state taxation in Finland and the respondents' gross monthly income in Korea. In South Africa, income denotes employed respondents' weekly earnings (the self-employed are not included).

Source: *OECD Time Use Database* (see Annex Table 5.A1.1 for more information); data for Germany as provided by the German Statistical Office based on the German Time Use Survey 2012-13 (Destatis, 2015).

In countries with higher female employment rates partnered men do slightly more unpaid work

In Norway, Finland and France, partnered men and women share paid and unpaid work (more) equally than in the other eight countries analysed (Figure 5.2). All three countries boast broad sets of public policies conducive to sharing, such as parental leave schemes and/or good child care provision (see Chapter 3 for a more detailed discussion). They also have more gender-equal attitudes on, for example, whether mothers should work (Chapter 2) and high female employment rates (see section on "Micro and macro level factors are associated with more equal sharing").

Where female employment rates are higher, as in Germany, Canada, France and the United States, partnered women do more work overall than men – albeit to a considerably smaller degree than in Italy and Spain. In Norway, which boasts the highest female employment rate, partnered men actually do more work overall than partnered women (Figure 5.6, Panel A). Broadly speaking, patterns are related to the behaviour of both sexes: partnered men devote more time to unpaid work in countries with the highest rates of female labour market participation and, at the same time and to a larger extent, partnered women spend less time on unpaid work. Overall, as female employment rates increase, the intensity of their unpaid work falls faster than the man's contribution rises (Figure 5.6, Panel B).

Figure 5.6. Couples share more evenly in countries with higher female employment rates

Gender gaps in overall work and unpaid work in minutes per day among partnered men and women aged 20 and over, and female employment rates of partnered women

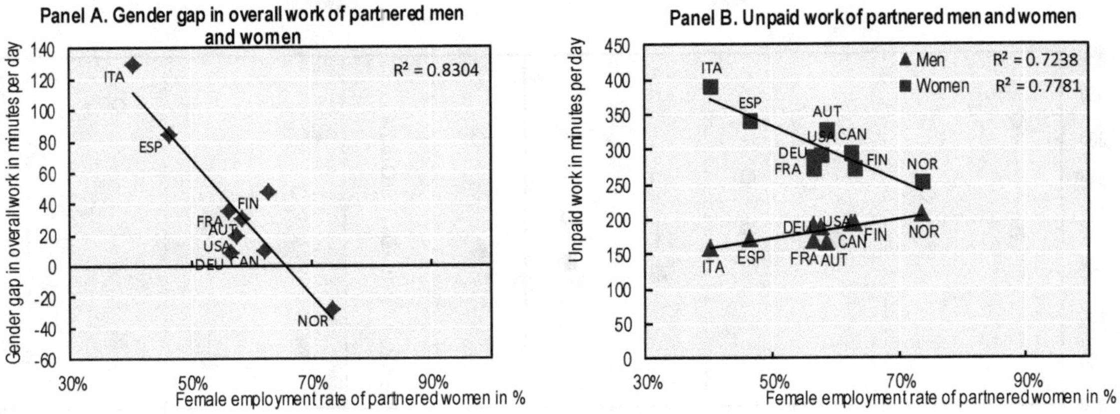

Note: Time use data for partnered men and women aged 20 and more who live in the same household as a spouse or cohabiting partner (married or not).

Employment rates for partnered women aged 20 or more and above who live in the same private household as a spouse or cohabiting partner (married or not). Employment rates in Norway refer to partnered women between 15 and 75 years old.

Source: *OECD Time Use Database* (see Annex Table 5.A1.1 for more information); data for Germany as provided by the German Statistical Office based on the German Time Use Survey 2012-13 (Destatis, 2015); OECD Secretariat estimates of female employment rates; employment rates for Norway supplied by Statistics Norway.

Couples with higher household income and higher education share more equally

Beyond societal attitudes, national socio-economic characteristics and policies, empirical studies have found that couples who share (more) equally are likely to be better educated and have higher household incomes (Box 5.2). Figure 5.7 shows that, in 8 countries save Austria and Korea, the gender gap in unpaid work is narrower in couples where both partners have a university-level degree than in couples with no such qualification degrees. Women in highly educated couples do less unpaid work – and men do a little more – than women in couples where partners do not hold higher education qualifications. Although, in Austria and Korea, men in more highly educated couples do participate more in unpaid work, their female partners devote even more time to unpaid work. As a result, the gender gap in unpaid work is similar to or even wider among well-educated couples in both countries.

Figure 5.7. Highly educated couples share unpaid work more equally in most countries

Gender gap in unpaid work, in minutes per day, in couples according to partners' combined educational status

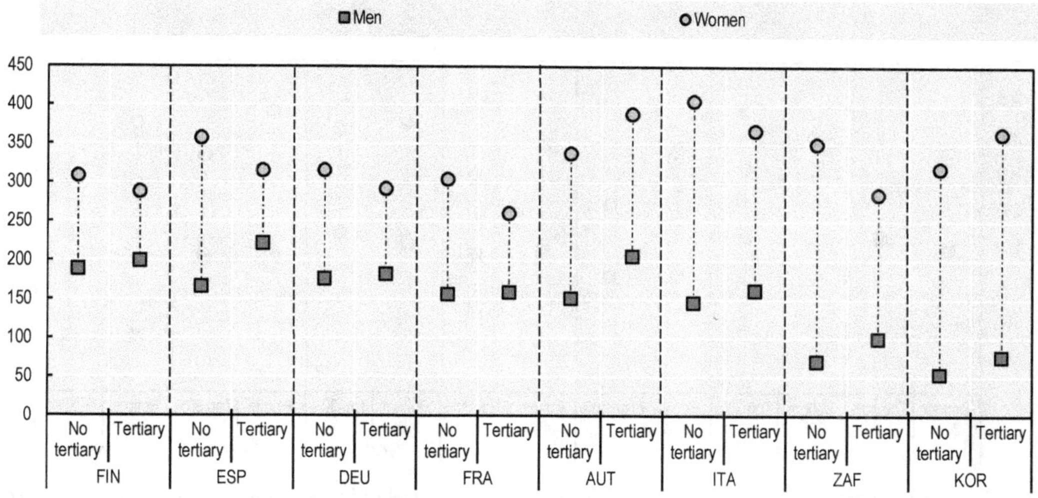

Note: Time use data for partnered men and women who live in the same household as a spouse or cohabitating partner (married or not), women's age restricted to the 25 to 45 year-old age bracket. Pensioners and students are excluded.

From left to right, countries are in ascending order of the gender gap in unpaid work among highly educated couples.

Source: *OECD Time Use Database* (see Annex Table 5.A1.1 for more information); data for Germany as provided by the German Statistical Office based on the German Time Use Survey 2012-13 (Destatis, 2015).

Education may be considered as an important vehicle of attitudinal and behavioural changes – the highly educated often set the trend for such changes before they are absorbed by the rest of society (Bianchi et al., 2000; Anderson and Kohler, 2015). Highly educated couples are more likely to have gender-equal attitudes (Chapter 2). Finland is a case in point. The country's relatively narrow gender gap in unpaid work in couples who are both highly educated but also a relatively small gender gap in couples with both partners without tertiary education (Figure 5.7) coincides with relatively more gender-egalitarian attitudes (Chapter 2) and a larger share of full-time dual-earner couples (Chapter 2, and Känsälä and Oinas, 2015). By contrast, in France and Spain and, to a lesser extent in Germany, the gender gap in unpaid work varies more widely from one education level to another. Although gender-equal behaviour in France and Spain may be similar to that among highly educated couples in Finland, it has not been emulated by the rest of society as in Finland. The unequal division of unpaid work in Austria and Korea, both countries with traditional attitudes (Chapter 2), spans all education levels.

Household income is usually closely correlated with education status. In the countries where household income data are available (all countries except Italy, Austria and Korea), the gender gap in unpaid work is narrower among partnered men and women with higher household incomes (Figure 5.8). Partnered women from the top 30% of the household income distribution do less unpaid work than their peers from the less well-off households in the bottom 30% of the household income distribution. Partnered men in couples in high household income brackets do more or the same amount of unpaid work as in lower-income households. As is to be expected, couples with higher household incomes in all countries are more likely to be highly educated and dual earners couple, so spending more hours in paid work than low-income couples.

Figure 5.8. Couples with higher household income share unpaid work more equally

Unpaid work in couples by low and high household income, in minutes per day

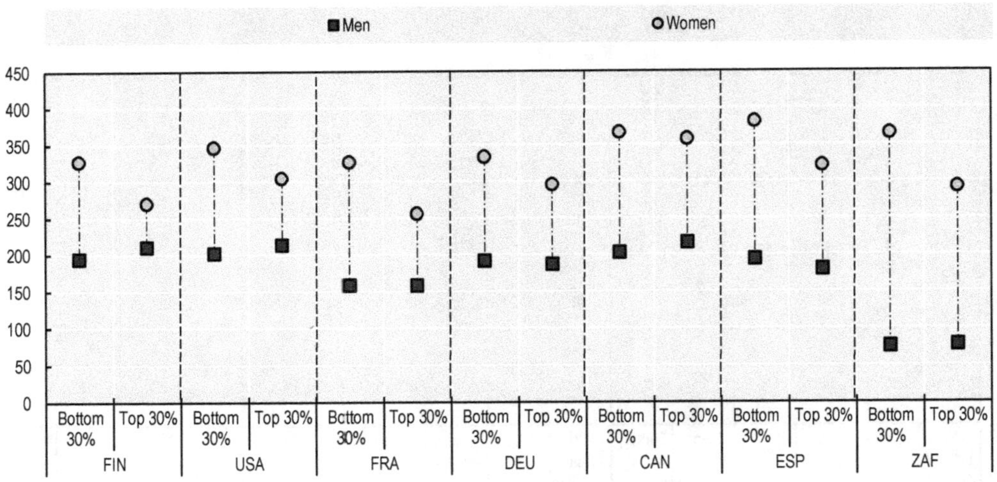

Note: Time use data for partnered men and women who live in the same household as a spouse or cohabiting partner (married or not), women's age restricted to the 25 to 45 year-old age bracket. Pensioners and students are excluded.

For Finland and France, the declared income of all household members is available as a continuous variable. For Canada and the United States, the categories refer to annual gross income; for Germany, Spain and South Africa the categories refer to gross monthly income. Time spent on unpaid work is shown for the households in the bottom and top 30% of the household income distribution of partnered households. If household income is a categorical variable, the categories are grouped by approximation.

From left to right, countries are arranged in ascending order of gender gap for the top 30% of the household income distribution.

Source: *OECD Time Use Database* (see Annex Table 5.A1.1 for more information); data for Germany as provided by the German Statistical Office based on the German Time Use Survey 2012-13 (Destatis, 2015).

Couples situated in the top 30% of the household income distribution of partnered couples (woman aged 25 to 45) in their country devote altogether less time to unpaid work than couples in the bottom 30% of the household income distribution. They may outsource household chores and/or employ others to do them (they may use dry-cleaning services, home helps and nannies) and/or buy more time-saving electronic appliances. Heisig (2011), for example, shows that richer households in 33 countries devote less time to housework and argues that the automation of domestic work plays a particularly important role in reducing time spent on housework.

4. Sharing among parents

The presence of young children leads to more traditional task sharing among men and women

A critical moment that may determine women's future labour market attachment and the sharing of housework is when couples have their first child (see Box 5.3 on the rise of part-time employment amongst mothers in the Netherlands). The evidence suggests that couples generally change markedly their sharing practices when they become parents, often reverting to (more) traditional gender roles (Pfahl, 2014; Baxter, 2008; Barnes, 2015). Figure 5.11 shows the correlation of the gender gaps in aggregate and unpaid work with the female employment rate of partnered women between 25 and 44 years of age in couples with and without children separately in order to capture the effect of parenthood on sharing.[5]

When it comes to young working-age partners without children in the household the gender gap in aggregate work and men's unpaid work is not closely associated with the female employment rate (Figure 5.11, Panel A). While young partnered women without children devote more time to unpaid work than men, they do so less in countries with higher female labour market attachment (Figure 5.11, Panel B).

The picture is quite different when it comes to couples with child care responsibilities. In Austria, Canada and Germany, fathers do more work than mothers on aggregate, while in Finland, Norway, and the United States mothers and fathers do much the same amount (Figure 5.11, Panel C). Altogether higher female labour market attachment is associated with narrower gender gaps in aggregate work among young parents. Panel D in Figure 5.11 breaks down the gender gap in unpaid work and shows that fathers in countries with higher maternal employment rates spend more time on unpaid work. Like women without children, mothers devote more time to unpaid work than men, though even more so in countries with lower female employment rates.

Box 5.3. Mothers' part-time work and unpaid work in the Netherlands over time

Female labour force participation in the Netherlands was, at 30%, low by international standards until the 1970s (Visser et al., 2004). However, between 1975 and 2010, it climbed from 30% to 70%. The bulk of the rise went to part-time work, while the employment rate of women who work full-time has oscillated around 21% since the early 1990s (Dijkgraaf en Portegijs, 2008).

Part-time employment started to expand in response to the recession in the early 1970s, which caused a steep rise in unemployment and social spending (de Beer and Luttikhuizen, 1998; Visser and Hemerijck, 1998). To curb expenditure spending and fight youth unemployment, public policy during the 1970s and 1980s provided subsidies to employers who split existing full-time jobs into two part-time jobs. In turn, employers made use of part-time work to get around union demands for collective reductions in the standard working week to less than 38 hours.

Figure 5.9. The Netherlands have high proportions of women and men in part-time work compared to other OECD countries

Percentages of men and women in part-time employment, selected OECD countries, 2000 and 2014

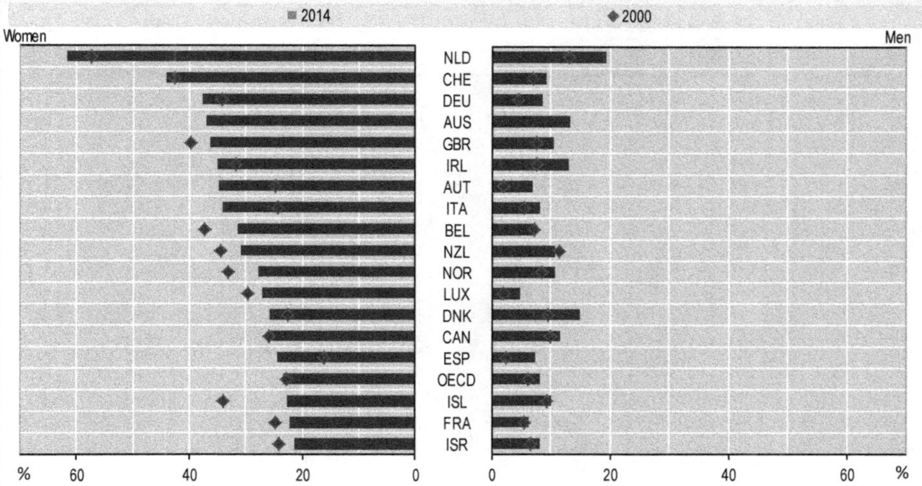

Note: From top to bottom, countries are arranged in descending order of the proportion of women working part-time. Data on countries with less than 20% of employed women working part-time are not presented here.

Part-time employment refers main jobs of less than 30 hours per week.

Source: *OECD Employment Database*, www.oecd.org/employment/emp/onlineoecdemploymentdatabase.htm.

Box 5.3. Mothers' part-time work and unpaid work in the Netherlands over time *(cont.)*

Rise in part-time work attributable to change in attitudes

However, part-time work really took off in the Netherlands not because of a redistribution of work among younger or older workers, but because women, particularly mothers, wanted to be in and stay in work. That perception was related to a sea-change in attitudes. In 2005, about three-quarters of women had no issue with mothers who had young children being in paid work and using care facilities, three times more than in 1970. However, because of the constraints of child care and out-of-school-hours care, women have widely chosen to work part- rather than full-time (Ribberink, 1998). In all, only one in ten mothers with a child not yet ten years of age was in paid work in the Netherlands in 1971. A quarter of a century later that proportion had increased to over 50%. The "normalisation" of part-time work in the Netherlands has been formalised in a range of legislative measures, such as laws that stipulate equal pay per working hour regardless of weekly working hours, employees' right to request changes in weekly working hours, and the entitlement to request parental leave on a part-time basis (Visser et al., 2004).

The change in women's employment patterns since the 1970s in the Netherlands has contributed to change in the sharing of unpaid work (Hook, 2006; Kan et al., 2011). Overall, the time that women devote to unpaid work has fallen, especially among those in employment (data not shown here), and increased moderately among men. Nevertheless, although employed 25-to-45 year-old women living with a partner have gradually come to spend less time on unpaid work, the fall has been more pronounced among childless women (white diamond vs. light blue square in Figure 5.10). It is related to a general trend increase in time devoted to child care activities by parents and a falling trend in other unpaid housework. By contrast, partnered employed men without children have been doing marginally less unpaid work over time. Partnered fathers, for their part, are doing more unpaid work, mainly because of their greater involvement in parenting, but also because they actually do more unpaid housework (white diamond Figure 5.10). All these factors have contributed to a narrowing gender gap in unpaid work in the Netherlands.

Figure 5.10. The time that women in the Netherlands spend on unpaid work has fallen, but the gender gap persists when children are present in the household

Unpaid work in minutes per day, 1975 to 2005

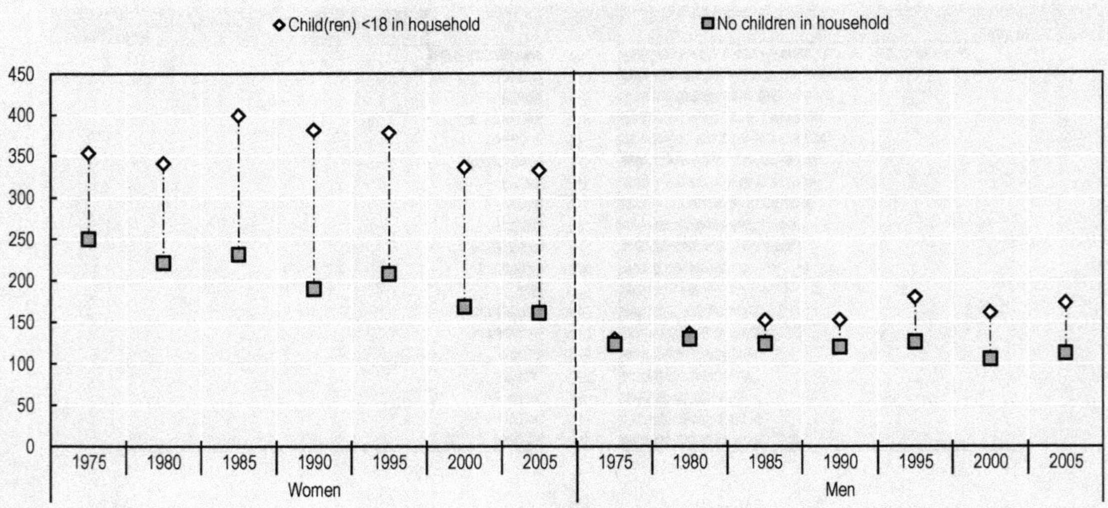

Note: Employed men and women living in partnership in the Netherlands, aged 25 to 45 years old, with or without dependent children under 18 in the household.

Source: Secretariat estimate based on data from the Multinational Time Use Study (MTUS, 2015) for the Netherlands.

Figure 5.11. Young, working-age partners share aggregate work and unpaid work less equally, particularly in countries with lower female employment rates, when they have children

Gender gaps in aggregate work and unpaid work, in minutes per day, of partnered men and women aged 20 or above and female employment rates of partnered women, with and without children

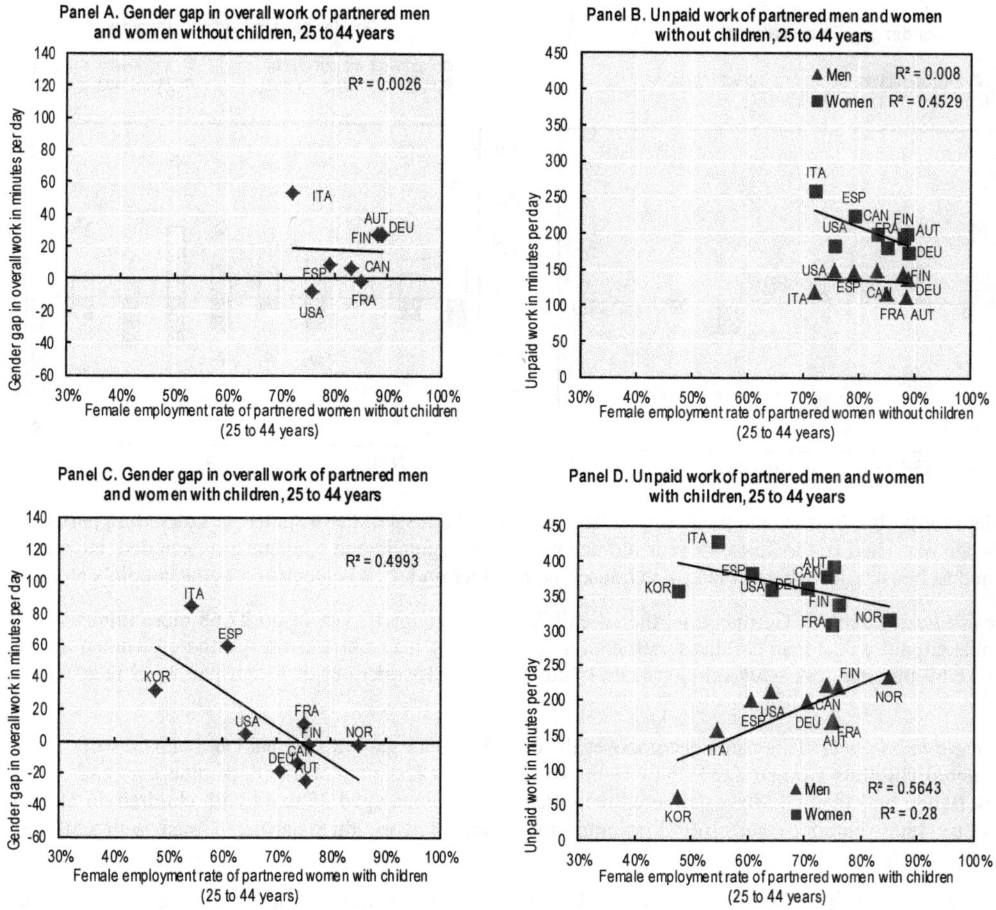

Note: Time use for men and women living in the same household with their partner. Pensioners and students excluded. Households with children are defined as households where a household member below the age of 18 is identified as the couple's child.

For the employment rate estimates, children are defined as between 0 and 14 years old inclusive (0 and 17 inclusive in the United States) who live in the same household as and are identified as the child of the respondent. Maternal employment rates for Korea for 2013 for mothers of children below 15 years.

Source: *OECD Time Use Database* (see Annex Table 5.A1.1 for more information); data for Germany as provided by the German Statistical Office based on the German Time Use Survey 2012-13 (Destatis, 2015); OECD Secretariat estimates of female employment rates.

Across countries the gender gap in aggregate work is not uniformly larger or smaller in couples with children than in couples without children (Figure 5.12, left-hand panel). The aggregate gap disguises considerable differences in gender gaps in paid and unpaid work taken separately (Figure 5.12, right-hand panel). The presence of young children increases the polarisation of paid and unpaid work, with gender gaps in both yawning wider. Fathers do relatively more paid work (except in Norway, Korea and South Africa) and mothers do relatively more unpaid work than men and women in childless couples.

Figure 5.12. Young working-age parents share paid and unpaid work more traditionally than their childless peers

Gender gaps in paid, unpaid and aggregate work, in minutes per day, among 25-to-44 year-old partnered men and women with and without children

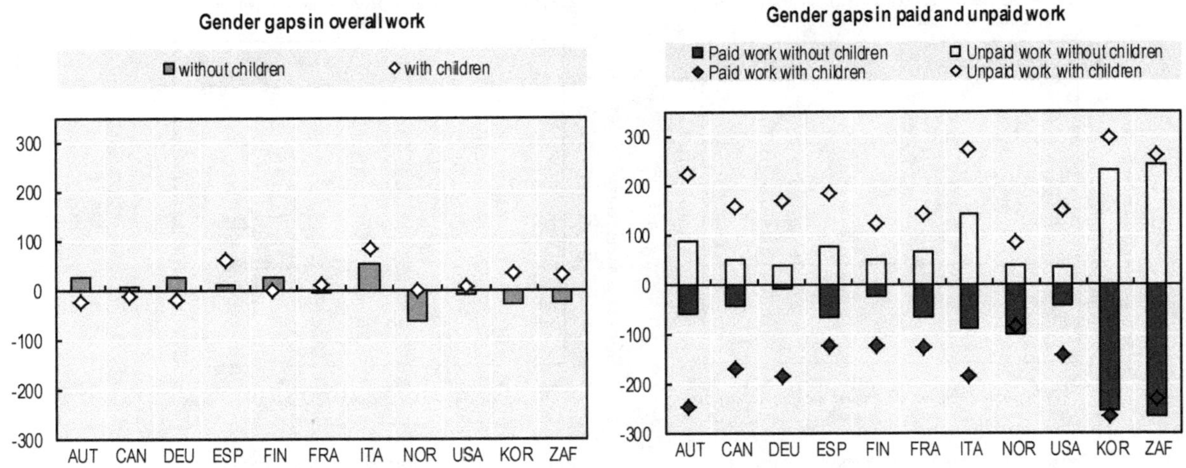

Note: Time use data for partnered men and women who live in the same household as a spouse or cohabiting partner (married or not), women's age restricted to the 25-to-45 year-old age bracket. Pensioners and students are excluded. Households with children are defined as households where at least one household member under 18 is identified as the couple's child.

Reading note for left hand panel: In Germany, partnered childless women aged 25 to 44 do 27.68 more minutes of work on aggregate (paid plus unpaid work) than childless partnered men (dark grey bar). On average, partnered women aged 25 to 44 with children do 18.69 minutes less work on aggregate (paid and unpaid work) per day than partnered men with children (white diamond).

Reading note for right hand panel: This panel decomposes the overall gender gap into the paid and unpaid work gender gaps. In Germany, partnered childless women aged 25 to 44 do 10.22 minutes less paid work (dark blue bar) and 37.9 minutes more unpaid work (white bar) than childless partnered men. Partnered women aged 25 to 44 with children do 185.3 minutes less paid work (dark blue diamond) and 166.51 minutes more unpaid work than partnered men with children (white diamond).

Source: *OECD Time Use Database* (see Annex Table 5.A1.1 for more information); data for Germany as provided by the German Statistical Office based on the German Time Use Survey 2012-13 (Destatis, 2015).

Partnered fathers spend between 8 and 28 minutes per day more in paid work than partnered men without children, except in Austria, Korea, Norway and South Africa. Among partnered women the difference in paid work time is considerably wider, with mothers often withdrawing fully or partly from the labour market. The greatest differences between partnered women with and without children come in Austria and Germany (respectively 203 and 135 minutes per day), whereas in Norway the difference is only 15 minutes per day.

The findings demonstrate that the transition to parenthood is a critical time that determines whether couples will go on sharing paid and unpaid work. As discussed in Chapter 3 and Box 5.4, parental leave, particularly the months for the exclusive use of fathers, is an important policy lever for encouraging young couples to keep up egalitarian sharing patterns when they become parents. Tax and benefit systems are also important financial incentives for parents to remain dual-earner couples and not to revert to traditional male-breadwinner models.

Box 5.4. "Daddy months" or how fathers' parental leave affects sharing and involvement with children

Mothers may be the main users of child-related leave provisions, but there is growing debate on leave arrangements that target or are available only to fathers. As well as affording fathers the opportunity to support the mother and child directly after child birth, father-specific leaves are likely to encourage them to engage in parenting and, to some degree at least, promote male unpaid work within the household. Moreover, father-specific leave is likely to reduce grounds for leave-associated employer discrimination against female employees: As long as mothers remain the main, almost exclusive, users of leave, there is a risk of employers not hiring young women on permanent or regular employment contracts and investing less in their career opportunities and training than in men's. That risk could be tempered by large numbers of young fathers taking up child-related leave not just for one or two days, but for months at a time (Levtov et al., 2015 on the "state of the world's fathers").

Evidence from across the OECD suggests that the provision of father-specific leave may also affect fathers' involvement in parenting and/or housework, their working hours, their own well-being, and the well-being of their children.

Across the OECD, fathers' take-up of leave is associated with their involvement in child care activities and at least some redistribution of unpaid work (Nepomnyaschy and Waldfogel, 2007; Tanaka and Waldfogel, 2007; Huerta et al., 2013; Schober, 2013; Almqvist and Duvander, 2014; Schober 2014a). Using data from the United Kingdom, for example, Tanaka and Waldfogel (2007) found that fathers who took paternity or parental leave were more likely to engage in child-related tasks such as changing diapers, feeding the child and/or getting up to care for the child at night. Huerta et al. (2013) corroborated some of those findings in a study of four OECD countries (Australia, Denmark, the United Kingdom and the United States), where it emerged that they were most likely to materialise when fathers took leave for two weeks or more.

Importantly, such benefits usually last: fathers who engage early are more likely to remain involved as their children grow (Baxter and Smart, 2010; Brandth and Gislason, 2012). In a study on Sweden, which introduced a so-called "daddy-month" of paid parental leave for the exclusive use of fathers in 1995, Almqvist and Duvander (2014) found that when fathers took long leave, parents shared both household tasks and parenting more equally. Fifteen years after Norway introduced its four-week paternity leave in 1993, Kotsadam and Finseraas (2011) found that eligible fathers were more likely to share housework in a gender-equal manner with their partner. However, evidence on the impact of paternity leave on fathers' labour market involvement is mixed. Cools et al. (2015) found no effect on fathers' working hours, whereas Rege and Solli (2013) found a negative effect on father's earnings which, they suggest, stems from reduced working hours. As for Sweden, Duvander and Jans (2009) found that long paternity leave has a negative impact on fathers' working hours, whereas Ekberg et al. (2013) found no substantial effect on parents' long-term wages or employment.

Fathers' well-being may also benefit from increased involvement around the home. Fathers who contribute more to unpaid work are less prone to divorce than less involved fathers (Sigle-Rushton, 2010), while fathers who engage more with their children report greater life satisfaction and better physical and mental health (Eggebeen and Knoester, 2001; WHO, 2007).

Greater paternal involvement in parenting and family life is also associated with positive cognitive and emotional outcomes for their children (Cabrera et al., 2007; Lamb, 2010; OECD, 2012; Huerta et al., 2013; Schober, 2015). Children's physical health also benefits (WHO, 2007). Similarly, Lamb (2012) found that fathers spend a greater share of their child care time with more interactive, "quality activities" (such as playing) than mothers. In sum, greater paternal involvement in parenting not only has advantages for female labour force participation, it is good for children, too.

Leave for fathers in Germany

With its reform of parental leave in 2007, Germany introduced earnings-related compensation for parents on leave and two bonus months reserved for their partner (read "the father"). The reform increased fathers' involvement in parenting according to most studies (Wrohlich et al., 2012; Lauber et al., 2014; Schober, 2014b; Bünning, 2015; Pfahl et al., 2014), although one study that focuses on the immediate effects in the child's first year found no effects (Kluve and Tamm, 2013).

Box 5.4. "Daddy months" or how fathers' parental leave affects sharing and involvement with children *(cont.)*

In line with international evidence, fathers' parenting involvement increases with the length of leave taken and when the father takes leave at a different time than his partner ("solo leave"). Bünning (2015) also showed that fathers' working hours fall when they take parental leave, and that their participation in housework increases if they took more than two months parental leave or "solo leave".

Pfahl et al. (2014) used in-depth interviews and an online survey to analyse the lingering medium-term effect on German couples, particularly fathers, of parental leave even after it ends. The survey and interviews took place in 2012-13 and questioned fathers who took parental leave between 2007 and 2013. Results suggest that, in couples who share parental leave months more equally, fathers are more likely to work part-time during and after parental leave. Fathers who take three months or more of leave tend to share housework more equally. They also reported a greater intensity in their relationships with their children which has outlasted the parental leave period itself. However, fathers who took leave for three months or more – particularly those who reduced their working hours after the parental leave period – reported that they believed that their careers had suffered or were likely to suffer as a result.

Partnered mothers are more involved in child care than partnered fathers but the gap closes at weekends and once the youngest child enters school

Parenthood ushers in much extra unpaid work for parents that includes more housework and such child-related tasks as physical care, playing and reading. While parents spend a considerable part of their day with children present, what they do is not always exclusively child-related – like having a family dinner as opposed to reading to the children. In time use surveys, respondents may record a primary activity, such as cooking, and also note a secondary activity, like listening to the radio while cooking. In most countries, respondents also indicate who was with them while they were doing what they were doing. They might not therefore record a child-related activity as primary (or secondary), even though they might still be with the children – for example, cooking while listening to the radio and supervising a child in the household who is doing his or her homework.

Two different indicators measure these different dimensions of interaction with the children (Box 5.1):

- time spent in the presence of household children, which sums up the total time spent in the presence of children in the household,
- participation rates in child care that show the percentage of mothers (fathers) out of all mothers (fathers) who recorded any type of child care as a primary activity during a day.

These indicators must be interpreted with caution, however, as not all countries use the same age thresholds to record the presence of children (see notes to Figure 5.13).

Women spend a lot more time than men with children regardless of their primary and secondary activity (Figure 5.13, Panel A). The gender gap also prevails in rates of participation in child care as a primary activity (Panel B). Outright child care like reading, playing and physical care make up the smaller share of the total time that either parent spends with the children. In families with children under school age, partnered mothers in Finland spend a comparatively large share of their time with children in pure child care, as do Finnish fathers – respectively 65% and 60% of total time spent with children. In Italy, child care accounts for 25% of the time that partnered mothers with their children, and 18% of the partnered fathers time. However, caution should once again be exercised in interpreting the results, as Finnish parents seem to spend considerably less time in the presence of their children than Italian parents. In all 11 countries, the time spent on child care as a primary activity lessens as children go to school. Box 5.5 illustrates the time that Australian parents and children spend together – but from the children's perspective.

Box 5.5. Time spent with parents from children's perspective in Australia

The Longitudinal Study of Australian Children (LSAC) collects data on how young children spend their day. It complements parents' information collected in the regular time use surveys with data from children's perspective. A nationally representative study of Australian children, the LSAC is a unique opportunity to examine how children's time with fathers and mothers varies with their paid working hours – and how it varies over the early years, as the LSAC follows children over time (longitudinal data).

The LSAC commenced in 2004 and collects data every two years. The youngest LSAC cohort data from which this report draws time use data relates to the age groups 0 to 1, 2 to 3 and 4 to 5 years old. Information collected on who was with the child ("Who else was in the same room or, if outside, nearby to the child?" with answer options "mother" and/or "father") is used to estimate how much time children spend per day:

- with both father and mother at the same time
- with only the father
- with only the mother.

For night-time hours (8 pm to 6 am), only the times when parents were present and children were awake were considered. The accounts in adult time use diaries of how children spend their time in couple families make it possible to relate children's time more closely to each parent's paid working hours.

While children are young fathers generally work long full-time hours, while mothers work part-time. Gendered patterns of paid and unpaid work time, which include child care, are thus apparent in Australian studies of parents' time use (Craig and Mullan, 2010) and in the LSAC:

- Based on parents' time use data, Craig, Powell, and Smyth (2014) report that Australian mothers spent more than 10 hours (617 minutes) per seven-day week on average with their children (0 to 14 years old), and fathers over 6 hours (401 minutes) per day in 2006.
- The child-based LSAC produce comparable estimates: children in the age groups 0 to 1, 2 to 3 and 4 to 5 years old spend an overall average of 572 minutes per day with their mothers and 313 minutes with their fathers. As parent-based estimates reflect parents' time with any number of children in the household, estimates of parental time from a single child's perspective (like those of the LSAC) are likely to be lower than those captured from adult time use diaries.

Figure 5.13 shows how children's time with parents in couple families differs according to the mother's employment status – denoted by the height of the bar. Children spend less time with parents in total on weekdays as mothers' paid working hours increase, which reflects the time spent in the care of non-parental adults (see "Average number of minutes children spend with other adults [not their parents]" at the bottom of the figure). As mothers' paid working hours lengthen, children's solo time with mothers falls, while with their fathers it increases. Multivariate methods, which take into account the longitudinal nature of the data, confirm these findings (Baxter, 2015). Yet both the total and solo time that children spend with the fathers declines as fathers' paid working week grows longer. And while associations between parental paid work hours and children's time use are weaker for weekends, the children of fathers who work long hours (55 hours or more per week) have the shortest weekend time with their father.

Finally, Baxter (2015) showed that children's time with parents correlates over time. Children who had more solo or total time with either parent at a very young age are likely to enjoy more such parental time at somewhat older ages. Policies that seek to enable parents, particularly fathers, to spend time with their young children may thus play an important role in greater father involvement as children grow older.

Box 5.5. Time spent with parents from children's perspective in Australia *(cont.)*

Figure 5.13. Children spend similar amounts of time with fathers and mothers when the mother works full-time

Children's weekday time with parents in couple families at the ages of 0-1, 2-3 and 4-5 years old, in minutes per weekday

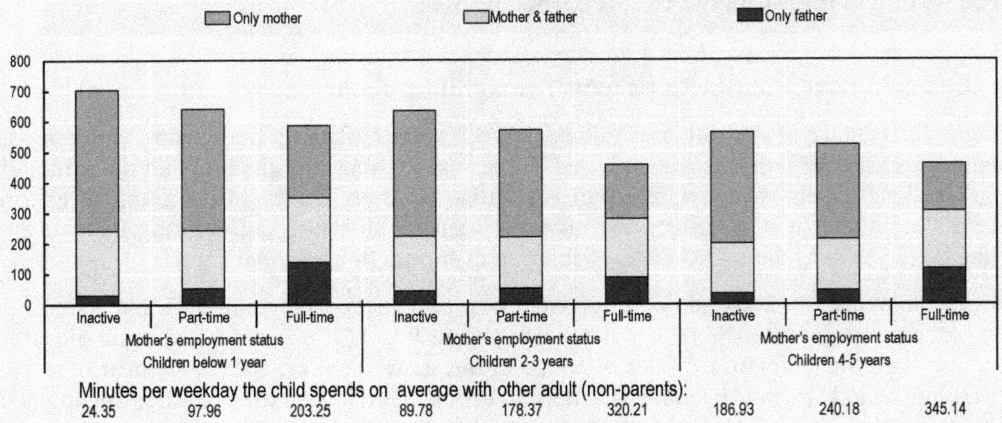

Note: Only children in couple families with diary data at three waves are included (N = 1 719).

Source: Baxter, J. (2015), "Children's Time With Fathers and Mothers Over the Pre-School Years: A Longitudinal Time-Use Study of Couple Families in Australia", *Family Science*, Vol. 6, No. 1.

In most families with young children, both parents report some kind of child care activity during the day. Such "dual child carer" families constitute 78% of families with at least one school-aged child in Spain and 62% in France, with other countries ranking in between (results not shown here). Families where only the mother reports at least one child care activity and the father none are the next largest group – "mother main carer" families, which account for 28% of families with at least one school-aged child in France, for example, and 17% in Spain. Among families with older children – as less outright child care is required and overall time with children lessens – the share of "dual child carer" families falls and that of "mother main carer" families rises.

Korea (57%) and South Africa (14%) have the lowest proportions of "dual carer" families of all 11 countries and mothers are more likely to be the only carer. However, in both countries the activity list restricts child care mainly to physical care and supervision and/or is geared mainly towards interaction with young children (Box 5.1). Various child care-related activities which the other countries have coded – such as talking to and teaching children – are not picked up to the same extent by the activity lists in Korea and South Africa.[6]

The gender gap in child care is narrower on weekends and closes once children are enrolled in school. And parents share participation in child care activities and time with the children more equally on weekends and when the children are older (Figure 5.14). At the weekend, parents of school-aged children in France, Finland and the United States spend nearly equal lengths of time in the presence of their children.[7] Hook and Wolfe (2012) confirm that, for the United States, Germany, Norway and the United Kingdom, fathers spend more time in interactive care and alone with children on weekends. But only Norwegian fathers increase both their rates of participation in child care and the time spent on physical care.

Figure 5.14. Partnered fathers are less involved than mothers with young children, but the gender gap seem smaller during weekends and when children start school

Panel A. Time spent in presence of children by youngest child's age and type of day, in minutes per day[1]

Panel B. Participation rates in child care by youngest child's age and type of day, in percentage[2]

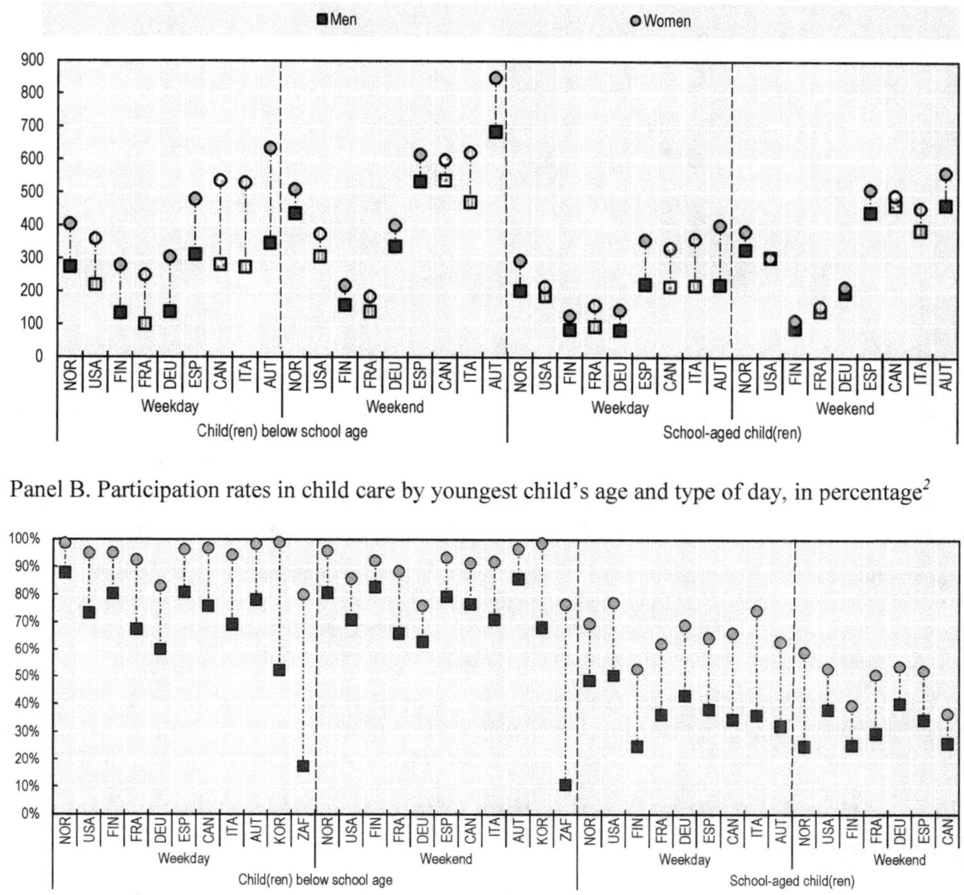

Note: Time use data for partnered men and women who live in the same household as a spouse or cohabitating partner (married or not), women's age restricted to the 25-to-45 year-old age bracket. Pensioners and students are excluded.

1. Minutes spent in the presence of children living in the household are recorded for all children under 18 in Italy, France, the United States (striped symbols), children under 15 in Canada (dotted symbols), children under 10 in Austria, Finland, Germany, and Spain (symbols without patterns). South Africa and Korea are not included because the presence of household children is not recorded at all in South Africa and in Korea only the presence of any other household member aged 10 or older is recorded.

2. Participation rates in child care capture the percentage of fathers or mothers that have recorded at least one child care activity (physical care, supervision, teaching, or reading, playing, and talking with the child) as a primary activity over the course of day entered in the diary. Participation rates are not shown for school-aged children in Korea and South Africa, as the child care activity list refers to activities with small children (see Box 5.1 for further details).

Source: OECD Time Use Database (see Annex Table 5.A1.1 for more information); data for Germany as provided by the German Statistical Office based on the German Time Use Survey 2012-13 (Destatis, 2015).

Highly educated couples are more likely to share more equally in many respects, including child care. The gender gap in child care participation between parents with higher education degrees is narrower than between parents with no such qualifications in all eight countries for which the education level of both parents is available (Figure 5.15). However, when it comes to time spent with children, highly educated couples are not significantly different from couples who have no university-level degree (results not shown here).

Figure 5.15. Highly educated couples participate more equally in child care activities

Gender gap in participation rates in child care by education level, in percentage

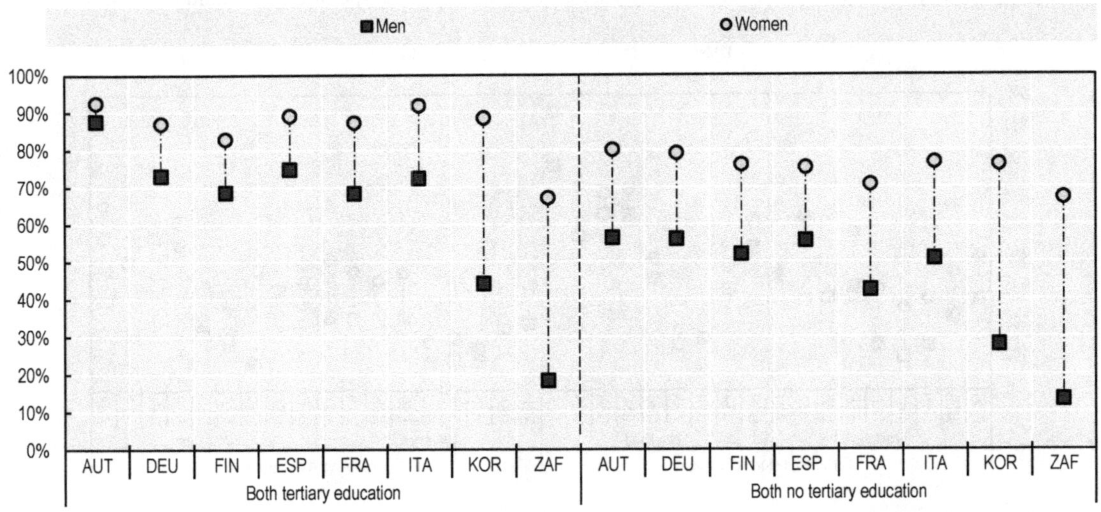

Note: Time use data for partnered men and women who live in the same household as a spouse or cohabitating partner (married or not), women's age restricted to the 25-to-45 year-old age bracket. Pensioners and students are excluded.

Participation rates in child care activities capture the percentage of fathers or mothers that have recorded at least one child care activity (physical care, supervision, teaching, reading, playing, and talking with the child) as a primary activity over the course of the diary day. Participation rates are not shown for school-aged children in Korea and South Africa due to the child care activity list referring to activities with small children (see Box 5.1 for further details).

Source: OECD Time Use Database (see Annex Table 5.A1.1 for more information); data for Germany as provided by the German Statistical Office based on the German Time Use Survey 2012-13 (Destatis, 2015).

Mothers have more hours of quality time with their children, but fathers have a higher proportion

In couple families where both parents are "carers" (see Box 5.1 for a definition) – i.e. participate in child care activities – mothers invest more time in child care activities than fathers (Figure 5.16, Panel A). However, the gender gap is narrower, or disappears, when the youngest child is enrolled in school. In families whose youngest child is under the compulsory school age, the gender gap between "carer parents" in time spent on child care varies from 51 minutes (in France) to 118 (in Korea). In Finnish families with school-aged children, "carer" fathers actually record more time in child care activities than "carer" mothers (see notes to Figure 5.16).

No agreed definition exists as to which child care activities should be considered as "quality time". Nevertheless, parents not only carry out routine care-giving tasks. They also interact educationally and creatively with their children in activities that are also likely to be associated with leisure. In that respect reading, playing, talking, teaching and taking children outdoors may be come under the heading of "quality time" or "quality activities".[8] Time spent on physical care, supervision, fetching children and non-specified child care is not considered "quality time" (Figure 5.16, Panel B).

Figure 5.16. Although fathers spend less time with young children, a greater share of that time is "quality time"

Panel A. The time that carer parents spend on child care activities, by youngest child's age, in minutes per day[1]

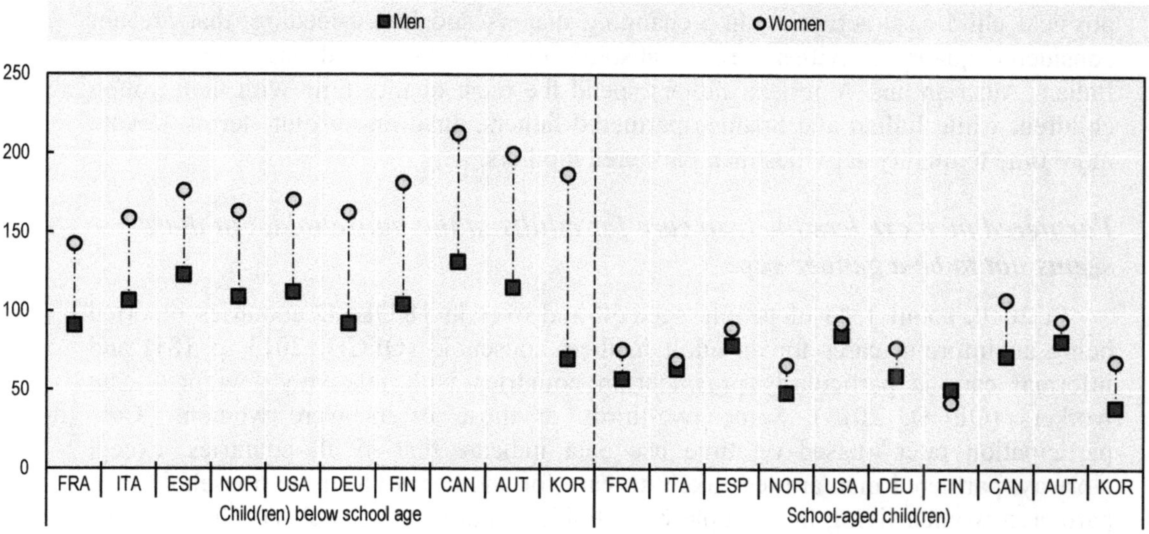

Panel B. The percentage of "quality time" in the total time that carer parents devote to child care activities by the youngest child's age[2]

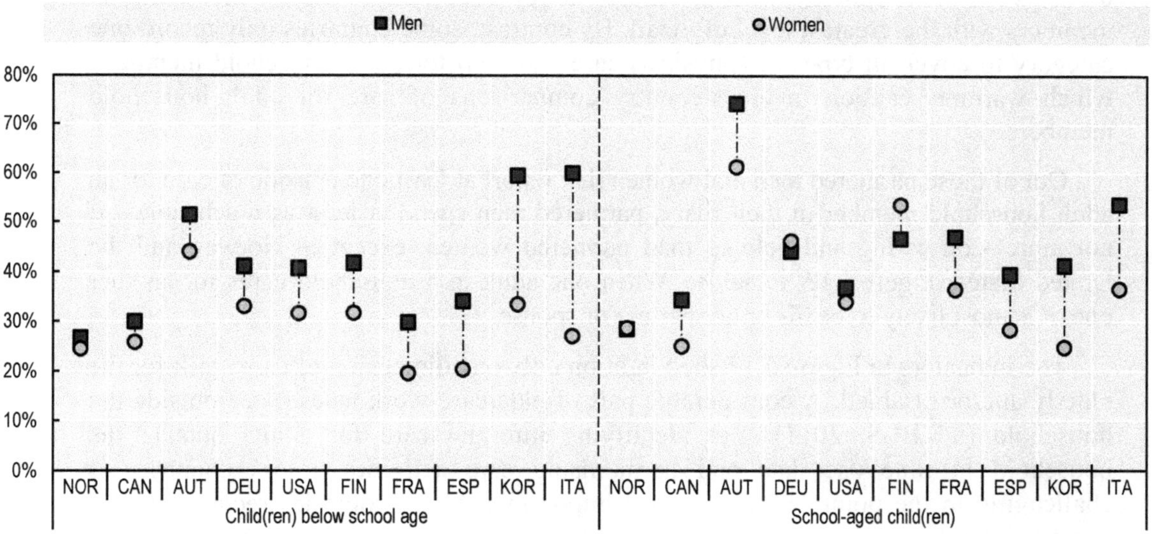

Note: Time use data for partnered men and women who live in the same household as a spouse or cohabitating partner (married or not), women's age restricted to the 25-to-45 year-old age bracket. Pensioners and students are excluded.

1. Data restricted to "carers", i.e. mothers and fathers who are engaged in at least one child care activity during the diary day (for detail see Box 5.1).

2. "Quality time" includes reading, playing, talking with children, taking them outdoors, teaching them. Physical care-giving, taking and fetching children and other unspecified child care activities are not considered quality time.

Source: *OECD Time Use Database* (see Annex Table 5.A1.1 for more information); data for Germany as provided by the German Statistical Office based on the German Time Use Survey 2012-13 (Destatis, 2015).

Fathers in couple families spend a larger proportion of their child care time in quality child care activities than mothers in all countries – with the exception of Norway and Finland and not if it comes to school-aged children (Figure 5.16, Panel B). Mothers, particularly those with infants, are often more engaged than fathers in physical child care activities, like changing diapers and breast-feeding, that are not considered quality activities here. In absolute terms, with around one hour per day, Italian, Austrian and American fathers spend the most quality time with their young children, while Italian and Spanish partnered fathers, again in absolute terms, devote more time to quality activities than partnered mothers.

Partnered men are less likely to care for adults in the household, but there seems not to be a gender gap

In 2010, about 15% of people aged 50 and over in 18 OECD countries reported being an informal carer for an adult in their household (OECD, 2013, p. 181) and informal care is particularly prevalent in countries with relatively few paid care workers (OECD, 2013). Some two-thirds of those carers were women. "Care participation rates" based on time use data indicate that in all countries, except Norway, partnered men are less likely to care for another adult in the household than partnered women living in a couple households (Figure 5.17, Panel A). The over-50s account for the bulk of carers.[9]

Countries report care for household adults at very different levels of detail in time use surveys. The United States time use survey records care for adult household members with the greatest level of detail. By contrast, some countries only record one category to cover all types of (physical) care and help for adult household members, which warrants caution in cross-country comparisons of care for adult household members.

Out of those partnered men and women that report at least one episode of care for an adult household member in their diary, partnered men spend at least as much time – if not more – on caring and helping than partnered women, except in Norway and the United States (Figure 5.17, Panel B). When one adult in a household cares for another one, it is most likely to be his or her partner or spouse.

The indicators in Figure 5.17 shed light on only one dimension of care work for the elderly and/or disabled. A considerable part of eldercare work takes place outside the household (US BLS, 2013). Yet identifying informal care for adults outside the household in time use data and harmonising care activities across countries is challenging to the point of being nearly impossible. Many countries record care for non-household adults separately, but lump together informal help for adults in other households and help for other households in a single category. A clear, consistent, cross-national identification of informal care for adults is beyond the scope of this analysis.[10]

Figure 5.17. Partnered men are less likely to care for adult household members than partnered women in first place, but once they are involved in care giving they devote similar amounts of time

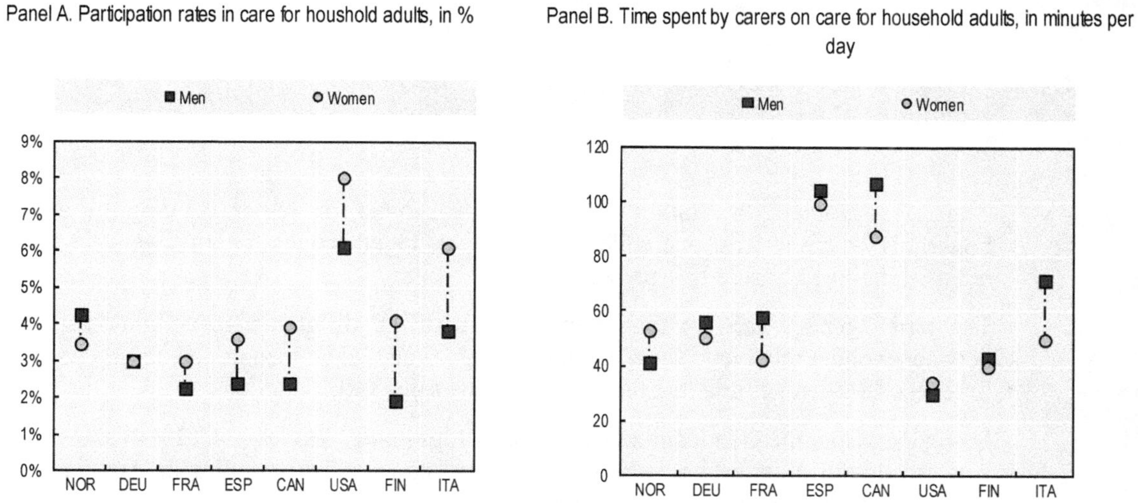

Note: Time use data for partnered men and women aged 18 or more.

Care for household adults" includes all care and help activities recorded. The indicator is not reported if less than 30 respondents participated in the activity.

Both indicators on care for adults in other households not reported for Finland and Spain because the activities with regard to care for an adult household member are lumped together with other activities.

Source: *OECD Time Use Database* (see Annex Table 5.A1.1 for more information); data for Germany as provided by the German Statistical Office based on the German Time Use Survey 2012-13 (Destatis, 2015).

5. Concluding remarks

Although women participate increasingly in paid employment, they widely work shorter weekly hours than their male partners. And even if they do work the same number of hours, couples do not yet share unpaid work equally.

Female partners spend twice as much time in unpaid work at home as their partners, although the gender gap in that respect is narrower in countries with higher female employment rates. In couples where women participate more in the labour market, couples share unpaid work more equally. The main reason, however, is that partnered women and dual-earner couples do less unpaid work overall, not because partnered men do more unpaid work. Education is an important contributory factor in more equally shared paid and unpaid work in most of the 11 countries for which time use data were analysed. Highly educated couples are more likely to be dual earners, and they generally share unpaid work more equally than couples who have no higher education qualifications.

Parenthood marks a turning point in the sharing behaviour of many couples. When they have a child, they often revert (albeit involuntarily) to more traditional gender roles than young couples with no children, who continue to share unpaid work more equally.

Mothers may spend more quality time with their children than fathers, but a larger proportion of fathers' child care time is quality time that comprises interactive activities such as reading, playing and talking with the children. Fathers in highly educated couples are also generally more involved in child care activities than fathers in less well educated couples.

Notes

1. "Parent", "mother" or "father" refers to the mother or father residing in a household where at least one child under 18 lives together with a couple (married or cohabitating) identified as his/her parents.

2. The term "gender gap" in this chapter refers to the difference in an indicator between women relative to men, e.g. the average time that women devote to unpaid time less the average time that men devote to the same task.

3. Using data from the Gender and Generations Programme, Aasve et al. (2014) show that couples in Norway share housework more equally than couples in Austria, Belgium, Bulgaria, France, Germany, Hungary, Romania, and the Russian Federation. The sharing variable is constructed from responses by one partner to questions on the intensity with which his or her partner usually takes on "standard" household tasks.

4. Respondents in the German Time Use Survey were selected through so-called "quota sampling": the target population is divided into several subgroups (e.g. by sex, age and geographic location), and respondents from those subgroups are then selected in a non-random procedure. The advantage of this approach is that it is less time-intensive and hence less costly than random sampling, and that the resulting response rates can be considerably higher. Survey results are not, however, necessarily representative of the entire population and "statistical inference" (including the construction of confidence intervals) therefore not possible (see Maier, 2014 for further details). Due to very low case numbers on the PT-FT combination in Finland and the rFT-rFT combination in Korea and South Africa, these combinations are not considered for these countries.

5. As the data do not distinguish between older couples who never had children and older couples whose children have already moved out of the household, the analysis is restricted to younger couples.

6. The South African activity list includes physical care, supervision, teaching and accompanying children but not reading, playing or talking with children. The South Korean activity list does not include talking to children or reading or playing with school-aged children.

7. Travel related to child care activities is not considered as child care in Figure 5.14. Yet child care-related travel can take up considerable time. However, defining travel related to child care as an additional child care activity does not change the patterns illustrated in Figure 5.14.

8. When defining "quality" time more narrowly as reading, playing, talking and taking the child outdoors only (not including teaching as a "quality" activity), fathers still spend a greater share of their time on quality child care activities than mothers.

9. The care participation rates based on daily time use presented in Figure 5.14 are systematically lower than the statistics on informal carers cited above as 1) age is

not restricted to the over-50s, 2) they are a result of limiting the analysis to household adults, and 3) in time use surveys people report their activities on one (or two) randomly picked days. In such a survey, anyone giving care informally, but not on a daily basis, has a lower chance of being recorded as involved in informal care than in response to a survey which asks whether he/she did any informal care work in the previous week.

10. In 2011 a series of elder care questions were added to the American Time Use Survey. Together with a detailed activity list, the expanded survey allows for a greater understanding of elder care in general and how elder care work is divided in couples. Surveys with a focus on ageing (like the 2007 General Social Survey of Canada, the Household, Income and Labour Dynamics in Australia Survey (HILDA), English Longitudinal Study of Ageing (ELSA) in England, and the Survey of Health, Ageing and Retirement in Europe (SHARE) in European Union countries) usually ask about how frequently care was provided (daily, weekly or monthly) and sometimes how many hours of care were provided per week. They do not, however, allow full mapping of the carer's (or his or her spouse's) day.

References

Aassve, A., G. Fuochi and L. Mencarini (2014), "Desperate Housework: Relative Resources, Time Availability, Economic Dependency, and Gender Ideology Across Europe", *Journal of Family Issues*, Vol. 35, No. 8, pp. 1000-1022.

Almqvist, A.-L. and A.-Z. Duvander (2014), "Changes in Gender Equality? Swedish Fathers' Parental Leave, Division of Childcare and Housework", *Journal of Family Studies*, Vol. 20, No. 1, pp. 19-27.

Barnes, M.W. (2015), "Gender Differentiation in Paid and Unpaid Work during the Transition to Parenthood", *Sociology Compass,* Vol. 9, No. 5, pp. 348-364.

Baxter, J. (2015), "Children's Time with Fathers and Mothers Over the Pre-School Years: A Longitudinal Time-Use Study of Couple Families in Australia", *Family Science*, Vol. 6, No. 1.

Baxter, J.A. (2005), "To Marry or Not to Marry: Marital Status and the Household Division of Labor", *Journal of Family Issues,* Vol. 26, No. 3, pp. 300-321.

Baxter, J.A. and D. Smart (2010), "Fathering in Australia among Couple Families with Young Children", *FaHCSIA Occasional Paper*, No. 37, Department of Families, Housing, Community Services and Indigenous Affairs, Canberra.

Baxter, J., B. Hewitt and M. Haynes (2008), "Life Course Transitions and Housework: Marriage, Parenthood, and Time on Housework", *Journal of Marriage and Family*, Vol. 70, No. 2, pp. 259-272.

Becker, G. (1981), *A Treatise on the Family*, Harvard University Press, Cambridge, United States.

Beer, P. de and R. Luttikhuizen (1998), "Le 'modèle polder' néerlandais : miracle ou mirage ? Réflexions sur le marché du travail et la politique de l'emploi aux Pays-Bas", in J.C. Barbier and J. Gautié (eds.), *Les politiques de l'emploi en Europe et aux États-Unis*, Presses Universitaires de France, Paris, pp. 113-134.

Bergemann, A. and R. Riphahn (2015), "Maternal Employment Effects of Paid Parental Leave", *IZA Discussion Paper*, No. 9073, Bonn.

Berk, S.F. (1985), *The Gender Factory: The Appointment of Work in American Households*, Plenum Press, New York.

Berkel, M. and N.D. de Graaf (1999), "By Virtue of Pleasantness? Housework and the Effects of Education Revisited", *Sociology*, Vol. 33, No. 4, pp. 785-808.

Bertrand, M., E. Kamenica and J. Pan (2015), "Gender Identity and Relative Income within Households", *Quarterly Journal of Economics*, Oxford University Press, Vol. 130, No. 2, pp. 571-614,

Bianchi, S.M. et al. (2000), "Is Anyone Doing the Housework? Trends in the Gender Division of Household Labor", *Social Forces*, Vol. 79, No. 1, pp. 191-228.

Bittman, M. and J. Wajman (2000), "The Rush Hour: The Character of Leisure Time and Gender Equity", *Social Forces,* Vol. 79, No. 1, pp. 165-189.

Blumstein, P. and P. Schwartz (1983), *American Couples: Money, Work, Sex*, William Morrow, New York.

Brandth, B. and I. Gislason (2012), "Family Policies and the Best Interest of Children", in B.G. Eydal and I. Gíslason (eds.), *Parental Leave, Childcare and Gender Equality in the Nordic Countries*, Nordic Council, Copenhagen.

Bünning, M. (2015), "What Happens after the 'Daddy Months'? Fathers' Involvement in Paid Work, Childcare, and Housework after Taking Parental Leave in Germany", *European Sociological Review*, first published online July 29, http://dx.doi.org/10.1093/esr/jcv072.

Cabrera, N.J., J.D. Shannon and C. Tamis-LeMonda (2007), "Fathers' Influence on their Children's Cognitive and Emotional Development: From Toddlers to Pre-K", *Applied Development Science*, Vol. 11, No. 4, pp. 208-213.

Ciano-Boyce, C. and L. Shelley-Sireci (2002), "Who Is Mommy Tonight? Lesbian Parenting Issues", *Journal of Homosexuality*, Vol. 43, No. 2, pp. 1-13.

Cools, S., J.H. Fiva and L.J. Kirkebøen (2015), "Causal Effects of Paternity Leave on Children and Parents", *Scandinavian Journal of Economics*, Vol. 117, No. 3, pp. 801-828.

Craig, L. and K. Mullan (2010), "Parenthood, Gender and Work Family Time in the United States, Australia, Italy, France, and Denmark", *Journal of Marriage and Family*, Vol. 72, No. 5, pp. 1344-1361.

Craig, L., A. Powell and C. Smyth (2014), "Towards Intensive Parenting? Changes in the Composition and Determinants of Mothers' and Fathers' Time with Children 1992–2006", *British Journal of Sociology*, Vol. 65, No. 3, pp. 555-579.

Davis, S. and T. Greenstein (2004), "Cross-national Variations in the Division of Household Labor", *Journal of Marriage and Family,* Vol. 66, No. 5, pp. 1260-1271.

Destatis – German Statistical Office (2015), "Time-use Survey 2012-2013" (Zeitverwendungserhebung 2012/2013), Wiesbaden.

Dijkgraaf, M. and W. Portegijs (2008), "Arbeidsdeelname en wekelijkse arbeidsduur van vrouwen", in W. Portegijs and S. Keuzenkamp (eds.), *Nederland deeltijdland, Vrouwen en deeltijdwerk*, Sociaal Cultureel Planbureau, Gravenhage.

Domínguez-Folgueras, M. (2012), "Is Cohabitation More Egalitarian? The Division of Household Labor in Five European Countries", *Journal of Family Issues*, Vol. 34, No. 12, pp. 1623-1646.

Dunne, G. (2000), "Opting into Motherhood: Lesbians Blurring the Boundaries and Transforming the Meaning of Parenthood and Kinship", *Gender & Society*, Vol. 14, No. 1, pp. 11-35.

Duvander, A.-Z., and A.-C. Jans (2009), "Consequences of Fathers' Parental Leave Use: Evidence from Sweden", *Finnish Yearbook of Population Research*, Vol. 44, pp. 49-62.

Eggebeen, D.J. and C. Knoester (2001), “Does Fatherhood Matter for Men?”, *Journal of Marriage and Family*, Vol. 63, No. 2, pp. 381-393.

Geist, C. (2005), “The Welfare State and the Home: Regime Differences in the Domestic Division of Labour”, *European Sociological Review*, Vol. 21, No. 1, pp. 23-41.

Gershuny, J., M. Bittman and J. Brice (2005), “Exit, Voice, and Suffering: Do Couples Adapt to Changing Employment Patterns?”, *Journal of Marriage and Family*, Vol. 67, No. 3, pp. 656-665.

Goñi-Legaz, S., A. Ollo-López, and A. Bayo-Moriones (2010), “The Division of Household Labor in Spanish Dual Earner Couples: Testing Three Theories”, *Sex Roles,* Vol. 63, pp. 515-529.

Gracia, P. (2014), “Fathers’ Child Care Involvement and Children’s Age in Spain: A Time Use Study on Differences by Education and Mothers’ Employment”, *European Sociological Review*, Vol. 30, No. 2, pp. 137-150.

Grunow, D., F. Schulz and H. Blossfeld (2012), “What Determines Change in the Division of Housework Over the Course of Marriage?”, *International Sociology*, Vol. 27, No. 3, pp. 289-307.

Heisig, J. (2011), “Who Does More Housework: Rich or Poor? A Comparison of 33 Countries”, *American Sociological Review*, Vol. 76, No. 1, pp. 74-99.

Hook, J. (2006), “Care in Context: Men’s Unpaid Work in 20 Countries, 1965-2003”, *American Sociological Review*, Vol. 71, No. 4, pp. 639-660.

Hook, J. and C. Wolfe (2012), “New Fathers? Residential Fathers’ Time With Children in Four Countries”, *Journal of Family Issues*, Vol. 33, No. 4, pp. 415-450.

Huerta, M.C. et al. (2013), “Fathers’ Leave, Fathers’ Involvement and Child Development: Are they Related?, Evidence from Four OECD Countries”, *OECD Social, Employment and Migration Working Papers*, No. 140, OECD Publishing, Paris, http://dx.doi.org/10.1787/5k4dlw9w6czq-en.

Kan, M.Y., O. Sullivan and J. Gershuny (2011), “Gender Convergence in Domestic Work: Discerning the Effects of Interactional and Institutional Barriers from Large-scale Data”, *Sociology*, Vol. 45, No. 2, pp. 234-251.

Kluve, J. and M. Tamm (2013), “Parental Leave Regulations, Mothers’ Labor Force Aattachment and Fathers’ Childcare Involvement: Evidence from a Natural Experiment”, *Journal of Population Economics*, Vol. 26, No. 3, pp. 983-1005.

Kotsadam, A. and H. Finseraas (2011), “The State Intervenes in the Battle of the Sexes: Causal Effects of Paternity Leave”, *Social Science Research*, No. 40, pp. 1611-1622.

Kühhirt, M. (2012), “Childbirth and the Long-term Division of Labour within Couples: How Do Substitution, Bargaining Power, and Norms Affect Parents’ Time Allocation in West Germany?”, *European Sociological Review*, Vol. 28, No. 5, pp. 565-582.

Kurdek, L. (2007), “The Allocation of Household Labor by Partners in Gay and Lesbian Couples”, *Journal of Family Issues*, Vol. 28, No. 1, pp. 132-148.

Lamb, M.E. (2010), *The Role of the Father in Child Development*, Fifth edition, Wiley, New York.

Lauber, V. et al. (2014), "Vereinbarkeit von Beruf und Familie von Paaren mit nicht schulpflichtigen Kindern unter spezifischer Berücksichtigung der Erwerbskonstellation beider Partner", *Politikberatung kompakt,* No. 88, DIW Berlin.

Levtov, R. et al. (2015), *State of the World's Fathers,* A MenCare Advocacy Publication, Promundo, Rutgers, Save the Children, Sonke Gender Justice, and the MenEngage Alliance, Washington, DC.

Lundberg, S. and R. Pollak (1996), "Bargaining and Distribution in Marriage", *Journal of European Social Policy*, Vol. 3, pp. 159-173.

Maier, L. (2014): "Methodik und Durchführung der Zeitverwendungserhebung 2012/2013", *Wirtschaft und Statistik*, November 2014, Statistisches Bundesamt (German Statistical Office), pp. 672-679.

Manser, M. and M. Brown (1977), "Bargaining Analyses of Household Decisions" in C.B. Lloyd and E.S. Andrews (eds.), *Women in the Labor Market*, Columbia University Press, New York, pp. 3-26.

Miranda, V. (2011), "Cooking, Caring and Volunteering: Unpaid Work around the World", *OECD Social, Employment and Migration Working Papers*, No. 116, OECD Publishing, Paris, http://dx.doi.org/10.1787/5kghrjm8s142-en.

MTUS – Multinational Time Use Study (2015), *MTUS Database*, Department of Sociology, University of Oxford, http://www.timeuse.org/mtus.html.

Nepomnyaschy, L. and J. Waldfogel (2007), "Paternity Leave and Fathers' Involvement with their Young Children: Evidence from the American Ecls–B", *Community, Work and Family*, Vol. 10, No. 4, pp. 427-453.

OECD (2013), *Health at a Glance 2013: OECD Indicators*, OECD Publishing, Paris, http://dx.doi.org/10.1787/health_glance-2013-en.

OECD (2012), *Closing the Gender Gap: Act Now*, OECD Publishing, Paris, http://dx.doi.org/10.1787/9789264179370-en.

OECD (2011), *Health at a Glance 2011: OECD Indicators*, OECD Publishing, Paris, http://dx.doi.org/10.1787/health_glance-2011-en.

Perlesz, A. et al. (2010), "Organising Work and Home in Same-sex Parented Families: Findings from the Work Love Play Study", *Australian and New Zealand Journal of Family Therapy*, Vol. 31, No. 4, pp. 374-391.

Pfahl, S. et al. (2014), "Nachhaltige Effekte der Elterngeldnutzung durch Väter", Berlin.

Rasmussen, A.W. (2010), "Increasing the Length of Parents' Birth-related Leave: The Effect on Children's Long-term Educational Outcomes", *Labour Economics*, Vol. 17, pp. 91-100.

Rege, M. and I.F. Solli (2013), "The Impact of Paternity Leave on Fathers' Future Earnings", *Demography,* Vol. 50, No. 6, pp. 2255-2277.

Ribberink, A. (1998), *Leidsvrouwen en zaakwaarneemsters, een geschiedenis van de aktiegroep Man Vrouw Maatschappij, 1968-1973*, Verloren b.v.

Schober, P. (2015), "Increasing Father Involvement in Child Care: What Do We Know about Effects on Child Development?", *DIW Roundup: Politik im Fokus*, No. 79.

Schober, P. (2014a), "Daddy Leave: Does It Change the Gender Division of Domestic Work?", *DIW Roundup No. 46*, German Institute for Economic Research (DIW), Berlin.

Schober, P. (2014b), "Parental Leave and Domestic Work of Mothers and Fathers: A Longitudinal Study of Two Reforms in West Germany", *Journal of Social Policy*, No. 43, pp. 351-372, http://dx.doi.org/10.1017/S0047279413000809.

Schober, P. (2013), "The Parenthood Effect on Gender Inequality: Explaining the Change in Paid and Domestic Work when British Couples Become Parents", *European Sociological Review*, Vol. 29, No. 1, pp. 74-85.

Shelton, B. and D. John (1993), "Does Marital Status Make a Difference? Housework among Married and Cohabiting Men and Women", *Journal of Family Issues*, Vol. 14, No. 3, pp. 401-420.

Sigle-Rushton, W. (2010), "Men's Unpaid Work and Divorce: Reassessing Specialization and Trade in British Families", *Feminist economics*, Vol. 16, No. 2, pp. 1-26.

Solomon, S., E. Rothblum and K. Balsam (2005), "Money, Housework, Sex, and Conflict: Same-Sex Couples in Civil Unions, Those Not in Civil Unions, and Heterosexual Married Siblings", *Sex Roles*, Vol. 52, No. 9/10, pp. 561-575.

Sullivan, O. (2010), "Changing Differences by Educational Attainment in Fathers' Domestic Labour and Child Care", *Sociology*, Vol. 44, No. 4, pp. 716-733.

Tanaka, S. (2005), "Parental Leave and Child Health across OECD Countries", *Economic Journal*, Vol. 115, pp. F7-F28.

Tanaka, S. and J. Waldfogel (2007), "Effects of Parental Leave and Work Hours on Fathers' Involvement with their Babies: Evidence from the Millennium Cohort Study", *Community, Work and Family*, Vol. 10, No. 4, pp. 409-426.

US BLS (2013), "Unpaid Eldercare in the United States – 2011-2012, Data from the American Yime Use Survey", Press release, 18 September, United States Bureau of Labor Statistics, http://www.bls.gov/news.release/pdf/elcare.pdf.

Visser, J. and A. Hemerijck (1998), *A Dutch Miracle: Job Growth, Welfare Reform and Corporatism in the Netherlands*, Amsterdam University Press.

Visser, J. et al. (2004), "The Netherlands: From Atypicality to a Typicality", in S. Sciarra, P. Davies and M. Freedland (eds.), *Employment Policy and the Regulation of Part-time Work in the European Union, A Comparative Analysis* , Cambridge University Press, Cambridge, pp. 190-223.

WHO (2007), "Fatherhood and Health Outcomes in Europe", WHO Regional Office for Europe, Copenhagen, Denmark.

Wrohlich, K. et al. (2012), "Elterngeld Monitor", *Politikberatung kompakt*, No. 61, DIW Berlin.

Annex 5.A1

Overview of the time use surveys analysed

Table 5.A1.1 shows the main features of the time use surveys used in this chapter. Methodological differences may affect the comparability of certain indicators across countries. The following lists the most important limitations for the indicators presented in this Chapter:

- Canada, Norway and the United States do not record both partners' time use in the household. Therefore, how a couple shares unpaid work is, cannot be computed. As for Finland and Spain, all household members ten years or older fill out the diary but people living in partnership within the same household cannot be identified through a personal identifier. So similar ages are used to identify partners.
- Austria, Finland, Germany Spain provide no information on time spent in the presence of household children unless they are young (below ten years), Canada only for household children under 15, Korea asks only whether a preschool-age child was present. South Africa does not ask who was present at all.
- Some countries define child care activities more narrowly. In Korea parents can record physical care, teaching, visiting the school and other activities with their school-age children. However, it lists reading and playing as separate activities only for pre-school age children. South Africa does not record reading, playing or talking with children as activities.
- The analysis is restricted to primary activities and does not take into account secondary activities [like watching TV (primary activity) while ironing (secondary activity)], because different countries record them quite differently. While in some countries, time use diaries include columns especially for secondary activities, the time use interviewers in countries like the United States do not ask specifically about simultaneous activities.
- Surveys that use self-written diaries usually record activities in much greater detail than retrospective interviews (used in Canada and the United States).
- Not all countries sample all year round. Some the field phase at a specific time of year – e.g. March and April 2009 in Austria, March and September in Korea, and October through December 2010 in South Africa.
- For South Africa subsistence farming and activities like selling fruit in the street are counted towards time in paid work.

Table 5.A1.1. Main features of the time use surveys

	Austria	Canada	Germany	Finland	France	Italy	Korea	Norway	Spain	United States	South Africa
Year of survey	2008-2009	2010	2012-2013	2009	2009-2010	2008	2009	2010	2009-2010	2010	2010
Season of survey	End March 2009 to April 2009	Jan. to Dec. 2010	1st Oct. 2009 to 30 Sept. 2010	April 2009 to May 2010	0	1st Feb. 2008 to 31 Jan. 2009	March and Sept.	15 Feb. 2010 to 14 Feb. 2011	1 Oct. 2009 to 30 Sept 2010	Around the year	Oct. to Dec. 2010
Approximate number of individuals surveyed	8 200	15 390	11 000	3 500	20 000	40 000	20 000	3 100	20 000	10 000	40 000
Time use diary filled out by respondent him/herself?	Yes	No, Retrospective interview	Yes	Yes	Yes	Yes	Yes	Yes	Yes	No, Retrospective interview	Yes
Secondary activity recorded?	Yes	Yes	Yes	Yes	Yes	Yes	Yes	Yes	Yes	Partially asked and coded	No
Other household members surveyed?	Yes, everyone age 10 or older	No	Yes, everyone age 10 or older	Yes, everyone age 10 or older	Yes, everyone age 10 or older	Yes, everyone age 10 or older	Yes, everyone age 10 or older	No	Yes, everyone age 10 or older	No	Yes, one other household member
Time-use of spouse documented?	Yes	No, but some basic information on time at work	Yes	Yes	Yes	Yes	Yes	No	Yes	No	Yes, for some spouses
Approximate number of couples surveyed, where female between 25 and 44	900	n.a.	3 400	800	3 350	3 650	3 900	n.a.	2 200	n.a.	1 150
Respondents document time spent in the presence of household children?	Yes, presence of children <10 years	Yes, presence of children < 15 years	Yes, presence of children <10 years	Yes, presence of children <10 years	Yes	Presence of son or daughter	Presence of pre-school age children	Yes	Yes, presence of children <10 years	Yes	No

Chapter 6

Equal sharing and having children in Germany and France

This chapter concludes Dare to Share *with a comparison of fertility behaviours in Germany and France. The point of departure is the disparity between France's high rates of fertility and Germany's low ones. The purpose is to explore how Germany might draw on French practices and policies to strengthen equal partnership in families so that German parents can have children and careers. Section 2 looks at the persistent fertility gap between the two countries, identifying France's family-friendly child care policies as a key factor. Section 3 then goes on to consider the discrepancy between mothers' desire for children and their childlessness, which is much higher in Germany than in France. Again policy is a critical determinant, though Germany's more traditional perceptions of gender roles also have a part to play. Section 4 stresses how couples' levels of educational attainment, earnings and length of working hours affect fertility. Some concluding remarks wrap up the chapter. They stress that policy changes since 2007 have helped ease the conflict between full-time work and parenthood. More equal sharing in families and public action to reconcile work and family life may further help to sustain tentatively rising fertility trends.*

1. Introduction and main findings

Partnership does not only have a bearing on sharing in the workplace and at home. Because it enables both adults in couple families to fulfil individual aspirations and helps them believe that combining work and family life are realistic prospects, more partnership could sustain birth-rates too.

For decades, fertility trends have been declining, as many potential parents postponed founding a family or decide to have fewer children or none at all. These choices are influenced by many different and often inter-related factors – the wish for a career before taking time off to care for children, the cost of children, which includes housing and education, and the growing acceptance of childlessness as a life choice.

In many OECD countries, there was an upswing in birth rates in the late 1990s, also driven by a combination of factors, such as the wish to catch up on motherhood after years of postponement, the development of policies to reconcile work and family commitments, and economic growth (Luci-Greulich and Thévenon, 2014). However, fertility rates flattened or fell with the onset of the Great Recession in 2007-08. In France, too, birth rates remained stable and in Germany they increased since 2009 but are still at a much lower level than in France.

Persistently low fertility rates below replacement level have implications for population growth, the make-up of future societies and macroeconomic growth patterns (Chapter 2; OECD, 2011; Bujard, 2015a). And when people do not have as many children as they wish, individual and family well-being both suffer. Accordingly, policy strives to help adults have as many children as they would like at the time of their choosing (OECD, 2011). Yet the role and effectiveness of policy in increasing fertility is under debate (Thévenon and Gauthier, 2011; Thévenon, 2015).

Chapter 3 examined the significant reforms to parental leave and child care policies which Germany introduced since the late 2000s. Might it be that such reform, which seeks to develop a package of policies that help reconcile work and family life, also exerts a positive influence on fertility outcomes and intentions? To what extent does the evidence from the experience of OECD countries support that conjecture?

To answer those questions, comparison between Germany and France is particularly interesting. Although they have achieved a comparable level of economic development, they are poles apart in the development of female labour force participation, policies to support families, and the combination of work-and-family and fertility trends over recent decades. In France, most women enter the labour market on a full-time basis, and working parents using formal care have received public support since the early 1980s. Fertility has remained at a high level by European standards. By contrast, part-time work is the more usual practice among working mothers in Germany (Chapter 4), and child care supports for fathers and mothers to women stay in work when they have children are comparatively recent. Moreover, full-time work often entails longer working hours in Germany than in France, where most full-time working mothers actually work between 35 and 39 hours. German fertility rates are among the lowest in Europe, although the recent upturn in fertility suggests that the fresh policy development can help to reverse the decline.

Against this backdrop, a close comparison of the interplay between partners' employment situations and fertility behaviour in Germany and France can provide insight into how changes in working patterns might positively affect fertility if they are backed by policies to reduce conflicts between work and family life.

This chapter looks in some detail at aspects of fertility behaviour in France and Germany. It first emphasises the persistent fertility gap between the two countries, and looks at the disparity between actual and would-be behaviour which may explain the gap. It identifies the effect of having children on female employment and working hours and national attitudes to the division of paid work and child care as key factors behind the differences in French and German fertility rates. Lastly, the chapter discusses how partners' educational attainment, earnings and working hours affect fertility. It stresses the greater opportunity cost of children and pronounced stratification of fertility by female employment status in Germany, attributable to the high degree of labour market segmentation and weaker support for the work-life balance than in France.

Main findings

- Since 1960 total fertility rates (TFRs) have declined across the OECD area to an average of 1.7 children per woman. In Germany, TFRs in the post re-unification period were lowest in 1994 at 1.24, but edged up thereafter to 1.47 children per women in 2014.
- Recent evaluations suggest that family-friendly policy reform (i.e. the 2007 parental leave reform and increase in public investment in child care services) have had a slight but positive effect on the TFR. The effect may further accrue when Germany expands its provision of early childhood education and care (ECEC). Nevertheless, its TFR is still low in comparison to countries that started to develop their work-life balance support at an earlier stage, such as France, Iceland and Sweden, whose TFRs are close to two children per women.
- The reconciliation of work and family life is an important determinant of fertility. Considered cross-nationally, countries with higher female employment rates are also among those whose fertility rates are close to two children per women. Women in Germany are less likely to work and bring up young children than their peers in France and many other OECD countries.
- In Germany, women are more likely to remain childless than in many other European countries, including France. Moreover, women who do have children have smaller families – 39% of women have 2 children or more in Germany, compared with 44% in France.
- Birth-rates in Germany vary much more widely than in France according to women's levels of educational attainment, labour market status, occupation and earnings.
    - In both countries, women with higher levels of educational attainment are less likely to have children, but more markedly so in Germany than in France.
    - At an individual level, women in employment in Germany are considerably less likely to have children than women who are not in paid work – women in France (and elsewhere), too, but to a much less pronounced extent.

  - Working full-time in Germany substantially lessens the likelihood of having a child, especially among women from a less well educated background.

- In Germany, fertility rates are higher in households with lower earnings, but rise steeply in couples where men earn significantly more than their partners. The pattern confirms the qualitative finding that male earnings are often considered crucial to the provision of the income security required to have children. By contrast, differences in earnings between partners do not affect the prospect of having children in France, all else being equal. This difference between the two countries reflects the greater influence of the male-breadwinner model and traditional gender roles and attitudes in Germany than in France.

- In Germany, women are more likely to have to choose both the occupation and the working hours that suit their desire for children. By contrast, in France, the provision of child care and out-of-school care services for longer hours without interruption seem to make fertility behaviour less dependent on working hours and occupations.

- The greater scope for balancing work and family life in France reduces the opportunity costs of having children, which thus becomes more likely as women's earnings increase.

- Comparison with France suggests that changes in working patterns in couple families are compatible with higher fertility in Germany, too, but only if support for the work-family balance is further developed to reconcile women's full-time employment with motherhood. If Germany were to continue to go down that avenue, fertility behaviour would become less dependent on partnered women working part-time and on the traditional household division of labour.

- The greater involvement of fathers in child care work after the birth of a first child may increase the likelihood of having another child. Evidence from Sweden suggests that father-specific leave entitlements foster paternal involvement in child care, which, in turn, heightens the probability of couples having a second child.

2. Fertility trends in Germany and the OECD

Since the late 1960s, birth rates have been falling across the OECD (Figure 6.1, Panel A). In some countries, the decline continued until the late 1990s since which, TFRs have generally remained below population replacement level of 2.1 children per woman (Chapter 2).[1]

Germany's TFR has been persistently below 1.5 children per woman since the mid-1980s, as in many of the so-called "lowest-low fertility countries" in Central, Eastern and Southern Europe (Kohler et al., 2002). By contrast, TFR rose in France, as in Northern Europe, from the late 1990s to the onset of the Great Recession in 2007-08. France's TFR has edged up significantly since its low point in the mid-1990s and has been close to 2 children per woman since the mid-2000s. In Germany, too, it rose from 1.36 to 1.47 in 2014, though it is still below 1.5 children per woman.

Differences in fertility behaviour between France and Germany are reflected in average completed family sizes (or completed fertility rates), the number of children born per women in a cohort of women by the end of their childbearing years (Figure 6.1, Panel B). In France, the average completed family size has remained persistently above two children per woman in all the generations born since the Second World War. By contrast, completed fertility rates (CFRs) have gradually declined to less than 1.5 on average in Germany,[2] where the western and the eastern *Länder* have followed different paths. CFRs hovered around 1.8 children per women in the eastern *Länder* in all cohorts born between the end of World War II and the early 1960s. There was then a steep fall in the average completed family size, as a result of which CFRs are no longer much higher than in the western *Länder*.

Figure 6.1. Fertility rates seem to have been edging up in Germany in recent years

Panel A. Total fertility rates, 1960-2014

Panel B. Completed fertility rates, for cohorts born 1935-1969

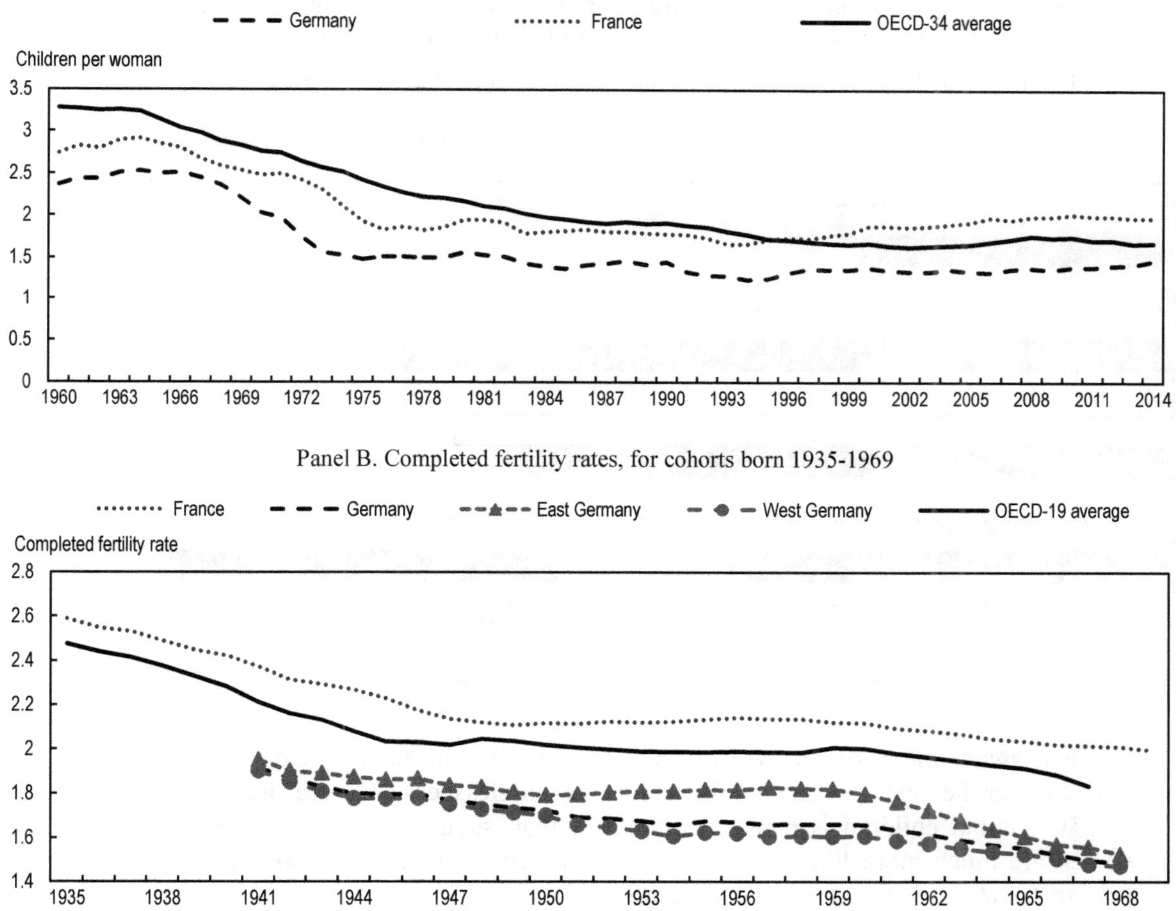

Source: Panel A: *OECD Family Database*, www.oecd.org/els/family/database.htm; Panel B: *Human Fertility Database*, http://www.humanfertility.org/cgi-bin/main.php.

The persistent gap between German and French fertility levels reflect two different fertility regimes. Although 36% of women aged 25 to 49 in Germany were childless in 2012, compared with only 28% in France (Figure 6.2), many of the youngest women in that cohort will, of course, have children in the future. One contributory factor, though not a major one, is that French women tend to start their families at a younger age than their German peers (when they do actually have children) – a woman's mean age at the birth of her first child was 28.1 in France and 29 in Germany in 2013. Moreover, when women do have children in Germany, they have fewer – 39% have 2 or more children, while the figure in France is 44%.

However, the most striking fact is that far fewer women have remained childless in France than in Germany – especially in the western *Länder* – by the end of their child-bearing years (Figure 6.3). Only 13% of women stay childless in France, a proportion of childlessness comparable to the Eastern Germany, where it remained constant in the post-war years before increasing with the cohort born in the 1950s and after. By contrast, childlessness started to rise continually and ever faster among women born after 1935 in western Germany, where around 23% of women born in the late 1960s and/or the early 1970s are childless. That proportion is also high by OECD standards.

Figure 6.2. Women in France are most likely to have two or more children, while women in Germany are more likely to remain childless

Distribution of the number of children per woman aged 25 to 49, France and Germany, 2012

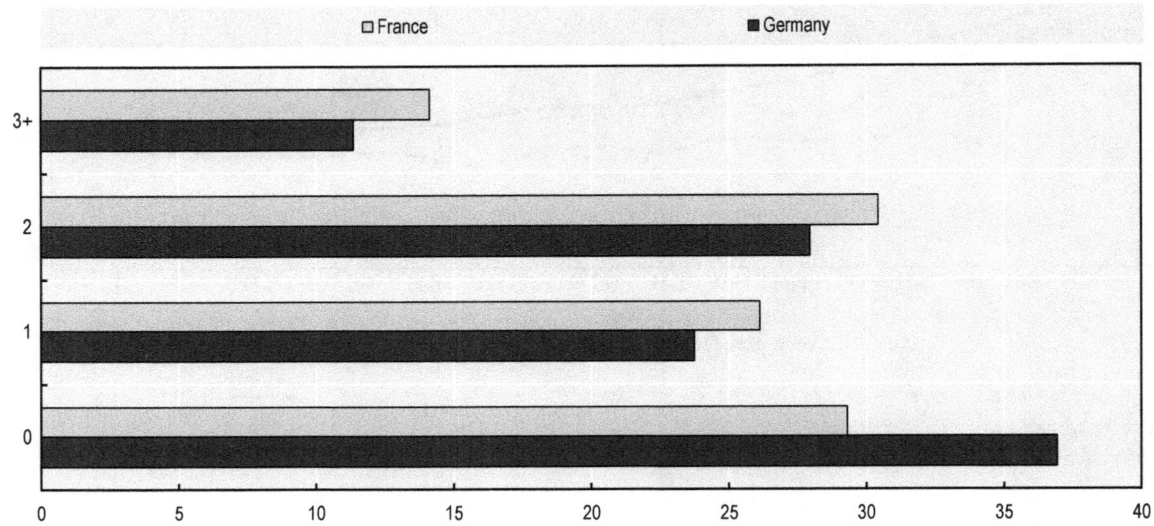

Source: 2012 European Union Labour Force Surveys for France; 2012 Mikrocensus for Germany.

Then again, many of the women in the 25-to-49 year-old age group will have children over the next 25 years, so that definitive childlessness as a measure of women over 50 without children is considerably lower than suggested above. Nevertheless, women are much more likely never to have children in Germany – especially in the western *Länder* – than in France (Figure 6.3).

Figure 6.3. Definitive childlessness in Germany is double the level in France

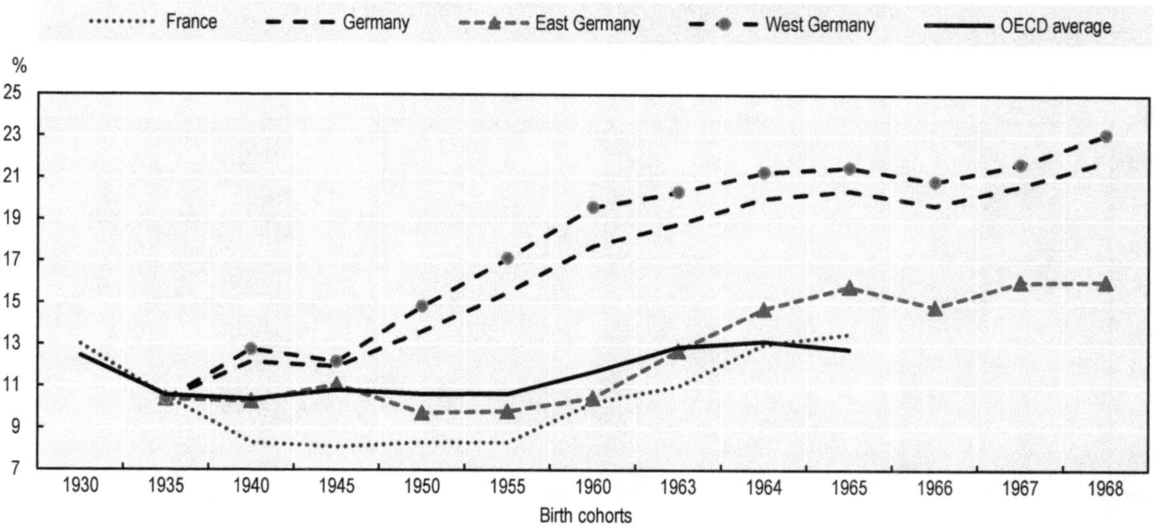

Source: *OECD Family Database*, www.oecd.org/els/family/database.htm; Bujard (2015b).

Childlessness is influenced by several factors in Germany (Dorbritz, 2008; Kreyenfeld and Konietzka, 2013; Bujard, 2015b). The likelihood of being childless is greater among women who have high levels of educational attainment, no migration background, are in full-time employment and live in urban areas (Bujard, 2015b). For instance, childlessness among poorly educated women is, at 15%, nearly half the level of 27% among women with university-level degrees – and migrant women make up a significant share of the poorly educated. Moreover, although the childlessness rate of highly educated women with no migration background in the cities of western Germany is 38%, it reaches 48% among those in full-time employment.

Trends in childlessness in Germany also point to growing incompatibility between motherhood and full-time employment (Bujard, 2015b; Thévenon, 2009).[3] Many women view motherhood as tantamount to cutting their hours of paid work or withdrawing from the labour force altogether, and a good number of those who embark on careers remain childless (Kreyenfeld and Konietzka, 2013; Bujard, 2015b).

3. The gap between actual and desired family size

Low fertility and childlessness do not always reflect individual preferences. In both France and Germany, the proportions of women who consider childlessness as their personal "ideal" are low – 3% and 7%, respectively (Figure 6.4), which are well below the percentages of childless women reported above. The inference is that many women in France, but particularly in Germany, experience unwanted childlessness.

Another difference between France and Germany comes in ideal family size. In 2011, a large share of women in France – 45% – stated that they would like to have three or more children. The proportion was only 18% in Germany, where two-thirds of respondents said their ideal family would have two children.

Figure 6.4. Two-child families are the dominant ideal in Germany

Distribution (%) of women, aged 15-39, by ideal number of children

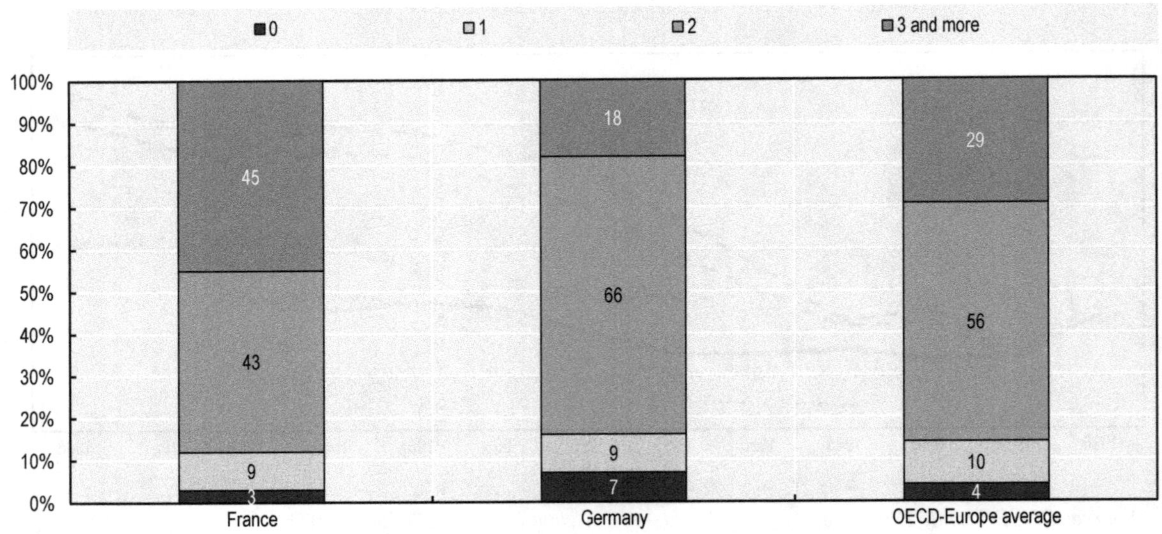

Source: Eurobarometer 2011 as calculated by Testa (2012).

France is a country where both intended and actual fertility rates are relatively high (Figure 6.5). By contrast, Germany belongs to a group of countries with low fertility aspirations and outcomes. The inference is that the interaction between cultural attitudes towards children and the internalisation of constraints on having children affects both fertility intentions and living up to them (Klobas and Ajzen, 2015).

Recent trends suggest that attitudes towards fertility are changing in Germany and moving away from the "lowest low" mindset. Dorbritz and Naderi (2013) detect an increase since the early 2000s in the number of children that adults would like to have. The increase emerges in different measures of fertility preferences. Dorbritz and Naderi observed, for instance, that the number of children that people between 20 and 39 years old would "realistically"[4] like to have increased from 1.44 in 2005 to 1.77 in 2011. A similar pattern in evolving fertility preferences is reported by IDA (2015) along changing perceptions – 33% of Germans considered their country child-friendly in 2013, compared to 25% in 2007. Fewer parents with children under 3 felt financially squeezed in 2013 than in 2007 (48% vs. 36%) and a much lower proportion found it difficult to get child care – 13% in 2013 compared to 29% in 2007).

Figure 6.5. Mean intended family sizes in EU OECD countries

Mean average actual and intended number of children, women (24-to-39 year-olds)

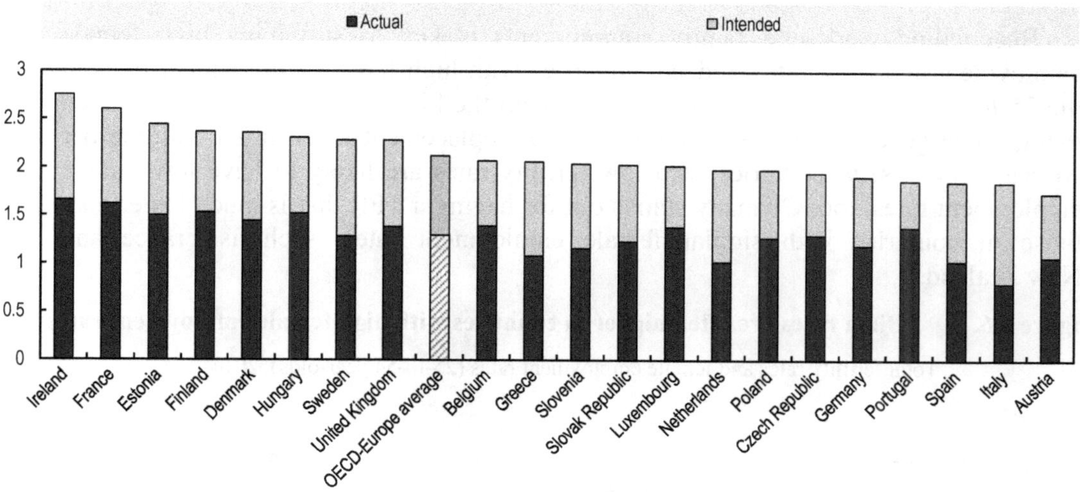

Source: Eurobarometer 2011: Fertility and Social Climate, http://ec.europa.eu/public_opinion/index_en.htm.

4. Combining work and family formation: a key determinant of fertility

Many factors affect cross-country differences in fertility trends (Goldstein et al., 2009; OECD, 2011). To some extent, the recovery in TFRs in many OECD countries that took place during the 1990s and 2000s was a logical consequence of post-war cohorts' postponement of childbearing and subsequent partial fertility recuperation (compensatory rise in fertility) among women in their 30s and early 40s (Bongaarts and Sobotka, 2012). The reasons for postponement are diverse, but two important ones are:

- the growing number of women who seek to establish themselves in the labour market before they have children,
- changes in attitudes towards household division of labour and child care.

Employment behaviour and fertility

Fertility behaviour has become increasingly associated with female employment status for many reasons (Anderson and Kohler, 2015; Luci-Greulich and Thévenon, 2014). First, the large gains in educational attainment among women put upward pressure on the cost of interrupting their employment spell to bear and/or rear children. In view of the growing risks associated with economic fluctuations and family break-up, it has also become increasingly important for women to secure their labour market situation before starting a family (Bernhardt, 1993; Blossfeld 1995). For that reason, employed women, particularly when they are highly educated, tend to have their first child earlier than those who are non-employed – but only, however, in Northern and Western European countries where they are more likely to have access to support for the work-life balance (Rendall et al., 2014; Wood et al, 2015). By contrast, in countries with limited provision for helping parents reconcile work and family life, the birth of a child often spells a significant reduction in family income, as at least one partner has to stop or scale back his/her employment participation in order to look after the child.

This income constraint appears to weigh particularly heavily on parents who would like to have more children, but who both have to work to sustain household income (Greulich et al., 2016).

Reconciling work and family commitments is key to sustaining high female employment and birth rates. Indeed, countries with high female employment rates in the 25-to-54 age group are often also those with the highest TFRs (Figure 6.6), even though they generally lie below the population-replacement level of 2.1 children per woman. Conversely, countries with low fertility rates are likely to have low female employment rates, too. Germany stands out for having a TFR that is much lower than those in countries with similar female employment rates, such as France and New Zealand.

Figure 6.6. Birth rates are often higher in countries with high female employment rates

Total fertility rates and female employment rates (25-to-54 year-olds), 2014[1]

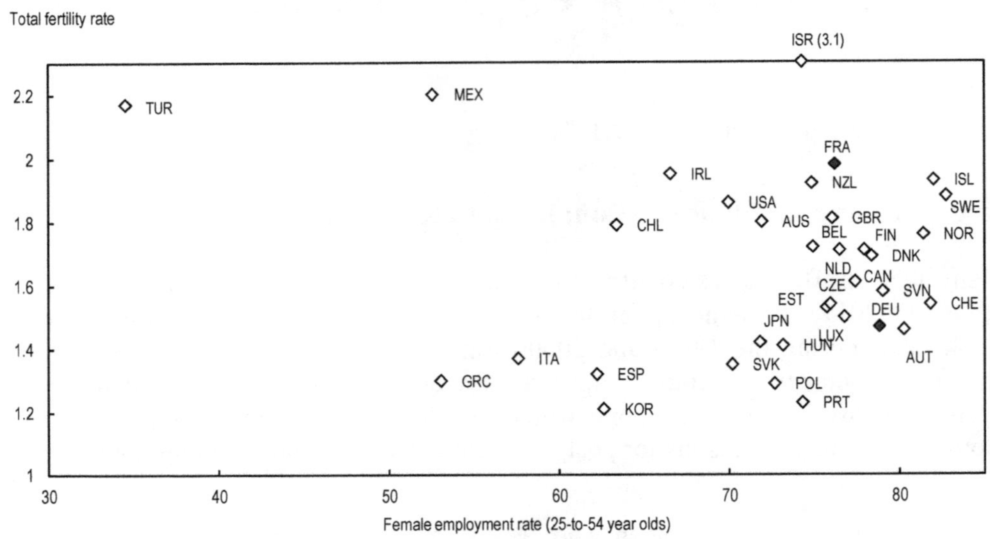

1. For the total fertility rate, data for Canada refer to 2012 and for Chile to 2013.

Source: *OECD Family Database*, www.oecd.org/els/family/database.htm.

Differences at the aggregate level in birth and female employment rates reflect differences at the individual level insofar female labour market participation is affected by the number and age of children in households. Female employment rates fall as family sizes increase in both France and Germany, but mothers with one or two children are considerably more likely to be in work in France (Figure 6.7). Women with children of preschool age are also more likely to work in France, and employment rates of mothers in Germany with children in the 0-to-2 year-old age-bracket are considerably lower. However, by the time the youngest child enters primary school differences in employment rates (not working hours) have almost disappeared.

More women are now returning to work after having had a child in Germany than a few years ago. In particular, the number of working mothers with children under three years of age rose significantly between 2006 and 2013 – i.e. after the introduction of parental allowance in 2007. Over that period, 10% more mothers resumed work two years after birth and 13% more in the third year (BMFSFJ, 2015).

Figure 6.7. Having children has a more adverse effect on female employment in Germany than in France

Employment rates (%) for mothers (15-to-64 years old) with children aged 0-14, by number of children aged 0-14 and by age of the youngest child, Germany, France and the OECD-27 average, 2013

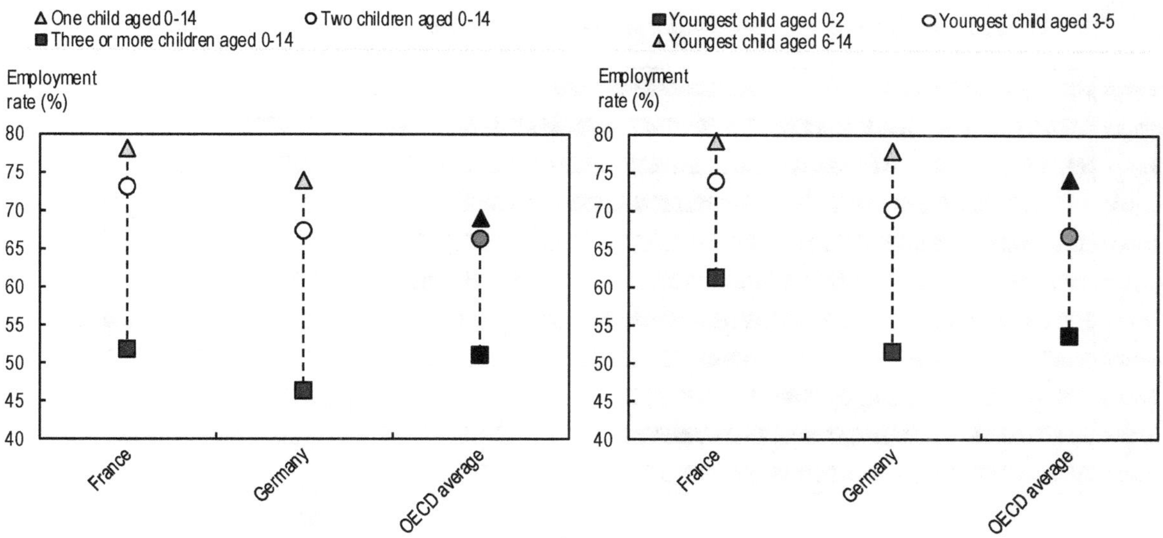

Source: *OECD Family Database*, www.oecd.org/els/family/database.htm.

Moreover, hours worked are more likely to be affected by the presence and number of children in Germany than in France. Thévenon (2009) identifies a growing polarisation since the early 1990s in women's employment status that is co-determined by the size of the family. In Germany, women with children have become increasingly likely to work short part-time hours (i.e. less than 20 hours a week), while those in full-time employment work comparatively long hours and seem increasingly childless. Such polarisation has not occurred in France, where 45% of female employees work for between 35 and 39 hours a week, and where the effect of the first and second child on full-time employment is much less pronounced than in Germany and in most other European countries. Many women in part-time employment in France also work for longer hours than in Germany – less than 9% of female employees work 20 hours or less in France and over 20% in Germany.

Attitudes towards work and family

Differences in female employment status also reflect, to a certain degree, variations in attitudes to the work-life balance and to couples sharing paid work. A high proportion of female employees in Germany who work more than 35 hours per week and whose partner works full-time are not satisfied with their working hours: almost 3 women in 4 report that they would like to work less (Figure 6.8, Panel A). The corresponding proportion is much lower in France at 48% and in Finland, Norway and Sweden (around 40%). By contrast, most women in Germany who work no more than 35 hours per week seem satisfied (Figure 6.8, Panel B) – only 15% report that they would like to work more, compared to 30% in France.

Figure 6.8. How many hours would you like to work?

Distribution (%) of employed women by ideal working hours relative to current working hours, for women with a full-time working partner, selected countries, 2010

Panel A. Women who more than 35 hours (and have a full-time working partner)

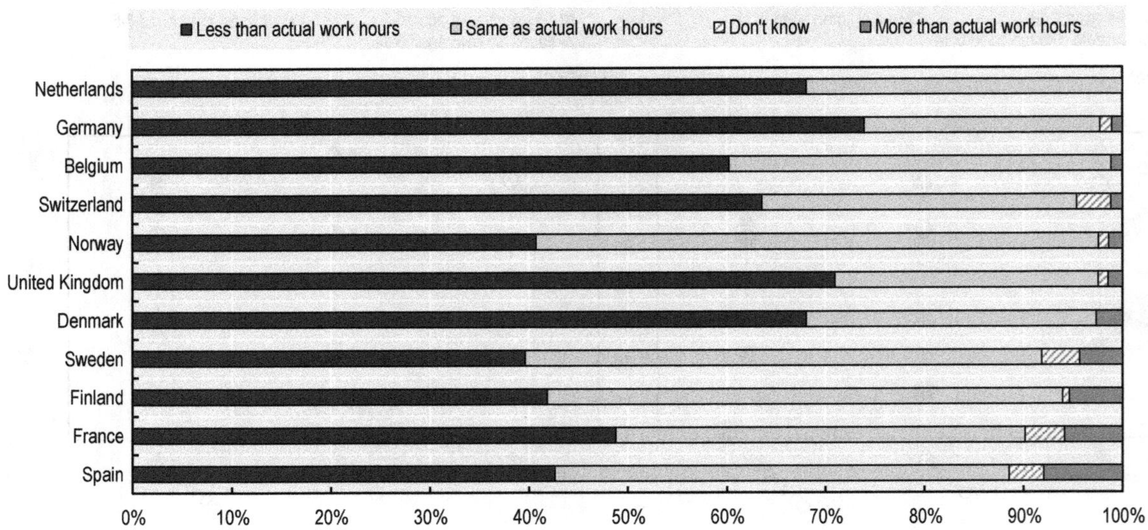

Panel B. Women who work less than 35 hours (and have a full-time working partner)

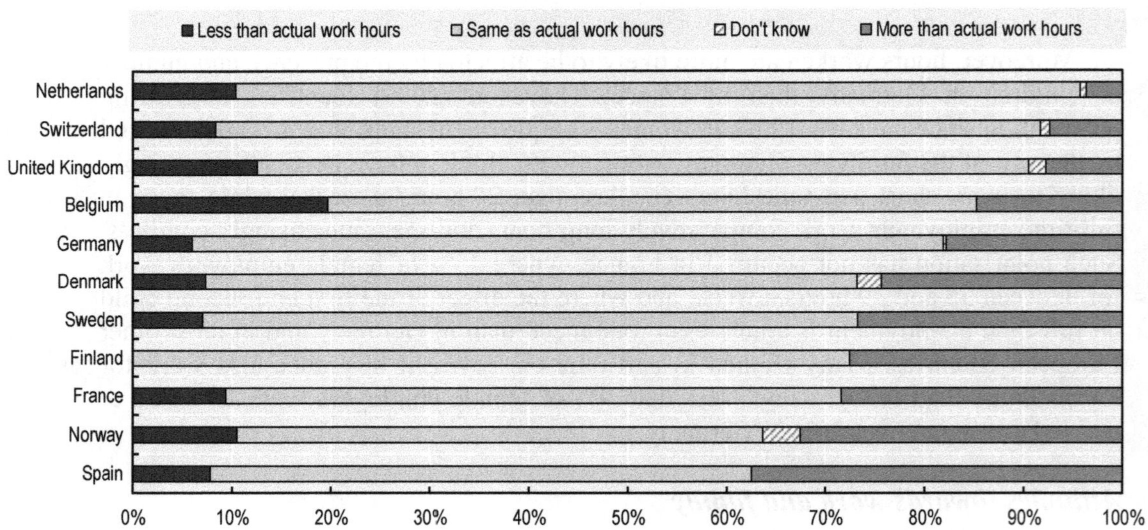

Source: OECD calculations based on the European Social Survey, Round 5 (2010), http://www.europeansocialsurvey.org/.

Chapter 2 looked at the hours which partnered men and women, with and without children of pre-school age, would prefer their partner to work. Preferences differ markedly by gender, as women would like their partners to work much longer average hours than the other way round. The same gender-related preferences hold true for all countries, but are more pronounced in Germany, the Netherlands and the United Kingdom than, for instance, in Sweden, Denmark and France. The cross-country variations suggest that the idea of the man as breadwinner is still very much alive in many countries.

Furthermore, Brachet et al. (2010) find that, in Germany more than in France, there is a general belief that men should secure an income base before getting married and having children. And, within Germany, that belief is more prevalent in West Germany than in East Germany (Bernardi et al., 2008)

Gender division of child care work and fertility

The literature on the relationship between fertility and gender equality in unpaid housework paints a mixed picture.[5] Some studies have found traditional gender role attitudes and behaviours to be associated with earlier, greater fertility, e.g. Bernhardt and Goldsheider (2006) and Westoff and Wiggins (2009). Others, by contrast, claim that gender-egalitarian behaviour and more equally shared domestic work increase birth rates (e.g. Cooke, 2009; Duvander and Andersson, 2006). And Duvander, Lappegard, and Andersson (2010) found that the involvement of fathers in caring for the first child particularly heightens the likelihood of couples having a second child in both Sweden and Norway.

Aassve et al. (2015) suggest that couples who share unpaid work in the household on a more gender-egalitarian basis are more likely to have second children in countries such as France, Hungary and Lithuania. However, the kind of unpaid work that each partner does, and how long each spends on it, has different bearings on the probability of further offspring. For instance, Miettinen et al. (2015) found that, in Finland, when women spend less time on housework, there appears to be a higher probability of subsequent birth. By contrast, a greater male contribution to housework does not seem to boost fertility. Their greater contribution to child care does, however. These recent findings are consistent with Cooke (2004), who found that German fathers' increased participation in child care heightens the odds of couples having a second child, while fathers sharing in unpaid housework appears non-significant.

Women's employment status, partnership and fertility behaviour in Germany and France

This report considers how the likelihood of couples in Germany and France having children is shaped by the interaction between women's labour market status, their working hours and partners' socio-economic attributes (see Annex 6.A1 for methodological details). It finds that having a child is linked more to educational attainment and women's employment status in Germany than in France – a consequence of the fact that balancing full-time work with family life is a greater challenge and that having children thereby generates higher opportunity costs.

- Women in Germany who have completed compulsory schooling only are almost twice as likely to have a child within a year as those with higher-education qualifications. In France, they are only 30% more likely.
- The employment status is a factor in both countries, but working women (regardless of how many hours they work) are much less likely to have a child in Germany than in France.
- Women who work part-time (especially those who do less than 20 hours a week in Germany) are much more likely to have a child than those in full-time employment. The influence of working hours also varies with women's educational attainment, though how level of education and working week interact differs from one country to the other. In France, irrespective of working hours,

women are 30% to 40% less likely to have a child when they hold a university-level degree than those who went no further than lower-secondary school. In Germany, however, women who work full-time are much less likely to have children when they hold a secondary-education qualification than women educated to university level who also work full-time. This finding reveals the considerable barriers to having children faced by women who work full-time in Germany, especially the less well educated who cannot afford to work and rear children.

- Women's choice of occupation also seems to affect fertility, regardless of working hours (see Annex 6.A1 for definitions of occupations). In Germany, for instance, there is a higher probability that professionals will have a child within a year than managers, who, in turn, are more likely than technicians, clerical workers and other low-skilled workers to become mothers. The association between occupation and fertility may be attributable to the fact that women's choice of occupation is based partly on how it fits with their fertility intentions. For instance, professionals may well have greater flexibility than machine operators as they seek to match work with family commitments. The same patterns can be seen in France, but it does not appear to affect fertility outcomes to the same extent.
- In France two women in the same occupation and earning the same wages are more likely, all else being equal, to have children when they work reduced full-time or part-time hours than those who do 40-hour weeks or more. The provision of child care and out-of-school care services – for longer hours and without interruption – seem to make fertility behaviour more responsive to working hours within occupations. In Germany, by contrast, the number of working hours *within* occupations has little bearing on fertility behaviour – which may be attributable to both occupation-specific working time constraints and the inadequate provision of care services. In Germany, women are more likely to have to choose (as far as possible) both the occupation and working hours that lend themselves to their fertility intentions.
- High-earning women generally face higher opportunity costs than low earners when they have children. It is therefore to be expected that they are less likely to do so, all else being equal. It is indeed the case in Germany, where there are much higher chances of low-income women becoming mothers than those in the middle or at the top of the earnings distribution. In France, by contrast, individual female earnings have a limited impact on fertility behaviour though high earners are slightly more likely to have children than low earners. The provision of support for the work-life balance lessens the opportunity costs of having children and, as a consequence, the likelihood of fertility increases with women's earnings.[6]

Last but not least, the educational level and earnings of male partners exert a much stronger influence on fertility behaviour in Germany than in France. Differences in earnings between partners do not affect the probability of having a child in France, all else being equal. In Germany, though, where male earnings are widely seen as crucial to securing the income required to have children, the likelihood of having a child increases considerably when men earn significantly more than their partners. The influence of male earnings on fertility reflects the fact that, in Germany much more than in France, the idea of the male as breadwinner still prevails, as do traditional gender roles and attitudes.

Comparison of Germany with France suggests that changes in working patterns in couple families are associated with higher fertility – but only if Germany strengthens its support for the work-family balance to make women's full-time employment and having children less mutually exclusive. Fertility behaviour would then become less dependent on partnered women working part-time in selected occupations and on the traditional household division of labour. Reconciliation policies – those which seek to balance employment and family commitments – are thus a critical component of environments that seek to foster higher fertility rates and the more equally balanced participation of men and women in the labour market.

5. What influence of reconciliation policies?

The recent and ongoing changes in family policies make it easier for many households to reconcile work and family commitments (Chapter 3). However, working parents, especially mothers, still receive far less support in Germany than France. In particular, the provision of child care services is far more developed in France where, since the mid-1990s, preschool and after-school care services frequently cover – albeit imperfectly – the needs of full-time workers. Longer school days, combined with a comprehensive provision of out-of-school care services, make balancing full-time work with family life much easier for many French families with school-aged children (Chapter 3). By contrast, in Germany most all-day primary schools provide no more than seven or eight hours of education and care, so most parents have to pick up their children in mid-afternoon. And, although the number of 3-to-6 year-olds enrolled full-time in kindergartens is growing, most children in that age group get formal care on a part-time basis only. In that context, many women have no option other than to choose between having children and pursuing a full-time career.

A large body of evidence shows that better opportunities for reconciling work and family life have a positive effect on fertility. The nature of family support matters, however. For example, one-off cash payments and baby grants may affect the timing of couples who plan to children, but do not necessarily affect the overall number of children in families (OECD, 2011; Thévenon and Gauthier, 2011).

Recent evidence also suggests that longer maternity and parental leave have a positive, but weak, effect on fertility trends (Luci-Greulich and Thévenon, 2013). The finding is consistent with evaluations of the 2007 parental leave reform which indicate that the fertility of German women in their mid-30s who have high levels of educational attainment has increased since the reform (Bujard and Passet, 2013; Stichnoth, 2014).

The extension of child care services for children below preschool age is another factor that studies have consistently found to have a positive effect on fertility trends (Luci-Greulich and Thévenon, 2013). In that regard, Hank and Kreyenfeld (2002) show that the low fertility rates in Germany can be explained by the limited availability of child care in Germany – a factor in the mutually exclusive choice of working full-time or having children (and working part-time). Indeed, the recent increase in the number of public child care places has contributed to a rise in fertility. Bauernschuster et al. (2013) suggest that the intended increase in public child care coverage to 39% under the terms of the 2007 development plan could increase boost TFR from 1.4 to 1.55 children per woman.

There is also evidence that the provision of father-specific leave entitlements fosters greater paternal involvement in parenting, which, in turn, may positively affect birth rates (Duvander and Andersson, 2006; Duvander et al., 2010; Lappegard, 2009; Skrede, 2005). Most of the evidence emanates from Nordic countries, where paternal leave entitlements are more generous than in other countries and administrative data enable comparisons of behaviour before and after reform. The effect of paternal leave provisions on fathers child care involvement is rather weak, however, and does not materialise in all countries. For instance, Duvander et al. (2015) found that Norwegian fertility did not change with the introduction in April 1993 of the father's quota in parental leave entitlements. By contrast, a significant rise in fertility seemed to have occurred in Sweden after it also introduced such a quota in 1995. There was a particular increase in the incidence of second or third children being born, especially in low-income households.

Family policies are also found to influence fertility intentions, especially decisions to have the first and second children (Billingsley and Ferrarini, 2014; Mills et al., 2008; Pailhé, 2009). Policies intended for both traditional male-breadwinner and dual-earner families seem to prompt the decision to have a first child, while support for dual-earner couples alone shapes the intention to have a second child. However, family policy does not seem to affect fertility intentions with regard to the third child or any more thereafter.

6. Concluding remarks

Total fertility rates have increased in Germany in recent years and emerging evidence points to the contribution of policy changes since the late 2000s to the upturn. The 2007 parental leave reform and the expansion of child care services in particular have help ease the conflict felt by many parents, especially mothers, torn between pursuing labour market aspirations and having children. What is more, 33% of Germans now perceive their country as child-friendly, compared to 25% in 2007 (IDA, 2015).

For the past 50 years, German women have had to grapple with the high opportunity costs of being a mother due to the lack of support for parents seeking to reconcile work with family commitments. The result has been a pronounced postponement of first births and a higher rise in childlessness than in most European countries (Burh and Huinink, 2015). However, patterns differ between the eastern and western German *Länder*. In the east, the increase in women's education did not considerably affect completed fertility which remained stable across generations up to those born in the 1960s, while in the western *Länder*, the lack of support for the work-family balance contributed to falling birth rates across all generations.

The evidence in this chapter shows that fertility rates in Germany are more closely associated with women's levels of education and their employment status than in France. In particular, women who engage in a full-time career in Germany are much more likely to remain childless than in France, while mothers are much more likely to work part-time and for particularly short hours (20 or less per week). Against that background, changes in work patterns that give parents more time with their children may encourage would-be parents to start a family or to have more children.

Policies to support working parents can have a positive influence on fertility. Indeed, today, many countries with higher female employment rates also have relatively high fertility rates, at close to two children per woman. The evidence points particularly to the increase in provision of child care services being one of the main policy drivers behind increased fertility in countries with higher FTRs than Germany. A more gender-egalitarian division of child care may also encourage households to have more children. What is more, one possible long-term effect of policies to support working parents could be to fuel fertility intentions, especially if parents start to think they no longer have to choose between having children *or* pursuing a career.

Changes in fertility behaviour are likely to materialise slowly, however, and existing household and workplace practices will have to evolve. Similarly, reconciliation policies can have but a limited impact, if they are not backed by changes in labour market institutions conducive to having children *and* pursuing a career. If recent analysis of fertility trends is anything to go by, a more gender-equal division of paid and unpaid child care work between parents may further sustain fertility trends.

Notes

1. The total fertility rate (TFR) expresses the average number of children born per woman over a lifetime given current age-specific fertility rates and assuming no female mortality during reproductive years. TFRs are generally computed as the sum of age-specific fertility rates defined over five-year intervals. Given child mortality rates and assuming no migration, a TFR of 2.1 children per woman is generally sufficient to generate a stable population within a given country – the so-called "replacement level".

2. Myrskyla et al. (2013), however, predict that completed fertility will stop declining in Germany and rise a little to around 1.6 children per woman among women born in 1970 and thereafter. The gap with France will persist, though, as Myrskyla et al. predict that the CFR will stabilise at around 2.1 children per women.

3. The prevalence of childlessness varies with the type of career that women pursue. For instance, childlessness has been traditionally high among academics in the western *Länder* of Germany, although it has slightly declined over recent years (Bujard, 2012).

4. The "realistic" number of children is obtained through questions that prompt respondents to consider their actual living conditions before stating how many children they want.

5. The ambiguous results are due partly to differences in how gender equality is defined and measured, as many studies do not measure "sharing" behaviours. The few studies that analysed everyday activities and the division of household work consider the relative contribution of each partner but ignore differences in the magnitude of domestic work between households (Miettinen, 2015).

6. This finding is consistent with those of Andersson et al. (2014) who compare the weight of female earnings in childbearing decisions in Germany and Denmark from 1980 to 2001. They find that female earnings are positively associated with fertility in Denmark, but adversely in western Germany. They interpret this finding as a consequence of opposite policy orientations in the two countries. Danish social policies encouraged women to become established in the labour market before having children, while German policy during the 1980s and 1990s was not designed to encourage maternal employment.

References

Aassve, A. et al. (2015), "What Is your Couple Type? Gender Ideology, Housework Sharing, and Babies", *Demographic Research*, Vol. 32, No. 30, pp. 835-858.

Anderson, T. and H. Kohler (2015), "Low Fertility, Socioeconomic Development, and Gender Equity", *Population and Development Review*, Vol. 41, No. 3, pp. 381-407.

Andersson, G., M. Kreyenfeld and T. Mika (2014), "Welfare State Context, Female Labour-market Attachment and Childbearing in Germany and Denmark", *Journal of Population Research*, Vol. 31, No. 4, pp. 287-316, http://dx.doi.org/10.1007/s12546-014-9135-3.

Bauernschuster, S., T. Hener and H. Rainer (2015), "Children of a (Policy) Revolution: The Introduction of Universal Child Care and its Effect on Fertility", *Journal of the European Economic Association*, http://dx.doi.org/ 10.1111/jeea.12158.

Bernardt, E. (1993), "Fertility and Employment", *European Sociological Review*, Vol. 9, No. 1, pp. 25-42, http://esr.oxfordjournals.org/content/9/1/25.full.pdf.

Bernhardt, E. and F. Goldsheider (2006), "Gender Equality, Parenthood Attitudes, and First Births in Sweden", *Vienna Yearbook of Population Studies*, No. 4, pp. 19-39.

Bernardi, L., A. Klärner and H. Von der Lippe (2008), "Job Insecurity and the Timing of Parenthood: A Comparison between Eastern and Western Germany", *European Journal of Population*, Vol. 24, No. 3, pp. 287-313, http://dx.doi.org/10.1007/s10680-007-9127-5.

Billingsley, S. and T. Ferrarini (2014), "Family Policy and Fertility Intentions in 21 European Countries", *Journal of Marriage and Family*, Vol. 76, No. 2, pp. 428-445.

Blossfeld, H.-P. (ed.) (1995), *The New Role of Women: Family Formation in Modern Societies*, Westview Press, Boulder.

BMFSFJ – Federal Ministry for Family Affairs, Senior Citizens, Women and Youth (2015), *Family Report 2014 – Benefits, Effects, Trends*, German Ministry of Family, Seniors, Women and Youth.

Bongaarts, J. and T. Sobotka (2012), "A Demographic Explanation for the Recent Rise in European Fertility", *Population and Development Review*, Vol. 38, No. 1, pp. 83-120, March, http://onlinelibrary.wiley.com/journal/10.1111/(ISSN)1728-4457.

Brachet, S., M-T. Letablier and A. Salles (2010), "Devenir parents en France et en Allemagne : normes, valeurs, représentations", *Politiques sociales et familiales*, No. 100, pp. 79-92. http://www.persee.fr/web/revues/home/prescript/revue/caf.

Breton, D. and F. Prioux (2009): "The One-child Family: France in the European Context", *Demographic Research*, Vol. 20, No. 27, pp. 657-692, http://www.demographic-research.org.

Buhr, P. and J. Huinink (2015), "The German Low Fertility: How We Got There and What We Can Expect for the Future", *European Sociological Review*, Vol. 31, No. 2, pp. 197-210, http://esr.oxfordjournals.org/content/31/2/197.abstract.

Bujard, M. (2015a), "Consequences of Enduring Low Fertility – A German Case Study. Demographic Projections and Implications for Different Policy Fields", *Comparative Population Studies*, Vol. 40, No. 2, pp. 131-164, http://www.comparativepopulationstudies.de/index.php/CPoS/article/viewFile/185/202.

Bujard, M. (2015b), "Kinderlosigkeit in Deutschland: Wie interagieren Bildung, Wohnort, Migrationshintergrund, Erwerbstätigkeit und Kohorte? Zeitschrift für Familienforschung", *Journal of Family Research*, Vol. 27, No. 3, pp. 1-25.

Bujard, M. (2012), "Talsohle bei Akademikerinnen durchschritten? Kinderzahl und Kinderlosigkeit in Deutschland nach Bildungs- und Berufsgruppen", *BiB Working Paper*, No. 4/2012, Bundesinstitut für Bevölkerungsforschung.

Bujard, M. (2011), "Family Policy and Demographic Effects: the Case of Germany", *Demografia*, Vol. 54, No. 5, English edition, pp. 56-78, http://demografia.hu/en/.

Bujard, M. and J. Passet (2013), "Wirkungen des *Elterngelds* auf Einkommen und Fertilität", *Zeitschrift für Familienforschung*, Vol. 25, No. 2, pp. 212-227, http://www.bib-demografie.de/SharedDocs/Publikationen/DE/BuchInfo/Bu_Zff_Wirkungen_Elterngeld.pdf?__blob=publicationFile&v=2.

Cooke, L. (2004), "The Gendered Division of Labor and Family Outcomes in Germany", *Journal of Marriage and the Family*, Vol. 66, No. 5, pp. 1246-1259.

Dorbritz, J. (2008), "Germany: Family Diversity with Low Actual and Desired Fertility", *Demographic Research*, No. 19, No. 17, pp. 557-598.

Dorbritz, J. and R. Naderi (2013), "Trendwende beim Kinderwunsch?", *Bevölkerungsforschung*, Vol. 34, No. 04/2013, Mitteilungen aus dem Bundesinstitut für Bevölkerungsforschung.

Duvander, A.Z. and G. Anderssen (2006), "Gender Equality and Fertility in Sweden: A Study on the Impact of the Father's Uptake of Parental Leave on Continued Childbearing", *Marriage and Family Review*, Vol. 39, No. 12, pp. 121-142.

Duvander, A.Z., T. Lappegard and G. Andersson (2010), "Family Policy and Fertility: A Comparative Study on the Impact of Fathers' and Mothers' Use of Parental Leave on Continued Childbearing in Norway and Sweden", *Journal of European Social Policy*, Vol. 20, No. 1, pp. 45-57.

Duvander, A.Z., T. Lappegard and M. Johansson (2015), "Family Policy Reform Impact on Continued Fertility in the Nordic Countries", Annual Conference of Families & Societies, Madrid, January.

Frejka, T. and J-P. Sardon (2007), "Cohort Birth Order, Parity Progression Ratio and Parity Distribution Trends in Developed Countries", *Demographic Research*, Vol. 16, No. 11, pp. 315-74, http://www.demographic-research.org/.

Frejka, T. and T. Sobotka (2008), "Fertility in Europe: Diverse, Delayed and Below Replacement", in T. Frejka et al. (eds.), *Childbearing Trends and Policies in Europe: Demographic Research*, Special Collection 7, Vol. 19, Article 3, pp. 15-46, http://www.demographic-research.org.

Goldstein, J., T. Sobotka and A. Jasilioniene (2009), "The End of 'Lowest-low Fertility?'", *Population and Development Review*, Vol. 35, No. 4, pp. 663-699, http://onlinelibrary.wiley.com/journal/10.1111/.

Greulich, A., O. Thévenon and M. Guergot-Larivière (2016), "Securing Women's Employment: A Fertility Booster in European Countries?", *CES Working Paper*, No. 2016/24, Université Paris 1 Sorbonne, ftp://mse.univ-paris1.fr/pub/mse/CES2016/16024.pdf.

Allensbach Intitut Für Demoskopie (2015), "Familienbilder in Deutschland und Frankreich", Untersuchung im Auftrag des Bundesministeriums für Familie, Senioren, Frauen und Jugend, Allensbach.

Klobas, J. and I. Ajzen (2015), "Making the Decision to Have a Child", in A. Liefbroer, J. Klobas and D. Philipov (eds.), *Reproductive Decision-Making in a Macro-Micro Perspective*, Springer.

Kohler, H.P., F. Billari and J. Ortega (2002), "The Emergence of Lowest-Low Fertility in Europe During the 1990s", *Population and Development Review*, Vol. 28, No. 4, pp. 641-680.

Kreyenfeld, M. and D. Konietzka (2013), *Ein Leben ohne Kinder: Ausmaß, Strukturen und Ursachen von Kinderlosigkeit in Deutschland*, Springer.

Luci-Greulich, A. and O. Thévenon (2014), "Does Economic Advancement 'Cause' a Re-increase in Fertility? An Empirical Analysis for OECD Countries (1960-2007)", *European Journal of Population*, Vol. 30, No. 2, pp. 187-221.

Luci-Greulich, A. and O. Thévenon (2013): "The Impact of Family Policies on Fertility Trends in Developed Countries", *European Journal of Population*, Vol. 29, No. 4, pp. 387-416, http://dx.doi.org/10.1007/s10680-013-9295-4.

Miettinen, A., L. Lainiala and A. Rotkirch (2015), "Women's Housework Decreases Fertility: Evidence from a Longitudinal Study among Finnish Couples", *Acta Sociologica*, Vol. 58, No. 2, pp. 139-154.

Myrskyla, M., J. Goldstein and Y.S. Cheng (2013), "New Cohort Fertility Forecasts for the Developed World: Rises, Falls, and Reversals", *Population and Development Review*, Vol. 39, No. 1, pp. 31-56.

OECD (2011), *Doing Better for Families*, OECD Publishing, Paris, http://dx.doi.org/10.1787/9789264098732-en.

Rendall, M. (2014), "Employment Impacts on Partnership and Parenthood Entry in Different Family-Policy Regimes", European Population Conference, http://epc2014.princeton.edu/.

Stichnoth, H. (2014), "Short-run Fertility Effects of Parental Leave Benefits: Evidence from a Structural Model", *Discussion Paper*, No. 14-069, ZEW (Zentrum for Europäisch Wirschafstforschung), http://ftp.zew.de/pub/zew-docs/dp/dp14069.pdf.

Testa, M.R. (2012), "Family Sizes in Europe: Evidence from the 2011 Eurobarometer Survey", *European Demographic Research Papers*, Vienna Institute of Demography, Vienna.

Thévenon, O. (2009), "Increased Women's Labour Force Participation in Europe: Progress in the Work-Life Balance or Polarization of Behaviors?", *Population*, Vol. 64, No. 2, pp. 235-272, http://www.cairn-int.info/journal-population.htm.

Thévenon, O. and A. Gauthier (2011), "Family Policies in Developed Countries: A Fertility Booster with Side-effects", *Community Work and Family*, Vol. 14, No. 2, pp. 197-216.

Westhoff, C.F, and J. Wiggins (2009), "Relationship between Men's Gender Attitudes and Fertility", Response to A. Puur et al. (2008), "Men's Childbearing Desires and Views of the Male Role in Europe at the Dawn of the 21st Century", *Demographic Research*, Vol. 21, No. 3, pp. 65-74.

Wood, J., J. Vergauwen and K. Neels (2015), "Economic Conditions and Variation in First Birth Hazards in 22 European Countries between 1970 and 2005", in K. Matthijs et al. (eds.), *Population Change in Europe, the Middle-East and North-Africa : Beyond the Demographic Divide*, Ashgate Publishing, pp. 45-80, http://www.ashgate.com/isbn/9781472439567.

Annex 6.A1

Jobs or babies? A comparison of fertility behaviour in Germany and France

The empirical analysis carried out seeks to compare the influence on fertility behaviour in France and Germany of:

- women's working status, occupation, earnings, educational level, and partnership status
- the employment status, educational level and earnings of women's partners.

The data used for the analysis are drawn from the EU Labour Force Surveys for the years 2003 to 2012 – such a wide sample range facilitates detailed analysis of the influence of work patterns. These patterns are captured by information on working hours, occupation and earnings. The data also make it possible to consider personal and partner's characteristics.

The analysis focuses on the probability of giving birth among women aged 25 to 49. Birth is identified by the presence in the household of a child not yet one year of age. Over the period under consideration, 8.1% of 25-to-49 year-old women are estimated to have given birth within a year in Germany. The proportion is one-third higher, at 12%, in France. This gap is consistent with the differences in TFRs.

The probability of giving birth is assumed to be influenced by a set of work-related factors, such as labour force status which encompasses:

- inactive women,[1]
- the unemployed,
- working women who work short hours (19 hours a week or less), long part-time (20 to 29 hours), reduced full-time (30 to 39 hours), and employees with long working hours (40 hours or more).

This information refers to the labour force status after child birth, *not* before, which precludes making statements about the causal effect of labour force status on fertility. It sheds light, however, on the widely different relationships between Germany and France in women's labour force status and fertility.

Employees' occupation is also taken into account by dividing into five groups the occupational categories in the Major Groups (one digit) of the International Standard *Classification* of Occupations (ISCO):

1. Women on parental leave are likely to be categorised as inactive if they were not working at all during the reference week.

- legislators, senior officials and managers – ISCO Major Group 1;
- professionals – ISCO Major Group 2;
- technicians, associate professionals, clerks, and service and sale workers – ISCO Major Groups 2,3 and 4;
- skilled agricultural, forestry and fishery workers and craft workers – ISCO Major Groups 6 and 7;
- plant and machine operators, assemblers and elementary occupations – ISCO Major Groups 8 and 9.

Individual earnings are also included as explanatory variables, although the information is available only from 2009 onwards. The model specification is also estimated without information on earnings in order to cover the longest possible period.

The other personal characteristics taken into account are:

- age, grouped into five brackets: 25-29; 29-34; 35-39; 40-44; 45-49,
- educational attainment with ISCED Level 1 distinction between at most lower secondary education, upper secondary education, and tertiary education;
- the partnership status of women which encompasses women who are single, have a non-cohabiting partner; are not married and living with a cohabiting partner are married and living with a cohabiting partner.

In addition, yearly dummies are included in the model estimation to control for year-specific factors (such as economic cycles) that may alter the relationship between fertility and the explanatory variables. Regional differences between the western and eastern parts of Germany are also accounted for with dummies that control for region-specific unobserved factors. Similarly, 8 regional dummies are included in the model for France to account for possibly unobserved heterogeneity.

Model estimations are run in two separate blocks. The first one includes women, partnered or not, while the second focuses on partnered women only to consider the effect of partners' attributes. Furthermore, the effect of the labour force status is linked with educational characteristics in order to consider possible differences in the effect of work intensity on fertility by level of educational attainment.

The estimated fertility equations are thus:

For the first block:

$$[1] \quad Ln\left(\frac{y=1}{y=0}\right) = \theta Age + \alpha Edu_w + \beta WS_w + \gamma Edu_w * WS_w + \delta Occup_w + \mu Earnings_w + \pi Partnership_w + \tau T + \varphi R$$

For the second block focusing on women with a cohabiting partner:

$$[2] \quad Ln\left(\frac{y=1}{y=0}\right) = \theta Age + \alpha Edu_w + \beta WS_w + \gamma Edu_w * WS_w + \delta Occup_w + \mu Earnings_w + \emptyset WS_m + \pi EduDiff_{w,m} + \omega EarningsDiff_{w,m} + \tau T + \varphi R$$

Where y (= 1 when there has been a child birth; 0 otherwise) is a logit function of the right-hand block of explanatory variables. Compared to the first equation, the second includes information on partner's working status, and on the differences in educational attainment and in earnings between the two partners.

The regressions are run separately for Germany and France in order to compare the magnitude of the association between the "explanatory" factors and "a child birth".

Table 6.A1.1 reports the results for all women, cohabiting with a partner or not. For each country, the first column shows the results of the model specification when the information on occupational groups and individual earnings are not taken into account. The second column includes information on occupations but not on earnings, while the third column also control for earnings levels. (The model specification is based on the three years of survey results for which this information is available.)

The main conclusions that can be drawn from this table include:

- Women with tertiary education are between 1.42 and 1.47 times more likely to give birth within a year than those with an upper-secondary degree. Conversely, a tertiary (university level) degree lowers the likelihood of having a child by 32 to 42%, compared to upper-secondary educated women. The respective differences by level of education are much lower in France.
- The work status of women plays a role in the two countries, but working women are much less likely to have a child in Germany, while the effect of employment on fertility is weaker in France. For instance, as shown in columns (3) and (3'), the likelihood that women working 20 hours or less have had a child relative to inactive women is twice as high in France (0.24) as in Germany (0.12).
- In both countries, professionals are more likely to have a child within a year than managers, who in turn are more likely than technicians, clerical workers and other low skilled workers.

Table 6.A1.1. Relationships between working patterns and fertility

Regression results – all women aged 25 to 49

	Germany			France		
	(-1)	(-2)	(-3)	(1')	(2')	(3')
Education (ref. upper secondary education)						
Lower secondary	1.47***	1.42***	1.48***	1.35***	1.24***	1.17***
	-0.024	-0.027	-0.05	-0.014	-0.014	-0.023
Tertiary	0.68***	0.66***	0.58***	0.79***	0.85***	0.87***
	-0.013	-0.014	-0.024	-0.01	-0.011	-0.019
Work status (ref. Inactive)						
Unemployed	0.09***	0.12***	0.13***	0.24***	0.28***	0.28***
	-0.004	-0.005	-0.012	-0.004	-0.005	-0.007
19 hours or less	0.28***	0.16***	0.12***	0.31***	0.23***	0.24***
	-0.006	-0.009	-0.015	-0.006	-0.006	-0.02
20 to 29 hours	0.21***	0.12***	0.13***	0.34***	0.24***	0.27***
	-0.005	-0.007	-0.016	-0.005	-0.006	-0.02
30 to 39 hours	0.17***	0.12***	0.12***	0.24***	0.18***	0.18***
	-0.003	-0.007	-0.015	-0.002	-0.004	-0.013
40 hours or more	0.13***	0.094***	0.10***	0.20***	0.14***	0.14***
	-0.003	-0.005	-0.012	-0.003	-0.004	-0.009
Interaction education*work status						
Lower secondary						
Unemployed	..	0.93	..	..	1.04	..
		-0.117			-0.049	
19 hours or less	..	1.19**	..	..	1.22***	..
		-0.066			-0.061	
20 to 29 hours	..	1.31***	..	..	1.40***	..
		-0.79			-0.053	
30 to 39 hours	..	0.65***	..	..	1.18***	..
		-0.033			-0.032	
40 hours or more	..	0.60***	..	..	1.23***	..
		-0.031			-0.045	
Tertiary (higher) education			..	..		..
Unemployed	..	1.34**	..	..	0.88*	..
		-0.152			-0.044	
19 hours or less	..	1.02	..	..	0.69***	..
		-0.073			-0.047	
20 to 29 hours	..	1.18*	..	..	0.84***	..
		-0.11			-0.044	
30 to 39 hours	..	0.74**	..	..	0.88***	..
		-0.074			-0.031	
40 hours or more	..	1.28**	..	..	0.87***	..
		-0.119			-0.054	
Occupation (ref. Managers)						
Professionals	..	1.18**	1.02	..	1.02	1.19***
		-0.072	-0.106		-0.025	-0.061
Technicians	..	0.947	0.64***	..	0.79***	0.89**
		-0.05	-0.065		-0.018	-0.046
Skilled agricultural and craft workers	..	0.92	0.52***	..	0.75***	0.74***
		-0.071	-0.077		-0.032	-0.062
Machine operators, and elementary occupations	..	0.59***	0.38***	..	0.55***	0.62***

Note: Standards errors in brackets. ***, ** and *: significant at 1%, 5% and 10%, respectively. The odd ratios are reported.

(1) and (1') report results without controlling for occupations nor earnings, and include data from 2003 to 2012.

(2) and (2') report results without controlling for earnings, and include data from 2003 to 2012.

(3) and (3') report results with the full list of covariates, and include data from 2009 to 2012.

- In both countries, women who work part-time are much more likely to have a child than those in full-time employment. However, once groups of occupations are controlled for, the likelihood of have a child no longer varies with working hours in Germany, while it does in France.
- The influence of working hours also varies with women's educational attainment, but the interaction differs between the two countries. In France, highly educated women have 30% to 40% less chance of giving birth than women who went no further than lower-secondary school, whatever their working hours are. In Germany, however, women who work full-time are much less likely to have children when they hold a secondary-education qualification than women educated to university level who also work full-time.
- The link between fertility and personal earnings is also different in the two countries. In Germany, there are much higher chances of low-income women becoming mothers than those in the middle or at the top of the earnings distribution. In France, by contrast, individual female earnings have a limited impact on fertility behaviour, and women with higher annual earnings are more likely to have a child within a year.

Table 6.A.2 shows the results for women who cohabit with a partner and may or may not be married. For reasons of space, only the influence of earnings and partner's characteristics is reported, although the estimation includes other covariates. As the table shows, partners' characteristics have a much stronger influence in Germany than they do in France:

- Households are more likely to have a child when women have a higher qualification than their partners, all else being equal. The association loses magnitude and significance once earnings are controlled for in France.
- Households where men earn significantly more than women are also much more likely to have a child. In France, the odds of having a child are not really affected by the gender gap in partners' earnings.

Table 6.A1.2. Associations between fertility and partners' characteristics

Regression results: women aged 25 to 49 and cohabiting with a partner

	Germany		France	
	(-1)	(-2)	(-1)	(-2)
Education gap with partner (ref. same level of education)				
Men with a **higher** degree than women	0.97	1.01	1.03**	0.98
	-0.026	-0.052	-0.014	-0.022
Men with a **lower** degree than women	1.17***	1.21***	1.14***	1.03
	-0.036	-0.069	-0.018	-0.028
Work status of the partner (ref. working full-time)				
Unemployed	1.12***	1.04	1.11***	1.18***
	-0.038	-0.085	-0.024	-0.043
Inactive	0.85***	0.93	0.89***	0.85***
	-0.036	-0.074	-0.024	-0.037
Short part-time	1	1.04	1.05*	0.99
	-0.042	-0.075	-0.029	-0.047
Long part-time	0.95**	0.97	1.01	1.01
	-0.017	-0.035	-0.011	-0.02
Earnings (ref. 3 quintile)				
1rst quintile		1.66***		0.86**
		-0.111		(0.04.)
2nd quintile		1.36***		1
		-0.081		-0.044
4th quintile		0.75***		0.98
		-0.055		-0.045
5th quintile		0.76**		1.15**
		-0.069		-0.065
Earnings gap between partners (ref. same quintile of income)				
Men earn more than women		1.36***		1.07**
		-0.075		-0.029
Men earn less than women		1.02		1.06*
		-0.049		-0.034
Number of observations	231175	65635	401060	114490
Log likelihood	-57787.55	-16782.67	-129681.1	-41041.62
McFadden Pseudo R2	0.239	0.254	0.224	0.223

Note: Standards errors in brackets. ***, ** and *: significant at 1%, 5% and 10%, respectively. The odd-ratios are reported.

(1) and (1') report results without controlling for earnings, and include data from 2003 to 2012.

(2) and (2') report results with the full list of covariates, and include data from 2009 to 2012.

ORGANISATION FOR ECONOMIC CO-OPERATION AND DEVELOPMENT

The OECD is a unique forum where governments work together to address the economic, social and environmental challenges of globalisation. The OECD is also at the forefront of efforts to understand and to help governments respond to new developments and concerns, such as corporate governance, the information economy and the challenges of an ageing population. The Organisation provides a setting where governments can compare policy experiences, seek answers to common problems, identify good practice and work to co-ordinate domestic and international policies.

The OECD member countries are: Australia, Austria, Belgium, Canada, Chile, the Czech Republic, Denmark, Estonia, Finland, France, Germany, Greece, Hungary, Iceland, Ireland, Israel, Italy, Japan, Korea, Latvia, Luxembourg, Mexico, the Netherlands, New Zealand, Norway, Poland, Portugal, the Slovak Republic, Slovenia, Spain, Sweden, Switzerland, Turkey, the United Kingdom and the United States. The European Union takes part in the work of the OECD.

OECD Publishing disseminates widely the results of the Organisation's statistics gathering and research on economic, social and environmental issues, as well as the conventions, guidelines and standards agreed by its members.

OECD PUBLISHING, 2, rue André-Pascal, 75775 PARIS CEDEX 16
(81 2016 11 1 P) ISBN 978-92-64-25914-0 – 2016

www.ingramcontent.com/pod-product-compliance
Lightning Source LLC
Chambersburg PA
CBHW061208240926
51846CB00006B/1145